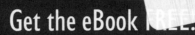

Get the eBook FREE!

(PDF, ePub, Kindle, and liveBook all included)

We believe that once you buy a book from us, you should be able to read it in any format we have available. To get electronic versions of this book at no additional cost to you, purchase and then register this book at the Manning website.

Go to https://www.manning.com/freebook and follow the instructions to complete your pBook registration.

That's it!
Thanks from Manning!

JUnit in Action

THIRD EDITION

CĂTĂLIN TUDOSE

MANNING
SHELTER ISLAND

Manning Publications Co.
20 Baldwin Road
PO Box 761
Shelter Island, NY 11964

Development editor:	Katie Sposato Johnson
Technical development editor:	John Guthrie
Review editor:	Mihaela Batinic
Production editor:	Deirdre S. Hiam
Copy editor:	Tiffany Taylor
Proofreader:	Katie Tennant
Technical proofreader:	David Cabrero
Typesetter and cover designer:	Marija Tudor

ISBN 9781617297045
Printed in the United States of America

*This book is dedicated to all those people who made it possible:
family, friends, colleagues, professors, students.*

Cătălin Tudose

contents

preface

I am fortunate to have been in the IT industry for almost 25 years. I started programming in C++ and Delphi, and that is how I spent my student years and the first years of my career. I made the step from my mathematics background as a teenager to computer science and always kept both studies in mind. In 2000, my attention turned for the first time to the Java programming language, which was very young, but many people were predicting a great future for it. I was part of a team developing online games, using a particular technology: applets, which were extremely fashionable during those years. Our team spent some time developing and some more time testing, which was mainly done manually: we played together in the network and tried to discover the corner cases by ourselves. We hadn't heard about JUnit or test-driven development, which were in the pioneering stages.

After 2004, Java dominated about 90% of my work life. It was the dawn of a new era for me, and things like code refactoring, unit testing, and test-driven development became part of my normal professional life. Nowadays, I cannot imagine a project (even if it is a smaller one) without automated testing, and neither can Luxoft, the company I work for. My fellow developers talk about how they do automated testing in their current work, what the client expectations are, how they measure and increase code coverage, and how they analyze the quality of tests. Not only are unit testing and test-driven development at the heart of the conversation, but so also is behavior-driven development. We now cannot imagine shipping a product to fulfill market expectations without solid tests: an actual pyramid of unit tests, integration tests, system tests, and acceptance tests.

I was also fortunate to get in contact with Manning after having already developed three courses about automated testing for Pluralsight. I didn't have to start this book from scratch: the second edition was already a best seller. But it was written for 2010 and JUnit 4, and 10 years look like centuries in the IT field! I made the big step to JUnit 5 and present-day hot technologies and working methodologies. Unit testing and JUnit have come a long way since their early days when I began working with them. The concept is simple, but careful consideration and planning are required when migrating from JUnit 4 to 5. The book effectively provides that information, with many practical examples. I hope that this approach will help you decide what to do when you face new situations in your current work.

acknowledgments

The Manning team helped to create a high-level book, and I am looking forward to more opportunities of this kind.

I would like to thank my professors and colleagues for all their support during the years and to the many participants in my face-to-face or online courses – they represented a stimulus for me in achieving top quality work and always looking for improvement. Thanks to the co-authors of the book, Petar Tahchiev, Felipe Leme, Vincent Massol, and Gary Gregory, for strong first editions that represented a good foundation. I hope to meet all of you in person some day. Best thoughts for my colleague and friend Vladimir Sonkin, with whom I share the steps in investigating new technologies.

I would also like to thank the staff at Manning: acquisition editor Mike Stephens, project editor Deirdre Hiam, development editor Katie Sposato Johnson, review editor Mihaela Batinic, technical development editor John Guthrie, technical proofer David Cabrero, senior technical development editor Al Scherer, copyeditor Tiffany Taylor, and proofreader Katie Tennant.

To all the reviewers: Andy Keffalas, Becky Huett, Burk Hufnagel, Conor Redmond, David Cabrero Souto, Ernesto Arroyo, Ferdinando Santacroce, Gaurav Tuli, Greg Wright, Gualtiero Testa, Gustavo Filipe Ramos Gomes, Hilde Van Gysel, Ivo Alexandre Costa Alves Angélico, Jean-François Morin, Joseph Tingsanchali, Junilu Lacar, Karthikeyarajan Rajendran, Kelum Prabath Senanayake, Kent R. Spillner, Kevin Orr, Paulo Cesar, Dias Lima, Robert Trausmuth, Robert Wenner, Sau Fai Fong, Shawn Ritchie, Sidharth Masaldaan, Simeon Leyzerzon, Srihari Sridharan, Thorsten P. Weber, Vittorio Marino, Vladimír Oraný, and Zorodzayi Mukuya. Your suggestions helped make this a better book.

about this book

JUnit in Action is a book about creating safe applications and how to greatly increase your development speed and remove much of the debugging nightmare—all with the help of JUnit 5 with its new features, and other tools and techniques that work in conjunction with JUnit 5.

The book focuses first on understanding the who, what, why, and how of JUnit. The first few chapters should convince you of the capabilities and power of JUnit 5. Following that, I take a deep dive into working effectively with JUnit 5: migrating from JUnit 4 to JUnit 5, testing strategies, working with JUnit 5 and different tools, working with modern frameworks, and developing applications with JUnit 5 according to present-day methodologies.

Who should read this book

This book is for application developers who are already proficient in writing Java Core code and are interested in learning how to develop safe and flexible applications. You should be familiar with object-oriented programming and have at least a working knowledge of Java. You will also need a working knowledge of Maven and be able to build a Maven project and open a Java program in IntelliJ IDEA, edit it, and launch it in execution. Some of the chapters require basic knowledge about technologies like Spring, Hibernate, REST, and Jakarta EE.

How this book is organized: A roadmap

This book has 22 chapters in five sections. Part 1 presents the JUnit 5 essentials:

- Chapter 1 gives you a quick introduction to the concepts of testing—knowledge you need to get started. You will get straight to the code, seeing how to write and execute a very simple test and see its results.

- Chapter 2 discusses JUnit in detail; you will see JUnit 5's capabilities and walk through the code that puts them in practice.
- Chapter 3 looks at the JUnit architecture.
- Chapter 4 discusses how to move from JUnit 4 to JUnit 5 and how to migrate projects between these versions of the framework.
- Chapter 5 is dedicated to tests as a whole. The chapter describes different kinds of tests and the scenarios to which they apply. It also discusses different levels of testing and the best scenarios in which to execute those tests.

Part 2 presents different testing strategies:

- Chapter 6 is dedicated to analyzing test quality. It introduces concepts such as code coverage, test-driven development, behavior-driven development, and mutating testing.
- Chapter 7 is dedicated to stubs, taking a look at a solution to isolate the environment and make tests seamless.
- Chapter 8 explains mock objects, providing an overview of how to construct and use them.
- Chapter 9 describes a different technique: executing tests in a container.

Part 3 shows how JUnit 5 works with other tools:

- Chapter 10 provides a very quick introduction to Maven and its terminology.
- Chapter 11 guides you through the same concepts, this time using another popular tool called Gradle.
- Chapter 12 investigates the way you can work with JUnit 5 by using the most popular IDEs today: IntelliJ IDEA, Eclipse, and NetBeans.
- Chapter 13 is devoted to continuous integration tools. This practice, which is highly recommended by extreme programmers, helps you maintain a code repository and automate the build on it.

Part 4 shows how JUnit 5 works with modern frameworks:

- Chapter 15 introduces HtmlUnit and Selenium. You will see how to test the presentation layer with these tools.
- Chapters 16 and 17 are dedicated to testing one of the most useful frameworks today: Spring. Spring is an open source application framework and inversion of control container for the Java platform. It includes several separate frameworks, including the Spring Boot convention-over-configuration solution for creating applications that you can run directly.
- Chapter 18 examines testing REST applications. Representational State Transfer is an application program interface that uses HTTP requests to GET, PUT, PATCH, POST, and DELETE data.

- Chapter 19 discusses alternatives for testing database applications, including JDBC, Spring, and Hibernate.

Part 5 shows how JUnit 5 works with modern software development methodologies:

- Chapter 20 discusses project development using one of today's popular development techniques: test-driven development.
- Chapter 21 discusses developing projects using behavior-driven development. It shows how to create applications that address business needs: applications that not only do things right but also do the right thing.
- Chapter 22 shows how to build a test pyramid strategy with the help of JUnit 5. It demonstrates testing from the ground level (unit testing) to the upper levels (integration testing, system testing, and acceptance testing).

In general, you can read this book from one chapter to the next. But, as long as you master the essentials presented in part 1, you can jump directly to any chapter that addresses your current needs.

About the code

This book contains (mostly) large blocks of code, rather than short snippets. Therefore, all the code listings are annotated and explained. In some chapters, annotations in listings and their explanations in text are marked with a number and the prime character to indicate comparisons with lines in similar listings. You can find the full source code for all these examples by downloading it from GitHub at https://github .com/ctudose/junit-in-action-third-edition.

liveBook discussion forum

Purchase of *JUnit in Action, Third Edition*, includes free access to a private web forum run by Manning Publications where you can make comments about the book, ask technical questions, and receive help from the authors and from other users. To access the forum, go to https://livebook.manning.com/#!/book/junit-in-action-third-edition/discussion. You can also learn more about Manning's forums and the rules of conduct at https://livebook.manning.com/#!/discussion.

Manning's commitment to our readers is to provide a venue where a meaningful dialogue between individual readers and between readers and the authors can take place. It is not a commitment to any specific amount of participation on the part of the authors, whose contribution to the forum remains voluntary (and unpaid). We suggest you try asking them some challenging questions lest their interest stray! The forum and the archives of previous discussions will be accessible from the publisher's website as long as the book is in print.

about the author

CĂTĂLIN TUDOSE is born in Piteşti, Argeş, Romania.

He graduated with a degree in computer science in 1997, in Bucharest, and also completed a PhD in this field in 2006. He has more than 15 years of experience in the Java area. He took part in projects in telecommunications and finance, working as a senior software developer or technical team leader. He is currently acting as a Java and Web Technologies expert at Luxoft Romania.

He taught more than 2000 hours of courses and applications as a professor at the Faculty of Automation and Computers in Bucharest. He taught more than 4000 hours of Java courses at Luxoft, including the Corporate Junior Program, which has prepared about 50 new Java programmers in Poland. He also developed corporate courses on Java topics inside the company.

He taught online courses at UMGC (University of Maryland Global Campus): Computer Graphics with Java (CMSC 405), Intermediate Programming in Java (CMIS 242), Advanced Programming in Java (CMIS 440), Software Verification and Validation (SWEN 647), Database Concepts (IFSM 410), SQL (IFSM 411), Advanced Database Concepts (IFSM 420).

He has developed 5 courses for Pluralsight: TDD with JUnit 5; Java: BDD Fundamentals; Implementing A Test Pyramid Strategy in Java; Spring Framework: Aspect Oriented Programming with Spring AOP; and Migrating from the JUnit 4 to the JUnit 5 Testing Platform.

Besides the professional IT domain, he is interested in mathematics, world culture, and soccer. He is a lifelong supporter of his hometown team, FC Argeş Piteşti.

about the cover illustration

The figure on the cover of *JUnit in Action, Third Edition* is captioned "Dame Walaque," or Walaque lady. The illustration is taken from a collection of dress costumes from various countries by Jacques Grasset de Saint-Sauveur (1757-1810), titled *Costumes de Différents Pays,* published in France in 1797. Each illustration is finely drawn and colored by hand. The rich variety of Grasset de Saint-Sauveur's collection reminds us vividly of how culturally apart the world's towns and regions were just 200 years ago. Isolated from each other, people spoke different dialects and languages. In the streets or in the countryside, it was easy to identify where they lived and what their trade or station in life was just by their dress.

The way we dress has changed since then and the diversity by region, so rich at the time, has faded away. It is now hard to tell apart the inhabitants of different continents, let alone different towns, regions, or countries. Perhaps we have traded cultural diversity for a more varied personal life—certainly for a more varied and fast-paced technological life.

At a time when it is hard to tell one computer book from another, Manning celebrates the inventiveness and initiative of the computer business with book covers based on the rich diversity of regional life of two centuries ago, brought back to life by Grasset de Saint-Sauveur's pictures.

Part 1

JUnit

Welcome to *JUnit in Action*, which covers the JUnit framework, started by Kent Beck and Erich Gamma in late 1995. Ever since then, the popularity of the framework has been growing; now JUnit is the de facto standard for unit testing Java applications.

This book is the third edition. The first edition was a best seller, written by Vincent Massol and Ted Husted in 2003 and dedicated to version 3.x of JUnit. The second edition was also a best seller, written by Petar Tahchiev, Felipe Leme, Vincent Massol, and Gary Gregory in 2010, and dedicated to version 4.x of JUnit.

In this edition, I cover version 5.x of JUnit—the newest version—and talk about lots of features included in it. At the same time, I focus on interesting details and techniques for testing your code: the architecture of the framework, test quality, mock objects, interaction with other tools, and JUnit extensions, as well as testing layers of your application, applying the test-driven development and behavior-driven development techniques, and so forth.

This part of the book explores JUnit itself. Chapter 1 gives you a quick introduction to the concepts of testing—knowledge you need to get started. I get straight to the code, showing you how to write and execute a very simple test and see its results. Chapter 2 introduces JUnit in detail. I show JUnit 5's capabilities and walk through the code that puts them in practice. Chapter 3 looks at JUnit architectures, and chapter 4 discusses how to make the step from JUnit 4 to JUnit 5 and how to migrate projects between these versions of the framework. Chapter 5 is dedicated to tests as a whole. The chapter describes different kinds of tests and the scenarios to which they apply. I discuss different levels of testing and the best scenarios in which to execute those tests.

JUnit jump-start

This chapter covers

- Understanding JUnit
- Installing JUnit
- Writing your first tests
- Running tests

Never in the field of software development was so much owed by so many to so few lines of code.

—Martin Fowler

All code needs to be tested. During development, the first thing we do is run our own programmer's acceptance test. We code, compile, and run. When we run, we test. The test may just consist of clicking a button to see whether it brings up the expected menu or looking at a result to compare it with the expected value. Nevertheless, every day, we code, we compile, we run, and *we test*.

When we test, we often find issues, especially during early runs. So we code, compile, run, and test again.

3

Most of us quickly develop a pattern for our informal tests: add a record, view a record, edit a record, and delete a record. Running a little test suite like this by hand is easy enough to do, so we do it—over and over again.

Some programmers like doing this type of repetitive testing. It can be a pleasant break from deep thought and hardcoding. When our little click-through tests finally succeed, we have a real feeling of accomplishment ("Eureka! I found it!").

Other programmers dislike this type of repetitive work. Rather than run the tests by hand, they prefer to create a small program that runs the tests automatically. Play-testing code is one thing; running automated tests is another.

If you're a "play-test" developer, this book is for you. It shows you that creating automated tests can be easy, effective, and even fun.

If you're already test-infected,[1] this book is also for you. We cover the basics in part 1 and move on to tough, real-life problems in parts 2–5.

1.1   Proving that a program works

Some developers feel that automated tests are essential parts of the development process: you cannot *prove* that a component works until it passes a comprehensive series of tests. In fact, two developers felt that this type of unit testing was so important that it deserved its own framework. In 1997, Erich Gamma and Kent Beck created a simple but effective unit testing framework for Java called *JUnit*: they were on a long plane trip, and it gave them something interesting to do. Erich wanted Kent to learn Java, and Erich was interested in knowing more about the SUnit testing framework that Kent created earlier for Smalltalk, and the flight gave them time to do both.

> **DEFINITION**   *Framework*—A semicomplete application that provides a reusable common structure to share among applications.[2] Developers incorporate the framework into their own applications and extend it to meet their specific needs. Frameworks differ from toolkits by providing a coherent structure rather than a simple set of utility classes. A framework defines a skeleton, and the application defines its own features to fill out the skeleton. The developer code is called appropriately by the framework. Developers can worry less about whether a design is good and focus more on implementing domain-specific functions.

If you recognize the names Erich Gamma and Kent Beck, that's for a good reason. Gamma is one of the Gang of Four who gave us the now-classic *Design Patterns* book.[3] Beck is equally well known for his groundbreaking work in the software discipline known as Extreme Programming (www.extremeprogramming.org).

---

[1] *Test-infected* is a term coined by Erich Gamma and Kent Beck in "Test-Infected: Programmers Love Writing Tests," *Java Report* 3 (7), 37–50, 1998.

[2] Ralph Johnson and Brian Foote, "Designing Reusable Classes," *Journal of Object-Oriented Programming* 1 (2): 22–35, 1988; www.laputan.org/drc/drc.html.

[3] Erich Gamma et al., *Design Patterns* (Reading, MA: Addison-Wesley, 1995).

JUnit quickly became the de facto standard framework for developing unit tests in Java. Today, JUnit (https://junit.org) is open source software hosted on GitHub, with an Eclipse Public License. And the underlying testing model, known as *xUnit*, is on its way to becoming the standard framework for any language. xUnit frameworks are available for ASP, C++, C#, Eiffel, Delphi, Perl, PHP, Python, Rebol, Smalltalk, and Visual Basic—to name just a few.

The JUnit team didn't invent software testing or even unit tests, of course. Originally, the term *unit test* described a test that examined the behavior of a single unit of work: a class or a method. Over time, the use of the term *unit test* broadened. The Institute of Electrical and Electronics Engineers (IEEE), for example, has defined unit testing as "testing of individual hardware or software units *or groups of related units*" (emphasis added).[4]

In this book, we use the term *unit test* in the narrower sense to mean a test that examines a single unit in isolation from other units. We focus on the type of small, incremental test that programmers apply to their own code. Sometimes, these tests are called *programmer tests* to differentiate them from quality-assurance or customer tests (http://c2.com/cgi/wiki?ProgrammerTest).

Here is a generic description of a typical unit test from the perspective of this book: "Confirms that the method accepts the expected range of input and that the method returns the expected value for each input." This description asks us to test the behavior of a method through its interface. If we give it value *x*, will it return value *y*? If we give it value *z* instead, will it throw the proper exception?

> **DEFINITION** *Unit test*—A test that examines the behavior of a distinct unit of work. A *unit of work* is a task that is not directly dependent on the completion of any other task. Within a Java application, the distinct unit of work is often, but not always, a single method. In contrast, *integration tests* and *acceptance tests* examine how various components interact.

Unit tests often focus on testing whether a method is following the terms of its API contract. Like a written contract between people who agree to exchange certain goods or services under specific conditions, an *API contract* is a formal agreement made by the signature of a method. A method requires its callers to provide specific object references or primitive values and returns an object reference or primitive value. If the method cannot fulfill the contract, the test should throw an exception, and we say that the method has *broken* its contract.

> **DEFINITION** *API contract*—A view of an application programming interface (API) as a formal agreement between the caller and the callee. Often, unit tests help define the API contract by demonstrating the expected behavior. The notion of an API contract arises from the practice of Design by Contract,

---

[4] *IEEE Standard Computer Dictionary: A Compilation of IEEE Standard Computer Glossaries* (New York: IEEE, 1990).

popularized by the Eiffel programming language (http://archive.eiffel.com/doc/manuals/technology/contract).

In this chapter, we walk through creating a unit test from scratch for a simple class. We start by writing a test and its minimal runtime framework so you can see how things used to be done. Then we roll out JUnit to show you how the right tools can make life much simpler.

1.2   *Starting from scratch*

For our first example, we will create a very simple `Calculator` class that adds two numbers. Our calculator, shown in the following listing, provides an API to clients and does not contain a user interface. To test its functionality, we'll first create our own pure Java tests and later move to JUnit 5.

> **Listing 1.1   The `Calculator` class to be tested**

```
public class Calculator {
    public double add(double number1, double number2) {
        return number1 + number2;
    }
}
```

Although the documentation isn't shown, the intended purpose of `Calculator`'s `add(double, double)` method is to take two `double`s and return the sum as a `double`. The compiler can tell you that the code compiles, but you should also make sure it works at runtime. A core principle of unit testing is, "Any program feature without an automated test simply doesn't exist."[5] The `add` method represents a core feature of the calculator. You have some code that allegedly implements the feature. What is missing is an automated test that proves the implementation works.

Isn't the add method too simple to break?

The current implementation of the `add` method is too simple to break with usual, everyday calculations. If `add` were a minor utility method, you might not test it directly. In that case, if `add` did fail, tests of the methods that used `add` would fail. The `add` method would be tested indirectly, but tested nonetheless. In the context of the calculator program, `add` is not just a method, but also a *program feature*. To have confidence in the program, most developers would expect there to be an automated test for the `add` feature, no matter how simple the implementation appears to be. In some cases, you can prove program features through automatic functional tests or automatic acceptance tests. For more about software tests in general, see chapter 5.

---

[5]   Kent Beck, *Extreme Programming Explained: Embrace Change* (Reading, MA: Addison-Wesley, 1999).

Yet testing anything at this point seems to be problematic. You do not even have a user interface with which to enter a pair of doubles. You could write a small command-line program that waited for you to type two double values and then displayed the result. Then, of course, you would also be testing your own ability to type a number and add the result yourself, which is much more than you want to do. You just want to know whether this unit of work actually adds two doubles and returns the correct sum. You do not want to test whether programmers can type numbers!

Meanwhile, if you are going to go to the effort of testing your work, you should also try to preserve that effort. It is good to know that the add(double, double) method worked when you wrote it. What you really want to know, however, is whether the method works when you ship the rest of the application or whenever you make a subsequent modification. If we put these requirements together, we come up with the idea of writing a simple test program for the add method.

The test program can pass known values to the method and see whether the result matches expectations. You can also run the program again later to be sure the method continues to work as the application grows. So what is the simplest possible test program you could write? What about this CalculatorTest program?

Listing 1.2 A simple test calculator program

```java
public class CalculatorTest {
    public static void main(String[] args) {
        Calculator calculator = new Calculator();
        double result = calculator.add(10, 50);
        if (result != 60) {
            System.out.println("Bad result: " + result);
        }
    }
}
```

CalculatorTest is simple indeed: it creates an instance of Calculator, passes two numbers to it, and checks the result. If the result does not meet your expectations, you print a message on standard output.

If you compile and run this program now, the test quietly passes, and all seems to be well. But what happens if you change the code so that it fails? You have to watch the screen carefully for the error message. You may not have to supply the input, but you are still testing your own ability to monitor the program's output. You want to test the code, not yourself!

The conventional way to signal error conditions in Java is to throw an exception. Let's throw an exception to indicate a test failure.

Meanwhile, you may also want to run tests for other Calculator methods that you have not written yet, such as subtract or multiply. Moving to a modular design will make catching and handling exceptions easier; it will also be easier to extend the test program later. The next listing shows a slightly better CalculatorTest program.

Listing 1.3　A (slightly) better test calculator program

```java
public class CalculatorTest {

    private int nbErrors = 0;

    public void testAdd() {
        Calculator calculator = new Calculator();
        double result = calculator.add(10, 50);
        if (result != 60) {
            throw new IllegalStateException("Bad result: " + result);
        }
    }

    public static void main(String[] args) {
        CalculatorTest test = new CalculatorTest();
        try {
            test.testAdd();
        }
        catch (Throwable e) {
            test.nbErrors++;
            e.printStackTrace();
        }
        if (test.nbErrors > 0) {
            throw new IllegalStateException("There were " + test.nbErrors
                + " error(s)");
        }
    }
}
```

❶

❷

At ❶, you move the test into its own `testAdd` method. Now it's easier to focus on what the test does. You can also add more methods with more unit tests later without making the `main` method harder to maintain. At ❷, you change the `main` method to print a stack trace when an error occurs; then, if there are any errors, you end by throwing a summary exception.

Now that you have looked at a simple application and its tests, you can see that even this small class and its tests can benefit from the little bit of skeleton code you created to run and manage test results. But as an application gets more complicated and the tests become more involved, continuing to build and maintain a custom testing framework becomes a burden.

Next, we take a step back and look at the general case for a unit testing framework.

1.2.1　*Understanding unit testing frameworks*

Unit testing has several best practices that frameworks should follow. The seemingly minor improvements in the `CalculatorTest` program in listing 1.3 highlight three rules that (in my experience) all unit testing frameworks should follow:

- Each unit test should run independently of all other unit tests.
- The framework should detect and report errors test by test.
- It should be easy to define which unit tests will run.

The "slightly better" test program comes close to following these rules but still falls short. For each unit test to be truly independent, for example, each should run in a different class instance.

1.2.2 *Adding unit tests*

You can add new unit tests by adding a new method and then adding a corresponding `try/catch` block to main. This is a step up but still short of what you would want in a real unit test suite. Experience tells us that large `try-catch` blocks cause maintenance problems. You could easily leave out a unit test and never know it!

It would be nice if you could just add new test methods and continue working, but if you did, how would the program know which methods to run? Well, you could have a simple registration procedure. A registration method would at least inventory which tests are running.

Another approach would be to use Java's reflection capabilities. A program could look at itself and decide to run whatever methods follow a certain naming convention, such as those that begin with `test`.

Making it easy to add tests (the third rule in the earlier list) sounds like another good rule for a unit testing framework. The support code that realizes this rule (via registration or reflection) would not be trivial, but it would be worthwhile. You'd have to do a lot of work up front, but that effort would pay off each time you add a new test.

Fortunately, the JUnit team has saved you the trouble. The JUnit framework already supports discovering methods. It also supports using a different class instance and class loader instance for each test and reports all errors on a test-by-test basis. The team has defined three discrete goals for the framework:

- The framework must help us write useful tests.
- The framework must help us create tests that retain their value over time.
- The framework must help us lower the cost of writing tests by reusing code.

We'll discuss these goals further in chapter 2.

Next, let's see how to set up JUnit.

1.3 *Setting up JUnit*

To use JUnit to write your application tests, you need to know about its dependencies. You'll work with JUnit 5, the latest version of the framework when this book was written. Version 5 of the testing framework is a modular one; you can no longer simply add a jar file to your project compilation classpath and your execution classpath. In fact, starting with version 5, the architecture is no longer monolithic (as discussed in chapter 3). Also, with the introduction of annotations in Java 5, JUnit has also moved to using them. JUnit 5 is heavily based on annotations—a contrast with the idea of extending a base class for all testing classes and using naming conventions for all testing methods to match the text *XYZ* pattern, as done in previous versions.

> **NOTE** If you are familiar with JUnit 4, you may wonder what's new in this version, as well as why and how to move toward it. JUnit 5 represents the next

generation of JUnit. You'll use the programming capabilities introduced start-ing with Java 8; you'll be able to build tests modularly and hierarchically; and the tests will be easier to understand, maintain, and extend. Chapter 4 dis-cusses the transition from JUnit 4 to JUnit 5 and shows that the projects you are working on may benefit from the great features of JUnit 5. As you'll see, you can make this transition smoothly, in small steps.

To manage JUnit 5's dependencies efficiently, it's logical to work with the help of a build tool. In this book, we'll use Maven, a very popular build tool. Chapter 10 is dedi-cated to the topic of running JUnit tests from Maven. What you need to know now are the basic ideas behind Maven: configuring your project through the pom.xml file, executing the `mvn clean install` command, and understanding the command's effects.

NOTE   You can download Maven from https://maven.apache.org. When this book was being written, the latest version was 3.6.3.

The dependencies that are always needed in the pom.xml file are shown in the follow-ing listing. In the beginning, you need only `junit-jupiter-api` and `junit-jupiter-engine`.

Listing 1.4   pom.xml JUnit 5 dependencies

```
<dependency>
    <groupId>org.junit.jupiter</groupId>
    <artifactId>junit-jupiter-api</artifactId>
    <version>5.6.0</version>
    <scope>test</scope>
</dependency>
<dependency>
    <groupId>org.junit.jupiter</groupId>
    <artifactId>junit-jupiter-engine</artifactId>
    <version>5.6.0</version>
    <scope>test</scope>
</dependency>
```

To be able to run tests from the command prompt, make sure your pom.xml configu-ration file includes a JUnit provider dependency for the Maven Surefire plugin. Here's what this dependency looks like.

Listing 1.5   Maven Surefire plugin configuration in pom.xml

```
<build>
    <plugins>
        <plugin>
            <artifactId>maven-surefire-plugin</artifactId>
            <version>2.22.2</version>
        </plugin>
    </plugins>
</build>
```

As Windows is the most commonly used operating system (OS), our example configuration details use Windows 10, the latest version. Concepts such as the path, environment variables, and the command prompt also exist in other OSs; follow your documentation guidelines if you will be running the examples on an OS other than Windows.

To run the tests, the bin folder from the Maven directory must be on the OS path (figure 1.1). You also need to configure the JAVA_HOME environment variable on your OS to point to the Java installation folder (figure 1.2). In addition, your JDK version must be at least 8, as required by JUnit 5.

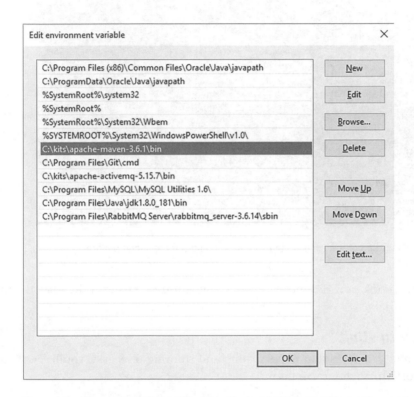

Figure 1.1   The configuration of the OS path must include the Apache Maven bin folder.

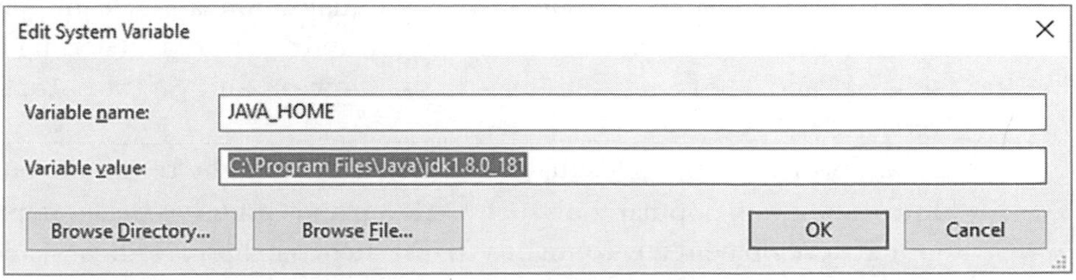

Figure 1.2   The configuration of the JAVA_HOME **environment variable**

You will need the source files from the chapter to get the results shown in figure 1.3. Open a command prompt into the project folder (the one containing the pom.xml file), and run this command:

```
mvn clean install
```

This command will take the Java source code, compile it, test it, and convert it into a runnable Java program (a jar file, in our case). Figure 1.3 shows the result of the test.

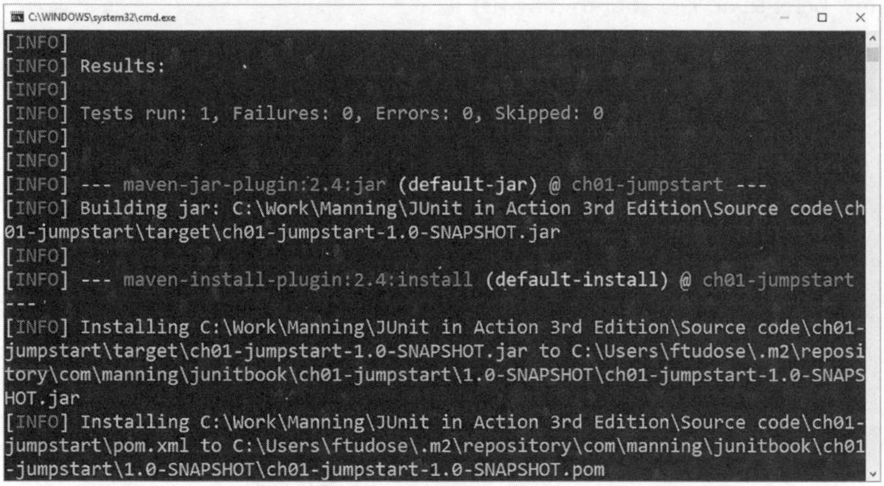

Figure 1.3   Execution of the JUnit tests using Maven and the command prompt

Part 3 of the book provides more details about running tests with the Maven and Gradle build tools.

1.4   *Testing with JUnit*

JUnit has many features that make writing and running tests easy. You'll see these features at work throughout this book:

- Separate test class instances and class loaders for each unit test to prevent side effects
- JUnit annotations to provide resource initialization and cleanup methods: @BeforeEach, @BeforeAll, @AfterEach, and @AfterAll (starting from version 5); and @Before, @BeforeClass, @After, and @AfterClass (up to version 4)
- A variety of assert methods that make it easy to check the results of your tests
- Integration with popular tools such as Maven and Gradle, as well as popular integrated development environments (IDEs) such as Eclipse, NetBeans, and IntelliJ

Without further ado, the next listing shows what the simple Calculator test looks like when written with JUnit.

Listing 1.6   JUnit `CalculatorTest` program

```
import static org.junit.jupiter.api.Assertions.assertEquals;
import org.junit.jupiter.api.Test;

public class CalculatorTest {

    @Test
    public void testAdd() {
        Calculator calculator = new Calculator();
        double result = calculator.add(10, 50);
        assertEquals(60, result, 0);
    }
}
```

① ② ③ ④ ⑤

Running such a test with the help of Maven results in behavior similar to that shown in figure 1.3. The test is very simple. At ①, you define a test class. It's common practice to end the class name with `Test`. JUnit 3 required extending the `TestCase` class, but this requirement was removed with JUnit 4. Also, up to JUnit 4, the class had to be public; starting with version 5, the top-level test class can be public or package-private, and you can name it whatever you want.

At ②, you mark the method as a unit test method by adding the `@Test` annotation. In the past, the usual practice was to name test methods following the test*XYZ* pattern, as was required up to JUnit 3. Now that doing so is no longer required, some programmers drop the prefix and use a descriptive phrase as the method name. You can name your methods as you like; as long as they have the `@Test` annotation, JUnit will execute them. The JUnit 5 `@Test` annotation belongs to a new package, `org.junit.jupiter.api`, and the JUnit 4 `@Test` annotation belongs to the `org.junit` package. This book uses JUnit 5's capabilities except in some clearly emphasized cases (such as to demonstrate migration from JUnit 4).

At ③, you start the test by creating an instance of the `Calculator` class (the object under test). And at ④, as before, you execute the test by calling the method to test, passing it two known values.

At ⑤, the JUnit framework begins to shine! To check the result of the test, you call an `assertEquals` method, which you imported with a static import on the first line of the class. The Javadoc for the `assertEquals` method is

```
/**
 * Assert that expected and actual are equal within the non-negative delta.
 * Equality imposed by this method is consistent with Double.equals(Object)
 * and Double.compare(double, double). */
public static void assertEquals(
    double expected, double actual, double delta)
```

In listing 1.6, you pass these parameters to `assertEquals`:

```
expected = 60
actual = result
delta = 0
```

Because you pass the calculator the values `10` and `50`, you tell `assertEquals` to expect the sum to be `60`. (You pass `0` as `delta` because you are expecting no floating-point errors when adding 10 and 50, as the decimal part of these numbers is 0.) When you call the `calculator` object, you save the return value in a local double named `result`. Therefore, you pass that variable to `assertEquals` to compare with the expected value (`60`). If the actual value is not equal to the expected value, JUnit throws an unchecked exception, which causes the test to fail.

Most often, the `delta` parameter can be `0`, and you can safely ignore it. This parameter comes into play with calculations that are not always precise, including many floating-point calculations. `delta` provides a range factor: if the actual value is within the range `expected – delta` and `expected + delta`, the test will pass. You may find this useful when you're performing mathematical computations with rounding or truncating errors or when you're asserting a condition about the modification date of a file, because the precision of these dates depends on the OS.

The remarkable thing about the JUnit `CalculatorTest` class in listing 1.6 is that the code is easier to write than the first `CalculatorTest` program in listings 1.2 or 1.3. In addition, you can run the test automatically through the JUnit framework.

When you run the test from the command line (figure 1.3), you see the amount of time it takes and the number of tests that passed. There are many other ways to run tests, from IDEs and from different build tools. This simple example gives you a taste of the power of JUnit and unit testing.

You may modify the `Calculator` class so that it has a bug—for example, instead of adding the numbers, it subtracts them. Then you can run the test and watch what the result looks like when a test fails.

In chapter 2, we will take a closer look at the JUnit framework classes (annotations and assertion mechanisms) and capabilities (nested and tagged tests, as well as repeated, parameterized, and dynamic tests). We'll show how they work together to make unit testing efficient and effective. You will learn how to use the JUnit 5 features in practice and differences between the old-style JUnit 4 and JUnit 5.

Summary

This chapter has covered the following:

- Why every developer should perform some type of test to see if code actually works. Developers who use automatic unit tests can repeat these tests on demand to ensure that new code works *and does not break existing tests.*
- Writing simple unit tests, which are not difficult to create without JUnit.
- As tests are added and become more complex, writing and maintaining tests becomes more difficult.
- Introduction to JUnit as a unit testing framework that makes it easier to create, run, and revise unit tests.
- Stepping through a simple JUnit test.

Exploring core JUnit

Mistakes are the portals of discovery.

—James Joyce

In chapter 1, we decided that we need a reliable, repeatable way to test programs. Our solution is to write or reuse a framework to drive the test code that exercises our program API. As our program grows, with new classes and new methods added to the existing classes, we need to grow our test code as well. Experience has taught us that classes sometimes interact in unexpected ways, so we need to make sure we can run all of our tests at any time, no matter what code changes have taken place. But how do we run multiple test classes? How do we find out which tests passed and which ones failed?

In this chapter, we look at how JUnit provides the functionality to answer those questions. The chapter begins with an overview of the core JUnit concepts: the test

15

class, methods, and annotations. Then we take a detailed look at the many testing mechanisms of JUnit 5 and the JUnit life cycle.

This chapter is written in the practical spirit of the Manning "in Action" series, looking mainly at the usage of the new core features. For comprehensive documentation of each class, method, and annotation, please visit the JUnit 5 user guide (https://junit.org/junit5/docs/current/user-guide) or the JUnit 5 Javadoc (https://junit.org/junit5/docs/current/api).

The chapter introduces Tested Data Systems Inc., an example company that uses the testing mechanisms. Tested Data Systems is an outsourcing company that runs several Java projects for a few customers. These projects use different frameworks and different build tools, but they have something in common: they need to be tested to ensure the high quality of the code. Some older projects are running their tests with JUnit 4; newer ones have already started using JUnit 5. The engineers have decided to acquire in-depth knowledge of JUnit 5 and to transmit it to the projects that need to move from JUnit 4 to JUnit 5.

2.1 *Core annotations*

The `CalculatorTest` program from chapter 1, shown in the following listing, defines a test class with a single test method, `testAdd`.

Listing 2.1 `CalculatorTest` **test case**

```
import static org.junit.jupiter.api.Assertions.assertEquals;
import org.junit.jupiter.api.Test;

public class CalculatorTest {

   @Test
   public void testAdd() {
      Calculator calculator = new Calculator();
      double result = calculator.add(10, 50);
      assertEquals(60, result, 0);
   }
}
```

These are the most important concepts:

- A *test class* may be a top-level class, a static member class, or an inner class annotated as `@Nested` that contains one or more test methods. Test classes cannot be abstract and must have a single constructor. The constructor must have no arguments, or arguments that can be dynamically resolved at runtime through dependency injection. (We discuss the details of dependency injection in section 2.6.) A test class is allowed to be package-private as a minimum requirement for visibility. It is no longer required that test classes be public, as was the case up to JUnit 4.x. The Java compiler will supply a no-args constructor for `CalculatorTest` because we do not define any constructors for the class.

- A *test method* is an instance method that is annotated with @Test, @Repeated-Test, @ParameterizedTest, @TestFactory, or @TestTemplate.
- A *life cycle method* is a method that is annotated with @BeforeAll, @AfterAll, @BeforeEach, or @AfterEach.

Test methods must not be abstract and must not return a value (the return type should be void).

The source files accompanying this book contain the code for all the examples. To use the imported classes, methods, and annotations needed for the test in listing 2.1, you'll need to declare their dependencies. Most projects use a build tool to manage them. (We have chosen to use Maven, as discussed in chapter 1. Chapter 10 covers running JUnit tests from Maven.)

You need to carry out only basic tasks in Maven: configure your project through the pom.xml file, execute the mvn clean install command, and understand the command's effects. The next listing shows the minimal JUnit 5 dependencies to be used in the pom.xml Maven configuration file.

> **Listing 2.2   pom.xml JUnit 5 dependencies**

```
<dependency>
    <groupId>org.junit.jupiter</groupId>
    <artifactId>junit-jupiter-api</artifactId>        ⬅── ❶
    <version>5.6.0</version>
    <scope>test</scope>
</dependency>
<dependency>
    <groupId>org.junit.jupiter</groupId>
    <artifactId>junit-jupiter-engine</artifactId>      ⬅── 
    <version>5.6.0</version>                               ❷
    <scope>test</scope>
</dependency>
```

This shows that the minimal needed dependencies are junit-jupiter-api ❶ and junit-jupiter-engine ❷.

JUnit creates a new instance of the test class before invoking each @Test method to ensure the independence of test methods and prevent unintentional side effects in the test code. Also, it is a universally accepted fact that the tests must produce the same result independent of the order of their execution. Because each test method runs on a new test class instance, you cannot reuse instance variable values across test methods. One test instance is created for the execution of each test method, which is the default behavior in JUnit 5 and all previous versions.

If you annotate your test class with @TestInstance(Lifecycle.PER_CLASS), JUnit 5 will execute all test methods on the same test instance. A new test instance will be created for each test class when using this annotation.

Listing 2.3 shows the use of the JUnit 5 life cycle methods in the lifecycle.SUT-Test class. One of the projects at Tested Data Systems is testing a system that will start up, receive regular and additional work, and close itself. The life cycle methods ensure that the system is initializing and then shutting down before and after each effective test. The test methods check whether the system receives regular and additional work.

Listing 2.3   Using JUnit 5 life cycle methods

```java
class SUTTest {
    private static ResourceForAllTests resourceForAllTests;
    private SUT systemUnderTest;

    @BeforeAll
    static void setUpClass() {
        resourceForAllTests =
            new ResourceForAllTests("Our resource for all tests");
    }

    @AfterAll
    static void tearDownClass() {
        resourceForAllTests.close();
    }

    @BeforeEach
    void setUp() {
        systemUnderTest = new SUT("Our system under test");
    }

    @AfterEach
    void tearDown() {
        systemUnderTest.close();
    }

    @Test
    void testRegularWork() {
        boolean canReceiveRegularWork =
            systemUnderTest.canReceiveRegularWork();

        assertTrue(canReceiveRegularWork);
    }

    @Test
    void testAdditionalWork() {
        boolean canReceiveAdditionalWork =
                systemUnderTest.canReceiveAdditionalWork();

        assertFalse(canReceiveAdditionalWork);
    }
}
```

❶ ❷ ❸ ❹ ❺ ❺

Following the life cycle of the test execution, you see that

- The method annotated with `@BeforeAll` ❶ is executed once: before all tests. This method needs to be static unless the entire test class is annotated with `@TestInstance(Lifecycle.PER_CLASS)`.
- The method annotated with `@BeforeEach` ❸ is executed before each test. In our case, it will be executed twice.

- The two methods annotated with @Test ❺ are executed independently.
- The method annotated with @AfterEach ❹ is executed after each test. In our case, it will be executed twice.
- The method annotated with @AfterAll ❷ is executed once: after all tests. This method needs to be static unless the entire test class is annotated with @TestInstance(Lifecycle.PER_CLASS).
- To run this test class, you can execute the following from the command line: mvn -Dtest=SUTTest.java clean install.

2.1.1 *The @DisplayName annotation*

The @DisplayName annotation can be used over classes and test methods. It helps the engineers at Tested Data Systems declare their own display name for an annotated test class or test method. Typically, this annotation is used for test reporting in IDEs and build tools. The string argument of the @DisplayName annotation may contain spaces, special characters, and even emojis.

The following listing demonstrates the use of the @DisplayName annotation through the class displayname.DisplayNameTest. The name that's displayed is usually a full phrase that provides significant information about the purpose of the test.

Listing 2.4 @DisplayName annotation

```
@DisplayName("Test class showing the @DisplayName annotation.")    ⬅
class DisplayNameTest {                                                  ❶
    private SUT systemUnderTest = new SUT();

    @Test
    @DisplayName("Our system under test says hello.")              ⬅
    void testHello() {                                                 ❷
        assertEquals("Hello", systemUnderTest.hello());
    }
                                        ❸
    @Test
    @DisplayName("😀")                            ⬅
    void testTalking() {
        assertEquals("How are you?", systemUnderTest.talk());
    }

    @Test
    void testBye() {
        assertEquals("Bye", systemUnderTest.bye());
    }
}
```

This example does the following:

- Shows the display name applied to the entire class ❶
- Applies a normal text display name ❷
- Uses a display name that includes an emoji ❸

A test that does not have an associated display name simply shows the method name. From IntelliJ, you can run a test by right-clicking on it and then executing the run command. The results of these tests in the IntelliJ IDE are shown in figure 2.1.

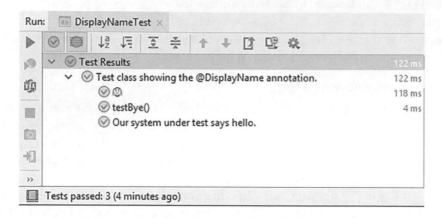

Figure 2.1   Running `DisplayNameTest` **in IntelliJ**

2.1.2   *The @Disabled annotation*

The `@Disabled` annotation can be used over classes and test methods. It signals that the annotated test class or test method is disabled and should not be executed. The programmers at Tested Data Systems use it to give their reasons for disabling a test so the rest of the team knows exactly why that was done. If this annotation is applied to a class, it disables all the methods of the test. Also, the disabled tests and the reasons for their being disabled are displayed differently on each programmer's console when the programmer runs them from the IDE.

The use of the annotation is demonstrated by the classes `disabled.Disabled-ClassTest` and `disabled.DisabledMethodsTest`. Listings 2.5 and 2.6 show the code for these classes.

Listing 2.5   `@Disabled` annotation used on a test class

```
@Disabled("Feature is still under construction.")
class DisabledClassTest {
    private SUT systemUnderTest= new SUT("Our system under test");    ❶

    @Test
     void testRegularWork() {
        boolean canReceiveRegularWork = systemUnderTest.
        canReceiveRegularWork();

        assertTrue(canReceiveRegularWork);
    }
```

```
@Test
void testAdditionalWork() {
    boolean canReceiveAdditionalWork =
            systemUnderTest.canReceiveAdditionalWork();

    assertFalse(canReceiveAdditionalWork);
}
```

The entire testing class is disabled, and the reason is provided ❶. This technique is recommended so that your colleagues (or even you) immediately understand why the test is not enabled.

Listing 2.6   @Disabled annotation used on methods

```
class DisabledMethodsTest {
    private SUT systemUnderTest= new SUT("Our system under test");

                                            ❶
    @Test
    @Disabled                           <──┘
    void testRegularWork() {
      boolean canReceiveRegularWork =
              systemUnderTest.canReceiveRegularWork ();

        assertTrue(canReceiveRegularWork);
    }

                                                            ❷
    @Test
    @Disabled("Feature still under construction.")    <──┘
    void testAdditionalWork() {
        boolean canReceiveAdditionalWork =
                systemUnderTest.canReceiveAdditionalWork ();

        assertFalse(canReceiveAdditionalWork);
    }
}
```

You see that

- The code provides two tests, both disabled.
- One of the tests is disabled without a reason given ❶.
- The other test is disabled with a reason that other programmers will understand ❷—the recommended approach.

2.2   Nested tests

An *inner class* is a class that is a member of another class. It can access any private instance variable of the outer class, as it is effectively part of that outer class. The typical use case is when two classes are tightly coupled, and it's logical to provide direct access from the inner class to all instance variables of the outer class. For example, we may test a flight that has two types of passengers trying to board. The behavior of the flight will be described in the outer test class, while the behavior of each type of passenger will be described in its own nested class. Each passenger is able to interact with the flight. The nested tests will follow the business logic and lead to writing clearer code, as you will be able to follow the testing process more easily.

Following this tight-coupling idea, nested tests give the test writer more capabilities to express the relationships among several groups of tests. Inner classes may be package-private.

The Tested Data Systems company works with customers. Each customer has a gender, a first name, a last name, sometimes a middle name, and the date when they became a customer (if known). Some parameters may not be present, so the engineers are using the builder pattern to create and test a customer.

The following listing demonstrates the use of the @Nested annotation on the class NestedTestsTest. The customer being tested is John Michael Smith, and the date when he became a customer is known.

Listing 2.7   Nested tests

```
public class NestedTestsTest {
    private static final String FIRST_NAME = "John";       ❷        ❶
    private static final String LAST_NAME = "Smith";

    @Nested                                    ❸
    class BuilderTest {
        private String MIDDLE_NAME = "Michael";

        @Test                                                          ❹
        void customerBuilder() throws ParseException {
            SimpleDateFormat simpleDateFormat =
                    new SimpleDateFormat("MM-dd-yyyy");
            Date customerDate = simpleDateFormat.parse("04-21-2019");

            Customer customer = new Customer.Builder(
                            Gender.MALE, FIRST_NAME, LAST_NAME)
                    .withMiddleName(MIDDLE_NAME)                       ❺
                    .withBecomeCustomer(customerDate)
                    .build();

            assertAll(() -> {
                assertEquals(Gender.MALE, customer.getGender());
                assertEquals(FIRST_NAME, customer.getFirstName());
                assertEquals(LAST_NAME, customer.getLastName());
                assertEquals(MIDDLE_NAME, customer.getMiddleName());   ❻
                assertEquals(customerDate,
                            customer.getBecomeCustomer());
            });
        }
    }
}
```

The main test is NestedTestsTest ❶, and it makes sense here that it is tightly coupled with the nested test BuilderTest ❸. First, NestedTestsTest defines the first name and last name of a customer that will be used for all nested tests ❷. The nested test, `BuilderTest`, verifies the construction of a `Customer` object ❹ with the help of the builder pattern ❺. The equality of the fields is verified at the end of the `customerBuilder` test ❻.

The source code file has another nested class, `CustomerHashCodeTest`, containing two more tests. You can follow along with it.

2.3 Tagged tests

If you are familiar with JUnit 4, *tagged tests* are replacements for JUnit 4 categories. You can use the `@Tag` annotation over classes and test methods. Later, you can use tags to filter test discovery and execution.

Listing 2.8 presents the `CustomerTest` tagged class, which tests the correct creation of Tested Data Systems customers. Listing 2.9 presents the `Customers-RepositoryTest` tagged class, which tests the existence and nonexistence of customers inside a repository. One use case may be to group your tests into a few categories based on the business logic and the things you are effectively testing. (Each test category has its own tag.) Then you may decide to run only some tests or alternate among categories, depending on your current needs.

Listing 2.8 `CustomerTest` tagged class

```
@Tag("individual")
public class CustomerTest {                                        ◀─── ❶
    private String CUSTOMER_NAME = "John Smith";

    @Test
    void testCustomer() {
        Customer customer = new Customer(CUSTOMER_NAME);

        assertEquals("John Smith", customer.getName());
    }
}
```

The `@Tag` annotation is added to the entire `CustomerTest` class ❶.

Listing 2.9 `CustomersRepositoryTest` tagged class

```
@Tag("repository")
public class CustomersRepositoryTest {                             ◀─── ❶
    private String CUSTOMER_NAME = "John Smith";
    private CustomersRepository repository = new CustomersRepository();

    @Test
    void testNonExistence() {
        boolean exists = repository.contains("John Smith");

        assertFalse(exists);
    }
```

```
@Test
void testCustomerPersistence() {
    repository.persist(new Customer(CUSTOMER_NAME));

    assertTrue(repository.contains("John Smith"));
}
}
```

Similarly, the @Tag annotation is added to the entire CustomersRepositoryTest class ①. Here is the Maven configuration file for these tests.

Listing 2.10   pom.xml configuration file

```
<plugin>
    <artifactId>maven-surefire-plugin</artifactId>
    <version>2.22.2</version>
    <!--
    <configuration>
        <groups>individual</groups>
        <excludedGroups>repository</excludedGroups>     ①
    </configuration>
    -->
</plugin>
```

To activate the tags, you have a few alternatives. One is to work at the level of the pom.xml configuration file. In this example, it's enough to uncomment the configuration node of the Surefire plugin ① and run mvn clean install.

Another alternative in the IntelliJ IDEA is to activate the tags by creating a configuration by choosing Run > Run > Edit Configurations > Tags (JUnit 5) as the test kind (figure 2.2). This is fine when you would like to quickly make some changes about which tests to run locally. However, it is strongly recommended that you make the changes at the level of the pom.xml file—otherwise, any automated build of the project will fail.

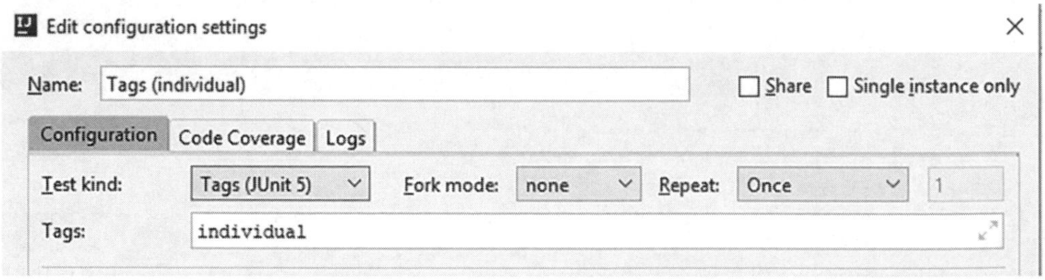

Figure 2.2   Configuring the tagged tests from the IntelliJ IDEA

2.4 Assertions

To perform test validation, you use the `assert` methods provided by the JUnit `Assertions` class. As you can see from the previous examples, we have statically imported these methods in our test class. Alternatively, you can import the JUnit `Assertions` class itself, depending on your taste for static imports. Table 2.1 lists some of the most popular `assert` methods.

Table 2.1   Sample JUnit 5 `assert` methods

assert method	What it is used for
`assertAll`	Overloaded method. It asserts that none of the supplied executables throw exceptions. An *executable* is an object of type `org.junit.jupiter.api.function.Executable`.
`assertArrayEquals`	Overloaded method. It asserts that the expected array and the actual array are equal.
`assertEquals`	Overloaded method. It asserts that the expected values and the actual values are equal.
`assertX(..., String message)`	Assertion that delivers the supplied message to the test framework if the assertion fails.
`assertX(..., Supplier<String> messageSupplier)`	Assertion that delivers the supplied message to the test framework if the assertion fails. The failure message is retrieved lazily from the supplied `messageSupplier`.

JUnit 5 provides a lot of overloaded assertion methods. It includes many assertion methods from JUnit 4 and adds a few that can use Java 8 lambdas. All JUnit Jupiter assertions belong to the `org.junit.jupiter.api.Assertions` class and are static methods. The `assertThat()` method that works with Hamcrest matchers has been removed. The recommended approach in such a case is to use the Hamcrest `MatcherAssert.assertThat()` overloaded methods, which are more flexible and in the spirit of the Java 8 capabilities.

> **DEFINITION**   *Hamcrest* is a framework that assists with the writing of software tests in JUnit. It supports the creation of customized assertion matchers (*Hamcrest* is an anagram of *matchers*), letting us define match rules declaratively. Later in this chapter, we discuss the capabilities of Hamcrest.

As stated previously, one of the projects at our previously introduced Tested Data Systems company is testing a system that starts up, receives regular and additional work, and closes itself. After we run some operations, we need to verify more than a single condition. In this case, we'll also use the lambda expressions introduced in Java 8.

Lambda expressions treat functionality as a method argument and code as data. We can pass around a lambda expression as if it were an object and execute it on demand.

This section presents a few examples provided by the assertions package. Listing 2.11 shows some of the overloaded assertAll methods. The heading parameter allows us to recognize the group of assertions within the assertAll() methods. The failure message of the assertAll() method can provide detailed information about every particular assertion within a group. Also, we're using the @DisplayName annotation to provide easy-to-understand information about what the test is looking for. Our purpose is the verification of the same system under test (SUT) class that we introduced earlier.

After the heading parameter from the assertAll method, we provide the rest of the arguments as a collection of executables—a shorter, more convenient way to assert that supplied executables do not throw exceptions.

Listing 2.11 assertAll method

```
class AssertAllTest {
    @Test
    @DisplayName(
        "SUT should default to not being under current verification")
    void testSystemNotVerified() {
        SUT systemUnderTest = new SUT("Our system under test");

        assertAll("By default,
                SUT is not under current verification",      ❶
            () -> assertEquals("Our system under test",       ❷
                systemUnderTest.getSystemName()),
            () -> assertFalse(systemUnderTest.isVerified())   ❸
        );
    }

    @Test
    @DisplayName("SUT should be under current verification")
    void testSystemUnderVerification() {
        SUT systemUnderTest = new SUT("Our system under test");

        systemUnderTest.verify();                             ❹

        assertAll("SUT under current verification",
            () -> assertEquals("Our system under test",       ❺
                systemUnderTest.getSystemName()),
            () -> assertTrue(systemUnderTest.isVerified())    ❻
        );
    }
}
```

The assertAll method will always check all the assertions that are provided to it, even if some of them fail—if any of the executables fail, the remaining ones will still be run. That is not true for the JUnit 4 approach: if you have a few assert methods, one under the other, and one of them fails, that failure will stop the execution of the others.

In the first test, the `assertAll` method receives as a parameter the message to be displayed if one of the supplied executables throws an exception ❶. Then the method receives one executable to be verified with `assertEquals` ❷ and one to be verified with `assertFalse` ❸. The assertion conditions are brief so that they can be read at a glance.

In the second test, the `assertAll` method receives as a parameter the message to be displayed if one of the supplied executables throws an exception ❹. Then it receives one executable to be verified with `assertEquals` ❺ and one to be verified with `assertTrue` ❻. Just like in the first test, the assertion conditions are easy to read.

The next listing shows the use of some assertion methods with messages. Thanks to `Supplier<String>`, the instructions required to create a complex message aren't provided in the case of success. We can use lambda or method references to verify our SUT; they improve performance.

Listing 2.12   Some assertion methods with messages

```
...
@Test
@DisplayName("SUT should be under current verification")
void testSystemUnderVerification() {
    systemUnderTest.verify();                                      ❶
    assertTrue(systemUnderTest.isVerified(),                            ❷
             () -> "System should be under verification");
}


@Test
@DisplayName("SUT should not be under current verification")
void testSystemNotUnderVerification() {                            ❸
    assertFalse(systemUnderTest.isVerified(),
            () -> "System should not be under verification.");
}                                                                 ❹


@Test
@DisplayName("SUT should have no current job")
void testNoJob() {                                          ❺
    assertNull(systemUnderTest.getCurrentJob(),                   ❻
            () -> "There should be no current job");
}
...
```

In this example:

- A condition is verified with the help of the `assertTrue` method ❶. In case of failure, a message is lazily created ❷.
- A condition is verified with the help of the `assertFalse` method ❸. In case of failure, a message is lazily created ❹.
- The existence of an object is verified with the help of the `assertNull` method ❺. In case of failure, a message is lazily created ❻.

The advantage of using lambda expressions as arguments for assertion methods is that all of them are lazily created, resulting in improved performance. If the condition at ❶ is fulfilled, meaning the test succeeded, the invocation of the lambda expression at ❷ does not take place, which would be impossible if the test were written in the old style.

There may be situations in which you expect a test to be executed within a given interval. In our example, it is natural for the user to expect that the system under test will run the given jobs quickly. JUnit 5 offers an elegant solution for this kind of use case.

The following listing shows the use of some `assertTimeout` and `assert-TimeoutPreemptively` methods, which replace the JUnit 4 `Timeout` rule. *The methods* need to check whether the SUT is performant enough, meaning it is executing its jobs within a given timeout.

Listing 2.13   Some `assertTimeout` methods

```
class AssertTimeoutTest {
    private SUT systemUnderTest = new SUT("Our system under test");

    @Test
    @DisplayName("A job is executed within a timeout")
    void testTimeout() throws InterruptedException {
        systemUnderTest.addJob(new Job("Job 1"));                          ❶
        assertTimeout(ofMillis(500), () -> systemUnderTest.run(200));   ◁─┘

    }

    @Test
    @DisplayName("A job is executed preemptively within a timeout")
    void testTimeoutPreemptively() throws InterruptedException {
        systemUnderTest.addJob(new Job("Job 1"));
        assertTimeoutPreemptively(ofMillis(500),
                                  () -> systemUnderTest.run(200));    ❷

    }

}
```

`assertTimeout` waits until the executable finishes ❶. The failure message looks something like this: `execution exceeded timeout of 500 ms by 193 ms`.

`assertTimeoutPreemptively` stops the executable when the time has expired ❷. The failure message looks like this: `execution timed out after 500 ms`.

In some situations, you expect a test to be executed and to throw an exception, so you may force the rest to run under inappropriate conditions or to receive inappropriate input. In our example, it is natural that the SUT that tries to run without a job assigned to it will throw an exception. Again, JUnit 5 offers an elegant solution.

Listing 2.14 shows the use of some `assertThrows` methods, which replace the JUnit 4 `ExpectedException` rule and the expected attribute of the `@Test` annotation. All assertions can be made against the returned instance of `Throwable`. This makes the tests more readable, as we are verifying that the SUT is throwing exceptions: a current job is expected but not found.

Listing 2.14 Some `assertThrows` methods

```
class AssertThrowsTest {
    private SUT systemUnderTest = new SUT("Our system under test");

    @Test
    @DisplayName("An exception is expected")
    void testExpectedException() {
        assertThrows(NoJobException.class, systemUnderTest::run);      ❶
    }

    @Test
    @DisplayName("An exception is caught")
    void testCatchException() {
        Throwable throwable = assertThrows(NoJobException.class,       ❷
                            () -> systemUnderTest.run(1000));
        assertEquals("No jobs on the execution list!",
                    throwable.getMessage());                           ❸
    }
}
```

In this example:

- We verify that the `systemUnderTest` object's call of the `run` method throws a `NoJobException` ❶.
- We verify that a call to `systemUnderTest.run(1000)` throws a `NoJob-Exception`, and we keep a reference to the thrown exception in the `throwable` variable ❷.
- We check the message kept in the `throwable` exception variable ❸.

2.5 *Assumptions*

Sometimes tests fail due to an external environment configuration or a date or time zone issue that we cannot control. We can prevent our tests from being executed under inappropriate conditions.

Assumptions verify the fulfillment of preconditions that are essential for running the tests. You can use assumptions when it does not make sense to continue the execution of a given test method. In the test report, these tests are marked as aborted.

JUnit 5 comes with a set of assumption methods suitable for use with Java 8 lambdas. The JUnit 5 assumptions are static methods belonging to the `org.junit` `.jupiter.api.Assumptions` class. The `message` parameter is in the last position.

JUnit 4 users should be aware that not all previously existing assumptions are provided in JUnit 5. There is no `assumeThat()` method, which we may regard as confirmation that matchers are no longer part of JUnit. The new `assumingThat()` method executes an assertion only if the assumption is fulfilled.

Suppose we have a test that needs to run only in the Windows OS and in the Java 8 version. These preconditions are turned into JUnit 5 assumptions. A test is executed only if the assumptions are true. The following listing shows the use of some assumption methods and verifies our SUT only under the environmental conditions we imposed: the OS needs to be Windows, and the Java version needs to be 8. If these conditions (assumptions) are not fulfilled, the check is not made.

Listing 2.15 Some assumption methods

```
class AssumptionsTest {
    private static String EXPECTED_JAVA_VERSION = "1.8";
    private TestsEnvironment environment = new TestsEnvironment(
            new JavaSpecification(
                System.getProperty("java.vm.specification.version")),
            new OperationSystem(
                System.getProperty("os.name"),
                System.getProperty("os.arch"))
            );

    private SUT systemUnderTest = new SUT();

    @BeforeEach
    void setUp() {                                              ◁──────❶
        assumeTrue(environment.isWindows());        ◁
    }

    @Test
    void testNoJobToRun() {
        assumingThat(
                () -> environment.getJavaVersion()             ❷
                            .equals(EXPECTED_JAVA_VERSION),  ◁───
                () -> assertFalse(systemUnderTest.hasJobToRun())); ◁─
    }                                                              ❸

    @Test
    void testJobToRun() {                                      ❹      ❺
        assumeTrue(environment.isAmd64Architecture());    ◁─
        systemUnderTest.run(new Job());                          ◁──
        assertTrue(systemUnderTest.hasJobToRun());    ◁─
    }                                                          ❻
}
```

In this example:

- The @BeforeEach annotated method is executed before each test. The test will not run unless the assumption that the current environment is Windows is true ❶.
- The first test checks that the current Java version is the expected one ❷. Only if this assumption is true does it verify that no job is currently being run by the SUT ❸.
- The second test checks the current environment architecture ❹. Only if this architecture is the expected one does it run a new job on the SUT ❺ and verify that the system has a job to run ❻.

2.6 Dependency injection in JUnit 5

The previous JUnit versions did not permit test constructors or methods to have parameters. JUnit 5 allows test constructors and methods to have parameters, but they need to be resolved through dependency injection.

The `ParameterResolver` interface dynamically resolves parameters at runtime. A parameter of a constructor or method must be resolved at runtime by a registered `ParameterResolver`. You can inject as many parameters as you want, in any order.

JUnit 5 now has three built-in resolvers. You must explicitly enable other parameter resolvers by registering appropriate extensions via `@ExtendWith`. The parameter resolvers that are automatically registered are discussed in the following sections.

2.6.1 TestInfoParameterResolver

If a constructor or method parameter is of type `TestInfo`, `TestInfoParameterResolver` supplies an instance of this type. `TestInfo` is a class whose objects are used to inject information about the currently executed test or container into the `@Test`, `@BeforeEach`, `@AfterEach`, `@BeforeAll`, and `@AfterAll` methods. Then `TestInfo` gets information about the current test: the display name, test class or method, and associated tags. The display name can be the name of the test class or test method or a custom name provided with the help of `@DisplayName`. Here's how to use a `TestInfo` parameter as an argument of a constructor and annotated methods.

Listing 2.16 `TestInfo` parameters

```
class TestInfoTest {
    TestInfoTest(TestInfo testInfo) {
        assertEquals("TestInfoTest", testInfo.getDisplayName());        ◄——  ❶
    }

    @BeforeEach
    void setUp(TestInfo testInfo) {
        String displayName = testInfo.getDisplayName();
        assertTrue(displayName.equals("display name of the method") ||
                displayName.equals(                                          ❷
                        "testGetNameOfTheMethod(TestInfo)"));
    }

    @Test
    void testGetNameOfTheMethod(TestInfo testInfo) {
        assertEquals("testGetNameOfTheMethod(TestInfo)",
                    testInfo.getDisplayName());                      ◄——  ❸
    }

    @Test
    @DisplayName("display name of the method")
    void testGetNameOfTheMethodWithDisplayNameAnnotation(TestInfo testInfo) {
        assertEquals("display name of the method",
                    testInfo.getDisplayName());                      ◄——
    }                                                                         ❹
}
```

In this example:

- A `TestInfo` parameter is injected into the constructor and into three methods. The constructor verifies that the display name is `TestInfoTest`: its own name **❶**. This is the default behavior, which we can vary using `@DisplayName` annotations.
- The `@BeforeEach` annotated method is executed before each test. It has an injected `TestInfo` parameter, and it verifies that the displayed name is the expected one: the name of the method or the name specified by the `@Display-Name` annotation **❷**.
- Both tests have an injected `TestInfo` parameter. Each parameter verifies that the displayed name is the expected one: the name of the method in the first test **❸** or the name specified by the `@DisplayName` annotation in the second test **❹**.
- The built-in `TestInfoParameterResolver` supplies an instance of `TestInfo` that corresponds to the current container or test as the value of the expected parameters of the constructor and of the methods.

2.6.2   *TestReporterParameterResolver*

If a constructor or method parameter is of type `TestReporter`, `TestReporter-ParameterResolver` supplies an instance of this type. `TestReporter` is a functional interface and therefore can be used as the assignment target for a lambda expression or method reference. `TestReporter` has a single `publishEntry` abstract method and several overloaded `publishEntry` default methods. Parameters of type `TestReporter` can be injected into methods of test classes annotated with `@BeforeEach`, `@AfterEach`, and `@Test`. `TestReporter` can also be used to provide additional information about the test that is run. Here's how to use a `TestReporter` parameter as an argument of `@Test` annotated methods.

Listing 2.17   `TestReporter` parameters

```
class TestReporterTest {

    @Test
    void testReportSingleValue(TestReporter testReporter) {          ❶
        testReporter.publishEntry("Single value");              ⟵
    }

    @Test
    void testReportKeyValuePair(TestReporter testReporter) {          ❷
        testReporter.publishEntry("Key", "Value");              ⟵
    }

    @Test
    void testReportMultipleKeyValuePairs(TestReporter testReporter) {  ❸
        Map<String, String> values = new HashMap<>();           ⟵
        values.put("user", "John");                          ❹
        values.put("password", "secret");
```

```
        testReporter.publishEntry(values);                    ◁──┐
    }                                                              │
                                                                   5
}
```

In this example, a `TestReporter` parameter is injected into three methods:

- In the first method, it is used to publish a single value entry ❶.
- In the second method, it is used to publish a key-value pair ❷.
- In the third method, we construct a map ❸, populate it with two key-value pairs ❹, and then use it to publish the constructed map ❺.
- The built-in `TestReporterParameterResolver` supplies the instance of `TestReporter` needed to publish the entries.

The result of the execution of this test is shown in figure 2.3.

```
⊘ Tests passed: 3 of 3 tests – 88 ms
 "C:\Program Files\Java\jdk1.8.0_181\bin\java" ...
 timestamp = 2019-05-11T22:51:37.086, Key = Value
 timestamp = 2019-05-11T22:51:37.103, password = secret, user = John
 timestamp = 2019-05-11T22:51:37.112, value = Single value
```

Figure 2.3   The result of executing `TestReporterTest`

2.6.3   *RepetitionInfoParameterResolver*

If a parameter in a method annotated with `@RepeatedTest`, `@BeforeEach`, or `@AfterEach` is of type `RepetitionInfo`, `RepetitionInfoParameterResolver` supplies an instance of this type. Then `RepetitionInfo` gets information about the current repetition and the total number of repetitions for a test annotated with `@RepeatedTest`. Repeated tests and examples are discussed in the following section.

2.7   *Repeated tests*

JUnit 5 allows us to repeat a test a specified number of times using the `@Repeated-Test` annotation, which has as a parameter the required number of repetitions. This feature can be particularly useful when conditions may change from one execution of a test to another. For example, some data that affects success may have changed between two executions of the same test, and an unexpected change in this data would be a bug that needs to be fixed.

A custom display name can be configured for each repetition using the `name` attribute of the `@RepeatedTest` annotation. The following placeholders are now supported:

- `{displayName}`—Display name of the method annotated with `@Repeated-Test`

- {currentRepetition}—Current repetition number
- {totalRepetitions}—Total number of repetitions

Listing 2.18 shows the use of repeated tests, display name placeholders, and RepetitionInfo parameters. The first repeated test verifies that the execution of the add method from the Calculator class is stable and always provides the same result. The second repeated test verifies that collections follow the appropriate behavior: a list receives a new element at each iteration, and a set does not get duplicate elements even if we try to insert such an element multiple times.

Listing 2.18   Repeated tests

```java
public class RepeatedTestsTest {

    private static Set<Integer> integerSet = new HashSet<>();
    private static List<Integer> integerList = new ArrayList<>();

    @RepeatedTest(value = 5, name =
"{displayName} - repetition {currentRepetition}/{totalRepetitions}")     ❶
    @DisplayName("Test add operation")
    void addNumber() {
        Calculator calculator = new Calculator();
        assertEquals(2, calculator.add(1, 1),
                    "1 + 1 should equal 2");
    }

    @RepeatedTest(value = 5, name = "the list contains
{currentRepetition} elements(s), the set contains 1 element")           ❷
    void testAddingToCollections(TestReporter testReporter,
                                 RepetitionInfo repetitionInfo) {
        integerSet.add(1);
        integerList.add(repetitionInfo.getCurrentRepetition());

        testReporter.publishEntry("Repetition number",
            String.valueOf(repetitionInfo.getCurrentRepetition()));      ❸
        assertEquals(1, integerSet.size());
        assertEquals(repetitionInfo.getCurrentRepetition(),
                    integerList.size());
    }
}
```

In this example:

- The first test is repeated five times. Each repetition shows the display name, the current repetition number, and the total number of repetitions ❶.
- The second test is repeated five times. Each repetition shows the number of elements in the list (the current repetition number) and checks whether the set always has only one element ❷.
- Each time the second test is repeated, the repetition number is displayed as it is injected into the RepetitionInfo parameter ❸.

The results of executing these tests are shown in figures 2.4 and 2.5. Each invocation of a repeated test behaves like the execution of a regular `@Test` method with full support for life cycle callbacks and extensions. That is why the list and the set in the example are declared as static.

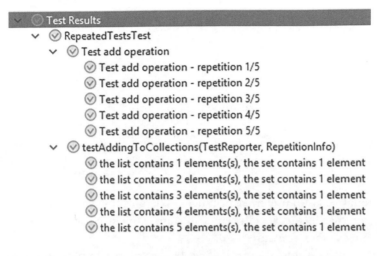

Figure 2.4   The names of the repeated tests at the time of execution

```
timestamp = 2019-05-12T17:26:34.783, Repetition number = 1
timestamp = 2019-05-12T17:26:34.798, Repetition number = 2
timestamp = 2019-05-12T17:26:34.803, Repetition number = 3
timestamp = 2019-05-12T17:26:34.813, Repetition number = 4
timestamp = 2019-05-12T17:26:34.817, Repetition number = 5
```

Figure 2.5   The messages shown on the console by the second repeated test

2.8   *Parameterized tests*

Parameterized tests allow a test to run multiple times with different arguments. The great benefit is that we can write a single test to be performed using arguments that check various input data. The methods are annotated with `@ParameterizedTest`. We must declare at least one source providing the arguments for each invocation. The arguments are then passed to the test method.

  `@ValueSource` lets us specify a single array of literal values. At execution, this array provides a single argument for each invocation of the parameterized test. The following test checks the number of words in some phrases that are provided as parameters.

Listing 2.19 @ValueSource annotation

```
class ParameterizedWithValueSourceTest {
    private WordCounter wordCounter = new WordCounter();        ❶

    @ParameterizedTest
    @ValueSource(strings = {"Check three parameters",
                            "JUnit in Action"})                  ❷
    void testWordsInSentence(String sentence) {
        assertEquals(3, wordCounter.countWords(sentence));
    }
}
```

In this example:

- We mark the test as being parameterized by using the corresponding annotation ❶.
- We specify the values to be passed as an argument of the testing method ❷. The testing method is executed twice: once for each argument provided by the @ValueSource annotation.

@EnumSource enables us to use enum instances. The annotation provides an optional names parameter that lets us specify which instances must be used or excluded. By default, all instances of an enum are used.

The following listing shows the use of the @EnumSource annotation to check the number of words in some phrases that are provided as enum instances.

Listing 2.20 @EnumSource annotation

```
class ParameterizedWithEnumSourceTest {
    private WordCounter wordCounter = new WordCounter();

    @ParameterizedTest
    @EnumSource(Sentences.class)                                 ❶
    void testWordsInSentence(Sentences sentence) {
        assertEquals(3, wordCounter.countWords(sentence.value()));
    }

    @ParameterizedTest
    @EnumSource(value=Sentences.class,
                names = { "JUNIT_IN_ACTION", "THREE_PARAMETERS" })   ❷
    void testSelectedWordsInSentence(Sentences sentence) {
        assertEquals(3, wordCounter.countWords(sentence.value()));
    }

    @ParameterizedTest #3
    @EnumSource(value=Sentences.class, mode = EXCLUDE, names =
                { "THREE_PARAMETERS" })                          ❸
    void testExcludedWordsInSentence(Sentences sentence) {
        assertEquals(3, wordCounter.countWords(sentence.value()));
    }
```

```
enum Sentences {
    JUNIT_IN_ACTION("JUnit in Action"),
    SOME_PARAMETERS("Check some parameters"),
    THREE_PARAMETERS("Check three parameters");

    private final String sentence;

    Sentences(String sentence) {
        this.sentence = sentence;
    }

    public String value() {
        return sentence;
    }
}
}
```

This example has three tests, which work as follows:

- The first test is annotated as being parameterized. Then we specify the enum source as the entire Sentences.class ❶. So this test is executed three times, once for each instance of the Sentences enum: JUNIT_IN_ACTION, SOME_PARAMETERS, and THREE_PARAMETERS.
- The second test is annotated as being parameterized. Then we specify the enum source as Sentences.class, but we restrict the instances to be passed to the test to JUNIT_IN_ACTION and THREE_PARAMETERS ❷. So, this test will be executed twice.
- The third test is annotated as being parameterized. Then we specify the enum source as Sentences.class, but we exclude the THREE_PARAMETERS instance ❸. So, this test is executed twice: for JUNIT_IN_ACTION and SOME_PARAMETERS.

We can use @CsvSource to express argument lists as comma-separated values (CSV), such as String literals. The following test uses the @CsvSource annotation to check the number of words in some phrases that are provided as parameters—this time, in CSV format.

Listing 2.21 @CsvSource annotation

```
class ParameterizedWithCsvSourceTest {
    private WordCounter wordCounter = new WordCounter();        ❶

    @ParameterizedTest
    @CsvSource({"2, Unit testing", "3, JUnit in Action",
                "4, Write solid Java code"})                    ❷
    void testWordsInSentence(int expected, String sentence) {
        assertEquals(expected, wordCounter.countWords(sentence));
    }
}
```

This example has one parameterized test, which functions as follows:

- The test is parameterized, as indicated by the appropriate annotation ❶.
- The parameters passed to the test are from the parsed CSV strings listed in the @CsvSource annotation ❷. So, this test is executed three times: once for each CSV line.
- Each CSV line is parsed. The first value is assigned to the expected parameter, and the second value is assigned to the sentence parameter.

@CsvFileSource allows us to use CSV files from the classpath. The parameterized test is executed once for each line of a CSV file. Listing 2.22 shows the use of the @CsvFileSource annotation, and listing 2.23 displays the contents of the word_counter.csv file on the classpath. The Maven build tool automatically adds the src/test/resources folder to the classpath. The test checks the number of words in some phrases that are provided as parameters—this time, in CSV format with a CSV file as resource input.

Listing 2.22   @CsvFileSource **annotation**

```
class ParameterizedWithCsvFileSourceTest {
    private WordCounter wordCounter = new WordCounter();

    @ParameterizedTest
    @CsvFileSource(resources = "/word_counter.csv")         ❶
    void testWordsInSentence(int expected, String sentence) {
        assertEquals(expected, wordCounter.countWords(sentence));
    }
}
```

Listing 2.23   **Contents of the word_counter.csv file**

```
2, Unit testing
3, JUnit in Action
4, Write solid Java code
```

This example has one parameterized test that receives as parameters the lines indicated in the @CsvFileSource annotation ❶. So, this test is executed three times: once for each CSV file line. The CSV file line is parsed, the first value is assigned to the expected parameter, and then the second value is assigned to the sentence parameter.

2.9   *Dynamic tests*

JUnit 5 introduces a dynamic new programming model that can generate tests at runtime. We write a factory method, and at runtime, it creates a series of tests to be executed. Such a factory method must be annotated with @TestFactory.

A @TestFactory method is not a regular test but a factory that generates tests. A method annotated as @TestFactory must return one of the following:

- A DynamicNode (an abstract class; DynamicContainer and DynamicTest are the instantiable concrete classes)

- An array of `DynamicNode` objects
- A `Stream` of `DynamicNode` objects
- A `Collection` of `DynamicNode` objects
- An `Iterable` of `DynamicNode` objects
- An `Iterator` of `DynamicNode` objects

As with the requirements for `@Test`-annotated methods, `@TestFactory`-annotated methods are allowed to be package-private as a minimum requirement for visibility, but they cannot be private or static. They may also declare parameters to be resolved by a `ParameterResolver`.

A `DynamicTest` is a test case generated at runtime, composed of a display name and an `Executable`. Because the `Executable` is a Java 8 functional interface, the implementation of a dynamic test can be provided as a lambda expression or as a method reference.

A dynamic test has a different life cycle than a standard test annotated with `@Test`. The methods annotated with `@BeforeEach` and `@AfterEach` are executed for the `@TestFactory` method but not for each dynamic test; other than these methods, there are no life cycle callbacks for individual dynamic tests. The behavior of `@BeforeAll` and `@AfterAll` remains the same; they are executed before all tests and at the end of all tests.

Listing 2.24 demonstrates dynamic tests. We want to check a predicate against a numerical value. To do so, we use a single factory to generate three tests to be created at runtime: one for a negative value, one for zero, and one for a positive value. We write one method but get three tests dynamically.

Listing 2.24 Dynamic tests

```java
class DynamicTestsTest {

    private PositiveNumberPredicate predicate = new
     PositiveNumberPredicate();

    @BeforeAll
    static void setUpClass() {                    ❶
        System.out.println("@BeforeAll method");
    }

    @AfterAll
    static void tearDownClass() {                 ❷
        System.out.println("@AfterAll method");
    }

    @BeforeEach                    ❸
    void setUp() {
        System.out.println("@BeforeEach method");
    }

    @AfterEach                        ❹
    void tearDown() {
```

```
            System.out.println("@AfterEach method");
    }

    @TestFactory
    Iterator<DynamicTest> positiveNumberPredicateTestCases() {
        return asList(
                dynamicTest("negative number",
                            () -> assertFalse(predicate.check(-1))),
                dynamicTest("zero",
                            () -> assertFalse(predicate.check(0))),
                dynamicTest("positive number",
                            () -> assertTrue(predicate.check(1)))
        ).iterator();
    }
}
```

In this example:

- The methods annotated with @BeforeAll ❶ and @AfterAll ❷ are executed once, as expected: at the beginning and at the end of the entire tests list, respectively.
- The methods annotated with @BeforeEach ❸ and @AfterEach ❹ are executed before and after the execution of the @TestFactory-annotated method, respectively ❺.
- This factory method generates three test methods labeled "negative number" ❻, "zero" ❼, and "positive number" ❽.
- The effective behavior of each test is given by the Executable provided as the second parameter of the dynamicTest method.

The result of executing these tests is shown in figure 2.6.

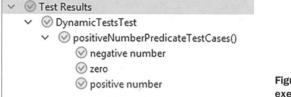

Figure 2.6   The result of executing dynamic tests

2.10   *Using Hamcrest matchers*

Statistics show that people easily become hooked on the unit-testing philosophy. When we get accustomed to writing tests and see how good it feels to be protected from possible mistakes, we wonder how it was possible to live without unit testing.

As we write more unit tests and assertions, we inevitably find that some assertions are big and hard to read. Our example company, Tested Data Systems, is working with customers whose data may be kept in lists. Engineers may populate a list with values like "Michael", "John", and "Edwin"; then they may search for customers like

"Oliver", "Jack", and "Harry", as in the following listing. This test is intended to fail and show the description of the assertion failure.

Listing 2.25 Cumbersome JUnit `assert` method

```
[...]
public class HamcrestListTest {
   private List<String> values;                         ❶

   @BeforeEach                                          ◄─┘
      public void setUp () {
          values = new ArrayList< >();
       values.add("Michael");
       values.add("John");
       values.add("Edwin");
       }
                                                        ❷
   @Test                                               ◄─┘
      @DisplayName("List without Hamcrest")
   public void testWithoutHamcrest() {
       assertEquals(3, values.size());
       assertTrue(values.contains("Oliver")
              || values.contains("Jack")             ❸
              || values.contains("Harry"));
       }
   }
```

This example constructs a simple JUnit test like those described earlier in this chapter:

- A `@BeforeEach` fixture ❶ initializes some data for the test. A single test method is used ❷.
- This test method makes a long, hard-to-read assertion ❸. (Maybe the assertion itself is not too hard to read, but what it does definitely is not obvious at first glance.)
- The goal is to simplify the assertion made in the test method.

To solve this problem, Tested Data Systems uses a library of matchers for building test expressions: Hamcrest. Hamcrest (https://code.google.com/archive/p/hamcrest) is a library that contains a lot of helpful `Matcher` objects (also known as *constraints* or *predicates*) ported in several languages, such as Java, C++, Objective-C, Python, and PHP.

The Hamcrest library

Hamcrest is not a testing framework itself, but it helps us declaratively specify simple matching rules. These matching rules can be used in many situations, but they are particularly helpful for unit testing.

The next listing provides the same test method as listing 2.25, this time written with the Hamcrest library.

Listing 2.26   Using the Hamcrest library

```
[...]
import static org.hamcrest.CoreMatchers.anyOf;
import static org.hamcrest.CoreMatchers.equalTo;
import static org.hamcrest.MatcherAssert.assertThat;
import static org.hamcrest.Matchers.*;
[...]

    @DisplayName("List with Hamcrest")
    public void testListWithHamcrest() {
        assertThat(values, hasSize(3));
        assertThat(values, hasItem(anyOf(equalTo("Oliver"),
                    equalTo("Jack"), equalTo("Harry"))));
  }

[...]
```

❶

❷

This example adds a test method that imports the needed matchers and the `assert-That` method ❶ and then constructs a test method. The test method uses one of the most powerful features of matchers: they can nest ❷. What Hamcrest gives us, and standard assertions do not, is a human-readable description of an assertion failure. Using assertion code with or without Hamcrest matchers is a personal preference.

The examples in the previous two listings construct a `List` with the customers `"Michael"`, `"John"`, and `"Edwin"` as elements. After that, the code asserts the presence of `"Oliver"`, `"Jack"`, or `"Harry"`, so the tests will fail on purpose. The result from the execution without Hamcrest is shown in figure 2.7, and the result from the execution with Hamcrest is shown in figure 2.8. As the figures show, the test that uses Hamcrest provides more details.

```
org.opentest4j.AssertionFailedError:
Expected :<true>
Actual   :<false>
 <Click to see difference>

 <4 internal calls>
    at com.manning.junitbook.ch02.core.hamcrest.HamcrestListTest.testListWithoutHamcrest(HamcrestListTest.java:53) <19 internal calls>
    at java.util.ArrayList.forEach(ArrayList.java:1257) <9 internal calls>
    at java.util.ArrayList.forEach(ArrayList.java:1257) <21 internal calls>
```

Figure 2.7   The result of the test execution without Hamcrest

```
java.lang.AssertionError:
Expected: a collection containing ("Oliver" or "Jack" or "Harry")
    but: mismatches were: [was "John", was "Michael", was "Edwin"]

    at org.hamcrest.MatcherAssert.assertThat(MatcherAssert.java:18)
    at org.hamcrest.MatcherAssert.assertThat(MatcherAssert.java:6)
    at com.manning.junitbook.ch02.hamcrest.HamcrestListTest.testListWithHamcrest(HamcrestListTest.java:60) <19 internal calls>
    at java.util.ArrayList.forEach(ArrayList.java:1257) <9 internal calls>
    at java.util.ArrayList.forEach(ArrayList.java:1257) <21 internal calls>
```

Figure 2.8   The result of the test execution with Hamcrest

To use Hamcrest in our projects, we need to add the required dependency to the pom.xml file.

```
<dependency>
    <groupId>org.hamcrest</groupId>
    <artifactId>hamcrest-library</artifactId>
    <version>2.1</version>
    <scope>test</scope>
</dependency>
```

To use Hamcrest in JUnit 4, you have to use the `assertThat` method from the `org.junit.Assert` class. But as explained earlier in this chapter, JUnit 5 removes the `assertThat()` method. The user guide justifies the decision this way:

> *[...]* `org.junit.jupiter.api.Assertions` *class does not provide an* `assertThat()` *method like the one found in JUnit 4's* `org.junit.Assert` *class, which accepts a Hamcrest Matcher. Instead, developers are encouraged to use the built-in support for matchers provided by third-party assertion libraries.*

This text means that if we want to use Hamcrest matchers, we have to use the `assertThat()` methods of the `org.hamcrest.MatcherAssert` class. As the previous examples illustrated, the overloaded methods take two or three method parameters:

- An error message shown when the assertion fails (optional)
- The actual value or object
- A `Matcher` object for the expected value

To create the `Matcher` object, we need to use one of the static factory methods provided by the `org.hamcrest.Matchers` class, as shown in table 2.2.

Table 2.2   Sample of common Hamcrest static factory methods

Factory method	Logical
anything	Matches absolutely anything; useful when we want to make the `assert` statement more readable
is	Used only to improve the readability of statements
allOf	Checks whether all contained matchers match (like the `&&` operator)
anyOf	Checks whether any of the contained matchers match (like the `||` operator)
not	Inverts the meaning of the contained matchers (like the `!` operator in Java)
instanceOf	Check whether objects are instances of one another

Table 2.2   Sample of common Hamcrest static factory methods *(continued)*

Factory method	Logical
sameInstance	Tests object identity
nullValue, notNullValue	Tests for null or non-null values
hasProperty	Tests whether a Java Bean has a certain property
hasEntry, hasKey, hasValue	Tests whether a given Map has a given entry, key, or value
hasItem, hasItems	Tests a given collection for the presence of an item or items
closeTo, greaterThan, greaterThanOrEqualTo, lessThan, lessThanOrEqualTo	Tests whether given numbers are close to, greater than, greater than or equal, less than, or less than or equal to a given value
equalToIgnoringCase	Tests whether a given string equals another one, ignoring the case
equalToIgnoringWhiteSpace	Tests whether a given string equals another one, ignoring white space
containsString, endsWith, startsWith	Tests whether a given string contains, starts with, or ends with a certain string

All of these methods are pretty straightforward to read and use. Also, remember that we can compose them into one another.

For each service provided to customers, Tested Data Systems charges a particular price. The following code tests the properties of a customer and some service prices using a few Hamcrest methods.

Listing 2.28   A few Hamcrest static factory methods

```java
public class HamcrestMatchersTest {

    private static String FIRST_NAME = "John";
    private static String LAST_NAME = "Smith";
    private static Customer customer = new Customer(FIRST_NAME, LAST_NAME);

    @Test
    @DisplayName("Hamcrest is, anyOf, allOf")
    public void testHamcrestIs() {
        int price1 = 1, price2 = 1, price3 = 2;

        assertThat(1, is(price1));
        assertThat(1, anyOf(is(price2), is(price3)));          ❶
        assertThat(1, allOf(is(price1), is(price2)));

    }

    @Test
    @DisplayName("Null expected")
    void testNull() {                          ❷
        assertThat(null, nullValue());
    }
```

```
@Test
@DisplayName("Object expected")
void testNotNull() {
    assertThat(customer, notNullValue());        ←──┐  ③
}

@Test
@DisplayName("Check correct customer properties")
void checkCorrectCustomerProperties() {
    assertThat(customer, allOf(
            hasProperty("firstName", is(FIRST_NAME)),        ④
            hasProperty("lastName", is(LAST_NAME))
    ));
}

}
```

This example shows

- The use of the is, anyOf, and allOf methods ❶
- The use of the nullValue method ❷
- The use of the notNullValue method ❸
- The use of the assertThat method ❶, ❷, ❸, and ❹, as described in table 2.2

We have also constructed a Customer object and check its properties with the help of the hasProperty method ❹.

Last but not least, Hamcrest is extremely extensible. Writing matchers that check a certain condition is easy: we implement the Matcher interface and an appropriately named factory method.

Chapter 3 analyzes the architectures of JUnit 4 and JUnit 5 and explains the move to the new architecture.

Summary

This chapter has covered the following:

- The core JUnit 5 classes related to assertions and assumptions.
- Using JUnit 5 methods and annotations: the methods from the assertions and assumptions classes, and annotations like @Test, @DisplayName, and @Disabled
- The life cycle of a JUnit 5 test, and controlling it through the @BeforeEach, @AfterEach, @BeforeAll, and @AfterAll annotations
- Applying JUnit 5 capabilities to create nested tests and tagged tests (annotation: @Tag)
- Implementing dependency injection with the help of test constructors and methods with parameters
- Applying dependency injection by using different parameter resolvers (Test-InfoParameterResolver, TestReporterParameterResolver)

- Implementing repeated tests (annotation: `@RepeatedTest`) as another application of dependency injection
- Parameterized tests, a very flexible tool for testing that consumes different data sets and dynamic tests created at runtime (annotations: `@Parameterized-Test`, `@TestFactory`)
- Using Hamcrest matchers to simplify assertions

JUnit architecture

This chapter covers
- Demonstrating the concept and importance of software architecture
- Comparing the JUnit 4 and JUnit 5 architectures

Architecture is the stuff that's hard to change later. And there should be as little of that stuff as possible.

—Martin Fowler

So far, we have broadly surveyed JUnit and its capabilities (chapter 1). We've also looked at JUnit core classes and methods and how they interact with each other, as well as how to use the many features of JUnit 5 (chapter 2).

This chapter looks at the architecture of the two most recent JUnit versions. It discusses the architecture of JUnit 4 to show where JUnit 5 started, where the big changes are between versions, and which shortcomings had to be addressed.

3.1   *The concept and importance of software architecture*

Software architecture refers to the fundamental structures of a software system. Such a system must be created in an organized manner. A software system structure comprises software elements, relationships among those elements, and properties of both elements and relationships.

Software architecture is like the architecture of a building. The architecture of a software system characterizes the foundation on which everything else sits, represented by the bottom boxes in figure 3.1. Foundational software architectural elements are as hard to move around and replace as are the foundational parts of physical architecture, because you have to move all the things on top to reach them.

Figure 3.1   The architecture represents the foundation of the system. At the bottom level, the architecture is hard to move around and replace. The intermediary boxes represent the design; the top ones represent the idioms.

The corollary to Fowler's definition of architecture is that you should construct the architectural elements so that they're easier to replace. The architecture of JUnit 5 emerged from the shortcomings of JUnit 4. To understand the significant impact of the architecture on the entire system, read the stories in the next two sections.

3.1.1   *Story 1: The telephone directories*

Once upon a time, two companies published telephone directories. The companies' books were identical in shape, size, and cost.

Neither company could gain a significant advantage. Clerks were buying both products for $1; they couldn't tell which book was better because the books contained similar information. Finally, company A hired a troubleshooter. The troubleshooter thought for a while and found a solution: "Let's make the format of our own book smaller than our competitor's book while keeping the same information."

When books are the same size, people often put the books near each other on their office desks. But when one book is large and flat, and the second is small but plump, people tend to put the small book on top of the large book (figure 3.2). At the end of the month, company A's customers realized that they had used only the top (small) directory; they never opened the large directory. So why spend a dollar on the larger one? This is one of the architectural changes from JUnit 4 to JUnit 5: smaller works better.

Figure 3.2 Changing the size of books is an architectural change that has a big impact. A small item is used and moved more easily and frequently than a big one.

3.1.2 Story 2: The sneakers manufacturer

A company began manufacturing sneakers in low-cost locations, expecting the net cost to be low. But losses from sneaker thefts were unexpectedly huge. The company tried to get more guards, but hiring guards increased the final price. The company needed a way to decrease the number of stolen sneakers without additional costs.

The company's analysts arrived at this solution: producing the left and right shoes in different locations (figure 3.3). Consequently, sneaker thefts decreased dramatically.

This scenario is another architectural change from JUnit 4 to JUnit 5: modularity improves the work. When we need some functionality, we can address the module that implements it. We depend on and load only a specific module instead of the entire testing framework, which saves time and memory.

Figure 3.3 Separating the production locations for left and right sneakers represents a major architectural change.

3.2 The JUnit 4 architecture

This book focuses on JUnit 5, but it also discusses JUnit 4 for some important reasons. One reason is that a lot of legacy code uses JUnit 4. Also, migration from JUnit 4 to JUnit 5 does not happen instantly (if ever), and projects may work with a hybrid

JUnit 4/JUnit 5 approach. Moreover, JUnit 5 was designed to work with old JUnit 4 code in existing legacy projects through JUnit Vintage. (Chapter 4 clarifies the best times to postpone or cancel migration from JUnit 4.)

The shortcomings of JUnit 4 helped JUnit 5 emerge, however. This section emphasizes some JUnit 4 characteristics that clearly show the need for the JUnit 5 approach: modularity, runners, and rules.

3.2.1   JUnit 4 modularity

JUnit 4, released in 2006, has a simple, monolithic architecture. All of its functionality is concentrated inside a single jar file (figure 3.4). If a programmer wants to use JUnit 4 in a project, all they need to do is add that jar file on the classpath.

junit.jar

Figure 3.4   The monolithic architecture of JUnit 4: a single jar file

3.2.2   JUnit 4 runners

A JUnit 4 *runner* is a class that extends the JUnit 4 abstract Runner class. A JUnit 4 runner is responsible for running JUnit tests. JUnit 4 remains a single jar file, but it's generally necessary to extend the functionality of this file. In other words, developers have the opportunity to add custom features to the functionality, such as executing additional things before and after running a test.

Runners may extend a test behavior by using reflection. Reflection breaks encapsulation, of course, but this technique was the only way to provide extensibility in JUnit 4 and earlier versions—one good reason for the JUnit 5 approach. You may need to keep existing JUnit 4 runners in your code for some time. (Extensions are the JUnit 5 equivalent of JUnit 4 runners and are introduced in chapter 4.)

In practice, you can work with existing runners, such as the runners for the Spring framework or for mocking objects with Mockito (chapter 8). We consider it very useful to demonstrate the creation and usage of custom runners, as they reveal the principles of runners in general. We can extend the JUnit 4 abstract Runner class, overriding its methods and working with reflection. This approach breaks encapsulation but was the only way to add custom functionality to JUnit 4. Revealing the shortcomings of working with custom runners in JUnit 4 opens the gate to understanding the capabilities and advantages of JUnit 5 extensions.

To demonstrate the use of JUnit 4 runners, we come back to our Calculator class.

Listing 3.1   Test Calculator class

```
public class Calculator {
    public double add(double number1, double number2) {
        return number1 + number2;
    }
}
```

We would like to enrich the behavior of tests that use this class by introducing an additional action before executing the test suite. We'll create a custom runner and use it as an argument of the @RunWith annotation to add custom features to the original JUnit functionality. The following listing demonstrates how to build a CustomTestRunner.

Listing 3.2 CustomTestRunner class

```java
public class CustomTestRunner extends Runner {

    private Class<?> testedClass;                                        ①

    public CustomTestRunner(Class<?> testedClass) {
        this.testedClass = testedClass;
    }

    @Override
    public Description getDescription() {
        return Description
                .createTestDescription(testedClass,                     ②
                    this.getClass().getSimpleName() + " description");
    }

    @Override
    public void run(RunNotifier notifier) {
        System.out.println("Running tests with " +
                this.getClass().getSimpleName() + ": " + testedClass);
        try {                                                           ③
            Object testObject = testedClass.newInstance();
            for (Method method : testedClass.getMethods()) {            ④
                if (method.isAnnotationPresent(Test.class)) {
                    notifier.fireTestStarted(Description
                            .createTestDescription(testedClass,         ⑤
                                            method.getName()));
                    method.invoke(testObject);                          ⑥
                    notifier.fireTestFinished(Description
                            .createTestDescription(testedClass,         ⑦
                                            method.getName()));
                }
            }
        } catch (InstantiationException | IllegalAccessException |
                InvocationTargetException e) {
            throw new RuntimeException(e);
        }
    }
}
```

In this listing:

- We keep a reference to the tested class, which is initialized inside the constructor ①.
- We override the abstract getDescription method inherited from the abstract Runner class. This method contains information that is later exported and may be used by various tools ②.

- We override the abstract `run` method inherited from the abstract `Runner` class. Inside it, we create an instance of the tested class ❸.
- We browse all public methods from the tested class and filter the `@Test`-annotated ones ❹.
- We invoke `fireTestStarted` to tell listeners that an atomic test is about to start ❺.
- We reflectively invoke the original `@Test`-annotated method ❻.
- We invoke `fireTestFinished` to tell listeners that an atomic test has finished ❼.

We'll use the `CustomTestRunner` class as an argument of the `@RunWith` annotation, to be applied to the `CalculatorTest` class.

Listing 3.3   `CalculatorTest` class

```
@RunWith(CustomTestRunner.class)
public class CalculatorTest {

    @Test
    public void testAdd()
    {
        Calculator calculator = new Calculator();
        double result = calculator.add(10, 50);
        assertEquals(60, result, 0);
    }
}
```

Figure 3.5 shows the result of executing this test. This example demonstrates how to add custom functionality to JUnit 4; using the recognized terminology, we are extending JUnit 4's functionality.

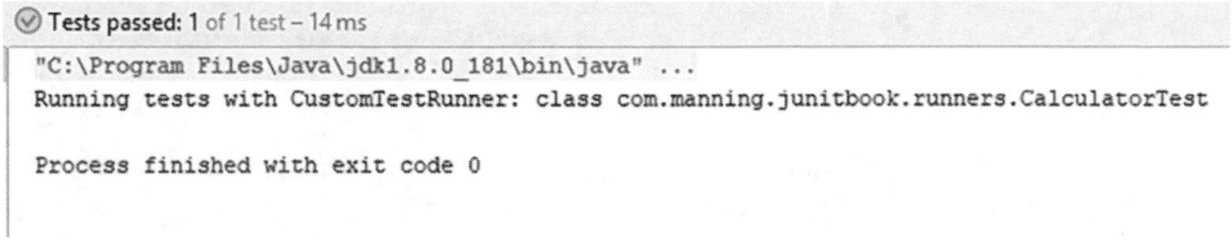

⊘ **Tests passed: 1** of 1 test – 14 ms

```
"C:\Program Files\Java\jdk1.8.0_181\bin\java" ...
Running tests with CustomTestRunner: class com.manning.junitbook.runners.CalculatorTest

Process finished with exit code 0
```

Figure 3.5   The result of executing `CalculatorTest` with a custom runner

3.2.3   *JUnit 4 rules*

A JUnit 4 *rule* is a component that intercepts test method calls; it allows you to do something before a test method is run and something else after a test method has run. Rules are specific to JUnit 4.

To add behavior to the executed tests, you must use the `@Rule` annotation on `TestRule` fields. This technique increases the flexibility of tests by creating objects that can be used and configured in the test methods.

As with runners, you may need to keep existing rules in your code for some time, as migration to JUnit 5 mechanisms is not straightforward. The equivalent approach in JUnit 5 forces programmers to implement extensions (covered in part 4).

We would like to add two more methods to the `Calculator` class, as shown next.

Listing 3.4 `Calculator` **class with additional functionality**

```
public class Calculator {

    ...

    public double sqrt(double x) {                                    ◄─┐
        if (x < 0) {                                                    │ ①
            throw new                                                   │
                IllegalArgumentException("Cannot extract the square    ② │
                                         root of a negative value");   │
        }                                                               │
        return Math.sqrt(x);                                           ◄─┘
    }

    public double divide(double x, double y) {            ◄─┐
        if (y == 0) {                                        │ ③
            throw new ArithmeticException("Cannot divide by zero");
        }                                                    │
        return x/y;                                         ◄─┘
④   }
}
```

The new logic of the `Calculator` class does the following:

- Declares a method to calculate the square root of a number ①. If the number is negative, an exception containing a message is created and thrown ②.
- Declares a method to divide two numbers ③. If the second number is zero, an exception containing a message is created and thrown ④.

We would like to test the newly introduced methods and see whether the appropriate exceptions are thrown for particular inputs. The following listing specifies which exception message is expected while executing the test code, using the new functionality of the `Calculator` class.

Listing 3.5 `RuleExceptionTester` **class**

```
public class RuleExceptionTester {
    @Rule
    public ExpectedException expectedException =                       ①
                            ExpectedException.none();

    private Calculator calculator = new Calculator();     ◄─┐ ②

    @Test
    public void expectIllegalArgumentException() {                    ③
        expectedException.expect(IllegalArgumentException.class);  ◄─┘
```

```
        expectedException.expectMessage("Cannot extract the square root
                                          of a negative value");          4
        calculator.sqrt(-1);            ←
    }
                                        5
    @Test
                                                             6
    public void expectArithmeticException() {
        expectedException.expect(ArithmeticException.class);     ←
        expectedException.expectMessage("Cannot divide by zero");   ←    #
        calculator.divide(1, 0);    ←
    }                                                                    7
}                                      8
```

In this example:

- We declare an `ExpectedException` field annotated with `@Rule`. The `@Rule` annotation must be applied to a public nonstatic field or a public nonstatic method ❶. The `ExpectedException.none()` factory method simply creates an unconfigured `ExpectedException`.

- We initialize an instance of the `Calculator` class whose functionality we are testing ❷.

- `ExpectedException` is configured to keep the type of exception ❸ and message ❹ before it is thrown by invoking the `sqrt` method ❺.

- `ExpectedException` is configured to keep the type of exception ❻ and message ❼ before it is thrown by invoking the `divide` method ❽.

In some situations, you need to work with temporary resources, such as creating files and folders to store only test-specific information. The `TemporaryFolder` rule allows you to create files and folders that should be deleted when the test method finishes (whether the test passes or fails).

The next listing shows a `TemporaryFolder` field annotated with `@Rule`. We are testing the existence of these temporary resources.

Listing 3.6   `RuleTester` **class**

```
public class RuleTester {
    @Rule                                                          1
    public TemporaryFolder folder = new TemporaryFolder();    ←
    private static File createdFolder;                            2
    private static File createdFile;

    @Test
    public void testTemporaryFolder() throws IOException {
        createdFolder = folder.newFolder("createdFolder");      3
        createdFile = folder.newFile("createdFile.txt");
        assertTrue(createdFolder.exists());                      4
        assertTrue(createdFile.exists());
    }
}

@AfterClass
public static void cleanUpAfterAllTestsRan() {
```

```
        assertFalse(createdFolder.exists());
        assertFalse(createdFile.exists());                    ⑤
    }
}
```

In this example:

- We declare a `TemporaryFolder` field annotated with `@Rule` and initialize it. The `@Rule` annotation must be applied to a public field or a public method ❶.
- We declare the static fields `createdFolder` and `createdFile` ❷.
- We use the `TemporaryFolder` field to create a folder and a file ❸, which are located in the Temp folder of our user profile in the operating system.
- We check the existence of the temporary folder and of the temporary file ❹.
- At the end of executing the tests, we check that the temporary resources do not exist any longer ❺.

We have demonstrated that two existing JUnit 4 rules—`ExpectedException` and `TemporaryFolder`—are working.

Now we would like to write a custom rule, which is useful for providing our own behavior before and after a test is run. We might like to start a process before executing a test and stop it after that, or connect to a database before executing a test and tear it down afterward.

To write a rule, we'll have to create a class that implements the `TestRule` interface (listing 3.7). Consequently, we'll override the `apply(Statement, Description)` method, which must return an instance of `Statement` (listing 3.8). Such an object represents the tests within the JUnit runtime, and `Statement#evaluate()` runs them. The `Description` object describes the individual test (listing 3.9); we can use this object to read information about the test through reflection.

Listing 3.7 `CustomRule` class

```
public class CustomRule implements TestRule {         ⟵──────┐
    private Statement base;                    ②              ❶
    private Description description;

    @Override
    public Statement apply(Statement base, Description description) {
        this.base = base;
        this.description = description;                       ③
        return new CustomStatement(base, description);
    }
}
```

In this example:

- We declare a `CustomRule` class that implements the `TestRule` interface ❶.
- We keep references to a `Statement` field and a `Description` field ❷, and we use them in the `apply` method that returns a `CustomStatement` ❸.

Listing 3.8   CustomStatement class

```
public class CustomStatement extends Statement {
    private Statement base;                              ②        ①
    private Description description;

    public CustomStatement(Statement base, Description description) {
        this.base = base;
        this.description = description;                  ③
    }

    @Override
    public void evaluate() throws Throwable {
        System.out.println(this.getClass().getSimpleName() + " " +
                    description.getMethodName() + " has started" );
        try {
            base.evaluate();                                          ④
        } finally {
            System.out.println(this.getClass().getSimpleName() + " " +
                    description.getMethodName() + " has finished");
        }
    }
}
```

In this example:

- We declare our CustomStatement class that extends the Statement class ①.
- We keep references to a Statement field and a Description field ②, and we use them as arguments of the constructor ③.
- We override the inherited evaluate method and call base.evaluate() inside it ④.

Listing 3.9   CustomRuleTester class

```
public class CustomRuleTester {

    @Rule
    public CustomRule myRule = new CustomRule();         ①

    @Test
    public void myCustomRuleTest() {                     ②
        System.out.println("Call of a test method");
    }
}
```

In this example, we use the previously defined CustomRule as follows:

- We declare a public CustomRule field and annotate it with @Rule ①.
- We create the myCustomRuleTest method and annotate it with @Test ②.

Figure 3.6 shows the result of executing this test. The effective execution of the test is surrounded by additional messages provided to the evaluate method of the CustomStatement class.

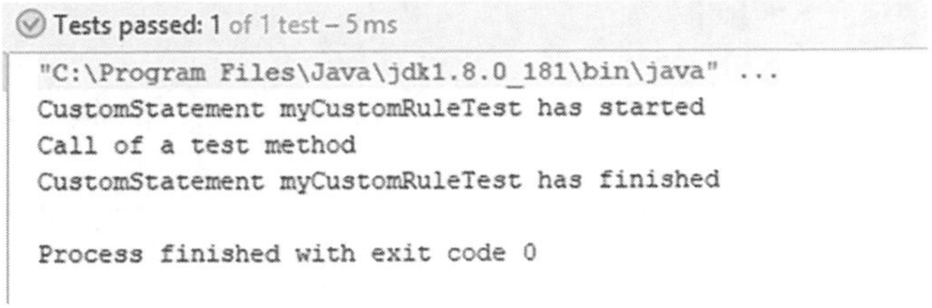

```
⊘ Tests passed: 1 of 1 test – 5 ms
 "C:\Program Files\Java\jdk1.8.0_181\bin\java" ...
 CustomStatement myCustomRuleTest has started
 Call of a test method
 CustomStatement myCustomRuleTest has finished

 Process finished with exit code 0
```

**Figure 3.6
The result of executing
`CustomRuleTester`**

As an alternative, we provide the `CustomRuleTester2` class, which keeps the `CustomRule` field private and exposes it through a public getter annotated with `@Rule`. This annotation works only on public and nonstatic fields and methods.

Listing 3.10 The `CustomRuleTester2` class

```java
public class CustomRuleTester2 {

    private CustomRule myRule = new CustomRule();

    @Rule
    public CustomRule getMyRule() {
        return myRule;
    }

    @Test
    public void myCustomRuleTest() {
        System.out.println("Call of a test method");
    }
}
```

The result of executing this test is the same (figure 3.6). The effective execution of the test is surrounded by the additional messages provided to the `evaluate` method of the `CustomStatement` class.

Writing your own rules is very useful when you need to add custom behavior to tests. Typical use cases include allocating a resource before a test is run and freeing it afterward, starting a process before executing a test and stopping it after that, and connecting to a database before executing a test and tearing it down after that.

By using runners and rules, you can extend the monolithic architecture of JUnit 4. You may still encounter a lot of JUnit 4 code that uses runners and rules; plus, migrating to the equivalent JUnit 5 mechanisms (extensions) is not straightforward. So you may keep runners and rules in your code for a while, even if you move your work to JUnit 5.

One more thing to look for in these examples of JUnit 4 runners and rules is the Maven pom.xml configuration file.

Listing 3.11 pom.xml configuration file

```xml
<dependencies>
    <dependency>
        <groupId>org.junit.vintage</groupId>
        <artifactId>junit-vintage-engine</artifactId>
```

```
        <version>5.6.0</version>
        <scope>provided</scope>
    </dependency>
</dependencies>
```

The only required dependency is `junit-vintage-engine`, which belongs to JUnit 5. JUnit Vintage (a component of the JUnit 5 architecture, discussed in section 3.3.4) ensures backward compatibility with previous versions of JUnit. Working wit JUnit Vintage, Maven transitively accesses the dependency to JUnit 4. As it may be tedious and time consuming to move the existing tests to JUnit 5, introducing this dependency can ensure the coexistence of JUnit 4 and JUnit 5 tests within the same project.

3.2.4   *Shortcomings of the JUnit 4 architecture*

Despite its apparent simplicity, the JUnit 4 architecture generated a series of problems that grew as time passed. JUnit was used not only by programmers, but also by many software programs, such as IDEs (Eclipse, NetBeans, and IntelliJ) and build tools (Ant and Maven). JUnit 4 is monolithic and was not designed to interact with these kinds of tools, but everyone wanted to work with such a popular, simple, useful framework.

The API provided by JUnit 4 was not flexible enough. Consequently, the IDEs and tools that were using JUnit 4 were tightly coupled to the unit testing framework—the API was not designed to provide classes and methods that were appropriate for the interaction with them. These tools needed to go into the JUnit classes and even use reflection to get the necessary information. If designers or JUnit decided to change the name of a private variable, this change could affect the tools that were accessing it reflectively. Maintaining the interaction with JUnit 4 was hard work, so the popularity and simplicity of the framework became obstacles.

Consequently, because everyone was using the same single jar and because all tools and IDEs were so tightly coupled to JUnit 4, its possibilities for evolution were seriously reduced. A new API designed for such tools resulted, along with a new architecture. As described in the stories in section 3.1, a need arose for smaller, modular things. This need was met with JUnit 5.

3.3   *The JUnit 5 architecture*

The new approach didn't come about instantly; it required time and analysis. The shortcomings of JUnit 4 were very good indicators of the needed improvements. Architects knew the problems, and they decided to take the path of breaking the single JUnit 4 jar file into several smaller files.

3.3.1   *JUnit 5 modularity*

A modular approach was needed to allow the JUnit framework to evolve. The architecture had to allow JUnit to interact with different programmatic clients that used different tools and IDEs. The logical separation of concerns required

- An API to write tests, mainly for use by developers
- A mechanism for discovering and running tests
- An API to allow easy interaction with IDEs and tools and to run tests from them

As a result, the JUnit 5 architecture contains three modules (figure 3.7):

- *JUnit Platform* serves as a foundation for launching testing frameworks on the Java virtual machine (JVM). It also provides an API to launch tests from the console, IDEs, and build tools.
- *JUnit Jupiter* combines the new programming and extension model for writing tests and extensions in JUnit 5. The name comes from the fifth planet of our solar system, which is also the largest.
- *JUnit Vintage* is a test engine for running JUnit 3– and JUnit 4–based tests on the platform, ensuring backward compatibility.

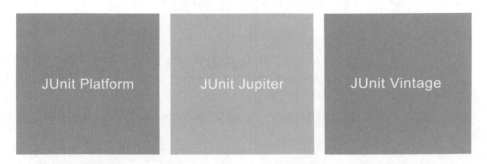

Figure 3.7   The modular architecture of JUnit 5

3.3.2   *JUnit Platform*

Going further with the modularity idea, let's take a brief look at the artifacts contained in the JUnit Platform:

- `junit-platform-commons`—A common internal library of JUnit intended solely for use within the JUnit framework. No use by external parties is supported.
- `junit-platform-console`—Provides support for discovering and executing tests on the JUnit Platform from the console.
- `junit-platform-console-standalone`—An executable jar with all dependencies included. This artifact is used by Console Launcher, a command-line Java application that lets us launch the JUnit Platform from the console. It can be used to run JUnit Vintage and JUnit Jupiter tests, for example, and to print test execution results to the console.
- `junit-platform-engine`—A public API for test engines.
- `junit-platform-launcher`—A public API for configuring and launching test plans, typically used by IDEs and build tools.
- `junit-platform-runner`—A runner for executing tests and test suites on the JUnit Platform in a JUnit 4 environment.
- `junit-platform-suite-api`—Contains the annotations for configuring test suites on the JUnit Platform.

- `junit-platform-surefire-provider`—Provides support for discovering and executing tests on the JUnit Platform by using Maven Surefire.
- `junit-platform-gradle-plugin`—Provides support for discovering and executing tests on the JUnit Platform by using Gradle.

3.3.3   JUnit Jupiter

JUnit Jupiter is a combination of the new programming model (annotations, classes, and methods) and an extension model for writing tests and extensions in JUnit 5. The Jupiter subproject provides a `TestEngine` for running Jupiter-based tests on the platform. Unlike the existing runner and rule extension points in JUnit 4, the JUnit Jupiter extension model consists of a single coherent concept: the `Extension` API, discussed in chapter 14.

The artifacts contained in JUnit Jupiter are as follows:

- `junit-jupiter-api`—JUnit Jupiter API for writing tests and extensions
- `junit-jupiter-engine`—JUnit Jupiter test engine implementation, required only at runtime
- `junit-jupiter-params`—Provides support for parameterized tests in JUnit Jupiter
- `junit-jupiter-migrationsupport`—Provides migration support from JUnit 4 to JUnit Jupiter and is required only for running selected JUnit 4 rules

3.3.4   JUnit Vintage

JUnit Vintage provides a `TestEngine` for running JUnit 3– and JUnit 4–based tests on the platform. It contains only `junit-vintage-engine`, the engine implementation to execute tests written in JUnit 3 or 4. For this purpose, of course, you also need the JUnit 3 or 4 jar.

This engine is very useful for interacting with old tests through JUnit 5. You may need to work on projects with JUnit 5 but still support many old tests, and JUnit Vintage is the solution in this situation.

3.3.5   The big picture of the JUnit 5 architecture

The JUnit Platform provides the facilities for running different kinds of tests: JUnit 3, 4, and 5 tests, as well as third-party tests (figure 3.8). Here are the details at the level of the jar files (figure 3.9):

- The test APIs provide the facilities for different test engines: `junit-jupiter-api` for JUnit 5 tests, `junit-4.12` for legacy tests, and custom engines for third-party tests.
- The test engines mentioned earlier are created by extending the `junit-platform-engine` public API, which is part of the JUnit Platform.
- The `junit-platform-launcher` public API provides the facilities to discover tests inside the JUnit Platform for build tools such as Maven and Gradle and for IDEs.

In addition to the modular architecture, JUnit 5 provides the extensions mechanism, which is discussed in chapter 4.

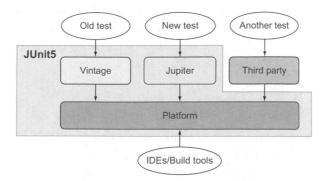

Figure 3.8 The big picture of the JUnit 5 architecture

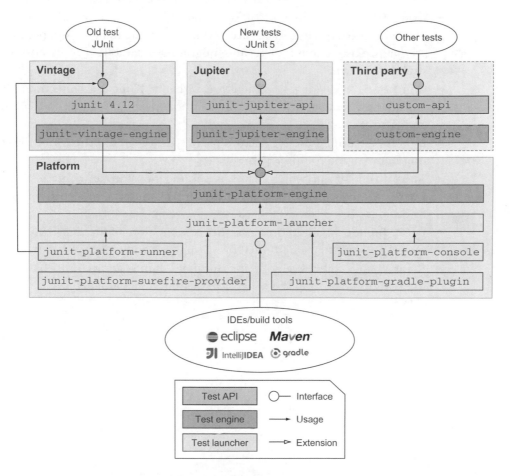

Figure 3.9 A detailed picture of the JUnit 5 architecture

The architecture of a system strongly determines its capabilities and behavior. Consider the runners and rules analyzed earlier in this chapter. Their way of working is generated by the JUnit 4 architecture that represents their foundation. Understanding the architectures of both JUnit 4 and JUnit 5 helps us apply their capabilities in practice, write efficient tests, and analyze alternative implementations, thereby quickening the pace at which we can master unit testing. In chapter 4, we analyze the process of migrating projects from JUnit 4 to JUnit 5 and the dependencies that are required.

Summary

This chapter has covered the following:

- The idea of software architecture as the fundamental structure of a software system. A software system structure comprises software elements, relationships among them, and properties of both elements and relationships.
- An analysis of the monolithic JUnit 4 architecture. It is simple, but real-life challenges like interactions with IDEs and build tools emphasize its shortcomings.
- Using JUnit 4 runners and rules, which represent possibilities to extend the monolithic architecture. They are and will continue to be in use, because there are many existing tests and because migrating them to JUnit 5 extensions is not straightforward.
- Contrasting the JUnit 4 architecture with the JUnit 5 architecture, which is modular and contains the following components: JUnit Platform, JUnit Jupiter, and JUnit Vintage.
- Details concerning the big picture of the JUnit 5 architecture and the interaction between the components.
- The JUnit Platform, which serves as a foundation for launching testing frameworks on the JVM and provides an API to launch tests from the console, IDEs, or build tools.
- JUnit Jupiter, which represents the combination of the new programming model and an extension model for writing tests and extensions in JUnit 5.
- JUnit Vintage, the test engine for running JUnit 3– and JUnit 4–based tests on the platform, ensuring the necessary backward compatibility.

Migrating from JUnit 4 to JUnit 5

This chapter covers

- Implementing the migration from JUnit 4 to JUnit 5
- Working with a hybrid approach for mature projects
- Comparing the needed JUnit 4 with JUnit 5 dependencies
- Comparing the equivalent JUnit 4 with JUnit 5 annotations
- Comparing JUnit 4 rules with JUnit 5 extensions

Nothing in this world can survive and remain useful without an update.

—Charles M. Tadros

So far, this book has introduced JUnit and its latest version, 5. We've discussed the core classes and methods and presented them in action so that you have a good understanding of how to build your tests efficiently. We've emphasized the importance of software architecture in general and shown the significant architectural changes between JUnit 4 and JUnit 5.

This chapter demonstrates how to make the step from JUnit 4 to JUnit 5 inside a project managed by our example company, Tested Data Systems Inc. The company keeps its customer information in a repository and addresses this repository to get the data. In addition, the company needs to track payments and other business rules.

JUnit 4 and JUnit 5 can work together within the same application. This fact is of particular benefit for implementing a migration in phases rather than all at once.

4.1   *Migration steps between JUnit 4 and JUnit 5*

JUnit 5 is a new paradigm introducing a new architecture. It also introduces new packages, annotations, methods, and classes. Some JUnit 5 features are similar to JUnit 4 features; others are new, providing new capabilities. The JUnit Jupiter programming and extension model does not natively support JUnit 4 features such as rules and runners. We do not need to update all existing tests, test extensions, and custom-built test infrastructure to migrate projects to JUnit Jupiter—at least, not instantly.

JUnit provides a migration path with the help of the JUnit Vintage test engine; table 4.1 summarizes the most important steps. This offers the possibility to execute tests based on old JUnit versions using the JUnit Platform infrastructure. All classes and annotations specific to JUnit Jupiter are located in the new `org.junit.jupiter` base package. All classes and annotations specific to JUnit 4 are located in the old `org.junit` base package. So, having both JUnit 4 and JUnit 5 Jupiter in the classpath does not result in a conflict. Consequently, your projects can keep previously implemented JUnit 4 tests together with JUnit Jupiter tests. JUnit 5 and JUnit 4 can coexist until you finalize your migration, whenever that may be, and the migration can be planned and executed slowly based on the priority of the tasks and the challenges of the various steps.

Table 4.1   Migrating from JUnit 4 and JUnit 5

Main step	Comments
Replace the needed dependencies.	JUnit 4 needs a single dependency. JUnit 5 requires more dependencies related to the features that are used. JUnit 5 uses JUnit Vintage to work with old JUnit 4 tests.
Replace the annotations, and introduce the new ones.	Some JUnit 5 annotations mirror those in JUnit 4. Some new annotations introduce new facilities and help us write better tests.
Replace the testing classes and methods.	JUnit 5 assertions and assumptions have been moved to different classes in different packages.
Replace the JUnit 4 rules and runners with the JUnit 5 extension model.	This step generally requires more effort than the other steps in this table. However, because JUnit 4 and JUnit 5 can coexist for an extended period, the rules and runners can remain in the code or be replaced much later.

Before developing and running JUnit tests,

- JUnit 4 requires Java 5 or later.
- JUnit 5 requires Java 8 or later.

Consequently, migrating from JUnit 4 to JUnit 5 can require an update of the Java version used in the project.

4.2   *Needed dependencies*

This section discusses the Tested Data Systems migration process from JUnit 4 to JUnit 5. The company has decided to migrate because it needs to create more testing code for its products and wants more flexibility and more clarity for writing these tests. JUnit 5 lets us label tests with display names using its nested tests and dynamic tests. Before Tested Data Systems can work effectively with these new JUnit 5 capabilities, the company needs to take the first step of creating JUnit 5 tests for its projects.

As we have explained, JUnit 4 has a monolithic architecture, so there is a single dependency in the Maven configuration that supports running JUnit 4 tests.

Listing 4.1   JUnit 4 Maven dependency

```
<dependencies>
    <dependency>
    <groupId>junit</groupId>
    <artifactId>junit</artifactId>
    <version>4.12</version>
    <scope>test</scope>
    </dependency>
</dependencies>
```

One JUnit 5 dependency, JUnit Vintage, can replace the dependency from listing 4.1 during migration. The first things Tested Data Systems needs to do in the migration process are at the level of the dependencies that are used.

The first dependency is `junit-vintage-engine` (listing 4.2). It belongs to JUnit 5 but ensures backward compatibility with previous versions of JUnit. Working with JUnit 5 Vintage, Maven transitively accesses the dependency to JUnit 4. Introducing this dependency is a first step in the migration Tested Data Systems has decided to implement for its projects. JUnit 4 and JUnit 5 tests can coexist within the same project until the migration process is finalized.

Listing 4.2   JUnit Vintage Maven dependency

```
<dependencies>
    <dependency>
        <groupId>org.junit.vintage</groupId>
        <artifactId>junit-vintage-engine</artifactId>
        <version>5.6.0</version>
        <scope>test</scope>
    </dependency>
</dependencies>
```

Running the JUnit 4 tests now, we can see that they are successfully executed, as shown in figure 4.1. Working with the JUnit 5 Vintage dependency instead of the old JUnit 4 dependency will not make any difference.

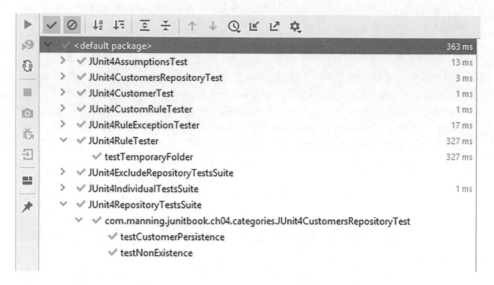

Figure 4.1   Running the JUnit 4 tests after replacing the old JUnit 4 dependency with JUnit 5 Vintage

After the company's programmers introduce the JUnit Vintage dependency, the migration path of Tested Data Systems' projects can continue with the introduction of JUnit 5 Jupiter annotations and features. The required dependencies are shown in the following listing.

Listing 4.3   The most useful JUnit Jupiter Maven dependencies

```
<dependencies>
    <dependency>
        <groupId>org.junit.jupiter</groupId>
        <artifactId>junit-jupiter-api</artifactId>
        <version>5.6.0</version>
        <scope>test</scope>
    </dependency>
    <dependency>
        <groupId>org.junit.jupiter</groupId>
        <artifactId>junit-jupiter-engine</artifactId>
        <version>5.6.0</version>
        <scope>test</scope>
    </dependency>
</dependencies>
```

To write tests using JUnit 5, we will always need the `junit-jupiter-api` and `junit-jupiter-engine` dependencies. The first represents the API for writing tests with

JUnit Jupiter (including the annotations, classes, and methods to be migrated to). The second represents the core JUnit Jupiter package for the execution test engine.

An additional dependency that we may need is `junit-jupiter-params` (for running parameterized tests). At the end of the migration process (when no more JUnit 4 tests are left), we can remove the first `junit-vintage-engine` dependency, presented in listing 4.2.

4.3 Annotations, classes, and methods

After making the move at the level of project dependencies, Tested Data Systems continues implementing the migration process. As explained earlier in this book, JUnit 5 provides features similar to JUnit 4 as well as a lot of new ones. Tested Data Systems hopes to benefit from the flexibility and clarity of these new features for the many tests that need to be developed for its projects. First, however, the company needs to migrate the equivalent features.

4.3.1 Equivalent annotations, classes, and methods

Tables 4.2, 4.3, and 4.4 summarize the equivalent annotations, assertions, and assumptions between JUnit 4 and JUnit 5.

Table 4.2 Annotations

JUnit 4	JUnit 5
@BeforeClass, @AfterClass	@BeforeAll, @AfterAll
@Before, @After	@BeforeEach, @AfterEach
@Ignore	@Disabled
@Category	@Tag

Table 4.3 Assertions

JUnit 4	JUnit 5
Assert class.	Assertions class.
Optional assertion message is the first parameter.	Optional assertion message is the last parameter.
assertThat method.	assertThat method has been removed. New methods are assertAll and assertThrows.

Table 4.4 Assumptions

JUnit 4	JUnit 5
Assume class.	Assumptions class.
assumeNotNull and assumeNoException.	assumeNotNull and assumeNoException have been removed.

Now the Tested Data Systems engineers decide to take the next step by applying the needed changes to the code from their projects. This section uses tests similar to the Tested Data Systems examples, which are built with both JUnit 4 and JUnit 5, to clarify the changes that have been introduced in JUnit 5.

We start with a class that simulates a system under test (SUT). This class can be initialized, can receive regular work but cannot receive additional work to execute, and can close itself.

Listing 4.4   Tested SUT class

```java
public class SUT {
    private String systemName;

    public SUT(String systemName) {
        this.systemName = systemName;
        System.out.println(systemName + " from class " +
            getClass().getSimpleName() + " is initializing.");
    }

    public boolean canReceiveRegularWork() {
        System.out.println(systemName + " from class " +
            getClass().getSimpleName() + " can receive regular work.");
        return true;
    }

    public boolean canReceiveAdditionalWork() {
        System.out.println(systemName + " from class " +
            getClass().getSimpleName() + " cannot receive additional
                                          work.");
        return false;
    }

    public void close() {
        System.out.println(systemName + " from class " +
            getClass().getSimpleName() + " is closing.");
    }
}
```

Listing 4.5 verifies the functionality of the SUT by using the JUnit 4 facilities, and listing 4.6 verifies the functionality of the SUT by using the JUnit 5 facilities. These examples also demonstrate the life cycle methods. As previously stated, the system can start up, can receive regular work but cannot receive additional work, and can close itself. The JUnit 4 and JUnit 5 life cycle and testing methods ensure that the system is initializing and then shutting down before and after each effective test. The test methods check whether the system can receive regular work and additional work. The annotations in the following listing will be discussed after listing 4.6.

Listing 4.5 `JUnit4SUTTest` class

```
public class JUnit4SUTTest {

   private static ResourceForAllTests resourceForAllTests;
   private SUT systemUnderTest;

   @BeforeClass
   public static void setUpClass() {                    ◁─┐
      resourceForAllTests =                                 ❶
         new ResourceForAllTests("Our resource for all tests");
   }

   @AfterClass
   public static void tearDownClass() {                 ◁─┐
      resourceForAllTests.close();                          ❷
   }
                                              ❸
   @Before
   public void setUp() {                      ◁─┘
      systemUnderTest = new SUT("Our system under test");
   }

   @After
   public void tearDown() {                   ◁─┐
      systemUnderTest.close();                    ❹
   }
                                    ❺
   @Test
   public void testRegularWork() {  ◁─┘
      boolean canReceiveRegularWork =
                     systemUnderTest.canReceiveRegularWork();

      assertTrue(canReceiveRegularWork);
   }

   @Test
   public void testAdditionalWork() {
      boolean canReceiveAdditionalWork =
            systemUnderTest.canReceiveAdditionalWork();
      assertFalse(canReceiveAdditionalWork);
   }
                              ❻
   @Test
   @Ignore                    ◁─┘
   public void myThirdTest() {
      assertEquals("2 is not equal to 1", 2, 1);
   }
}
```

We previously replaced the JUnit 4 dependency with the JUnit Vintage dependency. The result of running the `JUnit4SUTTest` class is the same in both cases (figure 4.2), and `myThirdTest` is marked with the `@Ignore` annotation. Now we can proceed to the effective migration of annotations, classes, and methods.

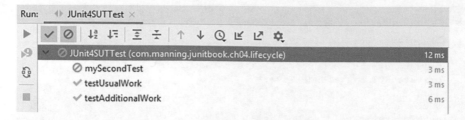

Figure 4.2   Running the `JUnit4SUTTestSuite` in IntelliJ using both the JUnit 4 dependency and the JUnit Vintage dependency

Listing 4.6   `JUnit5SUTTest` class

```java
class JUnit5UTTest {
    private static ResourceForAllTests resourceForAllTests;
    private SUT systemUnderTest;

    @BeforeAll
    static void setUpClass() {
        resourceForAllTests =
            new ResourceForAllTests("Our resource for all tests");
    }

    @AfterAll
    static void tearDownClass() {
        resourceForAllTests.close();
    }

    @BeforeEach
    void setUp() {
        systemUnderTest = new SUT("Our system under test");
    }

    @AfterEach
    void tearDown() {
        systemUnderTest.close();
    }

    @Test
    void testRegularWork() {
        boolean canReceiveRegularWork =
                systemUnderTest.canReceiveRegularWork();

        assertTrue(canReceiveRegularWork);
    }

    @Test
    void testAdditionalWork() {
        boolean canReceiveAdditionalWork =
                systemUnderTest.canReceiveAdditionalWork();

        assertFalse(canReceiveAdditionalWork);
    }
}
```

Annotations: ❶' ❷' ❸' ❹' ❺'

```
@Test                                    6'
@Disabled                          ←
void myThirdTest() {
    assertEquals(2, 1, "2 is not equal to 1");
}
}
```

Comparing the JUnit 4 and JUnit 5 methods, we see that

- The methods annotated with @BeforeClass (❶ in listing 4.5) and @Before-All (❶' in listing 4.6), respectively, are executed once, before all tests. These methods need to be static. In the JUnit 4 version, the methods also need to be public. In the JUnit 5 version, we can make the methods nonstatic and annotate the entire test class with @TestInstance(Life cycle.PER_CLASS).
- The methods annotated with @AfterClass (❷ in listing 4.5) and @AfterAll (❷' in listing 4.6), respectively, are executed once, after all tests. These methods need to be static. In the JUnit 4 version, the methods also need to be public. In the JUnit 5 version, we can make the methods nonstatic and annotate the whole test class with @TestInstance(Life cycle.PER_CLASS).
- The methods annotated with @Before (❸ in listing 4.5) and @BeforeEach (❸' in listing 4.6), respectively, are executed before each test. In the JUnit 4 version, the methods need to be public.
- The methods annotated with @After (❹ in listing 4.5) and @AfterEach (❹' in listing 4.6), respectively, are executed after each test. In the JUnit 4 version, the methods need to be public.
- The methods annotated with @Test (❺ in listing 4.5) and @Test (❺' in listing 4.6) are executed independently. In the JUnit 4 version, the methods need to be public. The two annotations belong to different packages: org.junit.Test and org.junit.jupiter.api.Test, respectively.
- To skip the execution of a test method, JUnit 4 uses the annotation @Ignore (❻ in listing 4.5), whereas JUnit 5 uses the annotation @Disabled (❻' in listing 4.6).

The access level has been relaxed for the test methods, from public to package-private. These methods are accessed only from within the package to which the test class belongs, so they didn't need to be made public.

4.3.2 Categories vs. tags

The Tested Data Systems engineers applied the equivalences presented in tables 4.2, 4.3, and 4.4 to the migration of their code. Now the company needs to verify its customers' information, as well as customers' existence or nonexistence. It wants to classify the verification tests in two groups: those that work with individual customers and those that check inside a repository. The company has used categories (in JUnit 4) and needs to switch to tags (in JUnit 5).

The following listing shows the two interfaces that need to be declared for the definition of JUnit 4 categories. These interfaces will be used as arguments of the JUnit 4 @Category annotation.

Listing 4.7   Interfaces created to define categories with JUnit 4

```java
public interface IndividualTests {

}

public interface RepositoryTests {

}
```

The next listing defines a JUnit 4 test that contains a method annotated as @Category(IndividualTests.class). This annotation assigns that test method as belonging to this category.

Listing 4.8   JUnit4CustomerTest class; one test method annotated with @Category

```java
public class JUnit4CustomerTest {
    private String CUSTOMER_NAME = "John Smith";

    @Category(IndividualTests.class)
    @Test
    public void testCustomer() {
        Customer customer = new Customer(CUSTOMER_NAME);

        assertEquals("John Smith", customer.getName());
    }
}
```

The following listing defines a JUnit 4 test class annotated as @Category(IndividualTests.class, RepositoryTests.class). This annotation assigns the two included test methods as belonging to these two categories.

Listing 4.9   JUnit4CustomersRepositoryTest class annotated with @Category

```java
@Category({IndividualTests.class, RepositoryTests.class})
public class JUnit4CustomersRepositoryTest {
    private String CUSTOMER_NAME = "John Smith";
    private CustomersRepository repository = new CustomersRepository();

    @Test
    public void testNonExistence() {
        boolean exists = repository.contains(CUSTOMER_NAME);

        assertFalse(exists);
    }

    @Test
    public void testCustomerPersistence() {
        repository.persist(new Customer(CUSTOMER_NAME));
```

```
        assertTrue(repository.contains("John Smith"));
    }
}
```

Listings 4.10, 4.11, and 4.12 describe three suites that look for particular test categories in the given classes.

Listing 4.10   JUnit4IndividualTestsSuite class

```
@RunWith(Categories.class)                              ←──────┐
@Categories.IncludeCategory(IndividualTests.class)   ←──────┤  ❶
@Suite.SuiteClasses({JUnit4CustomerTest.class,               ❷
    JUnit4CustomersRepositoryTest.class})   ←──────┐
public class JUnit4ndividualTestsSuite {             ❸
}
```

In this example, JUnit4IndividualTestsSuite

- Is annotated with @RunWith(Categories.class) ❶, informing JUnit that it has to execute the tests with this particular runner
- Includes the category of tests annotated with IndividualTests ❷
- Looks for these annotated tests in the JUnit4CustomerTest and JUnit4CustomersRepositoryTest classes ❸

The result of running this suite is shown in figure 4.3. All tests from the JUnit4-CustomerTest and JUnit4CustomersRepositoryTest classes will be executed, as all of them are annotated with IndividualTests.

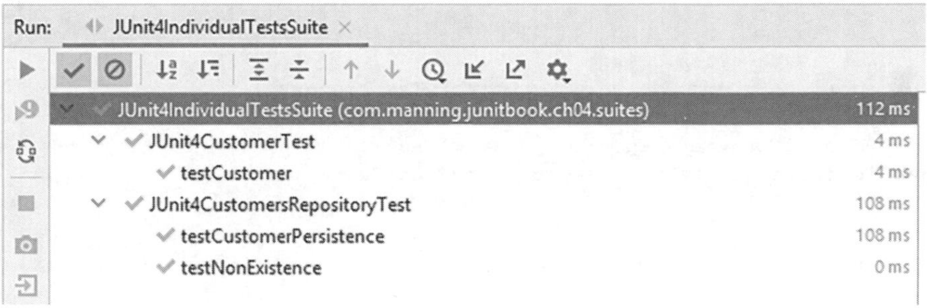

Figure 4.3   Running JUnit4IndividualTestsSuite in IntelliJ

Listing 4.11   JUnit4RepositoryTestsSuite class

```
@RunWith(Categories.class)                              ←──────┐
@Categories.IncludeCategory(RepositoryTests.class)   ←──────┤  ❶
@Suite.SuiteClasses({JUnit4CustomerTest.class,               ❷
    JUnit4CustomersRepositoryTest.class})   ←──────┐
public class JUnit4RepositoryTestsSuite {            ❸
}
```

In this example, JUnit4RepositoryTestsSuite

- Is annotated with @RunWith(Categories.class) ❶, informing JUnit that it has to execute the tests with this particular runner
- Includes the category of tests annotated with RepositoryTests ❷
- Looks for these annotated tests in the JUnit4CustomerTest and JUnit4CustomersRepositoryTest classes ❸

The result of running this suite is shown in figure 4.4. Two tests from the JUnit4-CustomersRepositoryTest class will be executed, as they are annotated with RepositoryTests.

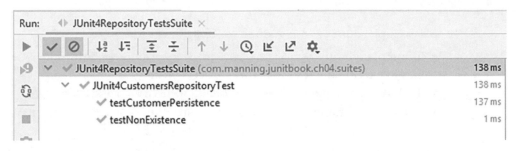

Figure 4.4   Running the JUnit4RepositoryTestsSuite **in IntelliJ**

Listing 4.12   JUnit4ExcludeRepositoryTestsSuite **class**

```
                                              ❶
@RunWith(Categories.class)            ◁──┘
@Categories.ExcludeCategory(RepositoryTests.class)      ◁──┐
@Suite.SuiteClasses({JUnit4CustomerTest.class,               ❷
    JUnit4CustomersRepositoryTest.class})      ◁──┐
public class JUnit4ExcludeRepositoryTestsSuite {      ❸
}
```

In this example, JUnit4ExcludeRepositoryTestsSuite

- Is annotated with @RunWith(Categories.class) ❶, informing JUnit that it has to execute the tests with this particular runner
- Excludes the category of tests annotated with RepositoryTests ❷
- Looks for these annotated tests in the JUnit4CustomerTest and JUnit4CustomersRepositoryTest classes ❸

The result of running this suite is shown in figure 4.5. One test from the JUnit4-CustomersTest class will be executed, as it is not annotated with Repository-Tests.

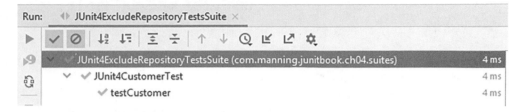

Figure 4.5   Running `JUnit4ExcludeRepositoryTestsSuite` **in IntelliJ**

The approach using JUnit 4 categories works, but it also has some shortcomings: it is a lot of code to write, and the team needs to define special test suites and special interfaces to be used solely as marker interfaces for thc tests. For that reason, the engineers at Tested Data Systems decide to switch to the JUnit 5 tags approach. Listing 4.13 introduces the `JUnit5CustomerTest` tagged class, and listing 4.14 shows the `CustomersRepositoryTest` tagged class.

Listing 4.13   `JUnit5CustomerTest` tagged class

```
@Tag("individual")
public class JUnit5CustomerTest {                              ◁─┐
    private String CUSTOMER_NAME = "John Smith";                 ❶

    @Test
    void testCustomer() {
        Customer customer = new Customer(CUSTOMER_NAME);

        assertEquals("John Smith", customer.getName());
    }
}
```

The `@Tag` annotation is added to the whole `JUnit5CustomerTest` class ❶.

Listing 4.14   `JUnit5CustomersRepositoryTest` tagged class

```
@Tag("repository")
public class JUnit5CustomersRepositoryTest {                   ◁─┐
    private String CUSTOMER_NAME = "John Smith";                 ❶
    private CustomersRepository repository = new CustomersRepository();

    @Test
    void testNonExistence() {
        boolean exists = repository.contains("John Smith");

        assertFalse(exists);
    }

    @Test
    void testCustomerPersistence() {
        repository.persist(new Customer(CUSTOMER_NAME));
```

```
        assertTrue(repository.contains("John Smith"));
    }
}
```

Similarly, the @Tag annotation is added to the whole JUnit5Customers-RepositoryTest class ❶.

To activate the JUnit 5 tags that replace the JUnit 4 categories, we have a few alternatives. For one, we can work at the level of the pom.xml configuration file.

Listing 4.15   pom.xml configuration file

```
<plugin>
    <artifactId>maven-surefire-plugin</artifactId>
    <version>2.22.2</version>
    <!--
    <configuration>
        <groups>individual</groups>                          ❶
        <excludedGroups>repository</excludedGroups>
    </configuration>
    -->
</plugin>
```

Here it is enough to uncomment the configuration node of the Surefire plugin ❶ and run mvn clean install. Or, from the IntelliJ IDEA, we can activate tag functionality by choosing Run > Edit Configurations and choosing Tags (JUnit 5) as the Test Kind (figure 4.6). However, the recommended way to go is to change pom.xml so the tests can be correctly executed from the command line.

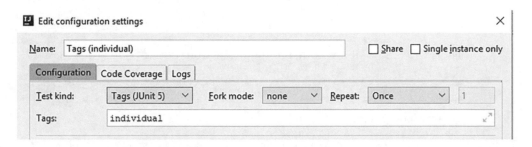

Figure 4.6   Configuring the tagged tests from the IntelliJ IDEA

Notice that we no longer define special interfaces for this goal; we no longer create many tedious suites at the level of the code. We simply annotate the classes with our own tags and then choose what to run by making the selections through the Maven configuration file or the IDE. We have less code to write and fewer changes to make at the level of the code itself. The Tested Data Systems engineers decide to take advantage of the JUnit 5 facilities.

4.3.3 *Migrating Hamcrest matcher functionality*

To continue our comparison of JUnit 4 and JUnit 5, we will look at the Hamcrest matcher functionality introduced in chapter 2. In this chapter, we use our collections example to put the two versions face to face. We will populate a list with values from Tested Data Systems' internal repository and then investigate whether its elements match some patterns using JUnit 4 (listing 4.16) and JUnit 5 (listing 4.17).

Listing 4.16 `JUnit4HamcrestListTest` class

```
import org.junit.Before;
import org.junit.Test;

public class JUnit4HamcrestListTest {

    private List<String> values;

    @Before
    public void setUp() {                          ◄——①
        values = new ArrayList<>();
        values.add("Oliver");
        values.add("Jack");
        values.add("Harry");
    }
                                              ②
    @Test                             ◄——
    public void testListWithHamcrest() {                    ③
        assertThat(values, hasSize(3));           ◄——
        assertThat(values, hasItem(anyOf(equalTo("Oliver"), equalTo("Jack"),  ④
            equalTo("Harry"))));                                        ◄——
        assertThat("The list doesn't contain all the expected objects, in
                    order", values, contains("Oliver", "Jack", "Harry"));
  ⑤  assertThat("The list doesn't contain all the expected objects",     ◄——
                values, containsInAnyOrder("Jack", "Harry", "Oliver"));
    }                                                                    ⑥
}
```

Listing 4.17 `JUnit5HamcrestListTest` class

```
import org.junit.jupiter.api.BeforeEach;
import org.junit.jupiter.api.DisplayName;
import org.junit.jupiter.api.Test;

public class JUnit5HamcrestListTest {

    private List<String> values;

    @BeforeEach                               ◄——
    public void setUp() {                      ①'
        values = new ArrayList<>();
        values.add("Oliver");
        values.add("Jack");
        values.add("Harry");
    }
```

```
    @Test
    @DisplayName("List with Hamcrest")
    public void testListWithHamcrest() {
        assertThat(values, hasSize(3));
        assertThat(values, hasItem(anyOf(equalTo("Oliver"), equalTo("Jack"),
            equalTo("Harry"))));
        assertThat("The list doesn't contain all the expected objects, in #
                    order", values, contains("Oliver", "Jack", "Harry"));
        assertThat("The list doesn't contain all the expected objects",
                    values, containsInAnyOrder("Jack", "Harry", "Oliver"));
    }
}
```

These examples are very similar (except for the `@Before`/`@BeforeEach` and `@Dis-playName` annotations). The old imports are gradually replaced by the new ones, which is why the annotations `org.junit.Test` and `org.junit.jupiter.api.Test` belong to different packages.

What do these programs do with the internal information managed at Tested Data Systems?

- We initialize the list to work with. The code is the same, but the annotations are different: `@Before` ❶ and `@BeforeEach` ❶'.
- The test methods are annotated with `org.junit.Test` ❷ and `org.junit.jupiter.api.Test` ❷', respectively.
- Verification ❸ uses the `org.junit.Assert.assertThat` method. JUnit 5 removes this method, so we use `org.hamcrest.MatcherAssert.assertThat` ❸'.
- We use the `anyOf` and `equalTo` methods from the `org.hamcrest.Matchers` class ❹ and the `anyOf` and `equalTo` methods from the `org.hamcrest.CoreMatchers` class ❹'.
- We use the same `org.hamcrest.Matchers.contains` method (❺ and ❺').
- We use the same `org.hamcrest.Matchers.containsInAnyOrder` method (❻ and ❻').

4.3.4   *Rules vs. the extension model*

A JUnit 4 rule is a component that lets us introduce additional actions when a method is executed, by intercepting its call and doing something before and after the execution of the method. To compare the JUnit 4 rules model and the JUnit 5 extension model, we'll revisit our extended `Calculator` class (listing 4.18). The developers at Tested Data Systems use this class to execute mathematical operations for verifying their SUTs. They are interested in testing the methods that can throw exceptions. One rule the Tested Data Systems test code uses extensively is `ExpectedException`, which can easily be replaced by the JUnit 5 `assertThrows` method.

Listing 4.18 Extended `Calculator` class

```
public class Calculator {

    ...

    public double sqrt(double x) {
        if (x < 0) {
            throw new
                IllegalArgumentException("Cannot extract the square
                                        root of a negative value");
        }
        return Math.sqrt(x);
    }

    public double divide(double x, double y) {
        if (y == 0) {
            throw new ArithmeticException("Cannot divide by zero");
        }
        return x/y;
    }
}
```

❶ ❷ ❸ ❹

The logic that can throw exceptions in the `Calculator` class does the following:

- Declares a method to calculate the square root of a number ❶. If the number is negative, an exception containing a message is created and thrown ❷.
- Declares a method to divide two numbers ❸. If the second number is zero, an exception containing a message is created and thrown ❹.

The following listing provides an example that specifies which exception message is expected during the execution of the test code, using the new functionality of the `Calculator` class (see listing 4.18).

Listing 4.19 `JUnit4RuleExceptionTester` class

```
public class JUnit4RuleExceptionTester {
    @Rule
    public ExpectedException expectedException =
                            ExpectedException.none();

    private Calculator calculator = new Calculator();

    @Test
    public void expectIllegalArgumentException() {
        expectedException.expect(IllegalArgumentException.class);
        expectedException.expectMessage("Cannot extract the square root
                                        of a negative value");
        calculator.sqrt(-1);
    }
}
```

❶ ❷ ❸ ❹ ❺

```
    @Test
    public void expectArithmeticException() {                              6
        expectedException.expect(ArithmeticException.class);      ◄───┘
        expectedException.expectMessage("Cannot divide by zero");    ◄───┐
        calculator.divide(1, 0);      ◄───┐                               7
    }                                      8
}
```

In this example:

- We declare an ExpectedException field annotated with @Rule. The @Rule annotation must be applied on a public nonstatic field or a public nonstatic method ❶. The ExpectedException.none() factory method simply creates an unconfigured ExpectedException.
- We initialize an instance of the Calculator class whose functionality we are testing ❷.
- ExpectedException is configured to expect the type of exception ❸ and the message ❹ before being thrown by invoking the sqrt method ❺.
- ExpectedException is configured to expect the type of exception ❻ and message ❼ before being thrown by invoking the divide method ❽.

The next listing shows the JUnit 5 approach.

Listing 4.20   `JUnit5ExceptionTester` class

```
public class JUnit5ExceptionTester {
    private Calculator calculator = new Calculator();     ◄───┐
                                                               ❶'
    @Test
    public void expectIllegalArgumentException() {
        Throwable throwable = assertThrows(
                    IllegalArgumentException.class,          ┤❷'
                    () -> calculator.sqrt(-1));
        assertEquals("Cannot extract the square root of a
                    negative value", throwable.getMessage());  ┤❸'

    }

    @Test
    public void expectArithmeticException() {
        Throwable throwable = assertThrows(ArithmeticException.class,  ┤❹'
                        () -> calculator.divide(1, 0));
        assertEquals("Cannot divide by zero", throwable.getMessage());  ◄───┐
                                                                            ❺'
    }
}
```

In this example:

- We initialize an instance of the Calculator class whose functionality we are testing ❶'.

- We assert that the execution of the supplied `calculator.sqrt(-1)` executable throws an `IllegalArgumentException` ❷', and we check the message from the exception ❸'.
- We assert that the execution of the supplied `calculator.divide(1, 0)` executable throws an `ArithmeticException` ❹', and we check the message from the exception ❺'.

A clear difference exists between JUnit 4 and JUnit 5 in the clarity and length of the code. The effective JUnit 5 testing code is 13 lines, whereas the effective JUnit 4 code is 20 lines. We do not need to initialize and manage any additional rules. The JUnit 5 testing methods contain one line each.

Another rule that Tested Data Systems would like to migrate is `TemporaryFolder`. The `TemporaryFolder` rule lets us create files and folders that should be deleted when the test method finishes (whether it passes or fails). Because the tests in Tested Data Systems' projects work intensively with temporary resources, this step is also a must. The JUnit 4 rule has been replaced by the `@TempDir` annotation in JUnit 5. The following listing presents the JUnit 4 approach.

Listing 4.21 `JUnit4RuleTester` class

```java
public class JUnit4RuleTester {
    @Rule
    public TemporaryFolder folder = new TemporaryFolder();        ❶

    @Test
    public void testTemporaryFolder() throws IOException {
        File createdFolder = folder.newFolder("createdFolder");   ❷
        File createdFile = folder.newFile("createdFile.txt");
        assertTrue(createdFolder.exists());                       ❸
        assertTrue(createdFile.exists());
    }
}
```

In this example:

- We declare a `TemporaryFolder` field annotated with `@Rule` and initialize it. The `@Rule` annotation must be applied on a public field or a public method ❶.
- We use the `TemporaryFolder` field to create a folder and a file ❷, located in the Temp folder of our user profile in the OS.
- We check the existence of the temporary folder and the temporary file ❸.

And here is the new JUnit 5 approach.

Listing 4.22 `JUnit5TempDirTester` class

```java
public class JUnit5TempDirTester {
    @TempDir                        ❶'
    Path tempDir;
```

```
    private static Path createdFile;

    @Test
    public void testTemporaryFolder() throws IOException {
        assertTrue(Files.isDirectory(tempDir));
        createdFile = Files.createFile(
                tempDir.resolve("createdFile.txt")
        );

        assertTrue(createdFile.toFile().exists());

    }

    @AfterAll
    public static void afterAll() {
        assertFalse(createdFile.toFile().exists());
    }

}
```

In this example:

- We declare a @TempDir annotated field ❶'.
- We declare the createdFile variable ❷'.
- We check the creation of this temporary directory before the execution of the test ❸'.
- We create a file within this directory and check its existence ❹'.
- After the execution of the tests, we check that the temporary resource has been removed ❺'. The temporary folder is removed after the execution of the afterAll method ends.

The advantage of the JUnit 5 extension approach is that we do not have to create the folder ourselves through a constructor; the folder is created automatically when we annotate a field with @TempDir.

4.3.5   *Custom rules*

Tested Data Systems has defined custom rules for its tests. Custom rules are particularly useful when some tests need similar additional actions before and after execution.

In JUnit 4, the Tested Data Systems engineers needed their additional actions to be executed before and after the execution of a test. So, they created their own classes to implement the TestRule interface (see listings 4.23–4.25). To do this, they had to override the apply(Statement, Description) method, which returns an instance of Statement. Such an object represents the tests within the JUnit runtime, and Statement#evaluate() runs them. The Description object describes the individual test. This object can be used to read information about the test through reflection.

Listing 4.23 `CustomRule` **class**

```
public class CustomRule implements TestRule {
    private Statement base;
    private Description description;

    @Override
    public Statement apply(Statement base, Description description) {
        this.base = base;
        this.description = description;
        return new CustomStatement(base, description);
    }

}
```

In this example:

- We declare our `CustomRule` class that implements the `TestRule` interface **①**.
- We keep references to a `Statement` field and a `Description` field **②**, and we use them in the `apply` method that returns a `CustomStatement` **③**.

Listing 4.24 `CustomStatement` **class**

```
public class CustomStatement extends Statement {
    private Statement base;
    private Description description;

    public CustomStatement(Statement base, Description description) {
        this.base = base;
        this.description = description;
    }

    @Override
    public void evaluate() throws Throwable {
        System.out.println(this.getClass().getSimpleName() + " " +
                description.getMethodName() + " has started");
        try {
            base.evaluate();
        } finally {
            System.out.println(this.getClass().getSimpleName() + " " +
                    description.getMethodName() + " has finished");
        }
    }
}
```

In this example:

- We declare our `CustomStatement` class that extends the `Statement` class **①**.
- We keep references to a `Statement` field and to a `Description` field **②**, and we use them as arguments of the constructor **③**.
- We override the inherited `evaluate` method and call `base.evaluate()` inside it **④**.

Listing 4.25   `JUnit4CustomRuleTester` class

```java
public class JUnit4CustomRuleTester {

    @Rule
    public CustomRule myRule = new CustomRule();          ❶

    @Test
    public void myCustomRuleTest() {
        System.out.println("Call of a test method");      ❷
    }
}
```

In this example, we use the previously defined `CustomRule` by doing the following:

- We declare a public `CustomRule` field and annotate it with `@Rule` ❶.
- We create the `myCustomRuleTest` method and annotate it with `@Test` ❷.

The result of executing this test is shown in figure 4.7. As the engineers from Tested Data Systems required, the effective execution of the test is surrounded by the additional messages provided to the `evaluate` method of the `CustomStatement` class.

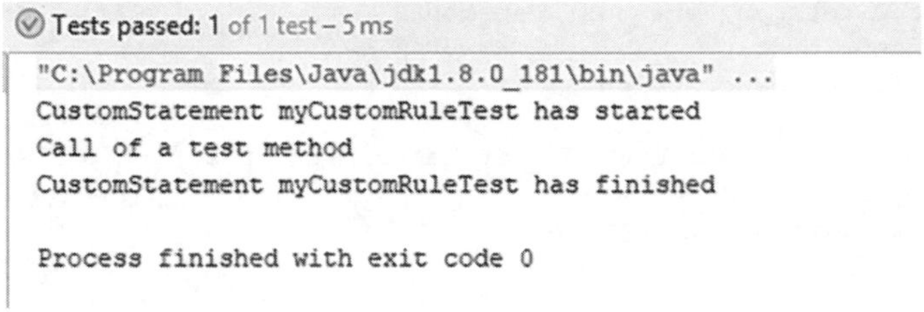

```
⊘ Tests passed: 1 of 1 test – 5 ms

"C:\Program Files\Java\jdk1.8.0_181\bin\java" ...
CustomStatement myCustomRuleTest has started
Call of a test method
CustomStatement myCustomRuleTest has finished

Process finished with exit code 0
```

Figure 4.7   **The result of executing `JUnit4CustomRuleTester`**

The engineers from Tested Data Systems would like to migrate their own rules as well. JUnit 5 allows effects similar to those of the JUnit 4 rules by introducing custom extensions that extend the behavior of test classes and methods. The code is shorter and relies on the declarative annotations style. First, we define the `CustomExtension` class, which is used as an argument of the `@ExtendWith` annotation on the tested class.

Listing 4.26   `CustomExtension` class

```java
public class CustomExtension implements AfterEachCallback,    ❶'
BeforeEachCallback {
    @Override
    public void beforeEach(ExtensionContext extensionContext)
                                          throws Exception {    ❷'
        System.out.println(this.getClass().getSimpleName() + " " +
                extensionContext.getDisplayName() + " has started" );
    }
```

```
    @Override
    public void afterEach(ExtensionContext extensionContext)
                                       throws Exception {
        System.out.println(this.getClass().getSimpleName() + " " +
            extensionContext.getDisplayName() + " has finished");
    }
}
```

In this example:

- We declare `CustomExtension` as implementing the `AfterEachCallback` and `BeforeEachCallback` interfaces ❶'.
- We override the `beforeEach` method, to be executed before each test method from the testing class that will be extended with `CustomExtension` ❷'.
- We override the `afterEach` method, to be executed after each test method from the testing class that will be extended with `CustomExtension` ❸'.

Listing 4.27 The `JUnit5CustomExtensionTester` class

```
@ExtendWith(CustomExtension.class)
public class JUnit5CustomExtensionTester {          ❶'

    @Test
    public void myCustomRuleTest() {                    ❷'
        System.out.println("Call of a test method");
    }
}
```

In this example:

- We extend `JUnit5CustomExtensionTester` with the `CustomExtension` class ❶'.
- We create the `myCustomRuleTest` method and annotate it with `@Test` ❷'.

The result of executing this test is shown in figure 4.8. Because the test class is extended with the `CustomExtension` class, the previously defined `beforeEach` and `afterEach` methods are executed before and after each test method, respectively.

Notice the clear difference between JUnit 4 and JUnit 5 in the clarity and length of the code. The JUnit 4 approach needs to work with three classes; the JUnit 5 approach

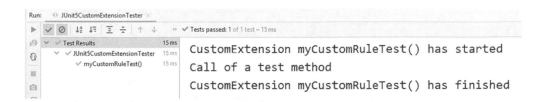

Figure 4.8 The result of executing `JUnit5CustomExtensionTester`

needs to work with only two. The code to be executed before and after each test method is isolated in a dedicated method with a clear name. We only need to annotate the testing class with `@ExtendWith`.

The JUnit 5 extension model can also be used to replace the runners from JUnit 4 gradually. For the extensions that have already been created, the migration process is simple:

- To migrate the Mockito tests, we need to replace the annotation `@Run-With(MockitoJUnitRunner.class)` in the tested class with the annotation `@ExtendWith(MockitoExtension.class)`.
- To migrate the Spring tests, we need to replace the annotation `@Run-With(SpringJUnit4ClassRunner.class)` in the tested class with the annotation `@ExtendWith(SpringExtension.class)`.

When this chapter was written, there was no extension for the Arquillian tests. The runners will be discussed in more detail in later chapters.

In chapter 5, we find out more about software testing principles and test types, the need to start from unit tests, and ways to advance to different testing levels.

Summary

This chapter has covered the following:

- Applying the steps needed by the migration from JUnit 4 to JUnit 5, and summarizing them into a guiding table: replace the dependencies, replace the annotations, replace the testing classes and methods, and replace the JUnit 4 rules and the runners with the JUnit 5 extension model.
- Using the needed dependencies in both cases, making the change from a single dependency in JUnit 4 to multiple dependencies in JUnit 5.
- Comparing and using the equivalent annotations, classes, and methods of JUnit 4 and JUnit 5, which drive similar effects: defining tests, controlling the life cycle of a test, and checking the results.
- Using examples to implement the effective changes in code when migrating from JUnit 4 to JUnit 5.

Software testing principles

This chapter covers

- Examining the need for unit tests
- Differentiating between types of software tests
- Comparing black-box and white-box testing

A crash is when your competitor's program dies. When your program dies, it is an "idiosyncrasy." Frequently, crashes are followed with a message like "ID 02." "ID" is an abbreviation for idiosyncrasy, and the number that follows indicates how many more months of testing the product should have had.

—Guy Kawasaki

Earlier chapters in this book took a very pragmatic approach to designing and deploying unit tests. We took a deep look at JUnit 5's capabilities and the architectures of both JUnit 4 and JUnit 5 and demonstrated how to migrate between the two versions. This chapter steps back to look at the various types of software tests and the roles they play in the application life cycle.

Why do you need to know all this information? Unit testing is not something you do without planning and preparation. To become a top-level developer, you need to contrast unit tests with functional and other types of tests. *Functional testing* simply means evaluating the compliance of a system or component with the requirements. When you understand why unit tests are necessary, you also need to know how far to take your tests. Testing in and of itself is not the goal.

5.1 The need for unit tests

The main goals of unit testing are to verify that your application works as expected and to catch bugs early. Although functional testing helps you accomplish the same goals, unit tests are extremely powerful and versatile and offer much more. Unit tests

- Allow greater test coverage than functional tests
- Increase team productivity
- Detect regressions and limit the need for debugging
- Give us the confidence to refactor and, in general, make changes
- Improve implementation
- Document expected behavior
- Enable code coverage and other metrics

5.1.1 Allowing greater test coverage

Unit tests are the first type of tests any application should have. If you have to choose between writing unit tests and functional tests, you should choose to write the second kind. In our experience, functional tests cover about 70% of the application code. If you want to go further and provide more test coverage, you need to write unit tests.

Unit tests can easily simulate error conditions, which is extremely difficult for functional tests to do (and impossible in some instances). Unit tests also provide much more than just testing, as explained in the following sections.

5.1.2 Increasing team productivity

Imagine that you are on a team working on a large application. Unit tests allow you to deliver quality code (tested code) without waiting for all the other components to be ready. On the other hand, functional tests are more coarse grained and need the full application, or a good part of it, to be ready before you can test it.

5.1.3 Detecting regressions and limiting debugging

A passing unit test suite confirms that your code works and gives you the confidence to modify your existing code, either for refactoring or to add and modify new features. As a developer, you can have no better feeling than knowing someone is watching your back and will warn you if you break something.

A suite of unit tests reduces the need to debug an application to find out why something is failing. Whereas a functional test tells you that a bug exists somewhere in the implementation of a use case, a unit test tells you that a specific method is failing for a specific reason. You no longer need to spend hours trying to find the problem.

5.1.4 *Refactoring with confidence*

Without unit tests, it is difficult to justify refactoring because there is always a relatively high chance that you will break something. Why would you risk spending hours of debugging time (and put delivery at risk) only to improve the implementation or change a method name? As shown in figure 5.1, unit tests provide the safety net that gives you the confidence to refactor.

Figure 5.1   Unit tests provide a safety net that gives you the confidence to refactor.

JUnit best practice: Refactoring

Throughout the history of computer science, many great teachers have advocated iterative development. Niklaus Wirth, for example, who gave us the now-ancient languages Algol and Pascal, championed techniques such as stepwise refinement.

(continued)

For a time, these techniques seemed to be difficult to apply to larger, layered applications. Small changes can reverberate throughout a system. Project managers looked to up-front planning as a way to minimize change, but productivity remained low.

The rise of the xUnit framework fueled the popularity of agile methodologies, which (once again) advocate iterative development. Agile methodologists favor writing code in vertical slices to produce a working use case, as opposed to writing code in horizontal slices to provide services layer by layer.

When you design and write code for a single use case or functional chain, your design may be adequate for this feature, but it may not be adequate for the next feature. To retain a design across features, agile methodologies encourage refactoring to adapt the code base as needed.

How do you ensure that *refactoring* (improving the design of existing code) does not break the existing code? The answer is that unit tests tell you when and where code breaks. In short, unit tests give you the confidence to refactor.

Agile methodologies try to lower project risks by enabling you to cope with change. They allow and embrace change by standardizing quick iterations and applying principles such as YAGNI (you ain't gonna need it) and "The Simplest Thing That Could Possibly Work." The foundation upon which all these principles rest, however, is a solid bed of unit tests.

5.1.5   *Improving implementation*

Unit tests are first-rate clients of the code they test. They force the API under test to be flexible and to be unit testable in isolation. Sometimes you have to refactor your code under test to make it unit testable. You may eventually use the test-driven development (TDD) approach, which by its own conception generates code that can be unit tested. We'll experiment with TDD in detail in chapter 20.

It is important to monitor your unit tests as you create and modify them. If a unit test is too long and unwieldy, the code under test usually has a design smell, and you should refactor it. You may also be testing too many features in one test method. If a test cannot verify a feature in isolation, the code probably is not flexible enough, and you should refactor it. Modifying code to test it is normal.

5.1.6   *Documenting expected behavior*

Imagine that you need to learn a new API. On the one hand, you have a 300-page document describing the API, and on the other hand, you have some examples of how to use the API. Which would you choose?

The power of examples is well known. Unit tests are examples that show how to use the API. As such, they make excellent developer documentation. Because unit tests match the production code, they *must* be up to date, unlike other forms of documentation.

To examine how tests effectively document the expected behavior, let's go back to the `Calculator` class that was introduced in previous chapters. Listing 5.1 illustrates how unit tests help provide documentation. The `expectIllegalArgument-Exception()` method shows that an `IllegalArgumentException` is thrown when we try to extract the square root from a negative number. The `expectArithmetic-Exception()` method shows that an `ArithmeticException` is thrown when we try to divide by zero.

Listing 5.1 Unit tests as automatic documentation

```java
public class JUnit5ExceptionTester {
    private Calculator calculator = new Calculator();        ←─┐  ❶

    @Test
    public void expectIllegalArgumentException() {
        assertThrows(IllegalArgumentException.class,
                          () -> calculator.sqrt(-1));        ❷
    }

    @Test
    public void expectArithmeticException() {
        assertThrows(ArithmeticException.class,
                          () -> calculator.divide(1, 0));    ❸
    }
}
```

In this example:

- We initialize an instance of the `Calculator` class whose functionality we are testing ❶.
- We assert that the execution of the supplied `calculator.sqrt(-1)` executable throws an `IllegalArgumentException` ❷.
- We assert that the execution of the supplied `calculator.divide(1, 0)` executable throws an `ArithmeticException` ❸.

The execution of the tests clearly shows the use cases. You can follow these use cases and examine what a particular execution will trigger, so the tests are an effective part of the project documentation.

5.1.7 Enabling code coverage and other metrics

Unit tests tell you, at the push of a button, whether everything still works. Furthermore, unit tests enable you to gather code-coverage metrics (see chapter 6) that show, statement by statement, what code execution the tests triggered and what code the tests did not touch. You can also use tools to track the progress of passing versus failing tests from one build to the next. Further, you can monitor performance and cause a test to fail if its performance has degraded from a previous build.

5.2   Test types

Figure 5.2 outlines four categories of software tests. There are other ways of categorizing software tests—other authors use different names—but these categories are the most useful for the purposes of this book. Please note that this section examines *software tests in general*, not just the automated unit tests covered elsewhere in the book.

In figure 5.2, the outermost tests are broadest in scope. The innermost tests are narrowest in scope. As you move from the inner boxes to the outer boxes, the software tests get more functional, requiring that more of the application be present.

Figure 5.2   The four types of tests, from the innermost (narrowest) to the outermost (broadest)

Earlier, we mentioned that each unit test focuses on a distinct unit of work. What about testing different units of work combined into a workflow? Will the result of the workflow do what you expect?

Different kinds of tests answer these questions. We categorize them in these varieties:

- Unit tests
- Integration tests
- System tests
- Acceptance tests

The following sections look at each test type, starting with the innermost (the narrowest in scope) and working out to the broadest in scope.

5.2.1   Unit testing

Unit testing is a software testing method in which individual units of source code (methods or classes) are tested to determine whether they are fit for use. Unit testing increases developer confidence in changing the code because, from the beginning, it serves as a safety net. If we have good unit tests and run them every time we change the code, we will be certain that our changes are not affecting the existing functionality.

We're focusing here on testing classes and methods in isolation. Suppose that the engineers at our example company, Tested Data Systems Inc., want to manage the company's customers. They will first test the creation of the customer. Then they will test the operations of searching for a customer and adding them to and removing them from the company database. Because a unit test is narrowest in scope, it may only require that some isolated classes be present.

5.2.2 *Integration software testing*

Individual unit tests are essential quality controls, but what happens when different units of work are combined into a workflow? When you have the tests for a class up and running, the next step is hooking up the class with other methods and services. Examining the interaction among components, possibly running in their target environment, is the job of integration testing. Table 5.1 differentiates the various cases under which components interact.

Table 5.1   Testing how objects, services, and subsystems interact

Interaction	Test description
Objects	The test instantiates objects and calls methods on these objects. You can use this test type to see how objects belonging to different classes cooperate to solve the problem.
Services	The test runs while a container hosts the application, which may connect to a database or attach to any other external resource or device. You can use this test type when you are developing an application that is deployed into a software container.
Subsystems	A layered application may have a frontend to handle the presentation and a backend to execute the business logic. Tests can verify that a request passes through the frontend and returns an appropriate response from the backend. You can use this test type in the case of an application with an architecture made of a presentation layer (web interface, for example) and a business service layer executing the logic.

Just as more traffic collisions occur at intersections, the points where objects interact are major contributors to bugs. Ideally, you should define integration tests before you write the application code. Being able to code to the test strongly increases a programmer's ability to write well-behaved objects. The engineers at Tested Data Systems will use integration testing to check whether the objects representing customers and offers cooperate well, such as when a customer is assigned only once to an offer. When the offer expires, the customer is automatically removed from the offer if they haven't accepted it; if we have added an offer on the customer side, the customer is added on the offer side.

5.2.3 *System software testing*

System testing of software is testing conducted on a complete, integrated system to evaluate the system's compliance with its specified requirements. The objective is to detect inconsistencies among units that are already integrated.

Test doubles or mock objects can simulate the behavior of complex, real objects and therefore are useful when a real object (such as some depended-on component) is impractical to incorporate into a test or when testing is impossible—at least for the moment—because the dependent component is not yet available. *Mock objects* may appear at the level of a unit test: their role is to replace a part of a system that is not available or impractical to incorporate into a test. *Test doubles* are simulated objects that mimic the behavior of real objects in a controlled way. They are created to test the behavior of some other objects that use them.

The engineers at Tested Data Systems will use test doubles when they are communicating with an external service; with an internal service that is not yet available or is slow, hard to configure, or difficult to access; or with a service that is not yet fully available. A test double is handy in that it relieves tests from waiting for the availability of that service.

The customers and offers that the Tested Data Systems engineers are managing, for example, need to be persisted to a database. This database is hard to set up and configure; the engineers must install the software and then create and populate the tables. These processes require time and people. The team will use a mock database for their programs.

5.2.4   *Acceptance software testing*

It is important that an application perform well, but the application must also meet the customer's needs. Acceptance tests are our final level of testing. The customer or a proxy usually specifies acceptance tests to ensure that the application meets whatever goals the customer or stakeholder has defined.

Acceptance tests are supersets of all other tests. They try to answer essential questions, such as whether the application addresses the business goals and is doing the right thing.

Acceptance tests may be expressed using the keywords Given, When, and Then. When you use these keywords, you are essentially following a scenario: the interaction of the user with the system. The verification in the Then step may look like a unit test, but it checks the end of the scenario and answers the question "Are we addressing the business goals?"

Tested Data Systems may implement acceptance tests such as these:

> Given that there is an economy offer,
> When we have a regular customer,
> Then we can add them to and remove them from the offer.

> Given that there is an economy offer,
> When we have a VIP customer,
> Then we can add them to the offer but not remove them from the offer.

Because acceptance tests are the broadest in scope, they are functional and require a larger part of the application to be present. The acceptance tests we just listed are anticipating the behavior-driven development (BDD) way of working, to be detailed in chapter 21.

5.3   *Black-box vs. white-box testing*

Before we close this chapter, we'll focus on one other category of software tests: black-box and white-box testing. This category is intuitive and easy to grasp, but developers often forget about it.

5.3.1 Black-box testing

A *black-box test* has no knowledge of the internal state or behavior of the system. The test relies solely on the external system interface to verify its correctness.

As the name of this methodology suggests, you treat the system as a black box. Imagine that the box is covered with buttons and LEDs. You do not know what is inside or how the system operates; you only know that when the correct input is provided, the system produces the desired output. All you need to know to test the system properly is the system's functional specification. The early stages of a project typically produce this kind of specification, which means we can start testing early. Anyone can take part in testing the system, such as a QA engineer, a developer, or even a customer.

The simplest form of black-box testing tries to mimic actions in the user interface manually. A more sophisticated approach is to use a tool for this task, such as Http-Unit, HtmlUnit, or Selenium. We will apply some of these tools in another part of the book (chapter 15).

At Tested Data Systems, black-box testing is used for applications that provide a web interface. The testing tool knows only that it has to interact with the frontend (selections, push-buttons, and so on) and verify the results (the result of the action, the content of the destination page, and so on).

5.3.2 White-box testing

At the other end of the spectrum is *white-box testing*, sometimes called *glass-box testing*. In this type of testing, we use detailed knowledge of the implementation to create tests and drive the testing process. In addition to understanding the component implementation, we need to know how this testing process interacts with other components. For these reasons, the implementers are the best candidates to create white-box tests.

White-box testing can be implemented at an earlier stage; there is no need to wait for the GUI to be available. You may cover many execution paths. Consider the scenarios from section 5.2.4:

> Given that there is an economy offer,
> When we have a regular customer,
> Then we can add them to and remove them from the offer.

> Given that there is an economy offer,
> When we have a VIP customer,
> Then we can add them to the offer but not remove them from the offer.

These scenarios are good examples of white-box testing. They require knowledge of the application internals (at least of the API) and cover different execution paths of which the external user is not aware. Each step corresponds to writing pieces of code that work with the existing API. Developers can apply the code from the early stages without needing a GUI.

5.3.3 *Pros and cons*

Which of the two approaches should you use? There is no absolute answer, so we suggest that you use both approaches. In some situations, you need user-centric tests (no need for details), and in others, you need to test the implementation details of the system. Tables 5.2 and 5.3 contrast black-box and white-box testing; let's consider the pros and cons of both approaches.

Table 5.2   The pros of black-box and white-box tests

Black-box tests	White-box tests
Tests are user-centric and expose specifications to discrepancies.	Testing can be implemented from the early stages of the project.
The tester may be a nontechnical person.	There is no need for an existing GUI.
Tests can be conducted independently of the developers.	Testing is controlled by the developers and can cover many execution paths.

Table 5.3   The cons of black-box and white-box tests

Black-box tests	White-box tests
A limited number of inputs may be tested.	Testing can be implemented only by skilled people with programming knowledge.
Many program paths may be left uncovered.	Tests will need to be rewritten if the implementation changes.
Tests may become redundant; the lack of details may mean covering the same execution paths.	Tests are tightly coupled to the implementation.

USER-CENTRIC APPROACH

Black-box testing first addresses user needs. We know that there is tremendous value in customer feedback, and one of our goals in extreme programming is to release early and release often. We are unlikely to get useful feedback, however, if we just tell the customer, "Here it is. Let us know what you think." It is far better to get the customer involved by providing a manual test script to run through. By making the customer think about the application, they can also clarify what the system should do. Interacting with the constructed GUI and comparing the results that are obtained with the expected ones is an example of testing that customers can run by themselves.

TESTING DIFFICULTIES

Black-box tests are more difficult to write and run[1] because they usually deal with a graphical frontend, whether it's a web browser or desktop application. Another issue is that a valid result on the screen does not always mean the application is correct.

---

[1] Black-box testing is getting easier with tools such as Selenium and HtmlUnit, which we examine in chapter 15.

White-box tests usually are easier to write and run than black-box tests, but the developers must implement them.

TEST COVERAGE

White-box testing provides better test coverage than black-box testing. On the other hand, black-box tests can bring more value than white-box tests. We focus on test coverage in chapter 6.

Although these test distinctions may seem to be academic, recall that "divide and conquer" does not have to apply only to writing production software; it can also apply to testing. We encourage you to use these different types of tests to provide the best code coverage possible, which will give you the confidence to refactor and evolve your applications.

Chapter 6, which starts part 2 of this book, looks at test quality. In it, we present best practices such as measuring test coverage and writing testable code, and we introduce test-driven development, behavior-driven development, and mutation testing.

Summary

This chapter has covered the following:

- Examining the need for unit tests. They offer greater test coverage than functional tests, increase team productivity, detect regressions, give us the confidence to refactor, improve implementation, document expected behavior, and enable code coverage.
- Comparing different types of software testing. From the narrowest to the broadest scope, they are as follows: unit testing, integration testing, system testing, and acceptance testing.
- Contrasting black-box testing and white-box testing. Black-box testing has no knowledge of the internal state or behavior of the system and relies solely on the external system interface to verify its correctness. White-box testing is controlled by the developer, can cover many execution paths, and provides better test coverage.

Part 2

Different testing strategies

This part of the book reveals different strategies and techniques in testing. Here, we take a more scientific and theoretical approach to explain the differences. We talk about test quality, describe incorporating mock objects and stubs, and dive into the details of in-container testing.

Chapter 6 is dedicated to the analysis of test quality. It introduces concepts such as code coverage, test-driven development, behavior-driven development, and mutating testing. Chapter 7 is dedicated to stubs, taking a look at a solution to isolate the environment and make tests seamless. Chapter 8 explains mock objects, providing an overview of how to construct and use them. The chapter also provides a real-world example showing not only where mock objects fit best, but also how to benefit by integrating them with JUnit tests.

Chapter 9 describes a different technique: executing tests inside a container. This solution is very different from the preceding ones, and like them, it has pros and cons. The chapter starts by providing an overview of in-container testing. The end of the chapter compares the mocks-stubs approach with the in-container approach.

Test quality

6

This chapter covers

- Measuring test coverage
- Writing testable code
- Investigating test-driven and behavior-driven development
- Introducing mutation testing
- Testing in the development cycle

I don't think anybody tests enough of anything.

—James Gosling

In the previous chapters, we introduced testing software, began to explore testing with JUnit, and presented different test methodologies. Now that you are writing test cases, it is time to measure how good these tests are by using a test-coverage tool to report what code is executed by the tests and what code is not. This chapter will also discuss how to write code that is easy to test and finish by taking a first look at test-driven development (TDD).

101

6.1   *Measuring test coverage*

Writing unit tests gives you the confidence to change and refactor an application. As you make changes, you run tests, which give you immediate feedback about new features under test and whether changes break the existing tests. The issue is that these changes may still break untested functionality.

To resolve this issue, you need to know precisely what code runs when you or the build invoke tests. Ideally, your tests should cover 100% of your application code. This section examines test coverage in detail.

Test coverage can ensure some of the quality of your programming, but it is also a controversial metric. High code coverage does not tell you anything about the quality of the tests. A good programmer should be able to see beyond the pure percentage obtained by running tests.

6.1.1   *Introduction to test coverage*

Using black-box testing, we can create tests that cover the public API of an application. Because we are using documentation—not knowledge of the implementation—as our guide, we do not create tests that use special parameter values to exercise special conditions in the code, for example.

Many metrics can be used to calculate test coverage. Some of the most basic are the percentage of program methods and the percentage of program lines called during execution of the test suite. Another metric of test coverage is tracking which methods the tests call. The result does not tell you whether the tests are complete, but it does tell you whether you have a test for a method. Figure 6.1 shows the partial test coverage typically achieved by black-box testing alone.

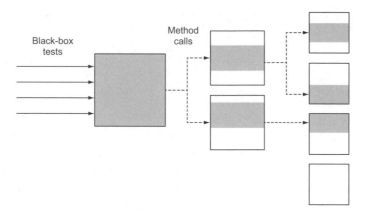

Figure 6.1   Partial test coverage with black-box tests. The boxes represent components or modules. The shaded areas represent the portions of the system effectively covered by tests, and the white areas represent the untested portions.

You *can* write a unit test with intimate knowledge of a method's implementation. If a method contains a conditional branch, you can write two unit tests, one for each branch. Because you need to see into the method to create such a test, this type of test falls in the category of white-box testing. Figure 6.2 shows 100% test coverage with white-box testing.

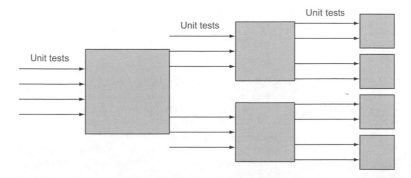

Figure 6.2 Complete test coverage with white-box tests. Each box represents a component or a module. The boxes are fully shaded, as they are fully covered by tests.

You can achieve higher test coverage by using white-box unit tests, because you have access to more methods and can control the inputs to each method and the behavior of secondary objects (using stubs or mock objects, as you'll see in later chapters). Because you can write white-box unit tests against protected, package-private, and public methods, you get more code coverage.

If you haven't been able to achieve high code coverage with black-box testing, you need more tests (you may have uncovered ways to use the application), or you may have superfluous code that does not contribute to the business goals. In either case, an analysis may be required to reveal the real causes.

A program with high test coverage, measured as a percentage, has more of its source code executed during testing, which suggests that it has a lower chance of containing undetected software bugs compared with a program with low test coverage. The metric is built by a tool that runs the test suite and analyzes the code that is effectively executed as a result.

6.1.2   *Tools for measuring code coverage*

This section demonstrates the use of tools to measure code coverage with the help of the source code provided for this chapter. We'll use the `com.manning.junit-book.ch06` package, which uses the `Calculator` and `CalculatorTest` classes.

A few code-coverage tools are well integrated with JUnit. A very convenient way to determine the code coverage is to work directly from IntelliJ IDEA. The IDE provides an option for executing the tests with coverage, as shown in figure 6.3.

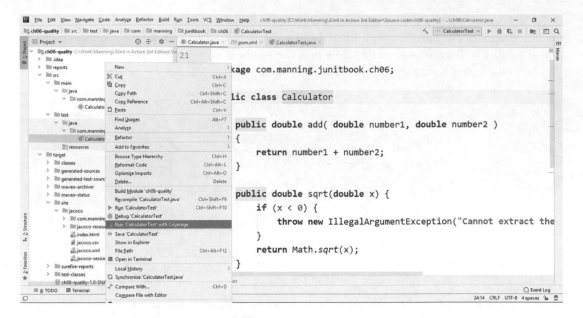

Figure 6.3   Running tests with coverage in IntelliJ

When you run the code with coverage, you get the report shown in figure 6.4. You can click Generate Coverage Report to create reports in HTML format.

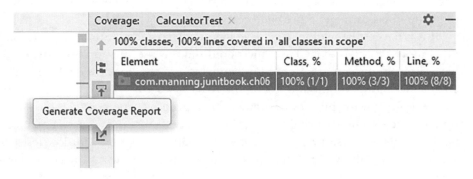

Figure 6.4   The result of running the tests with coverage

The HTML reports can be at the level of the `com.manning.junitbook.ch06` package (figure 6.5), the `Calculator` class (figure 6.6), or individual lines of code (figure 6.7).

[all classes]

Overall Coverage Summary

Package	Class, %
all classes	100% (1/ 1)

Coverage Breakdown

Package ▲	Class, %
com.manning.junitbook.ch06	100% (1/ 1)

Figure 6.5 The code-coverage report at the level of a package

[all classes] [com.manning.junitbook.ch06]

Coverage Summary for Package: com.manning.junitbook.ch06

Package	Class, %
com.manning.junitbook.ch06	100% (1/ 1)

Class ▲	Class, %
Calculator	100% (1/ 1)

Figure 6.6 The code-coverage report at the level of an individual class

```
22  package com.manning.junitbook.ch06;
23
24  public class Calculator
25  {
26      public double add( double number1, double number2 )
27      {
28          return number1 + number2;
29      }
30
31      public double sqrt(double x) {
32          if (x < 0) {
33              throw new IllegalArgumentException("Cannot extract the square root of a negative value");
34          }
35          return Math.sqrt(x);
36      }
37
38      public double divide(double x, double y) {
39          if (y == 0) {
40              throw new ArithmeticException("Cannot divide by zero");
41          }
42          return x/y;
43      }
```

Figure 6.7 The code-coverage report at the level of individual lines

The recommended way to work is to execute the tests from the command line with code coverage; this works fine in conjunction with the continuous integration/continuous development (CI/CD) pipeline. To do so, you can use the JaCoCo Java code coverage

```xml
<plugin>
    <groupId>org.jacoco</groupId>
    <artifactId>jacoco-maven-plugin</artifactId>
    <version>0.7.9</version>
    <executions>
        <execution>
            <goals>
                <goal>prepare-agent</goal>
            </goals>
        </execution>
        <execution>
            <id>report</id>
            <phase>test</phase>
            <goals>
                <goal>report</goal>
            </goals>
        </execution>
```

Figure 6.8   The JaCoCo plugin configuration in the Maven pom.xml file

tool. JaCoCo is an open source toolkit that is updated frequently and has very good integration with Maven. To make Maven and JaCoCo work together, you need to insert the JaCoCo plugin information in the pom.xml file (see figure 6.8).

Go to the command prompt, and run `mvn test` (figure 6.9). This command also generates—for the `com.manning.junitbook` package and the `Calculator` class—the code-coverage report, which you can access from the project folder, target\site\jacoco (figure 6.10). We've chosen to show an example that does not have 100% code coverage. You can also do this by removing some of the existing tests from the `CalculatorTest` class in the book's ch06-quality folder.

Figure 6.9   Running `mvn test` from the command prompt

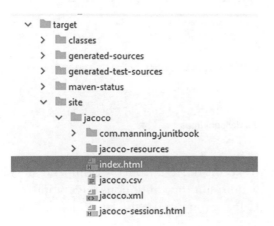

Figure 6.10   The code-coverage report, accessible in the project folder target\site\jacoco

From here, you can access the reports at the level of the `com.manning.junitbook` package (figure 6.11), `Calculator` class (figure 6.12), methods (figure 6.13), and individual lines (figure 6.14).

ch06-quality

Element	Missed Instructions	Cov.	Missed Branches	Cov.
com.manning.junitbook.ch06		84%		75%
Total	5 of 32	84%	1 of 4	75%

Figure 6.11   JaCoCo report at the package level

ch06-quality > com.manning.junitbook.ch06

com.manning.junitbook.ch06

Element	Missed Instructions	Cov.	Missed Branches	Cov.
Calculator		84%		75%
Total	5 of 32	84%	1 of 4	75%

Figure 6.12   JaCoCo report at the class level

ch06-quality > com.manning.junitbook.ch06 > Calculator

Calculator

Element	Missed Instructions	Cov.	Missed Branches	Cov.	
sqrt(double)		58%		50%	
divide(double, double)		100%		100%	
add(double, double)		100%		n/a	
Calculator()		100%		n/a	
Total	5 of 32	84%	1 of 4	75%	

Figure 6.13 JaCoCo report at the method level

```
21.
22. package com.manning.junitbook.ch06;
23.
24. public class Calculator
25. {
26.     public double add( double number1, double number2 )
27.     {
28.         return number1 + number2;
29.     }
30.
31.     public double sqrt(double x) {
32.         if (x < 0) {
33.             throw new IllegalArgumentException("Cannot extract the square root of a negative value");
34.         }
35.         return Math.sqrt(x);
36.     }
37.
38.     public double divide(double x, double y) {
39.         if (y == 0) {
40.             throw new ArithmeticException("Cannot divide by zero");
41.         }
42.         return x/y;
43.     }
44.
45.
```

Figure 6.14   JaCoCo report at the level of individual lines: covered lines are green, uncovered lines are red, and partially covered conditions are yellow.

6.2   *Writing testable code*

This chapter is dedicated to best practices in software testing. You're ready to move to the next level: writing code that is easy to test. Sometimes writing a single test case is easy; sometimes it isn't. Everything depends on the complexity of the application. A best practice is to avoid complexity as much as possible; code should be readable and testable.

In this section, we discuss best practices that can improve your design and code. Remember that it is always easier to write easily testable code than it is to refactor existing code to make it easily testable.

6.2.1   *Understanding that public APIs are contracts*

One principle in providing backward-compatible software states, "Never change the signature of a public method." An application code review shows that most calls are made from external applications, which play the role of clients of your API. If you change the signature of a public method, you need to change every call site in the application and unit tests. Even with refactoring wizards in tools such as IntelliJ and Eclipse, you must always perform this task with care. During initial development, especially if you're working with TDD, it is a great time to refactor the API as needed, because you do not yet have any public users. Things will change later!

In the open source world, and for any API made public by a commercial product, life can get even more complicated. Many people use your code, and you should be very careful about the changes you make to stay backward compatible. Public methods become the articulation points of an application between components, open source projects, and commercial products that usually do not know about one another's existence.

Imagine a public method that takes a distance as a `double` parameter and uses a black-box test to verify a computation. At some point, the meaning of the parameter changes from miles to kilometers. Your code still compiles, but the runtime breaks. Without a unit test to fail and tell you what is wrong, you may spend a lot of time debugging and talking to angry customers.

Mismatched units are the reason the NASA Mars Climate Observer was lost in 1999; one part of the system calculated the amount of thrust needed to adjust course and reduce speed, and another part used that information to determine how long to fire the thrusters. The problem was that one system used imperial measurements (foot-pounds), and the other used metric measurements (Newtons), and there was no test to catch the mistake! This example illustrates why you must test all public methods. For nonpublic methods, you need to go to a deeper level and use white-box tests.

6.2.2   *Reducing dependencies*

Remember that unit tests verify your code in isolation. Your unit tests should instantiate the class you want to test, use it, and assert its correctness. Your test cases should be simple. What happens when your class instantiates a new set of objects, directly or indirectly? Now your class depends on those classes. To write testable code, you should reduce dependencies as much as possible. If your classes depend on many other classes that need to be instantiated and set up with some state, your tests will be very complicated; you may need to use a complicated mock-objects solution (see chapter 8).

A solution that reduces dependencies separates methods that instantiate new objects (factories) from methods that provide your application logic. At Tested Data Systems Inc., one of the projects under development is in the automotive field. The project has to manage vehicles and drivers, and there are classes that shape them. Consider the following listing.

Listing 6.1 Reducing dependencies

```
class Vehicle {

    Driver d = new Driver();
    boolean hasDriver = true;

    private void setHasDriver(boolean hasDriver) {
        this.hasDriver = hasDriver;
    }
}
```

Every time the Vehicle class is instantiated with an object, the Driver class is also instantiated with an object. The concepts are mixed. The solution is to have the Driver instance passed to the Vehicle class.

Listing 6.2 Passing the Driver to the Vehicle

```
class Vehicle {

    Driver d;
    boolean hasDriver = true;

    Vehicle(Driver d) {
        this.d = d;
    }

    private void setHasDriver(boolean hasDriver) {
        this.hasDriver = hasDriver;
    }
}
```

This code allows us to produce a mock Driver object (see chapter 8) and pass it to the Vehicle class on instantiation. This process is called *dependency injection*—a technique in which a dependency is supplied to another object. We can mock any other type of Driver implementation. The requirements for the engineers at Tested Data Systems may introduce specific classes such as JuniorDriver and SeniorDriver, which are passed to the Vehicle class. Through dependency injection, the code supplies the Driver object to the Vehicle object by invoking the Vehicle(Driver d) constructor.

6.2.3 *Creating simple constructors*

By striving for better test coverage, you add more test cases. In each of these test cases, you

1 Instantiate the class to test.
2 Set the class to a particular state.
3 Do some action.
4 Assert the final state of the class.

By doing work in the constructor (other than populating instance variables), listing 6.3 mixes steps 1 and 2. It is a bad practice not only from the design point of view (we do the same work every time we instantiate the class) but also because we get the class in a predefined state. This code is hard to maintain and test. Setting the class to a particular state should be a separate operation, as shown in listings 6.3 and 6.4.

> **Listing 6.3   Setting the class to a particular state inside the constructor**

```
class Car {
   private int maxSpeed;

   Car() {
      this.maxSpeed = 180;
   }
}
```

> **Listing 6.4   Setting the class to a particular state by using a setter**

```
class Car {
   private int maxSpeed;

   public void setMaxSpeed(int maxSpeed) {
      this.maxSpeed = maxSpeed;
   }
}
```

6.2.4 *Following the Law of Demeter (Principle of Least Knowledge)*

The Law of Demeter, or Principle of Least Knowledge, states that one class should know only as much as it needs to know. The Law of Demeter can also be described this way:

Talk to your immediate friends.

Or

Don't talk to strangers.

Consider the following example violation.

> **Listing 6.5 Law of Demeter violation**

```
class Car {
   private Driver driver;

   Car(Context context) {
      this.driver = context.getDriver();
   }
}
```

In this example, you pass a `Context` object to the `Car` constructor. This object shapes some environmental attributes, such as whether the drive is long-distance, daytime, and/or nighttime. The code violates the Law of Demeter because the `Car` class needs to know that the `Context` object has a `getDriver` method. If you want to test this constructor, you need to get a valid `Context` object before calling the constructor. If the `Context` object has a lot of variables and methods, you could be forced to use mock objects (see chapter 8) to simulate the context.

The proper solution is to apply the Law of Demeter and pass references to methods and constructors only when you need to do so. In this example, you should pass the `Driver` to the `Car` constructor:

```
Car(Driver driver) {
   this.driver = driver;
}
```

These concepts are key: require objects, do not search for objects, and ask only for objects that your application requires.

Miško Hevery's society analogy

You can live in a society in which everyone (every class) declares who their friends (collaborators) are. If we know that Joe knows Mary, but neither Mary nor Joe knows Tim, it is safe for us to assume that if we give some information to Joe, he may give it to Mary, but under no circumstances will Tim get hold of it. Now imagine that everyone (every class) declares some of their friends (collaborators), but other friends are kept secret. We are left wondering how in the world Tim got the information we gave to Joe. This is the analogy that Miško Hevery provides on his blog.

Here is the interesting part. If you are the person who built the relationships (code), you know the true dependencies, but anyone who comes after you will be baffled, because the friends that are declared are not the sole friends of objects, and information flows into secret paths that are not clear. The ones coming after you live in a society full of liars.

6.2.5   *Avoiding hidden dependencies and global state*

Be very careful with the global state, because it allows many clients to share the global object. This sharing can have unintended consequences if the global object is not coded for shared access or if clients expect exclusive access to the global object.

At Tested Data Systems, the internal organization needs to install a database that is under the control of the database manager. Some reservations must be created for internal meetings and appointments. Consider the next example.

Listing 6.6   Global state in action

```
public void makeReservation() {
    Reservation reservation = new Reservation();
    reservation.makeReservation();
}

public class Reservation {
public void makeReservation() {
    manager.initDatabase(); //manager is a reference to a global
                            //DBManager, already initialized
    //require the global DBManager to do more action
}
}
```

`DBManager` implies a global state. Without instantiating the database, we will not be able to make a reservation. Internally, `Reservation` uses `DBManager` to access the database. Unless it's documented, the `Reservation` class hides its dependency on the database manager from the programmer, because the API does not provide any clues.

The following listing provides a better implementation. The `DBManager` dependency is injected into the `Reservation` object by calling the constructor with an argument.

Listing 6.7   Avoiding global state

```
public void makeReservation() {
    DBManager manager = new DBManager();
    manager.initDatabase();
    Reservation reservation = new Reservation(manager);
    reservation.makeReservation();
}
```

In this example, the `Reservation` object is constructed with a given database manager. Strictly speaking, the `Reservation` object should be able to function only if it has been configured with a database manager.

Avoid global state. When you provide access to a global object, you share not only that object, but also any object to which it refers.

6.2.6   *Favoring generic methods*

Static methods, like factory methods, are very useful, but large groups of static utility methods can introduce issues of their own. Recall that unit testing is testing in isolation. To achieve isolation, you need some articulation points where you can easily substitute your code for the test code. These points use polymorphism. With *polymorphism* (the ability of one object to pass more than one IS-A test), the method you are calling is not determined at compile time. You can easily use polymorphism to substitute application code for test code to force certain code patterns to be tested.

The opposite situation occurs when you use nothing but static methods. Then you practice procedural programming, and all your method calls are determined at compile time. You no longer have articulation points that you can substitute.

Sometimes the harm of static methods to your test is not great, especially when you choose a method that ends execution, such as `Math.sqrt()`. On the other hand, if you choose a method that lies in the heart of your application logic, every method that gets executed inside that static method becomes difficult to test.

Static code and the inability to use polymorphism in your application affect the application and tests equally. No polymorphism means no code reuse for both your application and your tests. This situation can lead to code duplication in the application and tests, which you should try to avoid.

Consequently, static utility methods that operate on parameterized types should be generic. Consider this method, which returns the union of two sets:

```java
public static Set union(Set s1, Set s2) {
    Set result = new HashSet(s1);
    result.addAll(s2);
    return result;
}
```

This method compiles, but with two warnings:

```
Union.java:5: warning: [unchecked] unchecked call to
HashSet(Collection<? extends E>) as a member of raw type HashSet
Set result = new HashSet(s1);
          ^
Union.java:6: warning: [unchecked] unchecked call to
addAll(Collection<? extends E>) as a member of raw type Set
result.addAll(s2);
                ^
```

To make the method typesafe and eliminate the warnings, you can modify it to declare a type parameter representing the element type for the three sets (the two arguments and the return value) and use this type parameter throughout the method. The type parameter list is `<E>`, and the return type is `Set<E>`:

```java
public static <E> Set<E> union(Set<E> s1, Set<E> s2) {
    Set<E> result = new HashSet<>(s1);
    result.addAll(s2);
    return result;
}
```

This method not only compiles without generating any warnings but also provides type safety, ease of use, and ease of testing.

6.2.7   *Favoring composition over inheritance*

Many people choose inheritance as a code-reuse mechanism. We think composition can be easier to test. At runtime, code cannot change an inheritance hierarchy, but you can compose objects differently. Strive to make your code as flexible as possible at runtime. This way, you can be sure it is easy to switch from one state of your objects to another, which makes the code easy to test.

It is safe to use inheritance within a package, where the subclass and the superclass are under the control of the same programmers. Inheriting from ordinary concrete classes across package boundaries may be risky.

Inheritance is appropriate only when the subclass is a subtype of the superclass. When you need classes A and B, you may ask yourself if you can relate them. Class B should extend class A only if an IS-A relationship exists between the two classes.

You'll also encounter violations of this principle in the Java platform libraries: a stack is not a vector, so `Stack` should not extend `Vector`. Similarly, a property list is not a hash table, so `Properties` should not extend `Hashtable`. In both cases, composition would be preferable.

6.2.8   *Favoring polymorphism over conditionals*

As we mentioned previously, all you do in your tests is

1 Instantiate the class to test.
2 Set the class to a particular state.
3 Assert the final state of the class.

Difficulties may arise at any of these points. Instantiating your class may be difficult if the class is too complex, for example.

One of the main ways to decrease complexity is to try to avoid long multiple-choice `switch` statements or `if` statements. Consider this listing.

Listing 6.8   Example of bad design with conditionals

```java
public class DocumentPrinter {
  [...]
    public void printDocument() {
        switch (document.getDocumentType()) {
        case WORD_DOCUMENT:
            printWORDDocument();
            break;
        case PDF_DOCUMENT:
            printPDFDocument();
            break;
        case TEXT_DOCUMENT:
            printTextDocument();
            break;
```

```
        default:
            printBinaryDocument();
            break;
        }
    }
    [...]
}
```

This implementation is awful for several reasons, and the code is hard to test and maintain. Every time you want to add a new document type, you need additional `case` clauses. If such a situation happens often in your code, you will have to change it in every place that it occurs.

> **TIP** Every time you use a long conditional statement, think of polymorphism. Polymorphism is a natural object-oriented way to avoid long conditionals by breaking a class into several smaller classes. Several smaller components are easier to test than one large, complex component.

In this example, you can avoid the conditional by creating different document types, such as `WordDocument`, `PDFDocument`, and `TextDocument`, each of which implements a `printDocument()` method (listing 6.9). This solution decreases the complexity of the code and makes it easier to read. When the `printDocument-(Document)` method of the `DocumentPrinter` class is called, it delegates to `printDocument()` from `Document`. The effective method to be executed is determined at runtime through polymorphism, and the code is easier to understand and test because it is not cluttered with conditionals.

Listing 6.9 Replacing conditionals with polymorphism

```
public class DocumentPrinter {
  [...]
    public void printDocument(Document document) {
        document.printDocument();
    }
}

public abstract class Document {
  [...]
    public abstract void printDocument();
}

public class WordDocument extends Document{
  [...]
    public void printDocument() {
        printWORDDocument();
    }
}

public class PDFDocument extends Document {
[...]
```

```
   public void printDocument() {
       printPDFDocument();
     }
}

public class TextDocument extends Document {
  [...]
    public void printDocument() {
        printTextDocument();
      }
}
```

6.3   *Test-driven development*

As you design an application, tests may help you improve the initial design. As you write more unit tests, positive reinforcement encourages you to write them earlier. As you design and implement, it becomes natural to wonder how you will test a class. Following this methodology, more developers are making the leap from test-friendly designs to TDD.

> **DEFINITION** *Test-driven development* (TDD)—A programming practice that instructs developers to write tests first and then write the code that makes the software pass those tests. Then the developer examines the code and refactors it to clean up any mess or improve things. The goal of TDD is clean code that works.

6.3.1   *Adapting the development cycle*

When you develop code, you design an application programming interface (API) and then implement the behavior promised by the interface. When you unit test code, you verify the promised behavior through an API. The test is a client of the API, just as your domain code is a client of the API.

The conventional development cycle goes something like this:

```
[code, test, (repeat)]
```

Developers who practice TDD make a seemingly slight but surprisingly effective adjustment:

```
[test, code, (repeat)]
```

The test drives the design and becomes the first client of the method, as opposed to software development that allows the addition of software that does not prove to meet requirements.

This approach has a few advantages:

- You write code that is driven by clear goals and can be sure that you address exactly what your application needs to do. Tests represent a means to design the code.

- You can introduce new functionality much faster. Tests drive you to implement code that does what it is supposed to do.
- Tests prevent you from introducing bugs into existing code that is working well.
- Tests serve as documentation, so you can follow them and understand what problems the code is supposed to solve.

6.3.2 Doing the TDD two-step

Earlier, we said that TDD tweaks the development cycle to go something like

```
[test, code, (repeat)]
```

The problem with this process is that it leaves out a key step. Development should go more like this:

```
[test, code, refactor, (repeat)]
```

Refactoring is the process of changing a software system in such a way that it improves the code's internal structure without altering its external behavior. To make sure external behavior is not affected, you need to rely on tests.

The core tenets of TDD are as follows:

- Write a failing test before writing new code.
- Write the smallest piece of code that will make the failing test pass.

Developers who follow this practice have found that test-backed, well-factored code is, by its very nature, easy and safe to change. TDD gives you the confidence to solve today's problems today and tomorrow's problems tomorrow. Carpe diem! Chapter 20 is dedicated to using TDD with JUnit 5.

JUnit best practice: Write failing tests first

If you take the TDD development pattern to heart, an interesting thing happens: before you can write any code, *you must write a test that fails*. Why does it fail? *Because you have not written the code to make it succeed*.

Faced with this situation, most of us begin by writing a simple implementation to let the test pass. When the test succeeds, you could stop and move on to the next problem. Being a professional, you would take a few minutes to refactor the implementation to remove redundancy, clarify intent, and optimize the investment in the new code. But as long as the test succeeds, technically, you're done.

If you always test first, you will never write a line of new code without a failing test.

6.4 Behavior-driven development

Behavior-driven development (BDD), which was originated by Dan North in the mid-2000s, is a methodology for developing IT solutions that satisfy business requirements directly. Its philosophy is driven by business strategy, requirements, and goals, which are refined and transformed into an IT solution. Whereas TDD helps you build good-quality software, BDD helps you build software that's worth building to solve the problems of the users.

BDD helps you write software in a way that lets you discover and focus your efforts on what really matters. You find out what features will benefit the organization and effective ways to implement them. You see beyond what the user asks for and build what the user actually needs.

A natural question that arises is, "What gives business value to the software?" The answer is that working features provide business value to the software. A *feature* is a tangible, deliverable piece of functionality that helps the business achieve its business goals. Also, software that can be easily maintained and enhanced is more valuable than software that is hard to change without breaking, so following a practice like BDD or TDD adds value.

To address business goals, a business analyst works with the customer to decide what software features achieve these goals. These features are high-level requirements, such as "Provide a way for a customer to choose among a few alternative routes to the destination" and "Provide a way for a customer to choose the optimal route to the destination." These features then need to be broken into *stories*. The stories might be, "Find the route between source and destination with the smallest number of flight changes" and "Find the quickest route between source and destination." Stories need to be described in terms of concrete examples, which become the acceptance criteria for the story.

Acceptance tests (introduced in chapter 5) are expressed BDD style in a way that can be automated later. The keywords are Given, When, and Then. Following is an example of acceptance criteria:

> *Given* the flights operated by company X,
> *When* we want to find the quickest route from Bucharest to New York from May 15 to 20,
> *Then* we will be provided the route Bucharest–Frankfurt–New York.

Chapter 21 discusses BDD with JUnit 5.

6.5   *Mutation testing*

If you strive for testing at different levels (from unit testing to acceptance testing) and obtain high code coverage (as close to 100% as possible), how can you be sure that your code is close to perfection? The bad news is that perfection may not be enough! Even 100% code coverage does not mean your code works perfectly—your tests may not be good enough. The simplest way for this to happen is to omit assertions in the tests; for example, the output may be too complex for the test to verify, so we display it or log it and let a person decide what to do next.

How can you check the quality of the tests and make sure they do what they are supposed to do? Mutation testing comes into play in this situation. *Mutation testing* (or *mutation analysis* or *program mutation*) is used to design new software tests and evaluate the quality of existing software tests.

The basic idea of mutation testing involves modifying a program in small ways. Each mutated version is called a *mutant*. The behavior of the original version differs from that of the mutant. Tests detect and reject mutants, which is called *killing the mutant*. Test suites are measured by the percentage of mutants that they kill. New tests can be designed to kill additional mutants.

Mutants are generated by well-defined mutation operators that exchange an existing operator for another one or invert some conditions. The goal is to support the creation of effective tests or to locate weaknesses in the test data used for the program or sections of the code that are seldom or never accessed during execution. Consequently, mutation testing is a form of white-box testing.

Given the following piece of code,

```
if(a) {
    b = 1;
} else {
    b = 2;
}
```

the mutation operation may reverse the condition so that the newly tested piece of code is

```
if(!a) {
    b = 1;
} else {
    b = 2;
}
```

A strong mutation test fulfills the following conditions:

1 The test reaches the `if` condition that has been mutated.
2 The test continues on a different branch from the initial correct one.
3 The changed value of b propagates to the output of the program and is checked by the test.
4 The test will fail because the method returned the wrong value for b.

Well-written tests must determine the failure of mutated tests to demonstrate that they initially covered the necessary logical conditions.

The best-known Java mutation testing framework is Pitest (https://pitest.org), which changes the Java bytecode to generate mutants. Mutation testing exceeds the scope of this book, but we wanted to introduce its primary ideas in the context of discussing test quality.

6.6 *Testing in the development cycle*

Testing occurs at different places and times during the development cycle. This section first introduces a development life cycle and then uses it as a basis for deciding what types of tests are executed when. Figure 6.15 shows a typical development cycle.

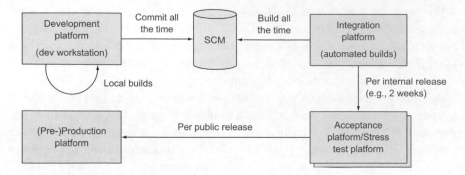

Figure 6.15   A typical application development life cycle, using the continuous integration principle

The life cycle is divided into the following platforms:

- *Development*—This coding happens on developers' workstations. One important rule is to *commit* (check in) to your source control management (SCM) system (Git, SVN, CVS, ClearCase, and so on) several times per day. After you commit, others can begin using your work. It is important to commit only something that works. To ensure this, you should first merge your changes with the current code in the repo. Then you should run a local build with Maven or Gradle. You can also watch the results of an automated build based on the latest changes to the SCM repository.

- *Integration*—This platform builds the application from its components (which may have been developed by different teams) and ensures that the components work together. This step is extremely valuable because problems are often discovered here. The step is so valuable, in fact, that you should automate it. After automation, the process is called *continuous integration* (see www.martinfowler .com/articles/continuousIntegration.html). You can achieve continuous integration by building the application automatically as part of the build process (see chapter 13).

- *Acceptance/stress test*—Depending on the resources available to your project, this can be one or two platforms. The stress-test platform exercises the application under load and verifies that it scales correctly (with respect to size and response time). The acceptance platform is where the project's customers accept (sign off on) the system. It is highly recommended that the system be deployed on the acceptance platform as often as possible to get user feedback.

- *(Pre)production*—The preproduction platform is the last staging area before production. This platform is optional, and small or noncritical projects can do without it.

Next, we discuss how testing fits into the development cycle. Figure 6.16 highlights the types of tests you can perform on each platform.

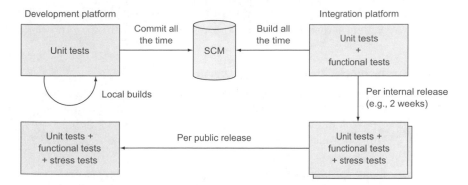

Figure 6.16   The different types of tests performed on each platform of the development cycle

On the *development platform*, you execute *logic unit tests* (tests that can be executed in isolation from the environment). These tests execute very quickly, and you usually execute them from your IDE to verify that any change you have made in the code has not broken anything. These tests are also executed by your automated build before you commit the code to your SCM. You could also execute integration tests, but they often take much longer because they need some part of the environment to be set up (database, application server, and so on). In practice, you execute only a subset of all integration tests, including any new integration tests that you have written.

The *integration platform* usually runs the build process automatically to package and deploy the application; then it executes unit and functional tests. *Functional testing* means evaluating the compliance of a system or component with the requirements. This black-box testing type usually describes what the system does. Generally, only a subset of all functional tests is run on the integration platform, because compared with the target production platform, integration is a simple platform that lacks elements. (It may be missing a connection to an external system being accessed, for example.) All tests are executed on the integration platform. Time is less important, and the whole build can take several hours with no effect on development.

On the *acceptance platform/stress test platform*, you execute the same tests executed by the integration platform; in addition, you run stress tests (to verify the robustness and performance of the software). The acceptance platform is extremely close to the production platform, and more functional tests can be executed here.

A good habit is to also run on the *(pre)production platform* the tests you ran on the acceptance platform. This technique acts as a sanity check, verifying that everything is set up correctly.

Human beings are strange creatures that tend to neglect details. In a perfect world, we would have all four platforms to run our tests on. In the real world, however, most software companies try to skip some of the platforms listed here, or the concept of testing as a whole. As a developer who bought this book, you've already made the right decision: more tests and less debugging.

Now, again, it is up to you. Are you going to strive for perfection, stick to everything that you've learned so far, and let your code benefit from that knowledge?

JUnit best practice: Continuous regression testing

Most tests are written for the here and now. You write a new feature, and you write a new test. You see whether the feature plays well with others and whether the users like it. If everyone is happy, you can lock the feature and move to the next item on your list. Most software is written in a progressive fashion: you add first one feature and then another.

Most often, each new feature is built on a path paved by existing features. If an existing method can service a new feature, you reuse the method and save the cost of writing a new one. The process is never quite that easy, of course. Sometimes you need to change an existing method to make it work with a new feature. In this case, you need to confirm that the old features still work with the amended method.

A strong benefit of JUnit is that it makes test cases easy to automate. When a change is made to a method, you can run the test for that method. If that test passes, you can run the rest. If any test fails, you can change the code (or the tests) until all tests pass again.

Using old tests to guard against new changes is a form of regression testing. Any kind of test can be used as a regression test, but running unit tests after every change is your first, best line of defense.

The best way to ensure that regression testing takes place is to automate your test suites.

Chapter 7 discusses test granularity and introduces *stubs*: programs that simulate the behavior of software components that a module under test depends on.

Summary

This chapter has covered the following:

- Techniques in unit testing that check the quality of the tests
- The concept of code coverage and tools that inspect it: you can do this from IntelliJ IDEA or with JaCoCo
- Designing improvements of the code to make it easily testable
- Investigating test-driven development (TDD) and behavior-driven development (BDD) as software development processes focused on quality
- Introduction to mutation testing, a technique to evaluate the quality of existing software tests by modifying programs in small ways
- Examining how testing in the development cycle using the continuous integration principle can start with coding (conventional development cycle) or with testing (TDD)

7

Coarse-grained
testing with stubs

This chapter covers

- Testing with stubs
- Using an embedded server in place of a real web server
- Implementing unit tests of an HTTP connection with stubs

And yet it moves.

—Galileo Galilei

As you develop your applications, you will find that the code you want to test depends on other classes, which themselves depend on other classes, which then depend on the environment (figure 7.1). You might be developing an application that uses Hibernate to access a database, a Java EE application (one that relies on a Java EE container for security, persistence, and other services), an application that accesses a filesystem, or an application that connects to some resource by using HTTP or another protocol.

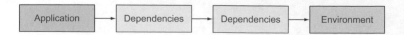

Figure 7.1   The application depends on other classes, which in turn depend on other classes, which then depend on the environment.

Starting in this chapter, we will look at using JUnit 5 to test an application that depends on external resources. We will include HTTP servers, database servers, and physical devices.

For applications that depend on a specific runtime environment, writing unit tests is a challenge. Your tests need to be stable, and when they run repeatedly, they need to yield the same results. You need a way to control the environment in which the tests run. One solution is to set up the real required environment as part of the tests and run the tests from within that environment. In some cases, this approach is practical and brings real benefits. (See chapter 9, which discusses in-container testing.) It works well only if you can set up the real environment on your development and build platforms, however, which is not always feasible.

If your application uses HTTP to connect to a web server provided by another company, for example, you usually will not have that server application available in your development environment. Therefore, you need a way to simulate that server so that you can still write and run tests for your code.

Alternatively, suppose that you are working with other developers on a project. What if you want to test your part of the application, but the other part is not ready? One solution is to simulate the missing part by replacing it with a fake that behaves similarly. There are two strategies for providing these fake objects: stubbing and using mock objects.

When you write stubs, you provide a predetermined behavior right from the beginning. The stubbed code is written outside the test, and it will always have a fixed behavior, no matter how many times or where you use the stub; its methods will usually return hardcoded values. The pattern of testing with a stub this: *initialize stub > execute test > verify assertions.*

A mock object does not have a predetermined behavior. When running a test, you are setting the expectations on the mock before effectively using it. You can run different tests, and you can reinitialize a mock and set different expectations on it. The pattern of testing with a mock object this: *initialize mock > set expectations > execute test > verify assertions.* This chapter is dedicated to stubbing; chapter 8 covers mock objects.

7.1   *Introducing stubs*

Stubs are mechanisms for faking the behavior of real code or code that is not ready yet. In other words, stubs allow you to test a portion of a system when the other part is not available. Stubs usually do not change the code you are testing; instead, they adapt to provide seamless integration.

DEFINITION *Stub*—A piece of code that is inserted at runtime in place of the real code to isolate the caller from the real implementation. The intent is to replace a complex behavior with a simpler one that allows independent testing of some part of the real code.

Here are some examples of when you might use stubs:

- You cannot modify an existing system because it is too complicated and fragile.
- You depend on an environment that you cannot control.
- You are replacing a full-blown external system such as a filesystem, a connection to a server, or a database.
- You are performing coarse-grained testing, such as integration testing between different subsystems.

Using stubs is not recommended in situations such as these:

- You need fine-grained tests to provide precise messages that underline the cause of the failure.
- You would like to test a small portion of the code in isolation.

In these situations, you should use mock objects (discussed in chapter 8).

Stubs usually provide very good confidence in the tested system. With stubs, you are not modifying the objects under test, and what you are testing is the same as what will execute in production. An automated build or a developer usually executes tests involving stubs in their running environment, providing additional confidence.

On the downside, stubs are usually hard to write, especially when the system to fake is complex. The stub needs to implement, in a brief, simplified way, the same logic as the code it is replacing, which is difficult to get right for complex logic. Here are some cons of stubbing:

- Stubs are often complex to write and need debugging themselves.
- Stubs can be difficult to maintain because they are complex.
- A stub does not lend itself well to fine-grained unit testing.
- Each situation requires a different stubbing strategy.

In general, stubs are better adapted than mocks for replacing coarse-grained portions of code.

7.2 Stubbing an HTTP connection

To demonstrate what stubs can do, we'll explain how the engineers at Tested Data Systems Inc. build stubs for an application that opens an HTTP connection to a URL and reads its content. The sample application (limited to a `WebClient.getContent` method) opens an HTTP connection to a remote web resource. The remote web resource is a servlet, which generates an HTML response. The web resource in figure 7.2 is what we call the *real code* in the stub definition.

Web client   **Web server**

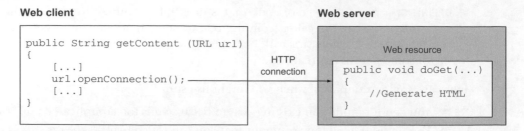

Figure 7.2   The sample application opens an HTTP connection to a remote web resource. The web resource is the real code in the stub definition.

The goal of the engineers at Tested Data Systems is to unit test the `getContent` method by stubbing the remote web resource, as demonstrated in figure 7.3. The remote web resource is not yet available, and the engineers need to progress with their part of the work in the absence of that resource. They replace the servlet web resource with the stub—a simple HTML page that returns whatever they need for the `TestWebClient` test case. This approach allows them to test the `getContent` method independently of the implementation of the web resource (which in turn could call several other objects down the execution chain, possibly down to a database).

Web client (being tested)   **Web server**

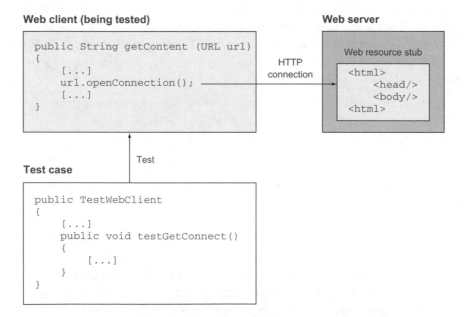

Figure 7.3   Adding a test case and replacing the real web resource with a stub

The important point to notice with stubbing is that getContent is not modified to accept the stub. The change is transparent to the application under test. For stubbing to be possible, the target code needs to have a well-defined interface and allow different implementations (a stub, in this case) to be plugged in. The interface is actually the public abstract class java.net.URLConnection, which cleanly isolates the implementation of the page from its caller.

Following is an example of a stub in action, using the simple HTTP connection example. The listing demonstrates a code snippet that opens an HTTP connection to a given URL and reads the content at that URL. The method is one part of a bigger application to be unit tested.

Listing 7.1 Sample method opening an HTTP connection

```
[...]
import java.net.URL;
import java.net.HttpURLConnection;
import java.io.InputStream;
import java.io.IOException;

public class WebClient {
    public String getContent(URL url) {
        StringBuffer content = new StringBuffer();
        try {
            HttpURLConnection connection = (HttpURLConnection)
                url.openConnection();                                    ❶
            connection.setDoInput(true);
            InputStream is = connection.getInputStream();
            byte[] buffer = new byte[2048];
            int count;                                                   ❷
            while (-1 != (count = is.read(buffer))) {
                content.append(new String(buffer, 0, count));
            }
        } catch (IOException e) {
            throw new RuntimeException(e);          ⟵
        }
        return content.toString();                  ❸
    }
}
```

In this listing:

- We start by opening an HTTP connection using the HttpURLConnection class ❶.
- We read the stream content until there is nothing more to read ❷.
- If an error occurs, we pack it into a RuntimeException and rethrow it ❸.

7.2.1 Choosing a stubbing solution

The example application has two possible scenarios: the remote web server (see figure 7.1) could be located outside the development platform (such as on a partner site), or it could be part of the platform where the application is to be deployed. In both cases, we need to introduce a server into the development platform to be able to unit test the WebClient class. One relatively easy solution would be to install an Apache test server and drop some test web pages in its document root. This stubbing solution is typical and widely used, but it has several drawbacks, as shown in table 7.1.

Table 7.1 Drawbacks of the chosen stubbing solution

Drawback	Explanation
Reliance on the environment	We need to be sure that the full environment is up and running before the test starts. If the web server is down, and we execute the test, it will fail, and we will spend time determining why it is failing. We will discover that the code is working fine and the problem was only a setup issue generating a false failure.
	When we are unit testing, it is important to be able to control as much as possible of the environment in which the tests execute, such that test results are reproducible.
Separated test logic	The test logic is scattered in two locations: in the JUnit 5 test case and on the test web page. We need to keep both types of resources in sync for the tests to succeed.
Difficult tests to automate	Automating the execution of the tests is difficult because it involves deploying the web pages on the web server, starting the web server, and running the unit tests.

Fortunately, an easier solution exists: using an embedded web server. Because the testing is in Java, the easiest solution is to use a Java web server that can be embedded in the test case. You can use the free, open source Jetty server for this purpose. The developers at Tested Data Systems will use Jetty to set up their stubs. (For more information about Jetty, visit www.eclipse.org/jetty.)

7.2.2 Using Jetty as an embedded server

We use Jetty because it is fast (important when running tests), it is lightweight, and the test cases can control it programmatically. Additionally, Jetty is a very good web, servlet, and JSP container that you can use in production.

Using Jetty allows us to eliminate the drawbacks outlined previously: the JUnit 5 test case starts the server, we write the tests in Java in one location, and automating the test suite becomes a nonissue. Thanks to Jetty modularity, the real task facing the developers at Tested Data Systems is stubbing the Jetty handlers, not the whole server from the ground up.

To understand how Jetty works, let's implement and examine an example of setting up and controlling it from the tests. The following listing demonstrates how to start Jetty from Java and how to define a document root (/) from which to start serving files.

Listing 7.2 Starting Jetty in embedded mode: `JettySample` class

```
[...]
import org.mortbay.jetty.Server;
import org.mortbay.jetty.handler.ResourceHandler;
import org.mortbay.jetty.servlet.Context;

public class JettySample {
    public static void main(String[] args) throws Exception {     ❶
        Server server = new Server(8081);

        Context root = new Context(server, "/");
        root.setResourceBase("./pom.xml");                         ❷
        root.setHandler(new ResourceHandler());

        server.start();                                            ❸
    }
}
```

In this listing:

- We start by creating the Jetty `Server` object ❶ and specifying in the constructor which port to listen to for HTTP requests (port 8081). Be sure to check that port 8081 is not already in use—you may change it in the source files, if necessary.
- Next, we create a `Context` object ❷ that processes the HTTP requests and passes them to various handlers. We map the context to the already created server instance, and to the root (/) URL. The setResourceBase method sets the document root from which to serve resources. On the next line, we attach a `ResourceHandler` to the root to serve files from the filesystem.
- Finally, we start the server ❸.

If you start the program from listing 7.2 and navigate your browser to http://localhost:8081, you should be able to see the content of the pom.xml file (figure 7.4). You get a similar effect by changing the code to set the base as `root.setResource-Base(".")`, restarting the server, and then navigating to http://localhost:8081/pom.xml.

Figure 7.4 demonstrates the results of running the code in listing 7.2 after opening a browser on http://localhost:8081. Now that you have seen how to run Jetty as an embedded server, the next section shows you how to stub the server resources.

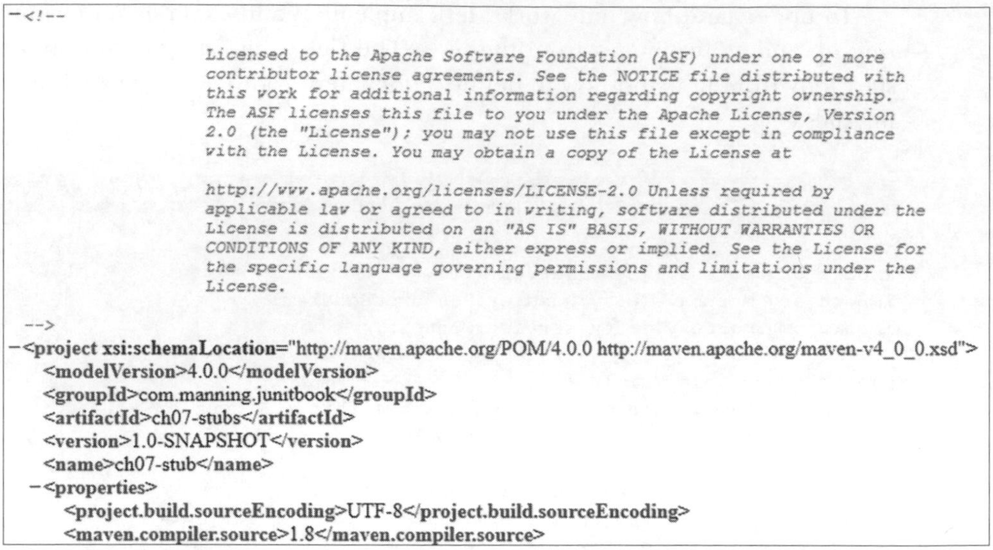

```
-<!--
              Licensed to the Apache Software Foundation (ASF) under one or more
              contributor license agreements. See the NOTICE file distributed with
              this work for additional information regarding copyright ownership.
              The ASF licenses this file to you under the Apache License, Version
              2.0 (the "License"); you may not use this file except in compliance
              with the License. You may obtain a copy of the License at

              http://www.apache.org/licenses/LICENSE-2.0 Unless required by
              applicable law or agreed to in writing, software distributed under the
              License is distributed on an "AS IS" BASIS, WITHOUT WARRANTIES OR
              CONDITIONS OF ANY KIND, either express or implied. See the License for
              the specific language governing permissions and limitations under the
              License.

  -->
-<project xsi:schemaLocation="http://maven.apache.org/POM/4.0.0 http://maven.apache.org/maven-v4_0_0.xsd">
    <modelVersion>4.0.0</modelVersion>
    <groupId>com.manning.junitbook</groupId>
    <artifactId>ch07-stubs</artifactId>
    <version>1.0-SNAPSHOT</version>
    <name>ch07-stub</name>
  -<properties>
      <project.build.sourceEncoding>UTF-8</project.build.sourceEncoding>
      <maven.compiler.source>1.8</maven.compiler.source>
```

Figure 7.4   Testing the `JettySample` in a browser. It displays the content of the pom.xml file to demonstrate how the Jetty web server works.

7.3   Stubbing the web server resources

This section focuses on the HTTP connection unit test. The developers at Tested Data Systems will write tests to verify that they can call a valid URL and get its content. These tests are the first steps in checking the functionality of web applications that are interacting with external customers.

7.3.1   Setting up the first stub test

To verify that the `WebClient` works with a valid URL, we need to start the Jetty server before the test, which we can implement in a test case `setUp` method. We can also stop the server in a `tearDown` method.

Listing 7.3   Skeleton of the first test to verify that `WebClient` works with a valid URL

```java
[...]
import java.net.URL;
import org.junit.jupiter.api.*;

public class TestWebClientSkeleton {

    @BeforeAll
    public static void setUp() {
        // Start Jetty and configure it to return "It works" when
        // the http://localhost:8081/testGetContentOk URL is
        // called.
    }
```

```
@AfterAll
public static void tearDown() {
   // Stop Jetty.
}

@Test
@Disabled(value = "This is just the initial skeleton of a test.
          Therefore, if we run it now, it will fail.")
public void testGetContentOk() throws MalformedURLException {
   WebClient client = new WebClient();
   String workingContent = client.getContent(new URL(
      "http://localhost:8081/testGetContentOk"));

   assertEquals ("It works", workingContent);
}
}
```

To implement the @BeforeAll and @AfterAll methods, we have two options. We can prepare a static page containing the text "It works", which we put in the document root (controlled by the call to root.setResourceBase(String) in listing 7.2). Alternatively, we can configure Jetty to use a custom handler that returns the string "It works" instead of getting it from a file. This technique is much more powerful because it lets us unit test the case when the remote HTTP server returns an error code to the WebClient client application.

CREATING A JETTY HANDLER
The next listing creates a Jetty Handler that returns the string "It works".

> **Listing 7.4 Creating a Jetty `Handler` that returns `"It works"`**

```
private static class TestGetContentOkHandler extends AbstractHandler {

   @Override                                                              ❶
   public void handle(String target, HttpServletRequest request,
      HttpServletResponse response, int dispatch) throws IOException {

      OutputStream out = response.getOutputStream();                      ❷
      ByteArrayISO8859Writer writer = new ByteArrayISO8859Writer();
      writer.write("It works");                                          ❸
      writer.flush();
      response.setIntHeader(HttpHeaders.CONTENT_LENGTH, writer.size());
      writer.writeTo(out);                                               ❹
      out.flush();
   }
}
```

In this listing:

- The class creates a handler ❶ by extending the Jetty AbstractHandler class and implementing a single method: handle.
- Jetty calls the handle method to forward an incoming request to our handler. After that, we use the Jetty ByteArrayISO8859Writer class ❷ to send back the string "It works", which we write in the HTTP response ❸.

- The last step is setting the response content length to the length of the string written to the output stream (required by Jetty) and then sending the response ❹.

Now that this handler is written, we can tell Jetty to use it by calling `context.set-Handler(new TestGetContentOkHandler())`.

WRITING THE TEST CLASS

We are almost ready to run the test that is the basis of verifying the functionality of the web applications interacting with the external customers of Tested Data Systems, as shown in the following listing.

Listing 7.5 Putting it all together

```java
[...]
import java.net.URL;
[...]

public class TestWebClient {
    private WebClient client = new WebClient();

  @BeforeAll
  public static void setUp() throws Exception() {
    Server server = new Server(8081);

    Context contentOkContext = new Context(server, "/testGetContentOk");
    contentOkContext.setHandler(new TestGetContentOkHandler());

    server.setStopAtShutDown(true);
    server.start();

  }


  @AfterAll
  public static void tearDown() {
    // Empty
  }


  @Test
  public void testGetContentOk() throws Exception {
    String workingContent = client.getContent(new URL(
      "http://localhost:8081/testGetContentOk"));
    assertEquals("It works", workingContent);
  }

  private static class TestGetContentOkHandler extends AbstractHandler {
    //Listing 7.4 here.
  }

}
```

The test class has become quite simple. The @BeforeAll setUp method constructs the Server object the same way as in listing 7.2. Then we have our @Test method. We leave our @AfterAll method empty intentionally because we programmed the server to stop at shutdown; the server instance is explicitly stopped when the JVM is shut down. If you run the test, you see the result in figure 7.5. The test passes.

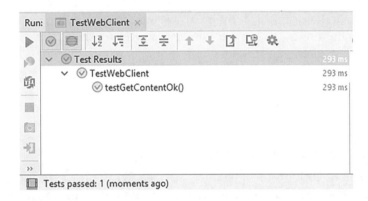

Figure 7.5 Result of the first working test using a Jetty stub. JUnit 5 starts the server before the first test, and the server shuts itself down after the last test.

7.3.2 *Reviewing the first stub test*

You have been able to fully unit test the getContent method in isolation by stubbing the web resource. What have you really tested? What kind of test have you achieved? You have done something quite powerful: unit tested the method and, at the same time, executed an integration test. In addition, you have tested not only the code logic but also the connection part that is outside the code (through the Java HttpURLConnection class).

The drawback of this approach is that it is complicated. At Tested Data Systems it can take a Jetty novice half a day to learn enough about Jetty to set it up correctly. In some instances, the novice will have to debug stubs to get them to work correctly. Keep in mind that the stub must stay simple, not become a full-fledged application that requires tests and maintenance. If you spend too much time debugging the stubs, a different solution may be called for.

In these examples, we need a web server—but another example and stub will be different and need a different setup. Experience helps, but different cases usually require different stubbing solutions.

The example tests the web application developed at Tested Data Systems, which is nice because it allows us to unit test the code and to perform some integration tests at the same time. This functionality, however, comes at the cost of complexity. More solutions that are lightweight focus on unit testing the code without performing integration tests. The rationale is that although we need integration tests, they could run in a separate test suite or as part of functional tests.

The next section looks at another solution that still qualifies as stubbing and is simpler in the sense that it does not require stubbing a whole web server. This solution brings us one step closer to the mock-object strategy, which is described in chapter 8.

7.4   *Stubbing the connection*

So far, we have stubbed the web server resources. Next, we will stub the HTTP connection instead. Doing so will prevent us from effectively testing the connection, which is fine because that is not the real goal at this point. We want to test the code in isolation. Functional or integration tests will test the connection at a later stage.

When it comes to stubbing the connection without changing the code, we benefit from the Java URL and HttpURLConnection classes, which let us plug in custom protocol handlers to process any kind of communication protocol. We can have any call to the HttpURLConnection class redirected to our own class, which will return whatever we need for the test.

7.4.1   *Producing a custom URL protocol handler*

To implement a custom URL protocol handler, we need to call the URL static method setURLStreamHandlerFactory and pass it a custom URLStreamHandlerFactory. The engineers at Tested Data Systems are using this approach to create their stub implementation of the URL stream handler. Whenever the URL openConnection method is called, the URLStreamHandlerFactory class is called to return a URLStream-Handler. The next listing shows the code that performs this action. The idea is to call setURLStreamHandlerFactory in the JUnit 5 setUp method.

Listing 7.6   Providing custom stream handler classes for testing

```
[...]
import java.net.URL;
import java.net.URLStreamHandlerFactory;
import java.net.URLStreamHandler;
import java.net.URLConnection;
import java.net.MalformedUrlException;

public class TestWebClient1 {

    @BeforeAll
    public static void setUp() {
        URL.setURLStreamHandlerFactory(new StubStreamHandlerFactory());   <─┐  ❶
    }

    private static class StubStreamHandlerFactory implements
        URLStreamHandlerFactory {
        @Override
        public URLStreamHandler createURLStreamHandler(String protocol) {    ❷
            return new StubHttpURLStreamHandler();
        }
    }
```

```
        private static class StubHttpURLStreamHandler
                        extends URLStreamHandler {
            @Override
            protected URLConnection openConnection(URL url)        ❸
                throws IOException {
                return new StubHttpURLConnection(url);
            }
        }
    }
    @Test
    public void testGetContentOk() throws MalformedURLException {
        WebClient client = new WebClient();
        String workingContent = client.getContent(
                                new URL("http://localhost"));
        assertEquals("It works", workingContent);
    }
}
```

In this listing:

- We start by calling setURLStreamHandlerFactory ❶ with our first stub class, StubStreamHandlerFactory.
- We use several (inner) classes (❷ and ❸) to use the StubHttpURLConnection class.
- In StubStreamHandlerFactory, we override the createURLStreamHandler method ❷, in which we return a new instance of our second private stub class, StubHttpURLStreamHandler.
- In StubHttpURLStreamHandler, we override one method, openConnection, to open a connection to the given URL ❸.

Note that we have not written the StubHttpURLConnection class yet. That class is the topic of the next section.

7.4.2 Creating a JDK HttpURLConnection stub

The last step is creating a stub implementation of the HttpURLConnection class so that we can return any value we want for the test. This simple implementation returns the string "It works" as a stream to the caller.

Listing 7.7 Stubbed HttpURLConnection class

```
[...]
import java.net.HttpURLConnection;
import java.net.ProtocolException;
import java.net.URL;
import java.io.InputStream;
import java.io.IOException;
import java.io.ByteArrayInputStream;

public class StubHttpURLConnection extends HttpURLConnection {
    private boolean isInput = true;
    protected StubHttpURLConnection(URL url) {
```

```
        super(url);
    }

    @Override
    public InputStream getInputStream() throws IOException {
        if (!isInput) {
            throw new ProtocolException(
                "Cannot read from URLConnection"
                + " if doInput=false (call setDoInput(true))");
        }
        ByteArrayInputStream readStream = new ByteArrayInputStream(
            new String("It works").getBytes());
        return readStream;
    }

    @Override
    public void connect() throws IOException {}

    @Override
    public void disconnect() {}

    @Override
    public boolean usingProxy() {
        return false;
    }
}
```

In this listing:

- HttpURLConnection is an abstract public class that does not implement an interface, so we extend it and override the methods wanted by the stub.
- In this stub, we provide an implementation for the getInputStream method, as it is the only method used by our code under test.
- If the code to be tested used more APIs from HttpURLConnection, we would need to stub these additional methods. This part is where the code would become more complex; we would need to reproduce the same behavior as the real HttpURLConnection.
- We test whether setDoInput(false) has been called in the code under test ❶. The isInput flag will tell if we use the URL connection for input. Then, a call to the getInputStream method returns a ProtocolException (the behavior of HttpURLConnection). Fortunately, in most cases, we need to stub only a few methods, not the whole API.

7.4.3   *Running the test*

We will test the getContent method by stubbing the connection to the remote resource using the TestWebClient1 test, which uses the StubHttpURLConnection. Figure 7.6 shows the result of the test.

As you can see, it is much easier to stub the connection than to stub the web resource. This approach does not provide the same level of testing (does not perform

Figure 7.6   Result of executing `TestWebClient1` **(which uses** `StubHttpURLConnection`**)**

integration tests), but it enables you to write a focused unit test for the `WebClient` logic more easily.

Chapter 8 demonstrates using mock objects, which allows fine-grained unit testing that is completely generic and (best of all) forces you to write good code. Although stubs are very useful in some cases, some people consider them to be vestiges of the past, when the consensus was that tests should be separate activities and should not modify existing code. The new mock-objects strategy not only allows modification of code but also favors it. Using mock objects is more than a unit testing strategy: it is a completely new way of writing code.

Summary

This chapter has covered the following:

- Analyzing when to use stubs: when you cannot modify an existing complex or fragile system, when you depend on an uncontrollable environment, to replace a full-blown external system, or for coarse-grained testing.
- Analyzing when not to use stubs: when you need fine-grained tests to provide precise messages that underline the exact cause of a failure, or when you would like to test a small portion of the code in isolation.
- Demonstrating how using a stub helps us unit test code accessing a remote web server using the Java `HttpURLConnection` API.
- In particular, implementing a stub for a remote web server by using the open source Jetty server. The embeddable nature of Jetty lets us concentrate on stubbing only the Jetty HTTP request handler, instead of having to stub the whole container.
- Implementing a more lightweight solution by stubbing the Java `HttpURL-Connection` class.

Testing with mock objects

This chapter covers

- Introducing and demonstrating mock objects
- Executing different refactorings with the help of mock objects
- Practicing on an HTTP connection sample application
- Working with and comparing the EasyMock, JMock, and Mockito frameworks

> *Programming today is a race between software engineers striving to build bigger and better idiot-proof programs, and the Universe trying to produce bigger and better idiots. So far, the Universe is winning.*
>
> —Rich Cook

Unit testing each method in isolation from other methods or the environment is certainly a nice goal. How do you perform this task? You saw in chapter 7 that the stubbing technique lets you unit test portions of code by isolating them from the environment (such as by stubbing a web server, the filesystem, a database, and so on). What about fine-grained isolation, such as being able to isolate a method call

138

to another class? Can you achieve this without deploying huge amounts of energy that would negate the benefits of having tests?

The answer is yes. The technique is called *mock objects*. Tim Mackinnon, Steve Freeman, and Philip Craig first presented the mock-objects concept at XP2000. The strategy allows you to unit test at the finest possible level. You develop method by method after having provided unit tests for each method.

8.1 Introducing mock objects

Testing in isolation offers strong benefits, such as the ability to test code that has not yet been written (as long as you at least have an interface to work with). In addition, testing in isolation helps teams unit test one part of the code without waiting for all the other parts.

The biggest advantage is the ability to write focused tests that test a single method, with no side effects resulting from other objects being called from the method under test. Small is beautiful. Writing small, focused tests is a tremendous help; small tests are easy to understand and do not break when other parts of the code are changed. Remember that one of the benefits of having a suite of unit tests is the courage it gives you to refactor mercilessly; the unit tests act as a safeguard against regression. If you have large tests, and your refactoring introduces a bug, several tests will fail. That result will tell you that there is a bug somewhere, but you will not know where. With fine-grained tests, potentially fewer tests are affected, and they provide precise messages that pinpoint the cause of the failure.

Mock objects (*mocks*, for short) are perfectly suited for testing a portion of code logic in isolation from the rest of the code. Mocks replace the objects with which your methods under test collaborate, thus offering a layer of isolation. In that sense, they are similar to stubs. The similarity ends there, however, because mocks do not implement any logic: they are empty shells that provide methods that let the tests control the behavior of all the business methods of the faked class.

A stub is created with a predetermined behavior, even a very simple one, and this behavior cannot be changed when running different tests. A mock does not have a predetermined behavior. When running a test, you are setting the expectations on the mock before effectively using it. You may run different tests, and you may reinitialize a mock and set different expectations on it. The pattern for testing with a mock is this: *initialize mock > set expectations > execute test > verify assertions*. We discuss when to use mock objects in section 8.6 at the end of this chapter, after we show them in action on some examples.

8.2 Unit testing with mock objects

In this section, we present an application and tests by using mock objects. Imagine a very simple use case in which we want to be able to make a bank transfer from one account to another (figure 8.1 and listings 8.1 and 8.2).

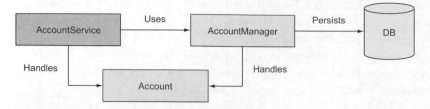

Figure 8.1   This simple bank account example uses a mock object to test an account transfer method.

The `AccountService` class offers services related to `Account` objects and uses `AccountManager` to persist data to the database (by using JDBC, for example). The service of interest to us materializes itself via the `AccountService.transfer` method, which makes the transfer. Without mocks, testing the `AccountService` `.transfer` behavior would imply setting up a database, presetting it with test data, deploying the code inside the container (Java EE application server, for example), and so forth. Although this process is required to ensure that the application works end to end, it is too much work when you want to unit test only your code logic.

Tested Data Systems Inc. creates software projects for other companies. One of the projects under development requires managing accounts and money transfers. The engineers need to design some solutions for it. The following listing presents a very simple `Account` object with two properties: an account ID and a balance.

Listing 8.1   The `Account` class

```
[...]
public class Account {
   private String accountId;
   private long balance;

   public Account(String accountId, long initialBalance) {
      this.accountId = accountId;
      this.balance = initialBalance;
   }

   public void debit(long amount) {
      this.balance -= amount;
   }

   public void credit(long amount) {
      this.balance += amount;
   }

   public long getBalance() {
      return this.balance;
   }
}
```

As part of the solution, the following `AccountManager` interface manages the life cycle and persistence of `Account` objects (limited to finding accounts by `ID` and updating accounts):

```
[...]
public interface AccountManager {
    Account findAccountForUser(String userId);
    void updateAccount(Account account);
}
```

The next listing shows the `transfer` method, designed for transferring money between two accounts. It uses the previously defined `AccountManager` interface to find the debit and credit accounts by `ID` and to update them.

Listing 8.2 The `AccountService` class

```
[...]
public class AccountService {
    private AccountManager accountManager;

    public void setAccountManager(AccountManager manager) {
        this.accountManager = manager;
    }

    public void transfer(String senderId, String beneficiaryId, long amount) {
        Account sender = accountManager.findAccountForUser(senderId);
        Account beneficiary =
                        accountManager.findAccountForUser(beneficiaryId);

        sender.debit(amount);
        beneficiary.credit(amount);
        this.accountManager.updateAccount(sender);
        this.accountManager.updateAccount(beneficiary);
    }
}
```

We want to be able to unit test the `AccountService.transfer` behavior. For that purpose, until the implementation of the `AccountManager` interface is ready, we use a mock implementation of the `AccountManager` interface because the `transfer` method is using this interface, and we need to test it in isolation.

Listing 8.3 The `MockAccountManager` class

```
[...]
import java.util.HashMap;

public class MockAccountManager implements AccountManager {
    private Map<String, Account> accounts = new HashMap<String, Account>();

    public void addAccount(String userId, Account account) {      ①
        this.accounts.put(userId, account);
    }
```

```
    public Account findAccountForUser(String userId) {
        return this.accounts.get(userId);                         ❷
    }

    public void updateAccount(Account account) {
        // do nothing                                             ❸
    }
}
```

In this listing:

- The `addAccount` method uses an instance variable to hold the values to return ❶. Because we have several `Account` objects that we want to be able to return, we store them in a `HashMap`. This step makes the mock generic and able to support different test cases. One test could set up the mock with one account, another test could set it up with two accounts or more, and so forth.
- We implement a method to retrieve the account from the `accounts` map ❷. We can retrieve only accounts that were added earlier.
- The `updateAccount` method does nothing for now, and it does not return any value ❸. Thus, we do nothing.

JUnit best practices: Do not write business logic in mock objects

The single most important rule to follow when writing a mock is that it should not have any business logic: a mock must be a dumb object that does only what the test tells it to do. In other words, it is purely driven by the tests. This characteristic is precisely the opposite of stubs, which contain all the logic (see chapter 7).

This point has two nice corollaries. First, mock objects can be generated easily. Second, because mock objects are empty shells, they are too simple to break and do not need testing themselves.

Now we are ready to write a unit test for `AccountService.transfer`. The following listing shows a typical test that uses a mock.

Listing 8.4   Testing `transfer` with `MockAccountManager`

```
[...]
public class TestAccountService {

  @Test
  public void testTransferOk() {
      Account senderAccount = new Account("1", 200);
      Account beneficiaryAccount = new Account("2", 100);

      MockAccountManager mockAccountManager = new MockAccountManager();
      mockAccountManager.addAccount("1", senderAccount);          ❶
      mockAccountManager.addAccount("2", beneficiaryAccount);

      AccountService accountService = new AccountService();
      accountService.setAccountManager(mockAccountManager);
```

```
        accountService.transfer("1", "2", 50);

        assertEquals(150, senderAccount.getBalance());
        assertEquals(150, beneficiaryAccount.getBalance());
    }
}
```

As usual, a test has three steps: setup ❶, execution ❷, and the verification of the result ❸. During the test setup, we create the `MockAccountManager` object and define what it should return when it's called for the two accounts we manipulate (the sender and beneficiary accounts). Practically, setting the expectations of the `mock-AccountManager` object by adding two accounts to it transforms it into our own defined mock. As stated earlier, one of the characteristics of a mock is that when you run a test, you are setting the expectations on the mock before effectively using it.

We have succeeded in testing the `AccountService` code in isolation from the other domain object, `AccountManager`, which in this case did not exist but could have been implemented with JDBC in real life.

JUnit best practices: Test only what could possibly break

You may have noticed that we did not mock the `Account` class. The reason is that this data-access-object class does not need to be mocked; it does not depend on the environment, and it is very simple. The other tests use the `Account` object, so they test it indirectly. If this class failed to operate correctly, the tests that rely on `Account` would fail and alert us to the problem.

At this point in the chapter, you should have a reasonably good understanding of mocks. The next section demonstrates that writing unit tests with mocks leads to refactoring the code under test—and that this process is a good thing.

8.3   *Refactoring with mock objects*

Some people used to say that unit tests should be fully transparent to the code under test and that runtime code should not be changed to simplify testing. *This is wrong!* Unit tests are first-class users of the runtime code and deserve the same consideration as any other user. If the code is too inflexible for the tests to use, we should correct the code.

Consider the following piece of code created by one of the engineers at Tested Data Systems. This engineer is taking care of the implementation of the `Account-Manager` class that we previously mocked until it is fully available.

Listing 8.5   The `DefaultAccountManager1` class

```
[...]
import java.util.PropertyResourceBundle;
import java.util.ResourceBundle;
import org.apache.commons.logging.Log;
import org.apache.commons.logging.LogFactory;
```

```
[...]
public class DefaultAccountManager1 implements AccountManager {
    private static final Log logger =
        LogFactory.getLog(DefaultAccountManager1.class);     ❶

    public Account findAccountForUser(String userId) {
        logger.debug("Getting account for user [" + userId + "]");
        ResourceBundle bundle =
            PropertyResourceBundle.getBundle("technical");   ❷
        String sql = bundle.getString("FIND_ACCOUNT_FOR_USER");
        // Some code logic to load a user account using JDBC
        [...]
    }
    [...]
}
```

In this listing:

- We create a `Log` object ❶.
- We retrieve an SQL command ❷.

Does the code look fine to you? We can see two issues, both of which relate to code flexibility and the ability to resist change. The first problem is that it is not possible to decide to use a different `Log` object, as it is created inside the class. For testing, for example, you probably would like to use a `Log` that does nothing, but you cannot do so.

As a rule, a class like this one should be able to use whatever `Log` it is given. The goal of this class is not to create loggers, but to perform some JDBC logic. The same goal applies to `PropertyResourceBundle`. It may sound OK right now, but what happens if we decide to use XML to store the configuration? Again, it should not be the goal of this class to decide what implementation to use.

An effective design strategy is to pass to an object any other object that is outside its immediate business logic. Ultimately, as you move up in the calling layers, the decision to use a given logger or configuration should be pushed to the top level. This strategy provides the best possible code flexibility and ability to cope with changes. And as we all know, change is the only constant. Taking these issues into consideration, the Tested Data Systems engineer who created the code will need to refactor it.

8.3.1   *Refactoring example*

Refactoring all code so that domain objects are passed around can be time consuming. You may not be ready to refactor the entire application just to be able to write a unit test. Fortunately, an easy refactoring technique lets you keep the same interface for the code but allows it to be passed domain objects that it should not create. As proof, the following listing shows what the refactored `DefaultAccountManager1` class could look like.

Listing 8.6   Refactoring `DefaultAccountManager2` for testing

```
[...]
public class DefaultAccountManager2 implements AccountManager {
    private Log logger;
    private Configuration configuration;                    ❶

    public DefaultAccountManager2() {
        this(LogFactory.getLog(DefaultAccountManager2.class),
            new DefaultConfiguration("technical"));
    }

    public DefaultAccountManager2(Log logger, Configuration configuration) {
        this.logger = logger;
        this.configuration = configuration;
    }

    public Account findAccountForUser(String userId) {
        this.logger.debug("Getting account for user [" + userId + "]");
        this.configuration.getSQL("FIND_ACCOUNT_FOR_USER");
        // Some code logic to load a user account using JDBC
    [...]
    }
[...]
}
```

At ❶, we swap the `PropertyResourceBundle` class from the previous listing in favor of a new `Configuration` field. This swap makes the code more flexible because it introduces an interface (which will be easy to mock), and the implementation of the `Configuration` interface can be anything we want (including using resource bundles). The design is better now because we can use and reuse the `DefaultAccount-Manager2` class with any implementation of the `Log` and `Configuration` interfaces (if we use the constructor that takes two parameters). The class can be controlled from the outside (by its caller). We have a no-args constructor and a constructor with arguments. The no-args constructor initializes the `logger` and `configuration` field members with default implementations.

8.3.2   Refactoring considerations

With this refactoring, we have provided a trap door for controlling the domain objects from the tests. We retain backward compatibility and pave an easy refactoring path for the future. Calling classes can start using the new constructor at their own pace.

Should you worry about introducing trap doors to make your code easier to test? Here's how Extreme Programming guru Ron Jeffries explains it:

> *My car has a diagnostic port and an oil dipstick. There is an inspection port on the side of my furnace and on the front of my oven. My pen cartridges are transparent so I can see if there is ink left.*

And if I find it useful to add a method to a class to enable me to test it, I do so. It happens once in a while, for example in classes with easy interfaces and complex inner function (probably starting to want an Extract Class).

I just give the class what I understand of what it wants, and keep an eye on it to see what it wants next.

Design patterns in action: Inversion of Control (IoC)

Applying the IoC pattern to a class means removing the creation of all object instances for which this class is not directly responsible and passing any needed instances instead. The instances may be passed by a specific constructor or a setter, or as parameters of the methods that need them. It becomes the responsibility of the calling code to set these domain objects correctly on the class that is called.[a]

---

[a] See Spring for a framework that implements the IoC pattern (https://spring.io).

IoC makes unit testing a breeze. To prove the point, here's how easily we can write a test for the `findAccountByUser` method.

Listing 8.7 The `testFindAccountByUser` method

```
public void testFindAccountByUser() {
    MockLog logger = new MockLog();                           ❶
    MockConfiguration configuration = new MockConfiguration();   ❷
    configuration.setSQL("SELECT * [...]");
    DefaultAccountManager2 am = new DefaultAccountManager2(logger,
                                                   configuration);   ❸

    Account account = am.findAccountForUser("1234");
    // Perform asserts here
    [...]
}
```

In this listing:

- We use a mock logger that implements the `Log` interface but does nothing ❶.
- Next, we create a `MockConfiguration` instance ❷ and set it up to return a given SQL query when `configuration.getSQL` is called.
- Finally, we create the instance of `DefaultAccountManager2` ❸ that we will test, passing to it the `Log` and `Configuration` instances.

We have been able to completely control the logging and configuration behavior from outside the code to test, in the test code. As a result, the code is more flexible and allows for any logging and configuration implementation to be used. We will implement more of these code refactorings in this chapter and later ones. For now, the developer from Tested Data Systems has solved the issues we previously examined by taking this approach.

One last point to note is that if we write the test first, we will automatically design the code to be flexible. Flexibility is a key point in writing a unit test. If we test first, we will not incur the cost of refactoring the code for flexibility later.

8.4   *Mocking an HTTP connection*

To see how mock objects work in a practical example, let's go back to the application developed at Tested Data Systems that opens an HTTP connection to a remote server and reads the content of a page. In chapter 7, we tested that application using stubs, but the developers from Tested Data Systems decided to move to a mock-object approach to simulate the HTTP connection. In addition, they will create mocks for classes that do not implement a Java interface (namely, the `HttpURLConnection` class).

In the full implementation scenario, we start with an initial testing implementation, improve the implementation as we go, and modify the original code to make it more flexible. We also use mocks to test for error conditions.

As we dive in, we will keep improving both the test code and the sample application, exactly as we might if we were writing the unit tests for the same application. In the process, you will learn how to reach a simple and elegant testing solution while making the application code more flexible and capable of handling change.

Figure 8.2 shows the sample HTTP application, which consists of a simple `Web-Client.getContent` method performing an HTTP connection to a web resource executing on a web server. We want to be able to unit test the `getContent` method in isolation from the web resource.

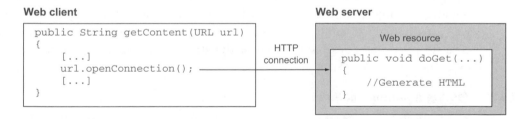

Figure 8.2   The sample HTTP application before the test is introduced

8.4.1   *Defining the mock objects*

Figure 8.3 illustrates a mock object. The `MockURL` class stands in for the real `URL` class, and all calls to the `URL` class in `getContent` are directed to the `MockURL` class. As you can see, the test is the controller: it creates and configures the behavior that the mock must have for this test, it (somehow) replaces the real `URL` class with the `MockURL` class, and it runs the test.

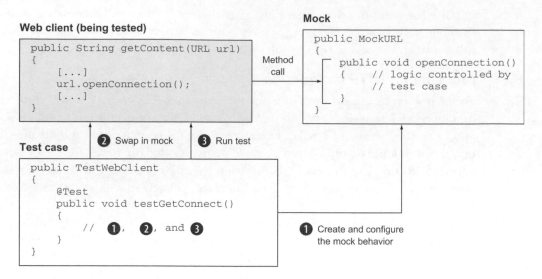

Figure 8.3   The steps involved in a test using mock objects: create and configure the mock object behavior, swap it in, and run the test.

Figure 8.3 shows an interesting aspect of the mock-objects strategy: the ability to swap in the mock in the production code. The perceptive reader will have noticed that because the URL class is final, it is not possible to create a MockURL class that extends it.

In the coming sections, we demonstrate how this feat can be performed in a different way (by mocking at another level). In any case, when using the mock-objects strategy, swapping in the mock instead of the real class is the hard part unless we are using dependency injection. This point may be viewed as negative for mock objects because you usually need to modify your code to provide a trap door. Ironically, modifying code to encourage flexibility is one of the strongest advantages of using mocks, as explained in sections 8.3.1 and 8.3.2.

8.4.2   Testing a sample method

The following code snippet opens an HTTP connection to a given URL and reads the content at that URL. Suppose that this code is one method of a bigger application that we want to unit test (see the WebClient class in chapter 7).

Listing 8.8   Sample method that opens an HTTP connection

```
[...]
import java.net.URL;
import java.net.HttpURLConnection;
import java.io.InputStream;
import java.io.IOException;
```

```
public class WebClient {
    public String getContent(URL url) {
        StringBuffer content = new StringBuffer();
            try {
            HttpURLConnection connection =
                (HttpURLConnection) url.openConnection();
            connection.setDoInput(true);
            InputStream is = connection.getInputStream();
            int count;
            while (-1 != (count = is.read())) {
                content.append( new String( Character.toChars( count ) ) );
            }
        } catch (IOException e) {
            return null;
        }
        return content.toString();
    }
}
```
①
②
③

In this listing:

- We open an HTTP connection ①.
- We read all the content that is received ②.
- If an error occurs, we return null ③. Admittedly, this is not the best possible error-handling solution, but it is good enough for the moment (and our tests will give us the courage to refactor later).

8.4.3 Try #1: Easy refactoring technique

The idea of this first refactoring technique applied at Tested Data Systems is to test the getContent method independently of a real HTTP connection to a web server. If you map the knowledge you acquired in section 8.2, it means writing a mock URL in which the url.openConnection method returns a mock HttpURLConnection. The MockHttpURLConnection class would provide an implementation that lets the test decide what the getInputStream method returns. Ideally, we would be able to write the following test.

Listing 8.9　testGetContentOk method

```
@Test
public void testGetContentOk() throws Exception {
    MockHttpURLConnection mockConnection = new MockHttpURLConnection();
    mockConnection.setupGetInputStream(
                    new ByteArrayInputStream("It works".getBytes()));
    MockURL mockURL = new MockURL();
    mockURL.setupOpenConnection(mockConnection);
    WebClient client = new WebClient();
    String workingContent = client.getContent(mockURL);
    assertEquals("It works", workingContent);
}
```
①
②
③
④

In this listing:

- We create a mock `HttpURLConnection` ❶.
- We create a mock `URL` ❷.
- We test the `getContent` method ❸.
- We assert the result ❹.

Unfortunately, this approach does not work! The JDK `URL` class is a final class, and no URL interface is available. So much for extensibility.

We need to find another solution and, potentially, another object to mock. One solution is to stub the `URLStreamHandlerFactory` class. We explored this solution in chapter 7, so we must find a technique that uses mock objects: refactoring the `get-Content` method. If you think about it, this method does two things: it gets an `Htt-pURLConnection` object and then reads the content from it. Refactoring leads to the following class. (Changes from listing 8.8 are shown in bold.) We have extracted the part that retrieved the `HttpURLConnection` object.

Listing 8.10   Extracting retrieval of the connection object from `getContent`

```java
public class WebClient1 {
   public String getContent(URL url) {
      StringBuffer content = new StringBuffer();
      try {
         HttpURLConnection connection = createHttpURLConnection(url);    ❶
         InputStream is = connection.getInputStream();
         int count;
         while (-1 != (count = is.read())) {
            content.append( new String( Character.toChars( count ) ) );
         }
      }
      catch (IOException e) {
         return null;
      }
      return content.toString();
   }

   protected HttpURLConnection createHttpURLConnection(URL url)
                                             throws IOException {    ❶
      return (HttpURLConnection) url.openConnection();
   }
}
```

In this listing, we call `createHttpURLConnection` ❶ to create the HTTP connection. How does this solution test `getContent` more effectively? It allows us to apply a useful trick, which writes a test helper class that extends the `WebClient1` class and overrides its `createHttpURLConnection` method, as follows:

```java
private class TestableWebClient extends WebClient1 {
   private HttpURLConnection connection;
   public void setHttpURLConnection(HttpURLConnection connection) {
      this.connection = connection;
```

```
    }
    public HttpURLConnection createHttpURLConnection(URL url)
                                                throws IOException {
        return this.connection;
    }
}
```

A common refactoring approach called *Method Factory* is especially useful when the class to mock has no interface. The strategy is to extend that class, add some setter methods to control it, and override some of its getter methods to return what we want for the test.

In the test, we can call the setHttpURLConnection method, passing it the mock HttpURLConnection object. Now the test becomes the following. (Differences are shown in bold.)

Listing 8.11 Modified testGetContentOk method

```
@Test
public void testGetContentOk() throws Exception {
    MockHttpURLConnection mockConnection = new MockHttpURLConnection();
    mockConnection.setupGetInputStream(
        new ByteArrayInputStream("It works".getBytes()));
    TestableWebClient client = new TestableWebClient();            ❶
    client.setHttpURLConnection(mockConnection);
    String workingContent =
                    client.getContent(new URL("http://localhost"));  ❷
    assertEquals("It works", workingContent);
}
```

In this listing:

- We configure TestableWebClient ❶ so that the createHttpURL-Connection method returns a mock object.
- Next, the getContent method is called ❷.
- In the case at hand, the Method Factory approach is OK, but it is not perfect. It is a bit like the Heisenberg Uncertainty Principle: the act of subclassing the class under test changes its behavior, so when you test the subclass, what are you truly testing?

This technique is useful as a means of opening an object to be more testable, but stopping here means testing something that is similar (but not identical) to the class you want to test. You are not writing tests for a third-party library and cannot change the code; you have complete control of the code to test. You can enhance the code and make it more test-friendly in the process.

8.4.4 *Try #2: Refactoring by using a class factory*

The developers at Tested Data Systems want to give another refactoring approach a try by applying the IoC pattern, which says that any resource we use needs to be passed to the getContent method or WebClient class. The only resource we use is the

`HttpURLConnection` object. We could change the `WebClient.getContent` signature to

```
public String getContent(URL url, HttpURLConnection connection)
```

This change means we are pushing the creation of the `HttpURLConnection` object to the caller of `WebClient`. The URL is retrieved from the `HttpURLConnection` class, however, and the signature does not look very nice. Fortunately, a better solution involves creating a `ConnectionFactory` interface, as shown in listings 8.12 and 8.13. The role of classes implementing the `ConnectionFactory` interface is to return an `InputStream` from a connection, whatever the connection may be (HTTP, TCP/IP, and so on). This refactoring technique is sometimes called a *Class Factory* refactoring.

> **Listing 8.12   The `ConnectionFactory` class**

```
[...]
import java.io.InputStream;
public interface ConnectionFactory {
   InputStream getData() throws Exception;
}
```

The `WebClient` code becomes as shown in the next listing.

> **Listing 8.13   Refactored `WebClient2` using `ConnectionFactory`**

```
[...]
import java.io.InputStream;

public class WebClient2 {
   public String getContent(ConnectionFactory connectionFactory) {
      String workingContent;
      StringBuffer content = new StringBuffer();
      try(InputStream is = connectionFactory.getData()) {
         int count;
         while (-1 != (count = is.read())) {
            content.append( new String( Character.toChars( count ) ) );
         }
         workingContent = content.toString();
      }
      catch (Exception e) {
         workingContent =  null;
      }
      return workingContent;
   }
}
```

This solution is better because we have made the retrieval of the data content independent of the way we get the connection. The first implementation worked only with URLs using the HTTP protocol. The new implementation can work with any standard protocol (file://, http://, ftp://, jar://, and so forth) or even a custom protocol. The next listing shows the `ConnectionFactory` implementation for the HTTP protocol.

Listing 8.14 The `HttpURLConnectionFactory` class

```
[...]
import java.io.InputStream;
import java.net.HttpURLConnection;
import java.net.URL;

public class HttpURLConnectionFactory implements ConnectionFactory {
    private URL url;
    public HttpURLConnectionFactory(URL url) {
        this.url = url;
    }
    public InputStream getData() throws Exception {
        HttpURLConnection connection =
            (HttpURLConnection) this.url.openConnection();
        return connection.getInputStream();
    }
}
```

Now we can easily test the `getContent` method by writing a mock for `Connection-Factory`.

Listing 8.15 The `MockConnectionFactory` class

```
[...]
import java.io.InputStream;

    public class MockConnectionFactory implements ConnectionFactory {
        private InputStream inputStream;

        public void setData(InputStream stream) {
            this.inputStream = stream;
        }
        public InputStream getData() throws Exception {
            return inputStream;
        }
    }
```

As usual, the mock does not contain any logic and is completely controllable from the outside (by calling the `setData` method). Now we can easily rewrite the test to use `MockConnectionFactory`.

Listing 8.16 Refactored test using `MockConnectionFactory`

```
[...]
import java.io.ByteArrayInputStream;

public class TestWebClient {
```

```
@Test
public void testGetContentOk() throws Exception {
    MockConnectionFactory mockConnectionFactory =
                                    new MockConnectionFactory();
    mockConnectionFactory.setData(
                new ByteArrayInputStream("It works".getBytes()));

    WebClient2 client = new WebClient2();
    String workingContent = client.getContent(mockConnectionFactory);
    assertEquals("It works", workingContent);
    }
}
```

We have achieved our initial goal: to unit test the code logic of the `WebClient.get-Content` method, which returns the content of a given URL. During this process, we had to refactor the method for the test, which led to a more extensible implementation that is better able to cope with change.

8.5   *Using mocks as Trojan horses*

Mock objects are Trojan horses, but they are not malicious. Mocks replace real objects from the inside without the calling classes being aware of it. Mocks have access to internal information about the class, making them quite powerful. In the examples so far, we have used them to emulate real behaviors, but we haven't mined all the information they can provide.

It is possible to use mocks as probes by letting them monitor the method calls that the object under test makes. Consider the HTTP connection example. One interesting call we could monitor is the `close` method on the `InputStream`, as we would like to make sure that the programmer will always close the stream; otherwise, we may experience a resource leak. A *resource leak* occurs when we do not close a reader, a scanner, a buffer, or another process that uses resources and needs to clean them out of memory. We have not used a mock object for `InputStream` so far, but we can easily create one and provide a `verify` method to ensure that `close` has been called. Then we can call the `verify` method at the end of the test to verify that all methods that should have been called were called (see listing 8.17). We may also want to verify that `close` has been called exactly once and raise an exception if it was called more than once or not at all. These kinds of verifications are often called *expectations*.

> **DEFINITION**   *Expectation*—When we're talking about mock objects, an expectation is a feature built into the mock that verifies whether the external class calling this mock has the correct behavior. A database connection mock, for example, could verify that the `close` method on the connection is called exactly once during any test that involves code using this mock.

To demonstrate the expectations that the resource has been closed and we avoid a resource leak, take a look at the following listing.

Listing 8.17 Mock `InputStream` with an expectation on `close`

```
[...]
import java.io.IOException;
import java.io.InputStream;

public class MockInputStream extends InputStream {
    private String buffer;
    private int position = 0;
    private int closeCount = 0;
    public void setBuffer(String buffer) {
        this.buffer = buffer;
    }
    public int read() throws IOException {
        if (position == this.buffer.length()) {
            return -1;
        }
        return this.buffer.charAt(this.position++);
    }
    public void close() throws IOException {
        closeCount++;
        super.close();
    }
    public void verify() throws java.lang.AssertionError {
        if (closeCount != 1) {
            throw new AssertionError ("close() should "
                        + "have been called once and once only");
        }
    }
}
```

❶
❷
❸

In this listing:

- We tell the mock what the `read` method should return ❶.
- We count the number of times `close` is called ❷.
- We verify that the expectations are met ❸.

In the case of the `MockInputStream` class, the expectation for `close` is simple: we always want it to be called once. Most of the time, however, the expectation for `closeCount` depends on the code under test. A mock usually has a method such as `setExpectedCloseCalls` so that the test can tell the mock what to expect.

Modify the `testGetContentOk` test method as follows to use the new `Mock-InputStream`:

```
[...]

public class TestWebClientFail {

    @Test
    public void testGetContentOk() throws Exception {
        MockConnectionFactory mockConnectionFactory =
                new MockConnectionFactory();
```

```
MockInputStream mockStream = new MockInputStream();
mockStream.setBuffer("It works");
mockConnectionFactory.setData(mockStream);
WebClient2 client = new WebClient2();
String workingContent = client.getContent(mockConnectionFactory);

assertEquals("It works", workingContent);
mockStream.verify();
    }
}
```

Instead of using a real `ByteArrayInputStream`, as in previous tests, we use `MockInputStream`. Note that we call the `verify` method of `MockInputStream` at the end of the test to ensure that all expectations are met. The result of the test is shown in figure 8.4.

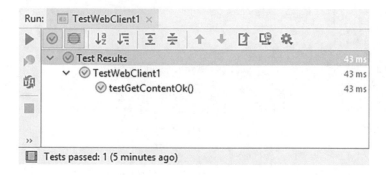

Figure 8.4   The result of running `TestWebClient1`

There are other handy uses for expectations. If you have a component manager calling different methods of your component life cycle, for example, you might expect them to be called in a given order. Or you might expect a given value to be passed as a parameter to the mock. The general idea is that in addition to behaving the way we want during a test, our mock can provide useful feedback on its use. The test can provide information regarding the number of method invocations, parameters that are passed to the methods, and the order in which methods are called.

The next section demonstrates the use of some of the most popular open source mocking frameworks. They are powerful enough for our needs, and we don't need to implement our mocks from the beginning.

8.6   *Introducing mock frameworks*

So far, the engineers at Tested Data Systems have implemented the mock objects from scratch. The task is not tedious, but it recurs. You might guess that we don't need to reinvent the wheel every time we need a mock, and you would be right: a lot of good existing frameworks can facilitate the use of mocks in our projects. In this section, we will take a closer look at three of the most widely used mock frameworks: EasyMock, JMock, and Mockito.

The developers at Tested Data Systems will try to rework the example HTTP connection application to demonstrate how to use the three frameworks and to come up with a basis for choosing one of the alternatives. People have their own experiences, preferences, and habits, and because the engineers have these three framework alternatives, they would like to compare them and make some conclusions.

8.6.1 Using EasyMock

EasyMock (https://easymock.org) is an open source framework that provides useful classes for mocking objects. To work with it, we need to add the following dependencies to the pom.xml file.

Listing 8.18 EasyMock dependencies from the pom.xml configuration file

```
<dependency>
    <groupId>org.easymock</groupId>
    <artifactId>easymock</artifactId>
    <version>4.2</version>
</dependency>
<dependency>
    <groupId>org.easymock</groupId>
    <artifactId>easymockclassextension</artifactId>
    <version>3.2</version>
</dependency>
```

While trying to introduce EasyMock, the developers at Tested Data Systems revise some of the mocks constructed in the previous sections. The start is simple: reworking the `AccountService` test from listing 8.2.

Listing 8.19 Reworking the `TestAccountService` test using EasyMock

```
[...]
import static org.easymock.EasyMock.createMock;
import static org.easymock.EasyMock.replay;            ❶
import static org.easymock.EasyMock.expect;
import static org.easymock.EasyMock.verify;

public class TestAccountServiceEasyMock
{
    private AccountManager mockAccountManager;         ❷

    @BeforeEach
    public void setUp()
    {
        mockAccountManager = createMock( "mockAccountManager",
                                    AccountManager.class );   ❸
    }
```

```
@Test
public void testTransferOk()
{
    Account senderAccount = new Account( "1", 200 );          ❹
    Account beneficiaryAccount = new Account( "2", 100 );

    // Start defining the expectations
    mockAccountManager.updateAccount( senderAccount );         ❺
    mockAccountManager.updateAccount( beneficiaryAccount );

    expect( mockAccountManager.findAccountForUser( "1" ) )
                            .andReturn( senderAccount );        ❻
    expect( mockAccountManager.findAccountForUser( "2" ) )
                            .andReturn( beneficiaryAccount );

    // we're done defining the expectations                    ❼
    replay( mockAccountManager );

    AccountService accountService = new AccountService();
    accountService.setAccountManager( mockAccountManager );    ❽
    accountService.transfer( "1", "2", 50 );

    assertEquals( 150, senderAccount.getBalance() );           ❾
    assertEquals( 150, beneficiaryAccount.getBalance() );
}

@AfterEach
public void tearDown()                                         ❿
{
    verify( mockAccountManager );
}
}
```

As you can see, the listing is pretty much the same length as listing 8.4, but we do not write additional mock classes. In this listing:

- We start by defining the imports that we need from the EasyMock library ❶. We rely heavily on static imports.
- We declare the object that we would like to mock ❷. Notice that our Account-Manager is an interface. The reason is simple: the core EasyMock framework can mock only interface objects.
- We call the createMock method to create a mock of the class we want ❸.
- As in listing 8.4, we create two Account objects that we are going to use in our tests ❹. After that, we start declaring our expectations.
- With EasyMock, we declare the expectations in two ways. When the method return type is void, we call it on the mock object ❺. When the method returns any kind of object, we use the expect and andReturn methods from the Easy-Mock API ❻.
- When we finish defining the expectations, we call the replay method. The replay method passes the mock from the phase where we record the method

we expect to be called to where we test. Before, we simply recorded the behavior, but the object was not working as a mock. After calling `replay`, the object works as expected **❼**.

- We call the `transfer` method to transfer some money between the two accounts **❽**.
- We assert the expected result **❾**.
- The `@AfterEach` method that is executed after every `@Test` method holds the verification of the expectations. With EasyMock, we can call the `verify` method with any mock object **❿** to verify that the method-call expectations we declared were triggered. Including the verification in the `@AfterEach` method allows us to introduce new tests easily, and we'll rely on the execution of the `verify` method from now on.

JUnit best practices: EasyMock object creation

Here is a nice-to-know tip on the `createMock` method. If you check the API of Easy-Mock, you see that the `createMock` method comes with numerous signatures. The signature that we use is

```
createMock(String name, Class claz);
```

but there's also

```
createMock(Class claz);
```

Which one should we use? `createMock(String name, Class claz)` is better. If we use `createMock(Class claz)` and our expectations are not met, we get an error message like the following:

```
java.lang.AssertionError:
  Expectation failure on verify:
    read(): expected: 7, actual: 0
```

As you see, this message is not as descriptive as it could be. If we use `create-Mock(String name, Class claz)` instead and map the class to a given name, we will get something like the following:

```
java.lang.AssertionError:
  Expectation failure on verify:
    name.read(): expected: 7, actual: 0
```

That was pretty easy, right? So how about moving a step forward and revising a more complicated example? Listing 8.20 demonstrates the reworked `WebClient` test from listing 8.16: verifying the correct value returned by the `getContent` method.

We want to test the `getContent` method of the `WebClient`. For this purpose, we need to mock all the dependencies to that method. In this example, we have two dependencies: `ConnectionFactory` and `InputStream`. It appears to be a problem because EasyMock can only mock interfaces, and `InputStream` is a class.

To mock the `InputStream` class, we are going to use the class extensions of Easy-Mock, which represent an extension project of EasyMock that lets you generate mock objects[1] for classes and interfaces. These class extensions are addressed by the second Maven dependency in the following listing..

> **Listing 8.20   Reworking the `WebClient` test using EasyMock**

```
[...]
import static org.easymock.classextension.EasyMock.createMock;
import static org.easymock.classextension.EasyMock.replay;          ❶
import static org.easymock.classextension.EasyMock.verify;

public class TestWebClientEasyMock {
    private ConnectionFactory factory;
    private InputStream stream;                                      ❷

    @BeforeEach
    public void setUp() {
        factory = createMock( "factory", ConnectionFactory.class );  ❸
        stream = createMock( "stream", InputStream.class );
    }

    @Test
    public void testGetContentOk() throws Exception {
        expect( factory.getData() ).andReturn( stream );
        expect( stream.read() ).andReturn( new Integer( (byte) 'W' ) );
        expect( stream.read() ).andReturn( new Integer( (byte) 'o' ) );
        expect( stream.read() ).andReturn( new Integer( (byte) 'r' ) );
        expect( stream.read() ).andReturn( new Integer( (byte) 'k' ) );  ❹
        expect( stream.read() ).andReturn( new Integer( (byte) 's' ) );
        expect( stream.read() ).andReturn( new Integer( (byte) '!' ) );
        expect( stream.read() ).andReturn( -1 );
        stream.close();                                ←              ❺

        replay( factory );                             ❻
        replay( stream );

        WebClient2 client = new WebClient2();                         ❼
        String workingContent = client.getContent( factory );  ←

        assertEquals( "Works!", workingContent );   ←
    }                                               ❽
[...]
    @Test
    public void testGetContentCannotCloseInputStream() throws Exception {
        expect( factory.getData() ).andReturn( stream );
        expect( stream.read() ).andReturn( -1 );
```

---

[1] Final and private methods cannot be mocked.

```
          stream.close();
          expectLastCall().andThrow(new IOException("cannot close"));

          replay( factory );
          replay( stream );
          WebClient2 client = new WebClient2();
          String workingContent = client.getContent( factory );

          assertNull( workingContent );
    }

    @AfterEach
    public void tearDown() {
        verify( factory );
        verify( stream );
    }
}
```

In this listing:

- We start by importing the objects that we need ❶. Notice that because we use the class extensions of EasyMock, we need to import the org.easymock .classextension.EasyMock object instead of org.easymock.EasyMock. Now we are ready to create mock objects of classes and interfaces by using the statically imported methods of the class extensions.
- As in the previous listings, we declare the objects that we want to mock ❷ and call the createMock method to initialize them ❸.
- We define the expectation of the stream when the read method is invoked ❹. (Notice that to stop reading from the stream, the last thing to return is -1.) Working with a low-level stream, we define how to read one byte at a time, as InputStream is reading byte by byte. We expect the close method to be called on the stream ❺.
- To denote that we are done declaring our expectations, we call the replay method ❻. The replay method passes the mock from the phase where we record the method that we expect to be called to where we test. Initially, the mock just records what it is supposed to do and will not react if called. But after calling replay, it will use the recorded behavior when called.
- The rest is invoking the method under test ❼ and asserting the expected result ❽.
- We also add another test to simulate a condition when we cannot close the InputStream. We define an expectation in which we expect the close method of the stream to be invoked ❾.
- On the next line, we declare that an IOException should be raised if this call occurs ❿.

As the name of the framework suggests, using EasyMock is very easy, and it is an option you may consider for your projects.

8.6.2   *Using JMock*

So far, you've seen how to implement your own mock objects and use the EasyMock framework. In this section, we introduce the JMock framework (http://jmock.org). We'll follow the same scenario that the engineers from Tested Data Systems are following to evaluate the capabilities of a mock framework and compare them with those of other frameworks: testing money transfers with the help of a mock `AccountManager`, this time using JMock. To work with JMock, we need to add the following dependencies to the pom.xml file.

Listing 8.21   JMock dependencies from the pom.xml configuration file

```
<dependency>
    <groupId>org.jmock</groupId>
    <artifactId>jmock-junit5</artifactId>
    <version>2.12.0</version>
</dependency>
<dependency>
    <groupId>org.jmock</groupId>
    <artifactId>jmock-legacy</artifactId>
    <version>2.5.1</version>
</dependency>
```

As in section 8.6.1, we start with a simple example: reworking listing 8.4 by means of JMock, as shown in the following listing.

Listing 8.22   Reworking the `TestAccountService` test using JMock

```
[...]
import org.jmock.Expectations;
import org.jmock.Mockery;                                    ❶
import org.jmock.junit5.JUnit5Mockery;

public class TestAccountServiceJMock {
    @RegisterExtension
    Mockery context = new JUnit5Mockery();                   ❷

    private AccountManager mockAccountManager;          ⟵
                                                             ❸
    @BeforeEach
    public void setUp() {
        mockAccountManager = context.mock( AccountManager.class );   ⟵
    }                                                            ❹

    @Test
    public void testTransferOk() {
        Account senderAccount = new Account( "1", 200 );
        Account beneficiaryAccount = new Account( "2", 100 );    ❺

        context.checking( new Expectations()          ⟵
        {                                               ❻
            {
```

```
            oneOf( mockAccountManager ).findAccountForUser( "1" );
            will( returnValue( senderAccount ) );
            oneOf( mockAccountManager ).findAccountForUser( "2" );
            will( returnValue( beneficiaryAccount ) );

            oneOf( mockAccountManager ).updateAccount( senderAccount );
            oneOf( mockAccountManager )
                    .updateAccount( beneficiaryAccount );
        }
    } );

    AccountService accountService = new AccountService();
    accountService.setAccountManager( mockAccountManager );
    accountService.transfer( "1", "2", 50 );

    assertEquals( 150, senderAccount.getBalance() );
    assertEquals( 150, beneficiaryAccount.getBalance() );
    }
}
```

7

8

9

In this listing:

- As always, we start by importing all the objects we need **1**. Unlike EasyMock, the JMock framework does not rely on any static import features.
- JUnit 5 provides a programmatic way to register extensions. For JMock, this way is annotating a `JUnit5Mockery` nonprivate instance field with `@Register-Extension`. (Part 4 of this book discusses the JUnit 5 extension model in detail.) The `context` object serves us to create mocks and define expectations **2**.
- We declare the `AccountManager` that we would like to mock **3**.
- In the `@BeforeEach` method that is executed before each of the `@Test` methods, we create the mock programmatically by means of the context object **4**.
- As in previous listings, we declare two accounts between which we are going to transfer money **5**.
- We start declaring the expectations by constructing a new `Expectations` object **6**.
- We declare the first expectation **7**, with each expectation having the form

```
invocation-count (mock-object).method(argument-constraints);
inSequence(sequence-name);
when(state-machine.is(state-name));
will(action);
then(state-machine.is(new-state-name));
```

All the clauses are optional except the bold ones: `invocation-count` and `mock-object`. We need to specify how many invocations will occur and on which object. After that, if the method returns an object, we can declare the return object by using the `will(returnValue())` construction.

- We start the transfer from one account to the other one **8** and then assert the expected results **9**. It's as simple as that!

But wait—what happened with the verification of the invocation count? In all the previous examples, we needed to verify that invocations of expectations happened the expected number of times. Well, with JMock, you don't have to do that. The JMock extension takes care of this task, and if the expected calls were not made, the test will fail.

Following the EasyMock pattern, we rework listing 8.20 and show the `WebClient` test, this time using JMock.

Listing 8.23 Reworking the `TestWebClient` test using JMock

```
[...]

public class TestWebClientJMock {
    @RegisterExtension
    Mockery context = new JUnit5Mockery() {                     ❶
        {
            setImposteriser( ClassImposteriser.INSTANCE );      ❷
        }
    };

    @Test
    public void testGetContentOk() throws Exception  {
        ConnectionFactory factory =
                        context.mock( ConnectionFactory.class );
        InputStream mockStream =                                 ❸
                        context.mock( InputStream.class );

        context.checking( new Expectations() {
            {
                oneOf( factory ).getData();
                will( returnValue( mockStream ) );              ❹

                atLeast( 1 ).of( mockStream ).read();
                will( onConsecutiveCalls(
                    returnValue( Integer.valueOf ( (byte) 'W' ) ),
                    returnValue( Integer.valueOf ( (byte) 'o' ) ),
                    returnValue( Integer.valueOf ( (byte) 'r' ) ),   ❺
                    returnValue( Integer.valueOf ( (byte) 'k' ) ),
                    returnValue( Integer.valueOf ( (byte) 's' ) ),
                    returnValue( Integer.valueOf ( (byte) '!' ) ),
                    returnValue( -1 ) ) );

                oneOf( mockStream ).close();
            }
        } );

        WebClient2 client = new WebClient2();                        ❻
        String workingContent = client.getContent( factory );

        assertEquals( "Works!", workingContent );
    }                                                               ❼
```

```
@Test
public void testGetContentCannotCloseInputStream() throws Exception {

    ConnectionFactory factory =
                        context.mock( ConnectionFactory.class );
    InputStream mockStream = context.mock( InputStream.class );

    context.checking( new Expectations() {
        {
            oneOf( factory ).getData();
            will( returnValue( mockStream ) );
            oneOf( mockStream ).read();
            will( returnValue( -1 ) );
            oneOf( mockStream ).close();
            will( throwException(
                    new IOException( "cannot close" ) ) );
        }
    } );

    WebClient2 client = new WebClient2();

    String workingContent = client.getContent( factory );

    assertNull( workingContent );
}
}
```

In this listing:

- We start the test case by registering the JMock extension. The `JUnit5Mockery` nonprivate instance field `context` is annotated with `@RegisterExtension` ❶. The JUnit 5 extension model will be analyzed in part 4.
- To tell JMock to create mock objects not only for interfaces but also for classes, we need to set the `imposteriser` property of the context ❷. Now we can continue creating mocks the normal way.
- We declare and programmatically initialize the two mock objects ❸.
- We start declaring the expectations ❹. Notice how we declare the consecutive execution of the `read()` method of the stream ❺ and the returned values.
- We call the method under test ❻.
- We assert the expected result ❼.
- For a full view of how to use the JMock mocking library, we also provide another `@Test` method that tests our `WebClient` under exceptional conditions. We declare the expectation of the `close()` method being triggered ❽, and we instruct JMock to raise an `IOException` when this trigger happens ❾.

As you can see, the JMock library is as easy to use as the EasyMock one but provides better integration with JUnit 5. We can register the `Mockery context` field programmatically. But we still need to look at the third proposed framework, Mockito, which is closer to the JUnit 5 paradigm.

8.6.3   *Using Mockito*

This section introduces Mockito (https://site.mockito.org), another popular mocking framework. The engineers at Tested Data Systems want to evaluate it and eventually introduce it into their projects. To work with Mockito, we need to add the following dependency to the pom.xml file.

Listing 8.24   Mockito dependency from the pom.xml configuration file

```xml
<dependency>
    <groupId>org.mockito</groupId>
    <artifactId>mockito-junit-jupiter</artifactId>
    <version>3.2.4</version>
    <scope>test</scope>
</dependency>
```

As with EasyMock and JMock, we rework the example from listing 8.4 (testing money transfers with the help of a mock `AccountManager`), this time by means of Mockito.

Listing 8.25   Reworking the `TestAccountService` test using Mockito

```
[...]

import org.junit.jupiter.api.extension.ExtendWith;
import org.mockito.Mock;                                          ❶
import org.mockito.Mockito;
import org.mockito.junit.jupiter.MockitoExtension;

                                                                 ❷
@ExtendWith(MockitoExtension.class)
public class TestAccountServiceMockito {

    @Mock
    private AccountManager mockAccountManager;                   ❸

    @Test
    public void testTransferOk() {
        Account senderAccount = new Account( "1", 200 );
        Account beneficiaryAccount = new Account( "2", 100 );    ❹

        Mockito.lenient()
            .when(mockAccountManager.findAccountForUser("1"))
            .thenReturn(senderAccount);
        Mockito.lenient()                                        ❺
            .when(mockAccountManager.findAccountForUser("2"))
            .thenReturn(beneficiaryAccount);

        AccountService accountService = new AccountService();    ❻
        accountService.setAccountManager( mockAccountManager );
        accountService.transfer( "1", "2", 50 );
```

```
        assertEquals( 150, senderAccount.getBalance() );
        assertEquals( 150, beneficiaryAccount.getBalance() );
    }
}
```
⑦

In this listing:

- As usual, we start by importing all the objects we need ❶. This example does not rely on static import features.
- We extend this test by using `MockitoExtension` ❷. `@ExtendWith` is a repeatable annotation that is used to register extensions for the annotated test class or test method. (We discuss the JUnit 5 extension model in detail in part 4.) For this Mockito example, we'll only note that this extension is needed to create mock objects through annotations ❸. This code tells Mockito to create a mock object of type `AccountManager`.
- As in the previous listings, we declare two accounts between which we are going to transfer money ❹.
- We start declaring the expectations by using the `when` method ❺. Additionally, we use the `lenient` method to modify the strictness of object mocking. Without this method, only one expectation declaration is allowed for the same `findAccountForUser` method, whereas we need two (one for the `"1"` argument and one for the `"2"` argument).
- We start the transfer from one account to the other ❻.
- We assert the expected results ❼.

Following the pattern in the previous sections, we rework listing 8.20, which shows the `WebClient` test, with Mockito.

Listing 8.26 Reworking the `TestWebClient` test using Mockito

```
[...]
import org.mockito.Mock;
import org.mockito.junit.jupiter.MockitoExtension;
import static org.mockito.Mockito.doThrow;              ❶
import static org.mockito.Mockito.when;
                                                         ❷
@ExtendWith(MockitoExtension.class)
public class TestWebClientMockito {
    @Mock
    private ConnectionFactory factory;                   ❸

    @Mock
    private InputStream mockStream;

    @Test                                                ❹
    public void testGetContentOk() throws Exception {
        when(factory.getData()).thenReturn(mockStream);
```

```
            when(mockStream.read()).thenReturn((int) 'W')
                                   .thenReturn((int) 'o')
                                   .thenReturn((int) 'r')
                                   .thenReturn((int) 'k')
                                   .thenReturn((int) 's')
                                   .thenReturn((int) '!')
                                   .thenReturn(-1);

        WebClient2 client = new WebClient2();

        String workingContent = client.getContent( factory );

        assertEquals( "Works!", workingContent );
    }

    @Test
    public void testGetContentCannotCloseInputStream()
        throws Exception {
        when(factory.getData()).thenReturn(mockStream);
        when(mockStream.read()).thenReturn(-1);
        doThrow(new IOException( "cannot close" ))
                             .when(mockStream).close();

        WebClient2 client = new WebClient2();

        String workingContent = client.getContent( factory );

        assertNull( workingContent );
    }
}
```

(annotations: ❺ on the read() thenReturn block; ❻ on the client = new WebClient2() line; ❼ on the assertEquals line; ❽ ❾ ❿ on the exceptional test block)

In this listing:

- We import the needed dependencies, static and nonstatic ❶.
- We extend this test by using `MockitoExtension` ❷.
- In this example, the extension is needed to create mock objects through annotations ❸. It tells Mockito to create one mock object of type `Connection-Factory` and one mock object of type `InputStream`.
- We start the declaration of the expectations ❹. Notice how we declare the consecutive execution of the `read()` method of the stream ❺ and the returned values.
- We call the method under test ❻.
- We assert the expected result ❼.
- We provide another `@Test` method that tests our `WebClient` under exceptional conditions. We declare the expectation of the `factory.getData()` method ❽, and we declare the expectation of the `mockStream.read()` method ❾. Then we instruct Mockito to raise an `IOException` when we close the stream ❿.

As you can see, the Mockito framework can be used with the new JUnit 5 extension model—not programmatically, like JMock, but by using the JUnit 5 `@ExtendWith` and the Mockito @Mock annotation. We use it to a greater extent in other chapters, as it is better integrated with JUnit 5.

Chapter 9 addresses another approach to unit testing components: in-container unit testing or integration unit testing.

Summary

This chapter has covered the following:

- Demonstrating the mock-objects technique. This approach lets you unit test code in isolation from other domain objects and the environment. When it comes to writing fine-grained unit tests, it helps you abstract yourself from the executing environment.
- Showing a nice side effect of writing mock-object tests: it forces you to rewrite some of the code under test. In practice, code is often not well written. With mock objects, you must think differently about the code and apply better design patterns, like interfaces and IoC.
- Implementing and comparing the Method Factory and Class Factory techniques for refactoring code that uses a mock HTTP connection.
- Using three mocking frameworks: EasyMock, JMock, and Mockito. Of the three frameworks, we demonstrated that at this time, Mockito has the best integration with JUnit 5, in particular with the JUnit 5 extension model.

In-container testing

The secret of success is sincerity. Once you can fake that you've got it made.

—Jean Giraudoux

This chapter examines one approach to unit testing components in an application container: in-container unit testing, or integration testing. These components are modules that may be developed by different programmers or teams and that need to be tested together or integrated. We will analyze in-container testing pros and cons and show what you can achieve by using the mock-objects approach introduced in chapter 8, where mock objects fall short, and how in-container testing enables you to write integration unit tests. We will also work with Arquillian, a Java EE container-agnostic framework for integration testing, and show you how to use it to conduct integration testing. Finally, we will compare the stub, mock-object, and in-container approaches covered in this part of this book.

9.1 Limitations of standard unit testing

Let's start with the example servlet in listing 9.1, which implements the `HttpServlet` method `isAuthenticated`, the method we want to unit test. A *servlet* is a Java software application that extends the capabilities of a server. Our example company, Tested Data Systems, uses servlets to develop web applications, one of which is an online shop that serves new customers. To access the online shop, users need to connect to the frontend interface. The online shop needs authentication mechanisms so that the client knows who is performing the operations, and the Tested Data Systems engineers would like to test a method that verifies whether a user is authenticated.

> Listing 9.1 Servlet implementing `isAuthenticated`

```
[...]
import javax.servlet.http.HttpServlet;
import javax.servlet.http.HttpServletRequest;
import javax.servlet.http.HttpSession;

public class SampleServlet extends HttpServlet {
    public boolean isAuthenticated(HttpServletRequest request) {
        HttpSession session = request.getSession(false);
        if (session == null) {
            return false;
        }
        String authenticationAttribute =
            (String) session.getAttribute("authenticated");
        return Boolean.valueOf(authenticationAttribute).booleanValue();
    }
}
```

This servlet, although it is simple enough, allows us to show the limitation of standard unit testing. To test the method `isAuthenticated`, we need a valid `HttpServletRequest`. Because `HttpServletRequest` is an interface, we cannot just call new `HttpServletRequest`. The `HttpServletRequest` life cycle and implementation are provided by the container (in this case, a servlet container). The same is true of other server-side objects, such as `HttpSession`. JUnit alone is not enough to write a test for the isAuthenticated method and for servlets in general.

> **DEFINITION** *Component* and *container*—A *component* is an application or a part of an application. A *container* is an isolated space where a component executes. A container offers services for the components it is hosting, such as life cycle, security, transactions, and so forth.

In the case of servlets and Java Server Pages (JSP), the container is a servlet container like Jetty or Tomcat. Other types of containers include JBoss (renamed WildFly), which is an Enterprise Java Beans (EJB) container. Java code can run in all these containers. As long as a container creates and manages objects at runtime, we should not use the standard JUnit techniques (the features of JUnit 5, stubs, and mock objects) to test those objects.

9.2   *The mock-objects solution*

The engineers at Tested Data Systems have to test the authentication mechanisms of the online shop. The first solution they consider for unit testing the isAuthenticated method (listing 9.1) is to mock the HttpServletRequest class using the approach described in chapter 8. Although mocking works, we need to write a lot of code to create a test. We can achieve the same result more easily by using the open source EasyMock framework (see chapter 8).

Listing 9.2   Testing a servlet with EasyMock

```
[...]
import javax.servlet.http.HttpServletRequest;
import static org.easymock.EasyMock.createStrictMock;
import static org.easymock.EasyMock.expect;
import static org.easymock.EasyMock.replay;                              ❶
import static org.easymock.EasyMock.verify;
import static org.easymock.EasyMock.eq;
import static org.junit.jupiter.api.Assertions.assertFalse;
import static org.junit.jupiter.api.Assertions.assertTrue;
[...]
public class TestSampleServletWithEasyMock {

    private SampleServlet servlet;
    private HttpServletRequest mockHttpServletRequest;                   ❷
    private HttpSession mockHttpSession;

    @BeforeEach
    public void setUp() {
        servlet = new SampleServlet();
        mockHttpServletRequest =
            createStrictMock(HttpServletRequest.class);                 ❸
        mockHttpSession = createStrictMock(HttpSession.class);
    }

    @Test
    public void testIsAuthenticatedAuthenticated() {
        expect(mockHttpServletRequest.getSession(eq(false)))
            .andReturn(mockHttpSession);
        expect(mockHttpSession.getAttribute(eq("authenticated")))       ❹
            .andReturn("true");
        replay(mockHttpServletRequest);                        ❺                ❻
        replay(mockHttpSession);
        assertTrue(servlet.isAuthenticated(mockHttpServletRequest));   ←
    }
```

```
@Test
public void testIsAuthenticatedNotAuthenticated() {
    expect(mockHttpSession.getAttribute(eq("authenticated")))
        .andReturn("false");
    replay(mockHttpSession);
    expect(mockHttpServletRequest.getSession(eq(false)))
        .andReturn(mockHttpSession);
    replay(mockHttpServletRequest);
    assertFalse(servlet.isAuthenticated(mockHttpServletRequest));
}

@Test
public void testIsAuthenticatedNoSession() {
    expect(mockHttpServletRequest.getSession(eq(false))).andReturn(null);
    replay(mockHttpServletRequest);
        replay(mockHttpSession);
        assertFalse(servlet.isAuthenticated(mockHttpServletRequest));
}

@AfterEach                              ❼
public void tearDown() {          ◀─┐
    verify(mockHttpServletRequest);      │  ❽
    verify(mockHttpSession);             │
}
}
```

In this listing:

- We start by importing the necessary classes and methods using static imports. We use the `EasyMock` class extensively ❶.
- Next, we declare instance variables for the objects ❷ we want to mock: `HttpServletRequest` and `HttpSession`.
- The `setUp` method annotated with `@BeforeEach` ❸ runs before each call to `@Test` methods; this is where we instantiate all the mock objects.
- Next, we implement our tests, following this pattern:
  - Set our expectations by using the EasyMock API ❹.
  - Invoke the `replay` method to finish declaring our expectations ❺. The `replay` method passes the mock from the phase where we record the method that we expect to be called to where we test. Initially, the mock just records what it is supposed to do and will not react if called. But after calling `replay`, it will use the recorded behavior when called.
  - Assert test conditions on the servlet ❻.
- The `@AfterEach` method executed after each `@Test` method ❼ calls the Easy-Mock `verify` API method ❽ to check whether the mocked objects met all of our programmed expectations.

Mocking a minimal portion of a container is a valid approach for testing components. But mocking can be complicated and require a lot of code. The source code provided with this book also includes the servlet testing versions for the JMock and Mockito frameworks. As with other kinds of tests, when the servlet changes, the test expectations must change to match. In the next section, the engineers at Tested Data Systems attempt to ease the task of testing the online shop's authentication mechanism.

9.3 *The step to in-container testing*

The next approach in testing the `SampleServlet` is running the test cases where the `HttpServletRequest` and `HttpSession` objects live: in the container itself. This approach eliminates the need to mock any objects; we simply access the objects and methods we need in the real container.

For our example of testing the online shop's authentication mechanism, we need the web request and session to be real `HttpServletRequest` and `HttpSession` objects managed by the container. Using a mechanism to deploy and execute our tests in a container, we have in-container testing. The next section covers options for in-container tests.

9.3.1 *Implementation strategies*

Two architectural choices drive in-container tests: server side and client side. We can drive the tests directly by controlling the server-side container and the unit tests. Alternatively, we can drive the tests from the client side, as shown in figure 9.1.

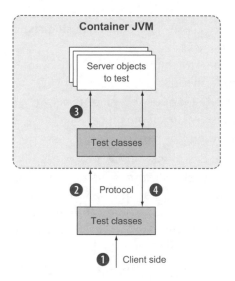

Figure 9.1   Life cycle of a typical in-container test: ❶ executing the client test classes, ❷ calling the same test case on the server side, ❸ testing the domain objects, and ❹ returning the results to the client

When the tests are packaged and deployed in the container and to the client, the JUnit test runner executes the test classes on the client ❶. A test class opens a connection via a protocol such as HTTP(S) and calls the same test case on the server side ❷. The server-side test case operates on server-side objects that are normally available (`HttpServletRequest`, `HttpServletResponse`, `HttpSession`, `BundleContext`, and so on) and tests our domain objects ❸. The server returns the result of the tests to the client ❹, which an IDE or Maven can gather.

9.3.2 In-container testing frameworks

As we have just seen, in-container testing is applicable when code interacts with a container and tests cannot create valid container objects (`HttpServletRequest` in the preceding section). Our example uses a servlet container, but many other types of containers are available, including Java EE, web server, applets, and EJB. In all these cases, the in-container testing strategy can be applied.

9.4 Comparing stubs, mock objects, and in-container testing

This section compares[1] the approaches we presented to test components: stubs, mocks, and in-container testing. It draws on many questions from forums and mailing lists.

9.4.1 Stubs evaluation

Chapter 7 introduces using stubs as an out-of-container testing technique. Stubs work well to isolate a given class for testing and assert the state of its instances. Stubbing a servlet container allows us to track the number of requests made, the state of the server, and which URLs were requested, for example. But stubs have some predefined behaviors from the beginning of their existence.

When using mock objects, we code and verify expectations. The engineers at Tested Data Systems were able to check the business logic and how many times tests call some particular methods.

One of the biggest advantages of stubs compared to mocks is that stubs are easier to understand. Stubs isolate a class with little extra code compared with mock objects, which require an entire framework to function. The drawbacks of stubs are that they rely on external tools and hacks and do not track the state objects they fake.

In chapter 7, the engineers at Tested Data Systems easily faked a servlet container with stubs. Doing so with mock objects would be much harder, however, because the engineers would need to fake container objects with state and behavior.

Here is a summary of stub pros and cons:

- *Pros:*
  - Fast and lightweight
  - Easy to write and understand
  - Powerful
  - More coarse-grained tests
- *Cons:*
  - Specialized methods required to verify the state
  - Do not test the behavior of faked objects

---

[1] For an in-depth comparison of stubs and mocks technology, see "Mocks Aren't Stubs," by Martin Fowler, at http://martinfowler.com/articles/mocksArentStubs.html.

– Time consuming for complicated interactions
– Require more maintenance when the code changes

9.4.2   *Mock-objects evaluation*

The greatest advantage of mock objects over in-container testing is that mocks do not require a running container to execute tests. Tests can be set up and run quickly. The main drawback is that the tested components do not run in the container in which we will deploy them. The tests cannot verify the interaction between components and the container. Also, the tests do not test the interactions among the components themselves as they run in the container.

We still need a way to perform integration tests—to check that modules developed by different developers or teams work together. Writing and running functional tests could achieve this goal. The problem with functional tests is that they are coarse grained and test only a full use case; we lose the benefits of fine-grained unit testing. We will not be able to test as many cases with functional tests as we can with unit tests.

Mock objects have other disadvantages. There are many mock objects to set up, for example, which may prove to be non-negligible overhead—the operating costs of managing all these mocks may be significant. Obviously, the cleaner the code (small and focused methods) is, the easier tests are to set up.

Another important drawback of mock objects is that to set up a test, we usually must know exactly how the mocked API behaves, which may require some knowledge of a domain outside our own. We know the behavior of our own API, but that may not be the case with other APIs, such as the Servlet API that the engineers at Tested Data Systems need to use for the online shop. Even though all containers of a given type implement the same API, not all containers behave the same way, so we may have to deal with bugs, tricks, and hacks for various third-party libraries in any project.

To wrap up this section, here are the pros and cons of unit testing with mock objects:

- *Pros:*
  - Do not require a running container to execute tests
  - Are quick to set up and run
  - Allow fine-grained unit testing
- *Cons:*
  - Do not test interactions with the container or between the components
  - Do not test the deployment of components
  - Require good knowledge of the API to mock, which can be difficult (especially for external libraries)
  - Do not provide confidence that the code will run in the target container
  - Offer more fine-grained testing, which may lead to testing code being swamped with interfaces
  - Like stubs, require maintenance when the code changes

9.4.3   *In-container testing evaluation*

So far, we have examined the advantages of in-container unit testing. This approach also has the disadvantages discussed in the following sections.

SPECIFIC TOOLS REQUIRED

A major drawback is that although the concept is generic, the tools that implement in-container unit testing are specific to the tested API, such as Jetty or Tomcat for servlets and WildFly for EJBs. With mock objects, because the concept is generic, you can test almost any API.

POOR IDE SUPPORT

A significant drawback of most in-container testing frameworks is the lack of good IDE integration. In most cases, you can use Maven or Gradle to execute tests in an embedded container, which also allows you to run a build in a continuous integration server (CIS; see chapter 13). Alternatively, IDEs can execute tests that use mock objects as normal JUnit tests.

In-container testing falls in the category of integration testing, which means you do not need to execute your in-container tests as often as normal unit tests and will most likely run them in a CIS, alleviating the need for IDE integration.

LONGER EXECUTION TIME

Another issue is performance. For a test to run in a container, you need to start and manage the container, which can be time consuming. The overhead in time and memory depends on the container. Startup overhead is not limited to the container. If a unit test hits a database, for example, the database must be in an expected state before the test starts. In terms of execution time, integration unit tests cost more than mock objects; consequently, you may not run them as often as unit tests.

COMPLEX CONFIGURATION

The biggest drawback of in-container testing is that the tests are complex to configure. Because the application and its tests run in a container, your application must be packaged (usually as a war or ear file) and deployed to the container. Then you must start the container and run the tests.

On the other hand, because you must perform the same tasks for production, it is a best practice to automate this process as part of the build and reuse it for testing purposes. As one of the most complex tasks of a Java EE project, providing automation for packaging and deployment becomes a win-win situation. The need to provide in-container testing drives the creation of this automated process at the beginning of the project, which facilitates continuous integration.

To further this goal, most in-container testing frameworks include support for build tools such as Maven and Gradle and allow the embedded startup of the container. This support helps hide the complexity involved in building various runtime artifacts, running tests, and gathering reports.

Taking into consideration the evaluation we have provided for in-container testing, the next section introduces Arquillian as a container-agnostic integration testing framework for Java EE.

9.5   *Testing with Arquillian*

Arquillian (http://arquillian.org) is a testing framework for Java that uses JUnit to execute test cases against a Java container. The Arquillian framework is broken into three major sections:

- Test runners (JUnit, in our case)
- Containers (WildFly, Tomcat, GlassFish, Jetty, and so on)
- Test enrichers (the injection of container resources and beans directly into the test class)

Despite the lack of integration with JUnit 5 (Arquillian does not have a JUnit 5 extension, at least when this chapter was written), it is very popular and has been largely adopted in projects up to JUnit 4. It greatly eases the task of managing containers, deployments, and framework initializations. On the other hand, as Arquillian is testing Java EE applications, its use in our examples requires some basic knowledge, in particular about Contexts and Dependency Injection (CDI)—a Java EE standard for the inversion of control design pattern.

ShrinkWrap is an external dependency used with Arquillian and a simple way to create archives in Java. Using the fluent ShrinkWrap API, developers at Tested Data Systems can assemble jar, war, and ear files to be deployed directly by Arquillian during testing. Such files are archives that may contain all the classes needed to run an application. ShrinkWrap helps define the deployments and the descriptors to be loaded to the Java container being tested against.

One project under development at Tested Data Systems is a flight-management application. The application creates and sets up flights; it also adds and removes passengers. The engineers want to test the integration between two classes: `Passenger` and `Flight`. The test will check whether each passenger can be added to or removed from a flight correctly, as well as whether the number of passengers exceeds the number of seats. (Nobody wants to get on a flight without having a seat!) The following two listings show the `Passenger` and `Flight` classes, as well as their logic.

Listing 9.3   `Passenger` class

```java
public class Passenger {

    private String identifier;                    ❶
    private String name;

    public Passenger(String identifier, String name) {     ❷
        this.identifier = identifier;
        this.name = name;
    }

    public String getIdentifier() {               ❸
        return identifier;
    }

    public String getName() {
```

```
        return name;
    }

    @Override
    public String toString() {           ←④
        return "Passenger " + getName() +
                " with identifier: " + getIdentifier();
    }
}
```

In this listing:

- We provide two fields—identifier and name—to describe a Passenger ❶.
- We provide a constructor with these two parameters ❷.
- We provide two getters ❸ and the overridden toString method ❹.

Listing 9.4 `Flight` **class**

```
public class Flight {

    private String flightNumber;
    private int seats;                           ❶
    Set<Passenger> passengers = new HashSet<>();

    public Flight(String flightNumber, int seats) {    ←
        this.flightNumber = flightNumber;                  ❷
        this.seats = seats;
    }

    public String getFlightNumber() {        ←
        return flightNumber;
    }

    public int getSeats() {                  ←     ❸
        return seats;
    }

    public int getNumberOfPassengers () {    ←
        return passengers.size();
    }
                                             ❹
    public void setSeats(int seats) {        ←
        if(passengers.size() > seats) {
            throw new RuntimeException(
            "Cannot reduce seats under the number of existing passengers!");
        }
        this.seats = seats;
    }                                                ❺
    public boolean addPassenger(Passenger passenger) {    ←
        if(passengers.size() >= seats) {
            throw new RuntimeException(
         "Cannot add more passengers than the capacity of the flight!");
        }
        return passengers.add(passenger);
    }
```

```
public boolean removePassenger(Passenger passenger) {          ←─┐
    return  passengers.remove(passenger);                        │  ❻
}

                                          ❼
@Override
public String toString() {          ←─┐
    return "Flight " + getFlightNumber();
}

}
```

In this listing:

- We provide three fields—flightNumber, seats, and passengers—to describe a Flight ❶.
- We provide a constructor with the first two mentioned parameters ❷.
- We provide three getters ❸ and one setter ❹ to address the fields we have defined. The setter on the seats field checks that the value of the field is not less than the number of existing passengers.
- The addPassenger method adds a passenger to the flight. It also compares the number of passengers with the number of seats so the flight will not be over-booked ❺.
- We provide the capability to remove a passenger from a flight ❻.
- We override the toString method ❼.

The next listing describes the 20 passengers on the flight by identifier and name. The list is stored in a CSV file.

Listing 9.5   flights_information.csv file

```
1236789; John Smith
9006789; Jane Underwood
1236790; James Perkins
9006790; Mary Calderon
1236791; Noah Graves
9006791; Jake Chavez
1236792; Oliver Aguilar
9006792; Emma McCann
1236793; Margaret Knight
9006793; Amelia Curry
1236794; Jack Vaughn
9006794; Liam Lewis
1236795; Olivia Reyes
9006795; Samantha Poole
1236796; Patricia Jordan
9006796; Robert Sherman
1236797; Mason Burton
9006797; Harry Christensen
1236798; Jennifer Mills
9006798; Sophia Graham
```

The next listing implements the `FlightBuilderUtil` class, which parses the CSV file and populates the flight with the corresponding passengers. Thus, the code brings the information from an external file to the memory of the application.

Listing 9.6   `FlightBuilderUtil` class

```
[..]
public class FlightBuilderUtil {

    public static Flight buildFlightFromCsv() throws IOException {          ❶
        Flight flight = new Flight("AA1234", 20);
        try(BufferedReader reader =
            new BufferedReader(new FileReader(                              ❷
                "src/test/resources/flights_information.csv")))
        {
            String line = null;
            do {                                                           ❸
                line = reader.readLine();
                if (line != null) {
                    String[] passengerString = line.toString().split(";"); ❹
                    Passenger passenger =
                            new Passenger(passengerString[0].trim(),       ❺
                                          passengerString[1].trim());
                    flight.addPassenger(passenger);                        ❻
                }
            } while (line != null);

        }

        return flight;                                                     ❼
    }
}
```

In this listing:

- We create a flight ❶.
- We open the CSV file to parse ❷.
- We read line by line ❸, split each line ❹, create a passenger based on the information that has been read ❺, and add the passenger to the flight ❻.
- We return the fully populated flight from the method ❼.

So far, all the classes that have been implemented for the development of the flight and passengers are pure Java classes; no particular framework and technology have been used. Arquillian is a testing framework that executes test cases against a Java container, so it requires some understanding of notions related to Java EE and CDI. Because it is a widely used framework for integration testing, we have decided to introduce it here; we'll explain the most important ideas so that you can quickly adopt it within your projects.

Arquillian abstracts the container or application startup logic from the unit tests; it drives a deployment runtime paradigm with the application, allowing the deployment of the program to a Java EE application server. Therefore, the framework is ideal for the in-container testing implemented in this chapter. In addition, it eliminates the need for specific tools that implement in-container testing.

Arquillian deploys the application to the targeted runtime to execute test cases. The targeted runtime can be an application server, embedded or managed. We need to add the following dependencies to the Maven pom.xml configuration file to work with Arquillian.

Listing 9.7   Required pom.xml dependencies

```
<dependencyManagement>
        <dependencies>
                <dependency>
                        <groupId>org.jboss.arquillian</groupId>        ①
                        <artifactId>arquillian-bom</artifactId>
                        <version>1.4.0.Final</version>
                        <scope>import</scope>
                        <type>pom</type>
                </dependency>
        </dependencies>
</dependencyManagement>
<dependencies>
        <dependency>
                <groupId>org.jboss.spec</groupId>                      ②
                <artifactId>jboss-javaee-7.0</artifactId>
                <version>1.0.3.Final</version>
                <type>pom</type>
                <scope>provided</scope>
        </dependency>
        <dependency>
                <groupId>org.junit.vintage</groupId>                   ③
                <artifactId>junit-vintage-engine</artifactId>
                <version>5.6.0</version>
                <scope>test</scope>
        </dependency>
        <dependency>
                <groupId>org.jboss.arquillian.junit</groupId>          ④
                <artifactId>arquillian-junit-container</artifactId>
                <scope>test</scope>
        </dependency>
        <dependency>
                <groupId>org.jboss.arquillian.container</groupId>      ⑤
                <artifactId>arquillian-weld-ee-embedded-1.1</artifactId>
                <version>1.0.0.CR9</version>
                <scope>test</scope>
        </dependency>
        <dependency>
                <groupId>org.jboss.weld</groupId>                      ⑥
                <artifactId>weld-core</artifactId>
                <version>2.3.5.Final</version>
                <scope>test</scope>
        </dependency>
</dependencies>
```

This listing adds

- The Arquillian API dependency **❶**.
- The Java EE 7 API dependency **❷**.
- The JUnit Vintage Engine dependency **❸**. As mentioned earlier, at least for the moment, Arquillian is not integrated with JUnit 5. Because Arquillian lacks a JUnit 5 extension, we'll have to use the JUnit 4 dependencies and annotations to run our tests.
- The Arquillian JUnit integration dependency **❹**.
- The container adapter dependencies **❺ ❻**. To execute our tests against a container, we must include the dependencies that correspond to that container. This requirement demonstrates one of the strengths of Arquillian: it abstracts the container from the unit tests and is not tightly coupled to specific tools that implement in-container unit testing.

An Arquillian test, as implemented in the following listing, looks just like a unit test, with some additions. The test is named `FlightWithPassengersTest` to show the goal of the integration testing between the two classes.

Listing 9.8 `FlightWithPassengersTest` class

```
[...]
@RunWith(Arquillian.class)
public class FlightWithPassengersTest {                    ❶

    @Deployment
    public static JavaArchive createDeployment() {
        return ShrinkWrap.create(JavaArchive.class)        ❷
                .addClasses(Passenger.class, Flight.class)
                .addAsManifestResource(EmptyAsset.INSTANCE, "beans.xml");
    }

    @Inject
    Flight flight;          ❸

    @Test(expected = RuntimeException.class)
    public void testNumberOfSeatsCannotBeExceeded() throws IOException {   ❹
        assertEquals(20, flight.getNumberOfPassengers());
        flight.addPassenger(new Passenger("1247890", "Michael Johnson"));
    }

    @Test
    public void testAddRemovePassengers() throws IOException {      ❺
        flight.setSeats(21);
        Passenger additionalPassenger =
                new Passenger("1247890", "Michael Johnson");
        flight.addPassenger(additionalPassenger);
        assertEquals(21, flight.getNumberOfPassengers());
        flight.removePassenger(additionalPassenger);
        assertEquals(20, flight.getNumberOfPassengers());
        assertEquals(21, flight.getSeats());
    }
}
```

As this listing shows, an Arquillian test case must have three things:

- A `@RunWith(Arquillian.class)` annotation on the class ❶. The `@RunWith` annotation tells JUnit to use Arquillian as the test controller.
- A public static method annotated with `@Deployment` that returns a Shrink-Wrap archive ❷. The purpose of the test archive is to isolate the classes and resources that the test needs. The archive is defined with ShrinkWrap. The microdeployment strategy lets us focus on precisely the classes we want to test. As a result, the test remains very lean and manageable. For the moment, we have included only the `Passenger` and the `Flight` classes. We try to inject a `Flight` object as a class member using the CDI `@Inject` annotation ❸. The `@Inject` annotation allows us to define injection points inside classes. In this case, `@Inject` instructs CDI to inject into the test a reference to an object of type `Flight`.
- At least one method annotated with `@Test` ❹ and ❺. Arquillian looks for a public static method with the `@Deployment` annotation to retrieve the test archive. Then each `@Test`-annotated method is run inside the container environment.

When the ShrinkWrap archive is deployed to the server, it becomes a real archive. The container has no knowledge that the archive was packaged by ShrinkWrap.

We have provided the infrastructure for using Arquillian in our project, and now we'll run our integration tests with its help! But we get an error (figure 9.2).

```
org.jboss.weld.exceptions.DeploymentException: WELD-001408: Unsatisfied dependencies for type Flight with qualifiers @Default
  at injection point [BackedAnnotatedField] @Inject com.manning.junitbook.ch09.airport.FlightWithPassengersTest.flight
  at com.manning.junitbook.ch09.airport.FlightWithPassengersTest.flight(FlightWithPassengersTest.java:0)
```

Figure 9.2   The result of running `FlightWithPassengersTest`

The error says `Unsatisfied dependencies for type Flight with qualifiers @Default`. It means the container is trying to inject the dependency, as it has been instructed to do through the CDI `@Inject` annotation, but it is unsatisfied. Why? What have the developers from Tested Data Systems missed? The `Flight` class provides only a constructor with arguments, and it has no default constructor to be used by the container for the creation of the object. The container does not know how to invoke the constructor with parameters and which parameters to pass to it to create the `Flight` object that must be injected.

What is the solution in this case? Java EE offers producer methods that are designed to inject objects that require custom initialization. The solution fixes the issue and is easy to put into practice, even by a junior developer.

Listing 9.9 `FlightProducer` class

```
[...]
public class FlightProducer {

    @Produces
    public Flight createFlight() throws IOException {
        return FlightBuilderUtil.buildFlightFromCsv();
    }
}
```

In this listing, we create the `FlightProducer` class with the `createFlight` method, which invokes `FlightBuilderUtil.buildFlightFromCsv()`. We can use such a method to inject objects that require custom initialization; in this case, we are injecting a flight that has been configured based on the CSV file. We annotated the `createFlight` method with `@Produces`, which is also a Java EE annotation. The container will automatically invoke this method to create the configured flight; then it injects the method into the `Flight` field, annotated with `@Inject` from the `Flight-WithPassengersTest` class.

Next we add the `FlightProducer` class to the ShrinkWrap archive.

Listing 9.10 Modified deployment method from `FlightWithPassengersTest`

```
[...]
@Deployment
public static JavaArchive createDeployment() {
        return ShrinkWrap.create(JavaArchive.class)
                .addClasses(Passenger.class, Flight.class,
                            FlightProducer.class)
                .addAsManifestResource(EmptyAsset.INSTANCE, "beans.xml");
}
```

If we run the tests now, they are green. The container injected the correctly configured flight (figure 9.3).

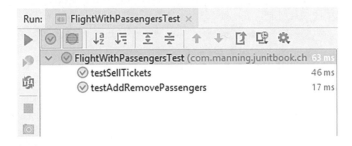

Figure 9.3 The result of running `FlightWithPassengersTest` after introducing the producer method

Considering the advantages of in-container testing, which eliminates tight coupling with specific tools, it is likely to receive more attention and attain greater applicability inside Tested Data Systems. The developers are waiting for one more thing: the creation of a JUnit 5 extension. (We are looking forward to it as well, so fingers crossed!)

Chapter 10 starts part 3 of this book by taking a deeper look at the integration of JUnit into the build process with Maven.

Summary

This chapter has covered the following:

- Analyzing the limitations of unit testing, including limitations of using mock objects: they cannot use objects whose implementation is provided by a container, they require a lot of code, the test expectations must continuously change to match the code evolution, and they do not provide an isolated running environment to run.
- Examining the need for and the steps to in-container testing: running the test cases where the objects actually live, in the container itself.
- Evaluating testing using stubs, mock objects, and in-container testing, and comparing their advantages and drawbacks.
- Working with Arquillian, a container-agnostic integration testing framework for Java EE, and implementing integration tests with its help. Despite its current lack of integration with JUnit 5 (it is missing a JUnit 5 extension), it has been used for many years in Java EE projects, as it uses JUnit to execute test cases against a Java container.

Part 3

Working with JUnit 5 and other tools

This part of the book deals with very important aspects of the development of every project: the build and the IDEs. The importance of the build is reconsidered more and more these days, especially in large projects. Also, an IDE that is comfortable for the developer strongly contributes to the speed of development and local testing. For these reasons, we dedicate a whole part of the book to integration of JUnit 5, build tools, and IDEs.

Chapter 10 provides a very quick introduction to Maven and its terminology. It shows you how to include the execution of your tests in the Maven build life cycle and how to produce nice HTML reports by means of some of the Maven plugins. Chapter 11 guides you through the same concepts, this time by means of another popular tool called Gradle. In chapter 12, you investigate the way that a developer may work with JUnit 5 by using the most popular IDEs today: IntelliJ IDEA, Eclipse, and NetBeans. Chapter 13 is devoted to continuous integration tools. This practice, which is highly recommended by extreme programmers, helps you maintain a code repository and automate the build on it. CI is a must for building large projects that depend on many other projects that change often (like any open source projects).

Running JUnit tests
from Maven 3

10

This chapter covers

- Creating a Maven project from scratch
- Testing the Maven project with JUnit 5
- Using Maven plugins
- Using the Maven Surefire plugin

The conventional view serves to protect us from the painful job of thinking.

—John Kenneth Galbraith

This chapter discusses a common build system tool called Maven. In the previous chapters, with provided Maven projects, you needed only to look at some external dependencies, run some simple commands, or run the tests from inside the IDE. This chapter gives you a brief introduction to the Maven build system, which will be very useful if you need a systematic way to start your tests.

Maven addresses two aspects of building software. First, it describes how software is built; then, it describes the needed dependencies. Unlike earlier tools, such as Apache Ant, it uses conventions for the build procedure, and only exceptions need to be written down. It relies on an XML file to describe its full configuration—most important are the meta-information about the software project being built, the needed dependencies on other external components, and the required plugins.

By the end of this chapter, you will know how to build Java projects with Maven, including managing their dependencies, executing JUnit tests, and generating JUnit reports. For basic Maven concepts and how to set up Maven, see appendix A.

10.1   Setting up a Maven project

If you have installed Maven, you are ready to use it. The first time you execute a plugin, your internet connection must be on, because Maven automatically downloads from the web all the third-party .jar files that the plugin requires.

First, create the C:\junitbook\ folder. This is your work directory and where you will set up the Maven examples. Type the following on the command line:

```
mvn archetype:generate -DgroupId=com.manning.junitbook
-DartifactId=maven-sampling
-DarchetypeArtifactid=maven-artifact-mojo
```

Press Enter, wait for the appropriate artifacts to be downloaded, and accept the default options. You should see a folder named maven-sampling being created. If you open the new project in IntelliJ IDEA, its structure should look like figure 10.1 (just note that the .idea folder is created not by Maven, but by the IDE).

What happened here? We invoked `maven-archetype-plugin` from the command line and told it to generate a new project from scratch with the given parameters. As a result, this Maven plugin created a new project with a new folder structure, following the convention for that folder structure. Further, it created a sample `App.java` class with the `main` method and a corresponding AppTest.java file that is a

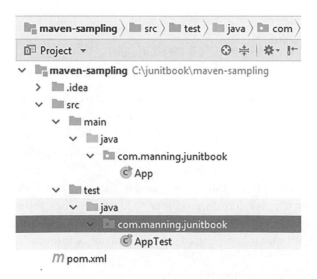

Figure 10.1   Folder structure after the project is created

unit test for our application. After looking at this folder structure, you should understand what files are in src/main/java and what files are in src/test/java.

The Maven plugin also generated a pom.xml file for us. Following are some parts of the descriptor.

Listing 10.1   pom.xml for the `maven-sampling` project

```
<project xmlns="http://maven.apache.org/POM/4.0.0"
         xmlns:xsi=http://www.w3.org/2001/XMLSchema-instance
         xsi:schemaLocation="http://maven.apache.org/POM/4.0.0
         http://maven.apache.org/maven-v4_0_0.xsd">

  <modelVersion>4.0.0</modelVersion>
  <groupId>com.manning.junitbook</groupId>
  <artifactId>maven-sampling</artifactId>
  <version>1.0-SNAPSHOT</version>
  <name>maven-sampling</name>
    <!-- FIXME change it to the project's website -->
  <url>http://www.example.com</url>
  [...]
  <dependencies>
    <dependency>
      <groupId>junit</groupId>
      <artifactId>junit</artifactId>
      <version>4.11</version>
      <scope>test</scope>
    </dependency>
  </dependencies>
  [...]
</project>
```

This code is the build descriptor for our project. It starts with a global `<project>` tag with the appropriate namespaces. Inside it, we place all of our components:

- `modelVersion`—Represents the version of the model of the `pom` being used. Currently, the only supported version is 4.0.0.
- `groupId`—Acts as the Java packaging in the filesystem, grouping different projects from one organization, company, or group of people. We provide this value in the command line when invoking Maven.
- `artifactId`—Represents the name that the project is known by. Again, the value here is the one we specified in the command line.
- `version`—Identifies the current version of our project (or project artifact). The `SNAPSHOT` ending indicates that this artifact is still in development mode; we have not released it yet.
- `dependencies`—Lists our dependencies.

Now that we have our project descriptor, we can improve it a little (listing 10.2). First, we need to change the version of the JUnit dependency, because we are using JUnit Jupiter 5.4.2, and the version that the plugin generated is 4.11. After that, we can insert some additional information to make the pom.xml more descriptive, such as a developers section. This information not only makes the pom.xml more descriptive but also will be included later when we build the website.

Listing 10.2   Changes and additions to pom.xml

```
<dependencies>
    <dependency>
        <groupId>org.junit.jupiter</groupId>
        <artifactId>junit-jupiter-api</artifactId>
        <version>5.6.0</version>
        <scope>test</scope>
    </dependency>
    <dependency>
        <groupId>org.junit.jupiter</groupId>
        <artifactId>junit-jupiter-engine</artifactId>
        <version>5.6.0</version>
        <scope>test</scope>
    </dependency>
</dependencies>

<developers>
    <developer>
        <name>Catalin Tudose</name>
        <id>ctudose</id>
        <organization>Manning</organization>
        <roles>
            <role>Java Developer</role>
        </roles>
    </developer>
    <developer>
        <name>Petar Tahchiev</name>
        <id>ptahchiev</id>
        <organization>Apache Software Foundation</organization>
        <roles>
            <role>Java Developer</role>
        </roles>
    </developer>
</developers>
```

We also specify organization, description, and inceptionYear.

Listing 10.3   Description elements in pom.xml

```
<description>
    "JUnit in Action III" book, the sample project for the "Running Junit
    tests from Maven" chapter.
</description>
<organization>
    <name>Manning Publications</name>
    <url>http://manning.com/</url>
</organization>
<inceptionYear>2019</inceptionYear>
```

Now we can start developing our software. What if you want to use a Java IDE other than IntelliJ IDEA, such as Eclipse? No problem. Maven offers additional plugins that let you import the project into your favorite IDE. To use Eclipse, open a terminal and navigate to the directory that contains the project descriptor (pom.xml). Then type the following and press Enter:

```
mvn eclipse:eclipse
```

This command invokes `maven-eclipse-plugin`, which, after downloading the necessary artifacts, produces the two files (.project and .classpath) that Eclipse needs to recognize the project as an Eclipse project. Next, you can import your project into Eclipse. All the dependencies listed in the pom.xml file are added to the project (figure 10.2).

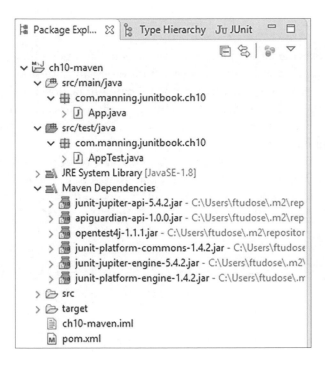

Figure 10.2   The imported project, with the Maven folders structure and needed dependencies (including the JUnit 5 ones)

Developers who use IntelliJ IDEA can import the project directly (refer to figure 10.1), as this IDE invokes the Maven plugin when such a project is open.

10.2 *Using the Maven plugins*

We have seen what Maven is and how to use it to start a project from scratch. We have also seen how to generate the project documentation and how to import a project into Eclipse and IntelliJ.

Whenever you would like to clean the project from previous activities, execute the following command:

```
mvn clean
```

This command causes Maven to go through the clean phase and invoke all the plugins that are attached to this phase—in particular, `maven-clean-plugin`, which deletes the target/ folder where your generated site resides.

10.2.1 *Maven compiler plugin*

Like any other build system, Maven is supposed to build our projects (compile our software and package in an archive). Every task in Maven is performed by an appropriate plugin, the configuration of which is in the <plugins> section of the project descriptor. To compile the source code, all you need to do is invoke the compile phase on the command line

```
mvn compile
```

which causes Maven to execute all the plugins attached to the compile phase (in particular, it will invoke `maven-compiler-plugin`). But before invoking the compile phase, as already discussed, Maven goes through the validate phase, downloads all the dependencies listed in the pom.xml file, and includes them in the classpath of the project. When the compilation process is complete, you can go to the target/classes/ folder and see the compiled classes there.

Next, we'll try to configure the compiler plugin, escaping from the convention-over-configuration principle. So far, the conventional compiler plugin has worked well. But what if we need to include the –source and –target attributes in the compiler invocation to generate class files for the specific version of the JVM? We can add the following code to the <build> section of our build file.

Listing 10.4 Configuring `maven-compiler-plugin`

```
<build>
   <plugins>
     <plugin>
       <artifactId>maven-compiler-plugin</artifactId>
        <version>2.3.2</version>
       <configuration>
          <source>1.8</source>
          <target>1.8</target>
       </configuration>
     </plugin>
   </plugins>
</build>
```

This code is a general way to configure each of our Maven plugins: enter a `<plugins>` section in our `<build>` section. There, we list each plugin that we want to configure—in this case, the `maven-compiler-plugin`. We need to enter the configuration parameters in the plugin `configuration` section. We can get a list of parameters for every plugin from the Maven website. Without the `<source>` and `<target>` parameters, the Java version to be used will be 5, which is quite old.

As we see in the declaration of the `maven-compiler-plugin` in listing 10.4, we have not set the `groupId` parameter. `maven-compiler-plugin` is one of the core Maven plugins that has an `org.apache.maven.plugins` groupId, and plugins with such a `groupId` can skip the `groupId` parameter.

10.2.2 *Maven Surefire plugin*

To process the unit tests from our project, Maven uses (of course) a plugin. The Maven plugin that executes the unit tests is called `maven-surefire-plugin`. The Surefire plugin executes the unit tests for our code, but these unit tests are not necessarily JUnit tests.

There are other frameworks for unit testing, and the Surefire plugin can execute their tests, too. The following listing shows the configuration of the Maven Surefire plugin.

Listing 10.5 The Maven Surefire plugin

```
<build>
   <plugins>
      <plugin>
        <artifactId>maven-surefire-plugin</artifactId>
          <version>2.22.2</version>
      </plugin>
   </plugins>
</build>
```

The conventional way to start `maven-surefire-plugin` is very simple: invoke the Maven test phase. This way, Maven first invokes all the phases that are supposed to come before the test phase (validate and compile) and then invokes all the plugins that are attached to the test phase, thus invoking `maven-surefire-plugin`. So by calling

```
mvn clean test
```

Maven first cleans the target/ directory, then compiles the source code and the tests, and finally lets JUnit 5 execute all the tests that are in the src/test/java directory (remember the convention). The output should be similar to figure 10.3.

That's great, but what if we want to execute only a single test case? This execution is unconventional, so we need to configure `maven-surefire-plugin` to do it.

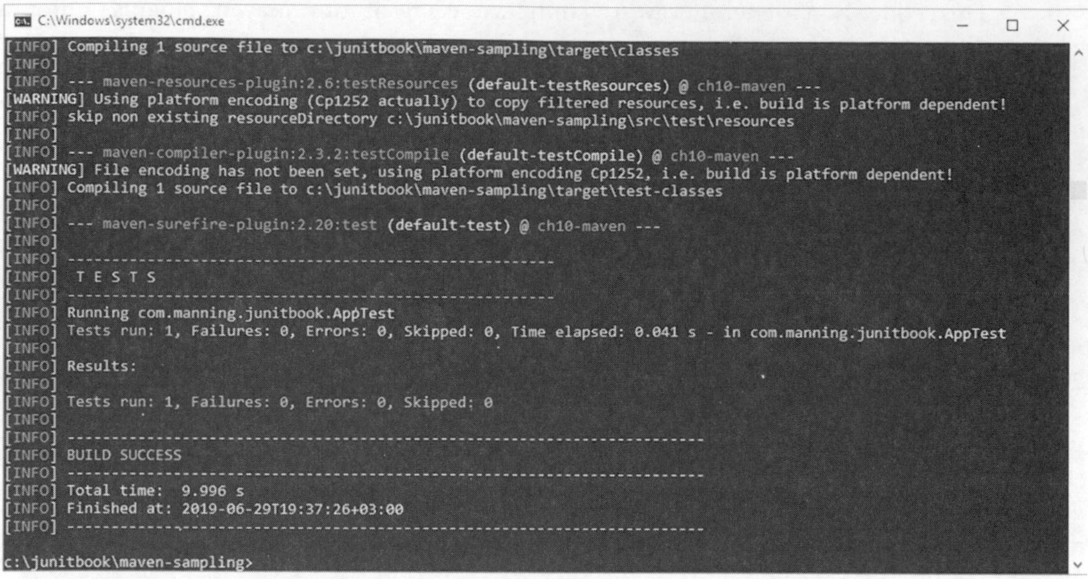

Figure 10.3   Execution of JUnit tests with Maven 3

Ideally, a parameter for the plugin allows us to specify the pattern of test cases that we want to execute. We configure the Surefire plugin in exactly the same way that we configure the compiler plugin.

Listing 10.6   Configuration of `maven-surefire-plugin`

```
<build>
   <plugins>
   [...]
     <plugin>
        <artifactId>maven-surefire-plugin</artifactId>
       <version>2.22.2</version>
        <configuration>
           <includes>**/*Test.java</includes>
        </configuration>
      [...]
     </plugin>
   [...]
   </plugins>
</build>
```

We have specified the `includes` parameter to denote that we want only the test cases matching the given pattern to be executed. But how do we know what parameters `maven-surefire-plugin` accepts? No one knows all the parameters by heart, of course, but we can always consult the `maven-surefire-plugin` documentation (and any other plugin documentation) on the Maven website (http://maven.apache.org).

The next step is generating documentation for the project. But wait a second—how are we supposed to do that with no files to generate the documentation from? This is another one of Maven's great benefits: with a little configuration and description, we can produce a fully functional website skeleton.

First, add the `maven-site-plugin` to the Maven pom.xml configuration file:

```
<plugin>
    <groupId>org.apache.maven.plugins</groupId>
    <artifactId>maven-site-plugin</artifactId>
    <version>3.7.1</version>
</plugin>
```

Then, type

```
mvn site
```

on the command line where the pom.xml file is. Maven should start downloading its plugins; and after their successful installation, it produces the website shown in figure 10.4.

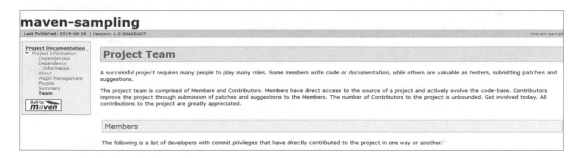

Figure 10.4   Maven produces a website documenting the project.

This website is generated in the Maven build directory—another convention. Maven uses the target/ folder for all the needs of the build itself. The source code is compiled in the target/classes/ folder, and the documentation is generated in target/site/.

Notice that the website is more like a skeleton of a website. Remember that we entered a small amount of data; we could enter more data and web pages in src/site, and Maven would include them on the website, thus generating full-blown documentation.

10.2.3   *Generating HTML JUnit reports with Maven*

Maven can generate reports from the JUnit XML output. Because, by default, Maven produces plain-text and XML-formatted output (by convention, they go in the target/ Surefire-reports/ folder), we do not need any other configuration to produce HTML Surefire reports for the JUnit tests.

As you may already guess, the job of producing these reports is done by a Maven plugin. The name of the plugin is `maven-surefire-report-plugin`, and by default, it is not attached to any of the core phases that we already know. (Many people do not need HTML reports every time they build software.) We can't invoke the plugin by running a certain phase (as we did with both the compiler plugin and the Surefire plugin). Instead, we have to call it directly from the command line:

```
mvn surefire-report:report
```

Maven tries to compile the source files and the test cases, and then it invokes the Surefire plugin to produce the plain-text and XML-formatted output of the tests. After that, the `surefire-report` plugin tries to transform all the XML from the target/ surefire-reports/ directory into an HTML report that will be placed in the target/site directory. (Remember that this is the convention for the folder—to keep all the generated documentation of the project—and that the HTML reports are considered to be documentation.) If we open the generated HTML report, it looks something like figure 10.5.

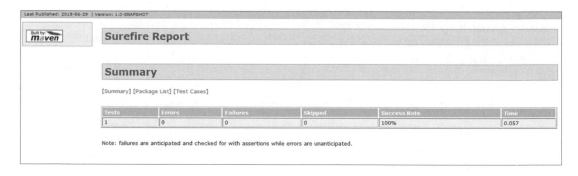

Figure 10.5   HTML report from the `maven-surefire-report` plugin

10.3   *Putting it all together*

This section demonstrates all the steps involved in creating a JUnit 5 project that is managed by Maven. As discussed in chapter 9, one of the projects under development at Tested Data Systems is a flight-management application. To start such an application, George, a project developer, creates the C:\Work\ folder, which will become the working directory and the one where he will set up the Maven project. He types the following on the command line:

```
mvn archetype:generate -DgroupId=com.testeddatasystems.flights
-DartifactId=flightsmanagement -DarchetypeArtifactid=maven-artifact-mojo
```

After pressing Enter and waiting for the appropriate artifacts to be downloaded, George accepts the default options (figure 10.6). Figure 10.7 shows the structure of the project: src/main/java/ is the Maven folder in which the Java code for the project resides, and src/test/java contains the unit tests. The .idea folder and the flightsmanagement.iml file are created by the IDE.

```
C:\WINDOWS\system32\cmd.exe - mvn archetype:generate -Dgroupid=com.testeddatasystems.flights -Dartifactid=flightsmanagement -DarchetypeArtifactid=maven-artifact-mojo    —    □    ×
2525: remote -> us.fatehi:schemacrawler-archetype-plugin-command (-)
2526: remote -> us.fatehi:schemacrawler-archetype-plugin-dbconnector (-)
2527: remote -> us.fatehi:schemacrawler-archetype-plugin-lint (-)
2528: remote -> ws.osiris:osiris-archetype (Maven Archetype for Osiris)
2529: remote -> xyz.luan.generator:xyz-gae-generator (-)
2530: remote -> xyz.luan.generator:xyz-generator (-)
2531: remote -> za.co.absa.hyperdrive:component-archetype (-)
Choose a number or apply filter (format: [groupId:]artifactId, case sensitive contains): 1449:
Choose org.apache.maven.archetypes:maven-archetype-quickstart version:
1: 1.0-alpha-1
2: 1.0-alpha-2
3: 1.0-alpha-3
4: 1.0-alpha-4
5: 1.0
6: 1.1
7: 1.3
8: 1.4
Choose a number: 8:
[INFO] Using property: groupId = com.testeddatasystems.flights
[INFO] Using property: artifactId = flightsmanagement
Define value for property 'version' 1.0-SNAPSHOT: .:
[INFO] Using property: package = com.testeddatasystems.flights
Confirm properties configuration:
groupId: com.testeddatasystems.flights
artifactId: flightsmanagement
version: 1.0-SNAPSHOT
package: com.testeddatasystems.flights
 Y: :
```

Figure 10.6   Creating a Maven 3 project and accepting the default options

Figure 10.7   The newly created flight-management project

George invokes `maven-archetype-plugin` from the command line and tells it to generate a new project from scratch with the given parameters. As a result, the Maven plugin creates a new project with the default folder structure, as well as a sample `App.java` class with the `main` method and a corresponding AppTest.java file that is a unit test for the application. The Maven plugin also generates a pom.xml file, as shown in the next listing.

Listing 10.7   pom.xml for the flight-management project

```
<project xmlns="http://maven.apache.org/POM/4.0.0"
        xmlns:xsi=http://www.w3.org/2001/XMLSchema-instance
        xsi:schemaLocation="http://maven.apache.org/POM/4.0.0
        http://maven.apache.org/maven-v4_0_0.xsd">

  <modelVersion>4.0.0</modelVersion>
  <groupId>com.testeddatasystems.flights</groupId>
  <artifactId>flightsmanagement</artifactId>
  <version>1.0-SNAPSHOT</version>
  <name> flightsmanagement </name>
     [...]
  <dependencies>
    <dependency>
      <groupId>junit</groupId>
      <artifactId>junit</artifactId>
      <version>4.11</version>
      <scope>test</scope>
    </dependency>
  </dependencies>
  [...]
</project>
```

This code is the build descriptor for the project. It includes the `modelVersion` (the version of the model of the POM being used, which currently is 4.0.0), the `groupId` (`com.testeddatasystems.flights`), the `artifactId` (the name by which the project is known—`flightsmanagement` in this case), and the version. `1.0-SNAPSHOT` indicates that the artifact is still in development mode. POM stands for *project object model*; the POM contains information about the project and its configuration, and is the fundamental unit of work in Maven.

George needs to change the version of the JUnit dependency because he is using JUnit Jupiter 5.6.0, and the one that the plugin generated is version 4.11.

Listing 10.8   Changes and additions to pom.xml

```
<dependencies>
    <dependency>
        <groupId>org.junit.jupiter</groupId>
        <artifactId>junit-jupiter-api</artifactId>
        <version>5.6.0</version>
        <scope>test</scope>
    </dependency>
```

```
        <dependency>
            <groupId>org.junit.jupiter</groupId>
            <artifactId>junit-jupiter-engine</artifactId>
            <version>5.6.0</version>
                    <scope>test</scope>
        </dependency>
    </dependencies>
</dependencies>
```

George removes the existing autogenerated App and AppTest classes and instead introduces the two classes that will start his application: Passenger (listing 10.9) and PassengerTest (listing 10.10).

Listing 10.9 Passenger class

```
    package com.testeddatasystems.flights;

public class Passenger {

    private String identifier;          ❶
    private String name;

    public Passenger(String identifier, String name) {
        this.identifier = identifier;   ❷
        this.name = name;
    }

    public String getIdentifier() {
        return identifier;
    }
                                        ❸
    public String getName() {
        return name;
    }

    @Override
    public String toString() {
        return "Passenger " + getName() +
                " with identifier: " + getIdentifier();   ❹
    }
}
```

The Passenger class contains the following:

- Two fields: identifier and name ❶
- A constructor, receiving as arguments identifier and name ❷
- Getters for the identifier and name fields ❸
- The overridden toString method ❹

Listing 10.10 PassengerTest class

```
    package com.testeddatasystems.flights;
[...]}
public class PassengerTest {
```

```
        @Test
        void testPassenger() {
            Passenger passenger =
                            new Passenger("123-456-789", "John Smith");
            assertEquals("Passenger John Smith with identifier:
                        123-456-789",
                        passenger.toString());
        }
    }
```
❶

The `PassengerTest` class contains one test: `testPassenger`, which verifies the output of the overridden `toString` method ❶.

Next, George executes the `mvn clean install` command at the level of the project folder (figure 10.8). This command first cleans the project, removing existing artifacts. Then it compiles the source code of the project, tests the compiled source code (using JUnit 5), packages the compiled code in JAR format (figure 10.9), and installs the package in the local Maven repository (figure 10.10). The local Maven repository is located at ~/.m2/repository/ in UNIX or C:\Documents and Settings\<*UserName*>\.m2\repository\ in Windows.

George has created a fully functional Maven project to develop the flight-management application and test it with JUnit 5. From now on, he can continue to add classes and tests and execute the Maven commands to package the application and run the tests.

```
C:\WINDOWS\system32\cmd.exe                                                           —   □   ×
[INFO] -------------------------------------------------------------
[INFO]  T E S T S
[INFO] -------------------------------------------------------------
[INFO] Running com.testeddatasystems.flights.PassengerTest
[INFO] Tests run: 1, Failures: 0, Errors: 0, Skipped: 0, Time elapsed: 0.091 s - in com.testeddatasystems.flights.Passen
gerTest
[INFO]
[INFO] Results:
[INFO]
[INFO] Tests run: 1, Failures: 0, Errors: 0, Skipped: 0
[INFO]
[INFO]
[INFO] --- maven-jar-plugin:3.0.2:jar (default-jar) @ flightsmanagement ---
[INFO] Building jar: C:\Work\flightsmanagement\target\flightsmanagement-1.0-SNAPSHOT.jar
[INFO]
[INFO] --- maven-install-plugin:2.5.2:install (default-install) @ flightsmanagement ---
[INFO] Installing C:\Work\flightsmanagement\target\flightsmanagement-1.0-SNAPSHOT.jar to C:\Users\ftudose\.m2\repository
\com\testeddatasystems\flights\flightsmanagement\1.0-SNAPSHOT\flightsmanagement-1.0-SNAPSHOT.jar
[INFO] Installing C:\Work\flightsmanagement\pom.xml to C:\Users\ftudose\.m2\repository\com\testeddatasystems\flights\fli
ghtsmanagement\1.0-SNAPSHOT\flightsmanagement-1.0-SNAPSHOT.pom
[INFO] -------------------------------------------------------------
[INFO] BUILD SUCCESS
[INFO] -------------------------------------------------------------
[INFO] Total time:  18.721 s
[INFO] Finished at: 2019-11-15T13:26:44+02:00
[INFO] -------------------------------------------------------------

C:\Work\flightsmanagement>_
```

Figure 10.8   Executing the `mvn clean install` command for the Maven project under development

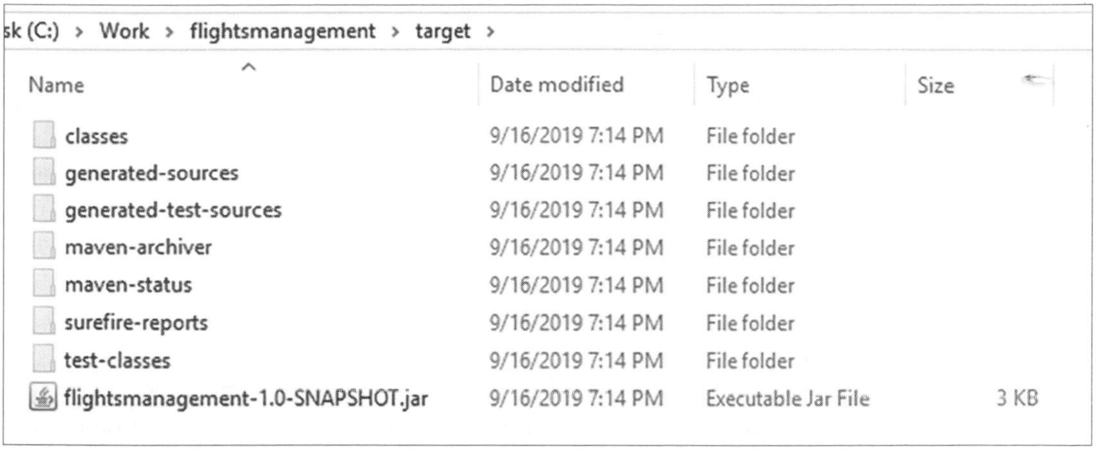

Figure 10.9 The jar-packaged file in the Maven `target` folder of the flight-management project

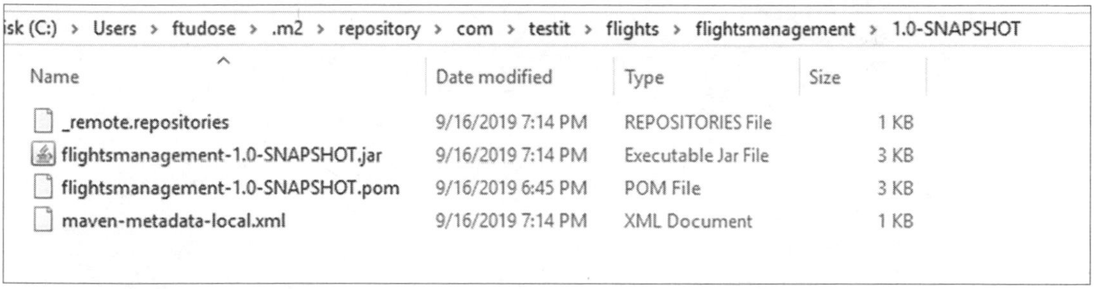

Figure 10.10 The local Maven repository containing the flight-management project's artifacts

10.4 *Maven challenges*

A lot of people who have used Maven agree that it is really easy to start using and that the idea behind the project is amazing. Things are more challenging when you need to do something unconventional, however.

What is great about Maven is that it sets up a frame for you and constrains you to think inside that frame—to think the Maven way and do things the Maven way. In most cases, Maven will not let you execute any nonsense. It restricts you and shows you the way things need to be done. But these restrictions may be a challenge if you are accustomed to doing things your own way and to having freedom of choice as a build engineer. Chapter 11 shows how to run JUnit tests with another build-automation tool inspired by Maven: Gradle.

Summary

This chapter has covered the following:

- A brief introduction to what Maven is and how to use it in a development environment to build your source code
- How to manage the project dependencies in the Maven style by adding them to the pom.xml file in a declarative way
- Creating a Maven project from scratch, opening it in IntelliJ IDEA, and testing it using JUnit 5
- Comparing how to prepare a Maven JUnit 5 project to be used with both Eclipse and IntelliJ IDEA
- Analyzing Maven plugins: using the compiler plugin, the Surefire plugin to process the unit tests from a project, the site plugin to build a site from a project, and the Surefire report plugin to build reports for the project

Running JUnit tests
from Gradle 6

This chapter covers

- Introducing Gradle
- Setting up a Gradle project
- Using Gradle plugins
- Creating a Gradle project from scratch and testing it with JUnit 5
- Comparing Gradle and Maven

Mixing one's wines may be a mistake, but old and new wisdom mix admirably.

—Bertolt Brecht

In this chapter, we will analyze the last part of the world of build system tools. Gradle is an open source build-automation system that started with the concepts of Apache Ant and Apache Maven. Instead of the XML form that Apache Maven uses, as you saw in chapter 10, Gradle introduces a domain-spccific languagc (DSL) based on Groovy for declaring the project configuration.

A DSL is a computer language dedicated to addressing a specific application domain. The idea is to have languages whose purpose is to solve problems belonging to a specific domain. In the case of builds, one of the results of applying the DSL idea is Gradle. Groovy is a Java-syntax-compatible object-oriented programming language that runs on the Java Virtual Machine (JVM).

11.1   Introducing Gradle

We'll take a look at various aspects of using Gradle to manage building and testing Java applications, with a focus on testing. We have worked with Maven, and you know from chapter 10 that it uses convention over configuration. Gradle also has a series of building conventions that we can follow when we do the build. This allows other developers who are also using Gradle to easily follow our build's configuration.

The conventions can easily be overridden. As we have explained, the build language of Gradle is a DSL based on Groovy; this makes it easy for developers to configure builds. The DSL replaces the XML approach promoted by Maven. XML has been used for years to store information. It is not surprising that XML is used to configure build files in Apache Ant and Apache Maven, as discussed in chapter 10. Maven came up with the idea of introducing convention over configuration, which was lacking in Ant. And we have discussed the Maven folder structure, support for dependencies, and build life cycles. Gradle has a declarative build language that expresses the intent of the build—this means you tell it *what* you would like to happen, not *how* you would like it to happen.

The engineers from Tested Data Systems Inc. are considering using Gradle for some of their projects. Consequently, they are weighing its capabilities, applying it to some pilot projects, and trying to differentiate it from other possible alternatives: mainly, Maven.

To get a first impression, the engineers at Tested Data Systems consider a simple Maven pom.xml configuration file (as you have previously seen; listing 11.1) and a simple build.gradle file (the default name of the build descriptor in Gradle; listing 11.2).

Listing 11.1   A simple Maven pom.xml file

```
<project>
    <modelVersion>4.0.0</modelVersion>
    <groupId>com.manning.junitbook</groupId>
    <artifactId>example-pom</artifactId>
    <packaging>jar</packaging>
    <version>1.0-SNAPSHOT</version>
    <dependencies>
        <dependency>
         <groupId>org.junit.jupiter</groupId>
         <artifactId>junit-jupiter-api</artifactId>
         <version>5.6.0</version>
         <scope>test</scope>
        </dependency>
        <dependency>
            <groupId>org.junit.jupiter</groupId>
            <artifactId>junit-jupiter-engine</artifactId>
            <version>5.6.0</version>
```

```
                <scope>test</scope>
            </dependency>
        </dependencies>
</project>
```

Listing 11.2 A simple Gradle build.gradle file

```
plugins {
    // Apply the java plugin to add support for Java
    id 'java'

    // Apply the application plugin to support building a CLI application
    id 'application'
}

repositories {
    // Use jcenter for resolving dependencies.
    // You can declare any Maven/Ivy/file repository here.
    jcenter()
}

dependencies {
    // Use JUnit Jupiter API for testing.
    testImplementation 'org.junit.jupiter:junit-jupiter-api:5.6.0'

    // Use JUnit Jupiter Engine for testing.
    testRuntimeOnly 'org.junit.jupiter:junit-jupiter-engine:5.6.0'
}

application {
    // Define the main class for the application
    mainClassName = 'com.manning.junitbook.ch11.App'
}

test {
    // Use junit platform for unit tests
    useJUnitPlatform()
}
```

You may be looking at this build.gradle configuration file and wondering what is happening in it. Its purpose is to give you a first taste of the way Gradle works. We'll get into details in this chapter. Additionally, many comments explain what is happening. The DSL approach, one of Gradle's strengths, is largely self-explanatory and relatively easy to maintain and manage. For the Gradle installation procedure and a brief explanation of its central concepts, see appendix B.

11.2 Setting up a Gradle project

It is time now for the engineers at Tested Data Systems to move on in their consideration of using Gradle for some of their projects by creating JUnit 5 pilot projects with Gradle. Oliver is involved in developing such a pilot project. He creates a new folder called junit5withgradle, opens a command prompt, and executes the gradle init command.

Then, he chooses the following options:

- Select Type of Project to Generate: Application
- Select Implementation Language: Java
- Select Build Script DSL: Groovy
- Select Test Framework: JUnit Jupiter

The result is shown in figure 11.1.

```
C:\Windows\system32\cmd.exe
C:\Work\Manning\junit5withgradle>gradle init

Select type of project to generate:
  1: basic
  2: application
  3: library
  4: Gradle plugin
Enter selection (default: basic) [1..4] 2

Select implementation language:
  1: C++
  2: Groovy
  3: Java
  4: Kotlin
Enter selection (default: Java) [1..4] 3

Select build script DSL:
  1: Groovy
  2: Kotlin
Enter selection (default: Groovy) [1..2] 1

Select test framework:
  1: JUnit 4
  2: TestNG
  3: Spock
  4: JUnit Jupiter
Enter selection (default: JUnit 4) [1..4] 4

Project name (default: junit5withgradle):

Source package (default: junit5withgradle): com.manning.junitbook.ch11


> Task :init
Get more help with your project: https://docs.gradle.org/5.5.1/userguide/tutorial_java_projects.html

BUILD SUCCESSFUL in 31s
2 actionable tasks: 2 executed
```

Figure 11.1   **The result of executing the `gradle init` command**

Because Oliver has initialized a new Java project with Gradle and chosen a few options, Gradle creates the project's folder structure, which follows Maven's structure:

- src/main/java contains the Java source code.
- src/test/java contains the Java tests.

To start the build, Oliver types `gradle build` at the command-line prompt, in the folder that contains the build.gradle file and the project that has just been created.

We'll now take a look at the build.gradle file that is created, explain its content, and demonstrate how Oliver can extend it.

> **Listing 11.3   Defining repositories in the build.gradle file**

```
repositories {
    // Use jcenter for resolving dependencies.
    // You can declare any Maven/Ivy/file repository here.
    jcenter()
}
```

By default, Gradle uses JCenter as the repository for the applications it manages. JCenter is the largest Java repository in the world. This means whatever is available on Maven Central is available on JCenter as well. Of course, we can specify that the Maven Central repository, our own repository, or multiple repositories should be used. The following listing shows that Oliver has chosen to use the Maven Central repository and the repository from Tested Data Systems, which allows access to proprietary dependencies.

> **Listing 11.4   Defining two repositories in the build.gradle file**

```
repositories {
    mavenCentral()

    testit {
     url "https://testeddatasystems.com/repository"
    }
}
```

Based on the options Oliver provides, Gradle adds some dependencies to the build.gradle file configuration.

> **Listing 11.5   Defining dependencies in the build.gradle file**

```
dependencies {
    // This dependency is used by the application.
    implementation 'com.google.guava:guava:27.1-jre'

    // Use JUnit Jupiter API for testing.
    testImplementation 'org.junit.jupiter:junit-jupiter-api:5.6.0'

    // Use JUnit Jupiter Engine for testing.
    testRuntimeOnly 'org.junit.jupiter:junit-jupiter-engine:5.6.0'
}
```

The dependency configuration declares the external dependencies that we would like to be downloaded from the repository or repositories in use. It defines the standard configurations listed in table 11.1.

Table 11.1   Standard dependency configurations and their meaning

Standard configuration	Meaning
`implementation`	The dependencies are required to compile the production source of the project.
`runtime`	The production classes require the dependencies at runtime. By default, the configuration also includes the compile-time dependencies.
`testImplementation`	The dependencies are required to compile the test source of the project. By default, the configuration includes compiled production classes and the compile-time dependencies.
`testRuntime`	The dependencies are required to run the tests. By default, the configuration includes runtime and test compile time dependencies.
`runtimeOnly`	The dependencies are required only at runtime, not at compile time.
`testRuntimeOnly`	The dependencies are required only at test runtime, not at test compile time.

Based on the option to create an application that Oliver provides, Gradle also adds the following configuration.

Listing 11.6   Configuring the main class of the application in the build.gradle file

```
application {
    // Define the main class for the application
    mainClassName = 'com.manning.junitbook.ch11.App'
}
```

This defines `com.manning.junitbook.ch11.App` as the main class of the application—the execution entry point.

The code in the next listing enables JUnit Platform support in build.gradle. More exactly, it specifies that JUnit Platform should be used to execute the tests—remember that we were allowed to choose among a few platforms when Gradle created the project for us.

Listing 11.7   Enabling JUnit Platform support in the build.gradle file

```
test {
    // Use junit platform for unit tests
    useJUnitPlatform()
}
```

`useJUnitPlatform` can take additional options. For example, we can specify tags to be included or excluded when the tests are executed. The configuration looks something like this.

Listing 11.8 Including and excluding tags to be executed in build.gradle

```
test {
    // Use junit platform for unit tests
    useJUnitPlatform {
        includeTags 'individual'
        excludeTags 'repository'
    }
}
```

These options mean the tests tagged by JUnit 5 as `'individual'` will be executed by Gradle, whereas tests tagged as `'repository'` will be excluded.

Listing 11.9 Gradle selectively executing differently tagged tests

```
@Tag("individual")
public class CustomerTest {
...
}

@Tag("repository")
public class CustomersRepositoryTest {
...
}
```

When Gradle creates a project, it also creates a *wrapper*. This wrapper represents a script that invokes a declared Gradle version, first downloading it if it is not available. The script is contained in the gradlew.bat or gradlew file (depending on the operating system). If you build a project and distribute it to your customers, they will quickly be able to run that project without any manual installation and with the certainty that they will be using exactly the same Gradle version used to create the project.

We can create reports concerning the execution of the tests. When running the `gradle test` command (or `gradlew test`, if we use the wrapper), a report is created in the build/reports/tests/test folder. Accessing the index.html file, we get the report shown in figure 11.2. We have included in our project the tagged tests introduced in chapter 2 and executed them through Gradle, including the individual tests and excluding the repository tests, as described in the build.gradle file.

At the time of writing, there are some known limitations regarding using JUnit 5 with Gradle: classes and tests are still displayed using their names instead of `@DisplayName`. This should be fixed in future releases of Gradle.

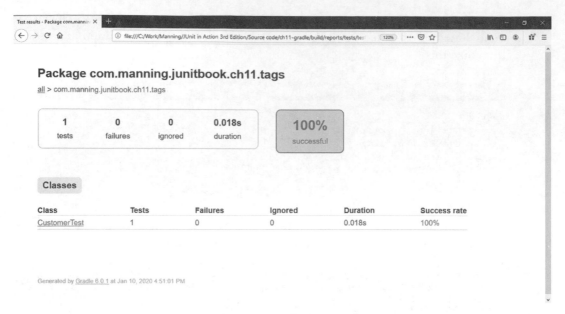

Figure 11.2   The report generated by Gradle includes the execution of `CustomerTest`, **tagged as** `'individual'`.

11.3   *Using Gradle plugins*

So far, so good—we have seen what Gradle is and how Oliver has used it to start a pilot project at Tested Data Systems from scratch. We have also seen how Gradle is able to manage dependencies by using a DSL.

Oliver would like to add plugins to his project. A Gradle plugin is a set of tasks. A lot of common tasks, such as compiling and setting up source files, are handled by plugins. Applying a plugin to a project means you allow the plugin to extend the project's capabilities.

There are two types of plugins in Gradle: script plugins and binary plugins. Script plugins represent tasks that are defined and can be applied from a script on the local filesystem or at a remote location. Of particular interest for us as Java developers using JUnit 5 are the binary plugins. Each binary plugin is identified by an ID: the core plugins use short names to be applied.

In the following listing, Oliver applies two plugins to the build.gradle file.

Listing 11.10   Applying plugins to the build.gradle file

```
plugins {
    // Apply the java plugin to add support for Java
    id 'java'

    // Apply the application plugin to add support for building a CLI
     application
    id 'application'
}
```

In this listing:

- Oliver applies the Java plugin to add support for the programming language—remember that during initialization with the `gradle init` command, Oliver chose Java as the language, and Gradle has added the needed support.
- He chooses "application" as the type of project to generate and adds the plugin that supports building a CLI application.

If we compare the code in listings 11.3–11.10, we get Oliver's Gradle configuration file from listing 11.2.

11.4 Creating a Gradle project from scratch and testing it with JUnit 5

We'll now demonstrate all the steps necessary to create a JUnit 5 project that is managed by Gradle. As we have discussed previously, one of the projects under development at Tested Data Systems is a flight-management application. In order to start such an application, Oliver, the project developer, creates the C:\Work\flightsmanagement folder that will become the working directory and where he will set up the Gradle project. He types the following on the command line:

```
gradle init
```

The result of running this command is shown in figure 11.3.

```
Select type of project to generate:
  1: basic
  2: application
  3: library
  4: Gradle plugin
Enter selection (default: basic) [1..4] 2

Select implementation language:
  1: C++
  2: Groovy
  3: Java
  4: Kotlin
Enter selection (default: Java) [1..4] 3

Select build script DSL:
  1: Groovy
  2: Kotlin
Enter selection (default: Groovy) [1..2] 1

Select test framework:
  1: JUnit 4
  2: TestNG
  3: Spock
  4: JUnit Jupiter
Enter selection (default: JUnit 4) [1..4] 4

Project name (default: flightsmanagement):
Source package (default: flightsmanagement): com.testeddatasystems.flightsmanagement
```

Figure 11.3 The result of executing the `gradle init` command to create the flight-management application

The structure of the project is shown in figure 11.4. src/main/java/ is the Gradle folder where the Java code for the project resides, and src/test/java contains the unit tests. The .idea folder is created by the IDE.

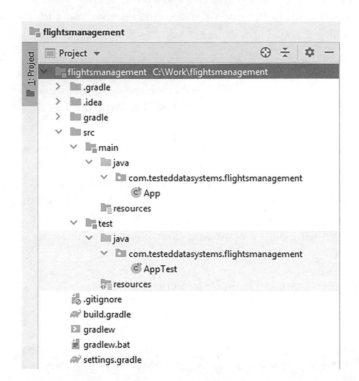

Figure 11.4   The newly created flight-management project

Executing the `gradle init` command also generates a build.gradle file.

Listing 11.11   build.gradle file for the flight-management application

```
plugins {
    // Apply the java plugin to add support for Java
    id 'java'

    // Apply the application plugin to add support for building a CLI appli-
      cation
    id 'application'
}

repositories {
    // Use jcenter for resolving dependencies.
    // You can declare any Maven/Ivy/file repository here.
    jcenter()
}
```

```
dependencies {
    // Use JUnit Jupiter API for testing.
    testImplementation 'org.junit.jupiter:junit-jupiter-api:5.6.0'

    // Use JUnit Jupiter Engine for testing.
    testRuntimeOnly 'org.junit.jupiter:junit-jupiter-engine:5.6.0'
}

application {
    // Define the main class for the application
    mainClassName = 'com.testeddatasystems.flightsmanagement.App'
}

test {
    // Use junit platform for unit tests
    useJUnitPlatform()
}
```

Oliver removes the existing autogenerated `App` and `AppTest` classes. He adds the two classes that will start his application: `Passenger` (listing 11.12) and `PassengerTest` (listing 11.13).

Listing 11.12　Passenger class

```
package com.testeddatasystems.flights;

public class Passenger {

    private String identifier;            ❶
    private String name;

    public Passenger(String identifier, String name) {
        this.identifier = identifier;     ❷
        this.name = name;
    }

    public String getIdentifier() {
        return identifier;
    }                                     ❸

    public String getName() {
        return name;
    }

    @Override
    public String toString() {
        return "Passenger " + getName() +      ❹
                " with identifier: " + getIdentifier();
    }

    public static void main (String args[]) {
        Passenger passenger = new Passenger("123-456-789", "John Smith");  ❺
        System.out.println(passenger);
    }

}
```

The Passenger class contains the following:

- Two fields, identifier and name ❶
- A constructor receiving as arguments identifier and name ❷
- Getters for the identifier and name fields ❸
- The overridden toString method ❹
- The main method will create and display a passenger ❺.

Listing 11.13   The PassengerTest class

```
package com.testeddatasystems.flights;
[...]

public class PassengerTest {

    @Test
    void testPassenger() {
        Passenger passenger = new Passenger("123-456-789",
                                            "John Smith");
        assertEquals("Passenger John Smith with identifier:
                    123-456-789",
                    passenger.toString());
    }
}
```
❶

The PassengerTest class contains one test: testPassenger, which verifies the output of the overridden toString method ❶.

In the build.gradle file, Oliver changes the main class to

```
application {
    // Define the main class for the application
    mainClassName = 'com.testeddatasystems.flightsmanagement.Passenger'
}
```

He then executes the gradle test command at the level of the project folder. This command simply runs the JUnit 5 test introduced in the application (figure 11.5).

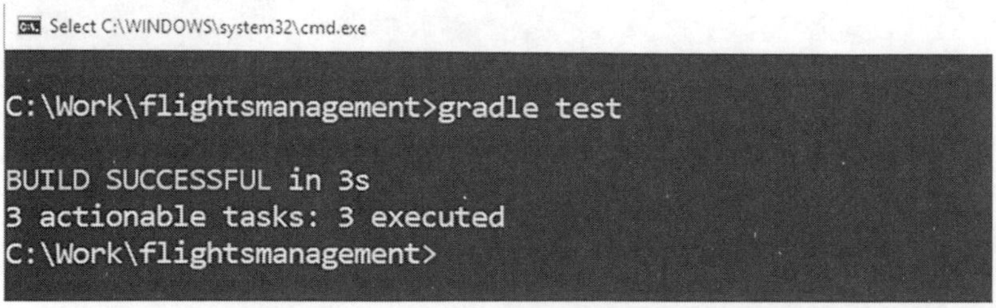

Figure 11.5   Executing the gradle test command for the Gradle project under development

Next, Oliver executes the `gradle run` command at the level of the project folder. This command runs the main class of the application, as described in the build.gradle file, and displays the information about passenger John Smith (figure 11.6). Running the `gradle build` command at the level of the project folder (figure 11.7) also creates the jar artifact in the build/libs folder (figure 11.8).

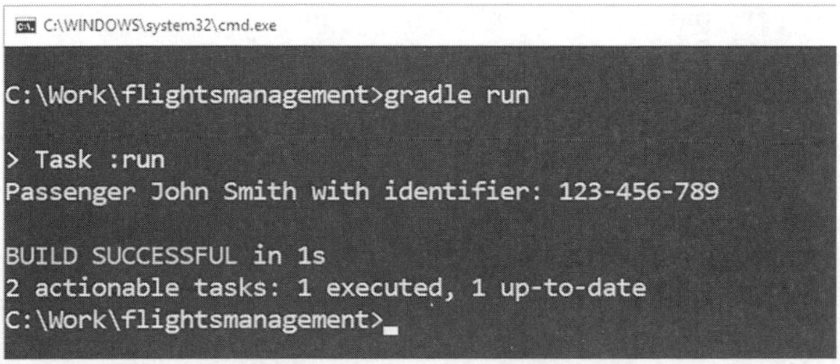

```
C:\WINDOWS\system32\cmd.exe

C:\Work\flightsmanagement>gradle run

> Task :run
Passenger John Smith with identifier: 123-456-789

BUILD SUCCESSFUL in 1s
2 actionable tasks: 1 executed, 1 up-to-date
C:\Work\flightsmanagement>
```

Figure 11.6   Executing the `gradle run` command

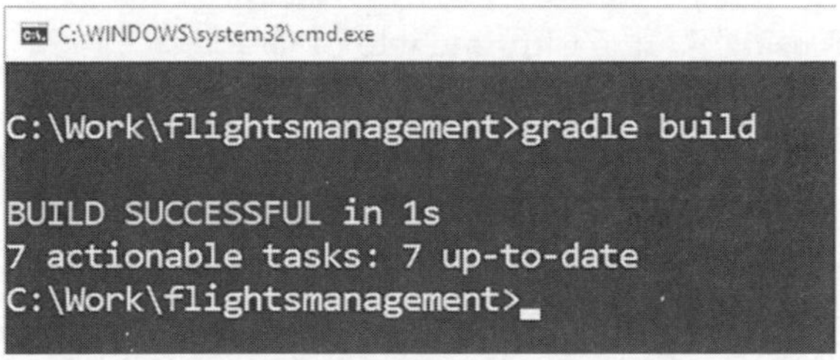

```
C:\WINDOWS\system32\cmd.exe

C:\Work\flightsmanagement>gradle build

BUILD SUCCESSFUL in 1s
7 actionable tasks: 7 up-to-date
C:\Work\flightsmanagement>
```

Figure 11.7   Executing the `gradle build` command

· Local Disk (C:) > Work > flightsmanagement > build > libs

Name	Date modified	Type	Size
📦 flightsmanagement.jar	11/15/2019 2:28 PM	Executable Jar File	2 KB

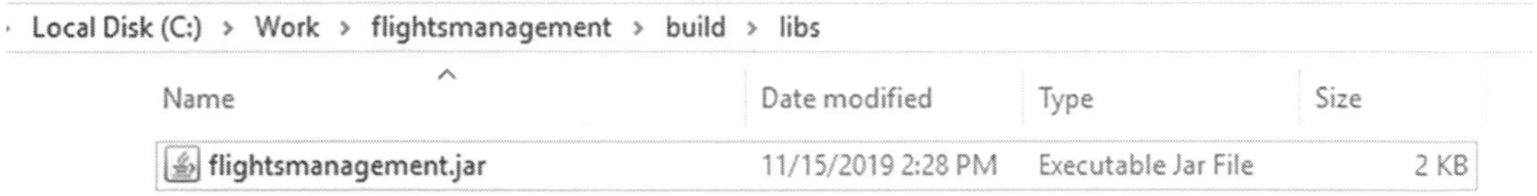

Figure 11.8   The jar file in the Gradle build/libs folder

At this time, Oliver has created a fully functional Gradle project to develop the flight-management application and test it using JUnit 5. From now on, he can continue to add new classes and tests and execute the Gradle commands to package the application and run the tests.

11.5   *Comparing Gradle and Maven*

We have now used and compared two build tools that will help us manage our JUnit 5 projects. The engineers at Tested Data Systems have some freedom of choice: some projects may use Maven, as it is an older and reliable tool that most of them know well. For other projects, they may decide to adopt Gradle: if they need to write custom tasks (which is harder to do with Maven), if they consider XML tedious and prefer to use a DSL that is close to Java, or if they are challenged to adopt something new. The choice may be a matter of personal or project preference—and it may be the same for you. In general, once you master one of these two build tools, joining a project that uses the other is not difficult.

We have mentioned that, at least of the time of writing, there are some known issues when using JUnit 5 with Gradle: classes and tests are still displayed with their names instead of @DisplayName. This is expected to be solved in future releases.

We should mention that projects at the global level still predominantly use Maven—about three-quarters of them, according to our research. In addition, the numbers are quite stable: Gradle hasn't advanced much in the market over the years. This is why, in this book, we mostly use Maven.

Summary

This chapter has covered the following:

- Creating a Java project using JUnit 5 with the help of Gradle
- Introduction to Gradle plugins
- Creating a Gradle project from scratch, opening it in IntelliJ IDEA, and testing it using JUnit 5
- Comparing Gradle and Maven as build tool alternatives

JUnit 5 IDE support

Enjoy the little things, for one day you may look back and realize they were the big things.

—Robert Brault

In this chapter, we will analyze and compare the leading IDEs that can be used to develop Java applications tested with the help of JUnit 5. An integrated development environment (IDE) is an application that provides software development facilities for computer programmers. Java IDEs are tools that let us write and debug Java programs more easily.

Many IDEs have been created to help Java developers. Of these, we have selected three of the most popular to analyze and compare: IntelliJ IDEA, Eclipse, and NetBeans. At the time of writing this chapter, IntelliJ IDEA and Eclipse each had about 40% of the market share. NetBeans had about 10%; we are including it in our analysis because it is the third option overall and particularly popular in some regions of the world.

Which of the possible IDEs you choose may be a matter of personal preference or project tradition. All of them may be used in the same company or even the same project. In fact, this is the case for our example company, Tested Data Systems Inc. We'll point out the reasons that determined which options the developers chose.

Our analysis and demonstration will focus on the capabilities of these IDEs using JUnit 5—the just-in-time information that you need now. For more comprehensive guidance, there are many other available sources, starting with the official documentation of each of the IDEs. We'll demonstrate using JUnit 5 with IntelliJ IDEA, then Eclipse, and finally NetBeans, as this is the order in which they were integrated with JUnit 5.

12.1 *Using JUnit 5 with IntelliJ IDEA*

IntelliJ IDEA is an IDE developed by JetBrains. It is available as an Apache 2 licensed community edition and in a proprietary commercial edition. For brief IntelliJ IDEA installation instructions, see appendix C.

We will demonstrate JUnit 5 in different IDEs using a selection of tests from chapter 2. Those tests covered the capabilities of JUnit 5 comprehensively, and we have chosen the ones that are significant in the context of an IDE. You can review the new JUnit 5 features and their use cases in chapter 2. Here, we are most interested in JUnit 5 within each IDE, but we'll briefly remind you in each case why you would use that particular feature.

Launch IntelliJ IDEA, and then open a project by choosing File > Open. When you open the project from this chapter's source code, the IDE will look as shown in figure 12.1. The project contains the tests that demonstrate JUnit 5's new features: capabilities such as displaying names and nested, parameterized, repeated, and dynamic tests using tags.

From here, you can execute all tests by right-clicking the highlighted test/java folder and then choosing Run > All Tests. You will get a result like that shown in figure 12.2. You will probably want to run all of the tests periodically while you are working on the implementation of a particular feature, to make sure the full project is working correctly and that your implementation does not affect the previously existing functionality.

Let's have a look at how to run particular test types with the help of IntelliJ IDEA. In figure 12.2, disabled tests are shown in gray, and they are marked as "ignored" after executing the whole suite. You can, however, force the execution of a particular test, even if it is disabled, by right-clicking it and running it directly, as shown in figure 12.3. You may want to do that occasionally to check whether the conditions that prevented the correct execution of that test have ceased to exist. For example, your test may wait for the implementation of a feature by a different team or for the availability of a resource, and you can verify fulfillment.

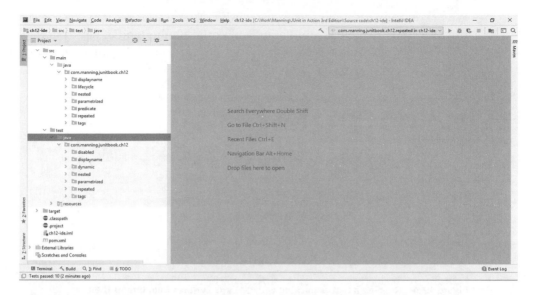

Figure 12.1 IntelliJ IDEA with an open JUnit 5 project

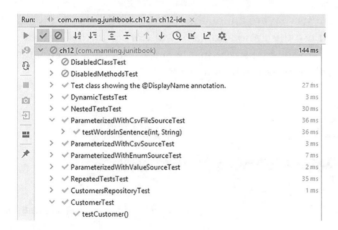

Figure 12.2 Executing all of the tests from inside IntelliJ IDEA

Figure 12.3 Forcing the execution of a disabled test from IntelliJ

When you run tests that are annotated with @DisplayName, they are shown as in figure 12.4. You will use this annotation and work with this kind of test from IntelliJ IDEA when you want to watch some significant information while you are developing from the IDE. We discussed this annotation in chapter 2.

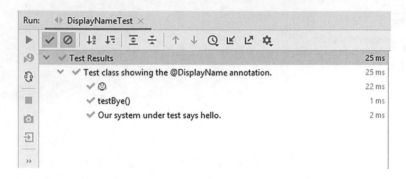

Figure 12.4   Running a test annotated with @DisplayName from IntelliJ IDEA

When you run dynamic tests that are annotated with @TestFactory, they are shown as in figure 12.5. You will use this annotation and will work with this kind of test from IntelliJ IDEA when you want to write a reasonable amount of code to generate tests at runtime. We discussed this annotation in chapter 2.

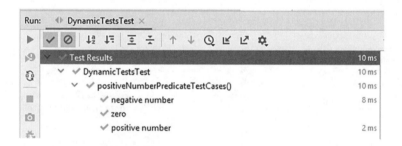

Figure 12.5   Running a dynamic test from IntelliJ IDEA

When you run nested tests, they are shown hierarchically, as in figure 12.6, where we have also taken advantage of the @DisplayName annotation's capabilities. You can use nested tests to express the relationships among several groups of tests that are tightly coupled; IntelliJ IDEA will display the hierarchy. We discussed the @Nested annotation in chapter 2.

When you run parameterized tests, they are displayed in detail, showing all of their parameters, as in figure 12.7. You can use parameterized tests to write a single test and then perform the testing using a series of different arguments. We discussed the annotation related to parameterized tests in chapter 2.

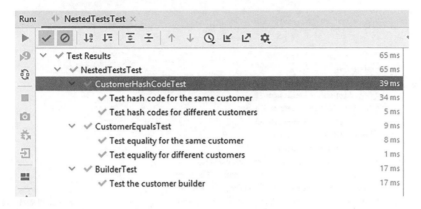

Figure 12.6   Running nested tests from IntelliJ IDEA

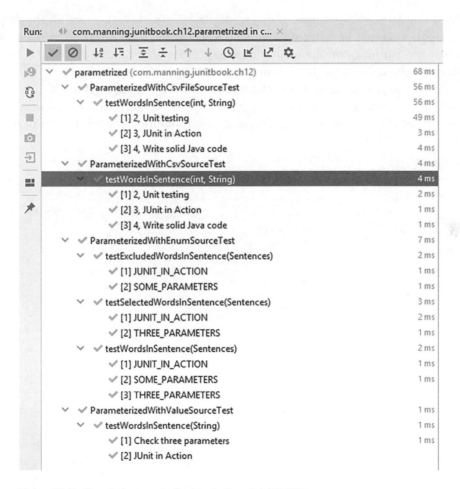

Figure 12.7   Running parameterized tests from IntelliJ IDEA

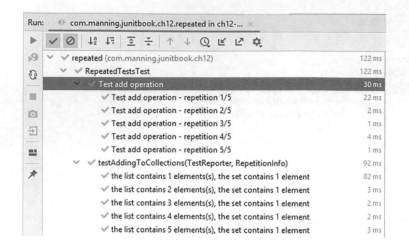

Figure 12.8   Running repeated tests from IntelliJ IDEA

When you run repeated tests, they are displayed in detail, showing all the required information about the currently repeated test, as in figure 12.8. You can use repeated tests if the running conditions may change from one test execution to the next. We discussed the `@RepeatedTest` annotation in chapter 2.

When you run the entire test suite from IntelliJ IDEA, the tagged tests are also run. If you want to run only particular tagged tests, choose Run > Edit Configurations and select from the Test Kind > Tags list, as shown in figure 12.9. You need to create the

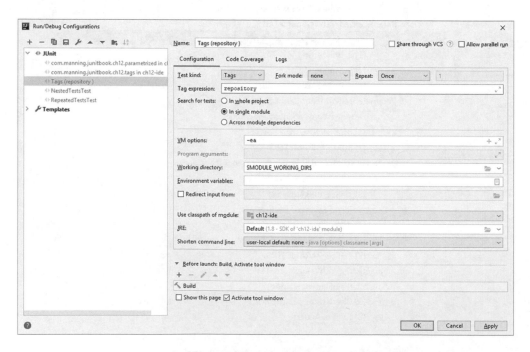

Figure 12.9   Configuring the option of running only tagged tests from IntelliJ IDEA

configuration by hand and execute it. Then you will be able to run only those particular tagged tests' configurations. You'll want to do this when you have a larger suite of tests and need to focus on particular tests rather than spend time with the entire suite. We discussed the @Tag annotation in chapter 2.

IntelliJ IDEA also makes it easy to run tests with code coverage. If you right-click the test or suite you want to run and choose Run with Coverage, you will see a table like that in figure 12.10. You can investigate at the class level and get information, as shown in figure 12.11. Or you can click the Generate Coverage Report button and obtain an HTML report, as in figure 12.12.

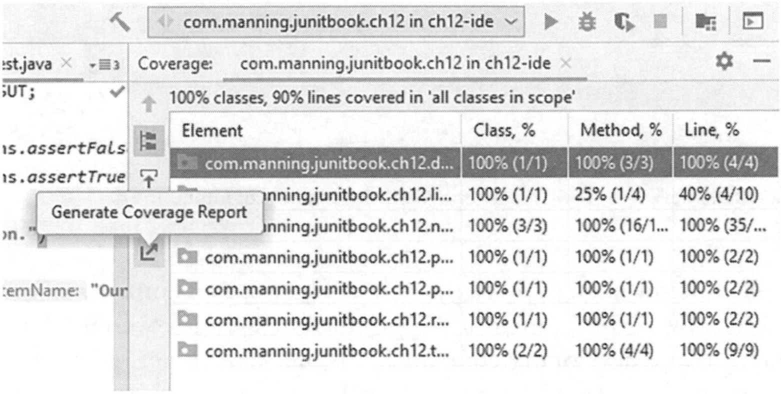

Figure 12.10 The table produced by IntelliJ IDEA after choosing Run with Coverage

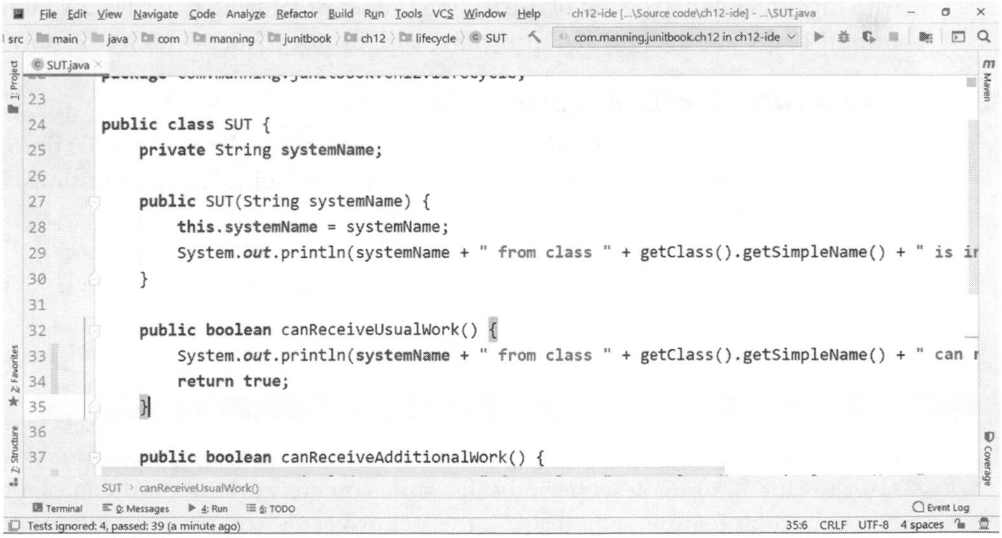

Figure 12.11 Code coverage at the individual class level

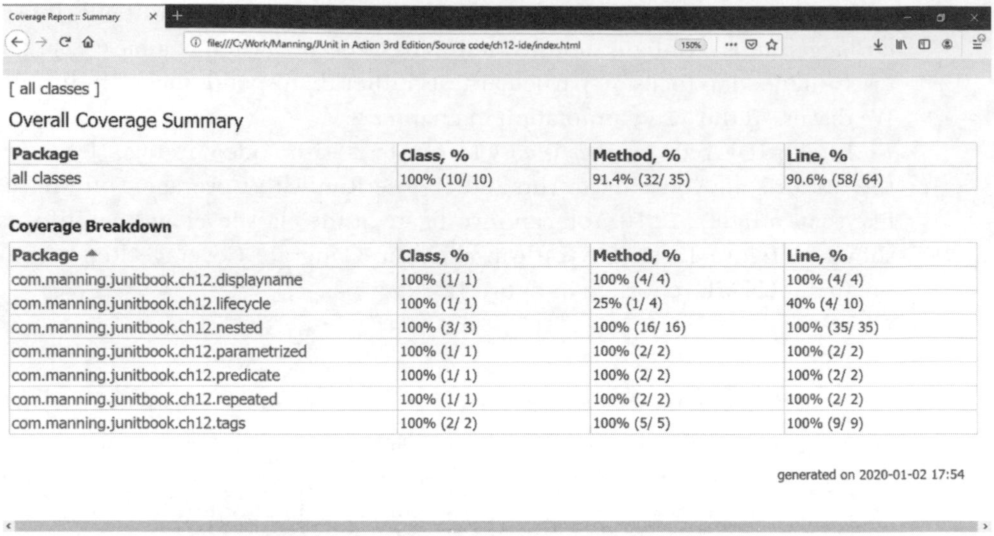

Package	Class, %	Method, %	Line, %
all classes	100% (10/ 10)	91.4% (32/ 35)	90.6% (58/ 64)

Coverage Breakdown

Package ▲	Class, %	Method, %	Line, %
com.manning.junitbook.ch12.displayname	100% (1/ 1)	100% (4/ 4)	100% (4/ 4)
com.manning.junitbook.ch12.lifecycle	100% (1/ 1)	25% (1/ 4)	40% (4/ 10)
com.manning.junitbook.ch12.nested	100% (3/ 3)	100% (16/ 16)	100% (35/ 35)
com.manning.junitbook.ch12.parametrized	100% (1/ 1)	100% (2/ 2)	100% (2/ 2)
com.manning.junitbook.ch12.predicate	100% (1/ 1)	100% (2/ 2)	100% (2/ 2)
com.manning.junitbook.ch12.repeated	100% (1/ 1)	100% (2/ 2)	100% (2/ 2)
com.manning.junitbook.ch12.tags	100% (2/ 2)	100% (5/ 5)	100% (9/ 9)

generated on 2020-01-02 17:54

Figure 12.12 Code coverage HTML report obtained with the help of IntelliJ IDEA

We discussed code coverage in more detail in chapter 6. Remember that it is a metric of test quality, showing how much of the production code is covered by the tests we are executing. While developing code and tests, we want to get quick feedback not only about whether the tests run successfully but also about their coverage. IntelliJ IDEA strongly supports both goals.

At Tested Data Systems, the developers who have decided to use IntelliJ for their projects are not only those who were using it before moving to JUnit 5, but also those who introduced this version of the testing framework during its early days. At that time, IntelliJ IDEA was the only IDE providing support for JUnit 5—it was the only option.

12.2 Using JUnit 5 with Eclipse

Eclipse is an IDE written mostly in Java. It can be used to develop applications in many programming languages, but its primary use is developing Java applications. For brief Eclipse installation instructions, see appendix C.

We'll walk through a demonstration similar to the one for IntelliJ IDEA: we selected tests from chapter 2 that are significant in the context of usage from inside an IDE. Launch Eclipse, import a project by selecting File > Import > General > Existing Projects into Workspace, and then choose the folder where the project is located. The IDE will look as shown in figure 12.13.

From here, you can execute all of the tests by right-clicking the project and choosing Run As > JUnit Test. You will see a result like that in figure 12.14. You will probably want to run all of the tests periodically while you are working on the implementation of a particular feature, to make sure the full project is working correctly and that your implementation does not affect the previously existing functionality.

Figure 12.13   Eclipse with an open JUnit 5 project

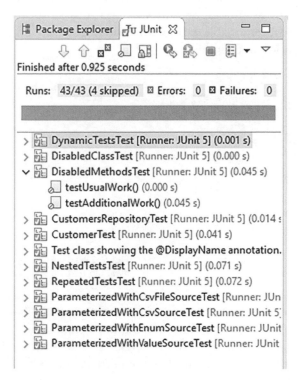

Figure 12.14   Executing all tests from inside Eclipse

Let's have a look at how to run particular test types with the help of Eclipse. In figure 12.14, disabled tests are shown in gray, and they are marked as "skipped" after executing the whole suite. In contrast to the capabilities of IntelliJ IDEA, you cannot force the execution of a particular disabled test.

When you run tests that are annotated with @DisplayName, they are shown as in figure 12.15. You will use this annotation and work with this kind of test from Eclipse when you want to watch some significant information while developing from the IDE. We discussed this annotation in chapter 2.

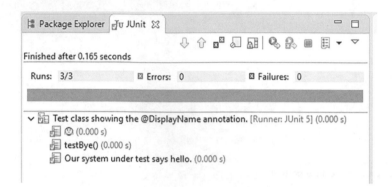

Figure 12.15   Running a test annotated with @DisplayName from Eclipse

When you run dynamic tests that are annotated with @TestFactory, they are shown as in figure 12.16. You can use this annotation and work with this kind of test from Eclipse when you want to write a reasonable amount of code to generate tests at runtime. We discussed this annotation in chapter 2.

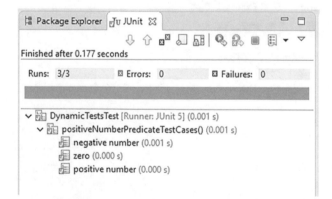

Figure 12.16   Running a dynamic test from Eclipse

When you run nested tests, they are shown hierarchically, as in figure 12.17, where we have also taken advantage of the @DisplayName annotation's capabilities. You can use nested tests to express the relationships among several groups of tests that are tightly coupled; Eclipse will display the hierarchy. We discussed @Nested in chapter 2.

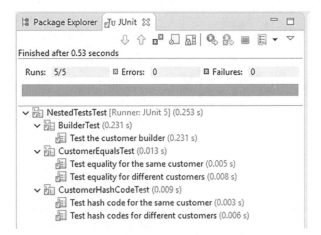

Figure 12.17 Running nested tests from Eclipse

When you run parameterized tests, they are displayed in detail, showing their parameters, as in figure 12.18. You can use parameterized tests to write a single test and then perform the testing using a series of different arguments. We discussed the annotation for parameterized tests in chapter 2.

Figure 12.18 Running parameterized tests from Eclipse

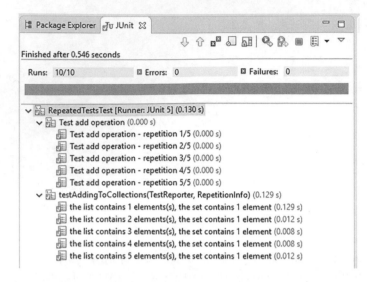

When you run repeated tests, they are displayed in detail, showing all the required information about the currently repeated test, as in figure 12.19. You can use repeated tests if running conditions may change from one test execution to the next. We discussed the `@RepeatedTest` annotation in chapter 2.

Figure 12.19   **Running repeated tests from Eclipse**

When you run the entire test suite from Eclipse, the tagged tests are also run. If you want to run only particular tagged tests, choose Run > Run Configurations > JUnit and select from Include Tags and Exclude Tags, as shown in figure 12.20.

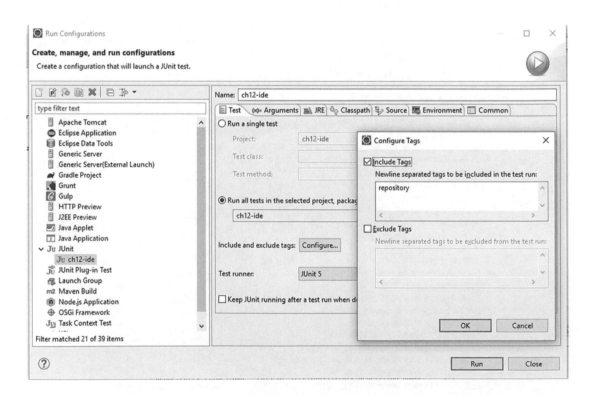

Figure 12.20   **Configuring the option to run only tagged tests from Eclipse**

Then you can run the configuration that only addresses tagged tests. You will do this when you have a larger suite of tests and need to focus on particular tests rather than spend time with the entire suite. We discussed the @Tag annotation in chapter 2.

Eclipse also makes it easy to run tests with code coverage. If you right-click the project, test, or suite to be run, and then choose Coverage As > JUnit Test, you will see a table like the one shown in figure 12.21. You can investigate at the individual class level and get information like that in figure 12.22. Or you can right-click the Coverage table, choose Export Session, and obtain an HTML report, as in figure 12.23.

Problems @ Javadoc Declaration Search Console Coverage ⊠ Gradle Tasks Gradle Executions

Element	Coverage	Covered Instructio...	Missed Instructions	Total Instructions
∨ ⌂ ch12-ide	88.9 %	776	97	873
∨ 🗁 src/main/java	81.0 %	255	60	315
∨ ⊞ com.manning.junitbook.ch12.lifecycle	28.2 %	22	56	78
> ⒥ SUT.java	28.2 %	22	56	78
∨ ⊞ com.manning.junitbook.ch12.nested	97.6 %	165	4	169
> ⒥ Customer.java	97.2 %	141	4	145
> ⒥ Gender.java	100.0 %	24	0	24
> ⊞ com.manning.junitbook.ch12.displayname	100.0 %	9	0	9
> ⊞ com.manning.junitbook.ch12.parametrized	100.0 %	8	0	8
> ⊞ com.manning.junitbook.ch12.predicate	100.0 %	9	0	9
> ⊞ com.manning.junitbook.ch12.repeated	100.0 %	7	0	7
> ⊞ com.manning.junitbook.ch12.tags	100.0 %	35	0	35
> 🗁 src/test/java	93.4 %	521	37	558

Figure 12.21 The table produced by Eclipse after running Coverage As > JUnit Test

```
⒥ SUT.java ⊠
 4⊕ " Licensed to the Apache Software Foundation (ASF) under one or more□
21
22  package com.manning.junitbook.ch12.lifecycle;
23
24  public class SUT {
25      private String systemName;
26
27⊝    public SUT(String systemName) {
28          this.systemName = systemName;
29          System.out.println(systemName + " from class " + getClass().getSimpleName() + " is initializing.");
30      }
31
32⊝    public boolean canReceiveUsualWork() {
33          System.out.println(systemName + " from class " + getClass().getSimpleName() + " can receive usual work.");
34          return true;
35      }
36
37⊝    public boolean canReceiveAdditionalWork() {
38          System.out.println(systemName + " from class " + getClass().getSimpleName() + " cannot receive additional work.");
39          return false;
40      }
41
42⊝    public void close() {
43          System.out.println(systemName + " from class " + getClass().getSimpleName() + " is closing.");
44      }
45
46
47  }
48
```

Figure 12.22 Code coverage at the individual class level

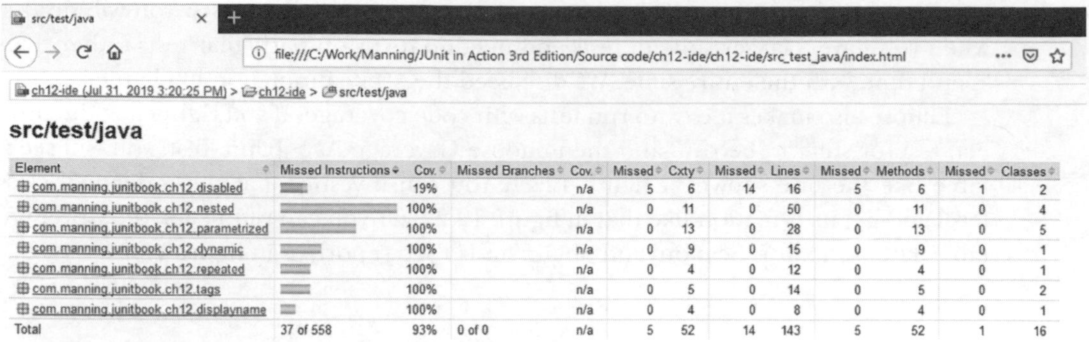

Figure 12.23　Code coverage HTML report obtained with the help of Eclipse

While developing code and tests, we want to get quick feedback not only about whether the tests run successfully but also about their coverage. Eclipse strongly supports both goals. Code coverage is a metric of test quality, showing how much of the production code is covered by the tests we are executing.At Tested Data Systems, the developers who have decided to use Eclipse for their projects are generally those who were already using it before moving to JUnit 5 and were not under pressure to adopt it. This is simply because Eclipse came with JUnit 5 support later than IntelliJ IDEA.

12.3　*Using JUnit 5 with NetBeans*

NetBeans is an IDE that we can use to write code in several programming languages, including Java. For brief NetBeans installation instructions, see appendix C.

We'll walk through a demonstration similar to that for IntelliJ IDEA and Eclipse. We have selected JUnit 5 tests from chapter 2 that are significant in the context of usage from inside an IDE: tests demonstrating capabilities such as displaying names and nested, parameterized, repeated, and dynamic tests, using tags.

Launch NetBeans using one of the executables from the netbeans/bin folder: netbeans or netbeans64, depending on the operating system. To open a project, select File > Open Project, and then choose the folder where the project is located. The IDE will look as shown in figure 12.24.

From here, you can execute all of the tests by right-clicking the project and choosing Run/Test project. You will get a result like that shown in figure 12.25. You will probably want to run all of the tests periodically while you are working on the implementation of a particular feature, to make sure the full project is working correctly and that your implementation does not affect the previously existing functionality.

In figure 12.25, disabled tests are shown in gray, and they are marked as "skipped" after executing the whole suite. In contrast to the capabilities of IntelliJ IDEA, you cannot force the execution of a particular disabled test.

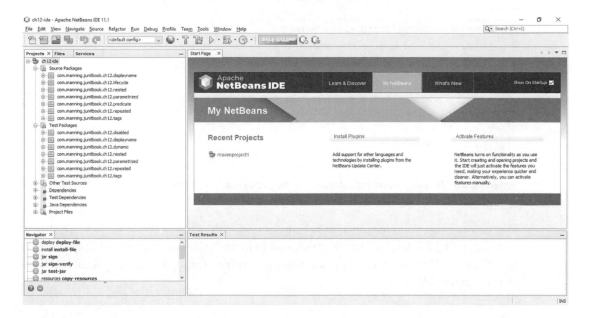

Figure 12.24   NetBeans with an open JUnit 5 project

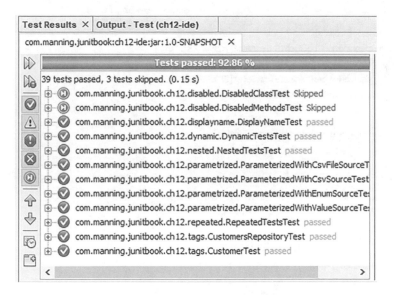

Figure 12.25   Executing all tests from inside NetBeans

When you run tests that are annotated with `@DisplayName`, they are shown as in figure 12.26. Unlike IntelliJ IDEA and Eclipse, NetBeans cannot use the information provided by this annotation and simply shows the names of tests that have been run. We discussed this annotation in chapter 2.

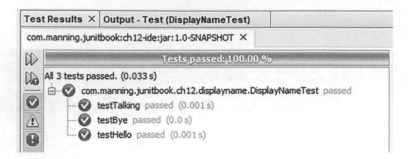

Figure 12.26   Running a test annotated with @DisplayName from IntelliJ

When you run dynamic tests that are annotated with @TestFactory, they are shown as in figure 12.27. Unlike IntelliJ IDEA and Eclipse, NetBeans cannot use the names of the dynamically generated tests and simply numbers them. We discussed this annotation in chapter 2.

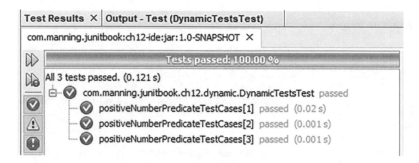

Figure 12.27   Running a dynamic test from NetBeans

When you run nested tests, they are not even recognized by NetBeans, as shown in figure 12.28. We discussed the @Nested annotation in chapter 2.

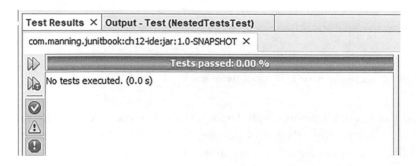

Figure 12.28   Running nested tests from NetBeans

When you run parameterized tests, they are displayed with numbers but without details of their parameters, unlike in IntelliJ IDEA and Eclipse. This is shown in figure 12.29. We discussed parameterized test annotations in chapter 2.

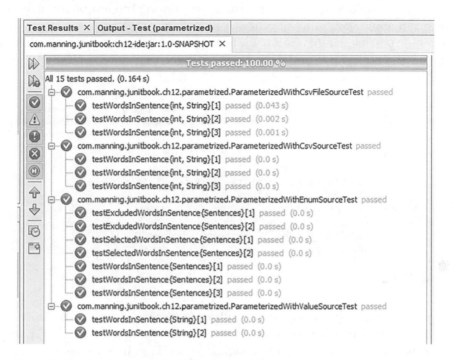

Figure 12.29 Running parameterized tests from NetBeans

When you run repeated tests, they are shown without any of the required information about the currently repeated test, as in IntelliJ IDEA and Eclipse. You can see the results in figure 12.30. We discussed the `@RepeatedTest` annotation in chapter 2.

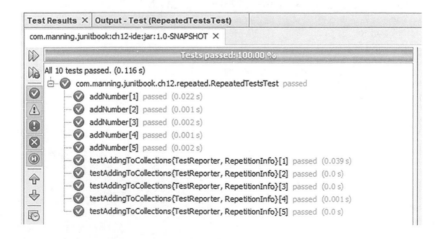

Figure 12.30 Running repeated tests from NetBeans

When running the whole test suite from NetBeans, tagged tests are also run. The IDE does not provide the option to run only particular tagged tests. If you are running a Maven project, you have to make changes at the level of the pom.xml file with the help of the Surefire plugin. This plugin is used during the test phase of a project to execute an application's unit tests; it may filter some of the executed tests or generate reports. A possible configuration is shown in the following listing, including tests tagged with `individual` and excluding tests tagged with `repository`. We discussed the `@Tag` annotation in chapter 2.

Listing 12.1   Possible filtering configuration for the Maven Surefire plugin

```
<build>
   <plugins>
      <plugin>
         <artifactId>maven-surefire-plugin</artifactId>
         <version>2.22.2</version>
         <configuration>
            <groups>individual</groups>
            <excludedGroups>repository</excludedGroups>
         </configuration>
      </plugin>
   </plugins>
</build>
```

It is not possible to run tests directly with code coverage from NetBeans. We can do this with the help of JaCoCo, an open source toolkit for measuring and reporting Java code coverage. If you are running a Maven project, you have to make changes at the level of the pom.xml file, using JaCoCo. The configuration of the JaCoCo plugin is shown next.

Listing 12.2   Configuration of the JaCoCo plugin

```
<plugin>
    <groupId>org.jacoco</groupId>
    <artifactId>jacoco-maven-plugin</artifactId>
    <version>0.7.7.201606060606</version>
    <executions>
        <execution>
            <goals>
                <goal>prepare-agent</goal>
            </goals>
        </execution>
        <execution>
            <id>report</id>
            <phase>prepare-package</phase>
            <goals>
                <goal>report</goal>
            </goals>
        </execution>
    </executions>
</plugin>
```

After you build the project (right-click and choose Build), the Code Coverage menu item appears when you right-click again on the project (figure 12.31). You can choose Show Report (figure 12.32) or investigate at the individual class level (figure 12.33).

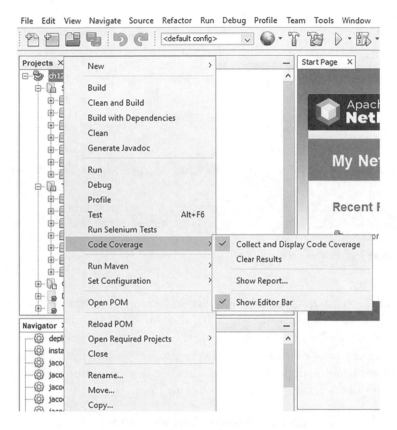

Figure 12.31   The newly added Code Coverage menu

Filename	Coverage	Total	Not Executed
com.manning.junitbook.ch12.lifecycle.SUT	40.00 %	10	6
com.manning.junitbook.ch12.parametrized.WordCounter	100.00 %	2	0
com.manning.junitbook.ch12.tags.Customer	100.00 %	4	0
com.manning.junitbook.ch12.tags.CustomersRepository	100.00 %	5	0
com.manning.junitbook.ch12.displayname.SUT	100.00 %	4	0
com.manning.junitbook.ch12.predicate.PositiveNumberPredicate	100.00 %	2	0
com.manning.junitbook.ch12.repeated.Calculator	100.00 %	2	0
com.manning.junitbook.ch12.nested.Customer	100.00 %	31	0
com.manning.junitbook.ch12.nested.Gender	100.00 %	2	0
Total	90.32 %	62	6

Total Coverage: 90.32 %

Figure 12.32   Code coverage as shown from NetBeans, with the help of the JaCoCo plugin

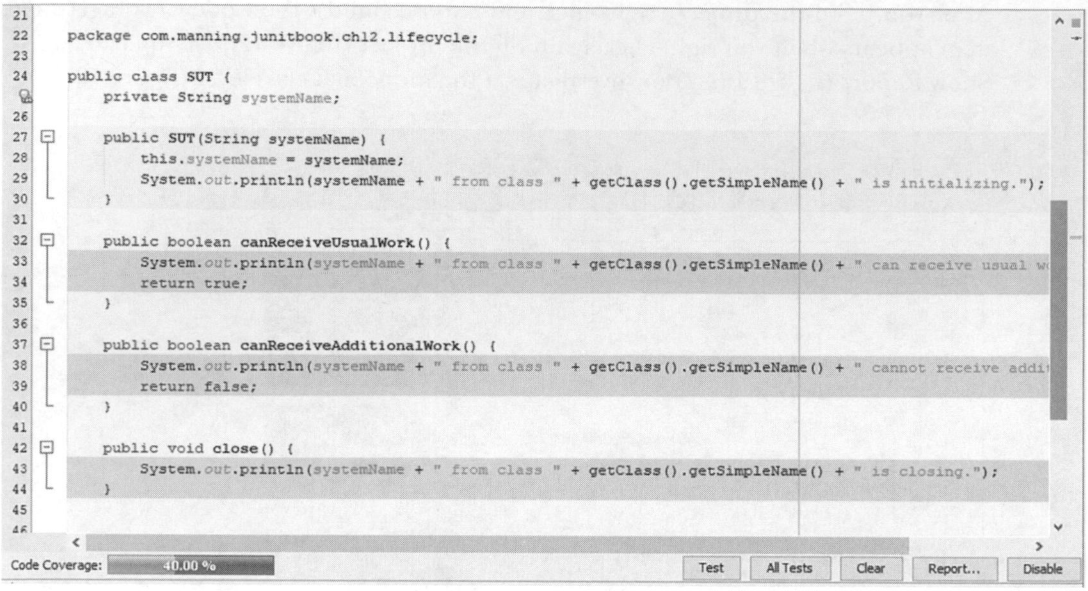

```
21
22    package com.manning.junitbook.ch12.lifecycle;
23
24    public class SUT {
          private String systemName;
26
27 ⊟        public SUT(String systemName) {
28              this.systemName = systemName;
29              System.out.println(systemName + " from class " + getClass().getSimpleName() + " is initializing.");
30          }
31
32 ⊟        public boolean canReceiveUsualWork() {
33              System.out.println(systemName + " from class " + getClass().getSimpleName() + " can receive usual wo
34              return true;
35          }
36
37 ⊟        public boolean canReceiveAdditionalWork() {
38              System.out.println(systemName + " from class " + getClass().getSimpleName() + " cannot receive addi
39              return false;
40          }
41
42 ⊟        public void close() {
43              System.out.println(systemName + " from class " + getClass().getSimpleName() + " is closing.");
44          }
45
46
```

Code Coverage: 40.00 %   [Test] [All Tests] [Clear] [Report...] [Disable]

Figure 12.33   Code coverage at the individual class level

Using NetBeans, you can get feedback about code coverage, but you need to use separate plugins, as we have demonstrated with JaCoCo. At Tested Data Systems, the developers who have decided to use NetBeans for their projects are generally those who have been using it a long time and moved very late to JUnit 5 (this IDE was the last one to introduce JUnit 5 support). Overall, they are not very interested in the user-friendly behavior of the testing framework's new features.

12.4   Comparing JUnit 5 usage in IntelliJ, Eclipse, and NetBeans

Table 12.1 summarizes our comparison of the three IDEs that can help you develop JUnit 5 projects. Remember that we used the latest version of each IDE at the time of writing; the IDE developers may focus on more integration in the future. IntelliJ IDEA now has the best integration, followed closely by Eclipse. NetBeans neglects most of the capabilities and user-friendly behavior provided by JUnit 5.

Which IDE you decide to use will depend on personal preference or project requirements. To make a good decision, consider the other capabilities of the IDEs, not only their integration with JUnit 5. Your research should include sources that present each IDE in detail, starting with the official documentation. Our purpose was to provide just-in-time information to evaluate IntelliJ IDEA, Eclipse, and NetBeans from the perspective of their relationship with the framework that is the topic of our book: JUnit 5.

Table 12.1   Comparison of JUnit 5's integration with IDEs

Feature	IntelliJ IDEA	Eclipse	NetBeans
Force running disabled tests	Yes	No	No
User-friendly display of `@DisplayName` tests	Yes	Yes	No
User-friendly display of dynamic tests	Yes	Yes	No
User-friendly display of nested tests	Yes	Yes	Does not execute nested tests
User-friendly display of parameterized tests	Yes	Yes	No
User-friendly display of repeated tests	Yes	Yes	No
User-friendly execution of tagged tests	Yes	Yes	Only with the help of the Surefire plugin
Run with code coverage from inside the IDE	Yes	Yes	Only with the help of the JaCoCo plugin

In the next chapter, we'll investigate the capabilities of JUnit 5 related to another important type of software it is used in conjunction with: continuous integration tools.

Summary

This chapter has covered the following:

- IDEs and the importance of using them with Java and JUnit 5 to gain productivity
- Executing JUnit 5 tests from IntelliJ IDEA, and the capabilities of this IDE for addressing the features of the testing framework
- Executing JUnit 5 tests from Eclipse, and the capabilities of this IDE for addressing the features of the testing framework
- Executing JUnit 5 tests from NetBeans, and the capabilities of this IDE for addressing the features of the testing framework
- Comparing IntelliJ IDEA, Eclipse, and NetBeans as IDE alternatives for working on JUnit 5 projects, focusing on how each of them can work with the new capabilities of the testing framework

Continuous integration with JUnit 5

13

This chapter covers

- Customizing and configuring Jenkins
- Practicing continuous integration on a development team
- Working on tasks in a continuous integration environment

Life is a continuous exercise in creative problem solving.

—Michael J. Gelb

In chapters 10 and 11, we implemented ways to automatically execute tests by using tools such as Maven and Gradle. The build then triggered our tests. Now it is time to go to the next level: automatically executing the build and the tests at regular intervals using other popular tools. In this chapter, we will explore the paradigm of continuous integration and demonstrate how to schedule projects to be built automatically at a particular time.

13.1 *Continuous integration testing*

Integration tests are usually time consuming, and as a single developer, you may not have all the different modules built on your machine. Therefore, it makes no sense to run all of the integration tests during development time. That is because, at development time, we are focused on our module, and all we want to know is whether it works as a single unit. At development time, we are mostly concerned that if we provide the right input data, the module behaves as expected and produces the expected result.

Integrating the execution of JUnit tests as part of your development cycle— [code : run : test : code], or [test : code : run : test] if you are using test-driven development (TDD)—is a very important concept in the sense that JUnit tests are unit tests: that is, they test a single component of your project in isolation. But many projects have a modular architecture, where different developers on the team work on different modules of the project. Each developer takes care of their own module and their own unit tests to make sure their module is well tested. Tested Data Systems Inc. is no exception: for a project that is under development, tasks are assigned to a few programmers who work independently and test their own code through JUnit 5 tests.

Different modules interact with each other, so we need to assemble all the modules to see how they work together. In order for the application to be test proven, we need other sorts of tests: integration or functional tests. We saw in chapter 5 that these test the interaction between different modules. At Tested Data Systems, the engineers will also need to test the integration of the code and of the modules they have developed independently.

TDD teaches us to test early and to test often. Executing all of our unit, integration, and functional tests every time we make a small change will slow us down immensely. To avoid this, we execute the unit tests only at development time—as early and as often as reasonable. What happens with the integration tests?

Integration tests should be executed independently from the development process. It's best to execute them at regular intervals (say, 15 minutes). This way, if something gets broken, we will hear about it in the next 15 minutes and have a better chance to fix it.

> **DEFINITION** *Continuous integration (CI)*—"A software development practice where members of a team integrate their work frequently, usually each person integrates at least daily—leading to multiple integrations per day. Each integration is verified by an automated build (including test) to detect integration errors as quickly as possible. Many teams find that this approach leads to significantly reduced integration problems and allows a team to develop cohesive software more rapidly."[1]

---

[1] This definition is taken from the marvelous article "Continuous Integration" by Martin Fowler and Matthew Foemmel. It can be found at www.martinfowler.com/articles/continuousIntegration.html.

To execute integration tests at regular intervals, we also need to have the system modules prepared and built. After the modules are built and the integration tests are executed, we want to see the results of the execution as quickly as possible. We need a software tool to perform all of the following steps automatically:

1 Check out the project from the source control system.
2 Build each of the modules and execute all of the unit tests to verify that the different modules work as expected in isolation.
3 Execute the integration tests to verify that the different modules integrate with each other as expected.
4 Publish the results from the tests executed in step 3.

Several questions may arise at this point. First, what is the difference between a human executing all these steps and a tool doing so? The answer is that there is no difference, and there shouldn't be! Apart from the fact that no one can stand to do such a job, if you take a close look at step 1, you see that we simply check out the project from the source control system. We do that as if we were a new member of the team and we just started with the project—with a clean checkout in an empty folder. Then, before moving on, we want to make sure all of the modules work properly in isolation—because if they don't, it doesn't make much sense to test whether they integrate well with the other modules, does it? The last step in the proposed scenario is to notify the developers about the test results. The notification could be done with an email, or simply by publishing the reports from the tests on a web server.

This overall interaction is illustrated in figure 13.1. The CI tool interacts with the source control system to get the project ❶. After that, it uses the build tool that the project is using to build the project and execute different kinds of tests (❷ and ❸). Finally ❹, the CI tool publishes the results and blows the whistle so that everybody can see them.

These four steps are very general and could be improved considerably. For instance, it would be better to check whether any changes have been made in the source control system before we start building. Otherwise, we waste the CPU power of the machine, knowing for sure that we will get the same results.

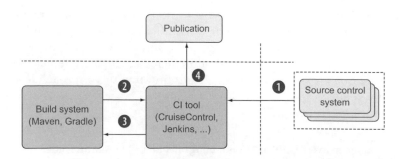

Figure 13.1 Continuous integration scheme: get the project; build it and execute tests; publish the results.

Now that we agree that we need a tool to integrate our projects continuously, let's look at one open source solution we might use: Jenkins (it makes no sense to reinvent the wheel when good tools are already available).

13.2 Introducing Jenkins

Jenkins (https://jenkins.io) is a CI tool alternative that is really worth considering. It has its roots in a similar CI project named Hudson. Initially developed at Sun Microsystems, Hudson was free software. Oracle bought Sun and intended to make Hudson a commercial version. The majority of the development community decided to continue the project under the name Jenkins in early 2011. Interest in Hudson strongly decreased after this, and Jenkins replaced it. Since February 2017, Hudson is no longer under maintenance.

For the Jenkins installation procedure, see appendix D. After the installation is completed, a folder structure is created, in which the most important element is the jenkins.war file (figure 13.2).

Program Files (x86) > Jenkins >

Name	Date modified	Type	Size
users	8/15/2019 5:22 PM	File folder	
war	8/15/2019 5:14 PM	File folder	
workflow-libs	8/15/2019 5:19 PM	File folder	
.lastStarted	8/15/2019 5:15 PM	LASTSTARTED File	0 KB
.owner	8/15/2019 9:26 PM	OWNER File	1 KB
config.xml	8/15/2019 5:23 PM	XML Document	2 KB
hudson.model.UpdateCenter.xml	8/15/2019 5:14 PM	XML Document	1 KB
hudson.plugins.git.GitTool.xml	8/15/2019 5:19 PM	XML Document	1 KB
identity.key.enc	8/15/2019 5:14 PM	Wireshark capture...	2 KB
jenkins.err.log	8/15/2019 8:49 PM	Text Document	157 KB
jenkins.exe	7/17/2019 6:08 AM	Application	363 KB
jenkins.exe.config	4/5/2015 10:05 AM	CONFIG File	1 KB
jenkins.install.InstallUtil.lastExecVersion	8/15/2019 5:23 PM	LASTEXECVERSIO...	1 KB
jenkins.install.UpgradeWizard.state	8/15/2019 5:23 PM	STATE File	1 KB
jenkins.model.JenkinsLocationConfigura...	8/15/2019 5:22 PM	XML Document	1 KB
jenkins.out.log	8/15/2019 5:14 PM	Text Document	1 KB
jenkins.pid	8/15/2019 5:13 PM	PID File	1 KB
jenkins.telemetry.Correlator.xml	8/15/2019 5:14 PM	XML Document	1 KB
jenkins.war	7/17/2019 6:08 AM	WAR File	75,566 KB
jenkins.wrapper.log	8/15/2019 9:57 PM	Text Document	3 KB
jenkins.xml	7/17/2019 6:08 AM	XML Document	3 KB
nodeMonitors.xml	8/15/2019 5:14 PM	XML Document	1 KB
secret.key	8/15/2019 5:14 PM	KEY File	1 KB
secret.key.not-so-secret	8/15/2019 5:14 PM	NOT-SO-SECRET ...	0 KB

Figure 13.2   The Jenkins installation folder with the jenkins.war file

Start the server from the Jenkins installation folder by executing the following command (figure 13.3):

```
java -jar jenkins.war
```

Figure 13.3   Launching the Jenkins server from the command line

To start using the server, navigate to the http://localhost:8080/ URL. You should see something similar to figure 13.4. Unlock Jenkins using the password generated in the previous step (see figure 13.3).

Figure 13.4   Accessing Jenkins from the web interface

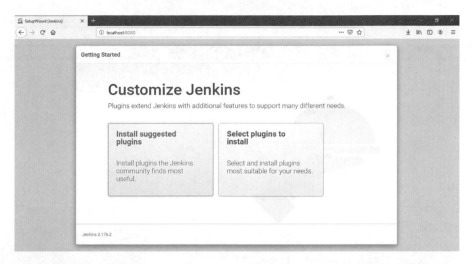

Figure 13.5 Customizing the Jenkins window: choosing the plugins to be installed

After entering the password, you will see the window shown in figure 13.5. Choose Install Suggested Plugins to install several useful plugins in a typical configuration: among these are the folders plugin (for grouping tasks), the monitoring plugin (for managing charts of CPU, HTTP response time, and memory), and the metrics plugin (provides health checks). For details about the plugins, see the Jenkins documentation at https://jenkins.io/doc.

After the plugins are installed, a window opens in which you are required to create the first admin user by providing new credentials (figure 13.6). Click Save and Continue, and you are directed to the window where you can start using Jenkins (figure 13.7).

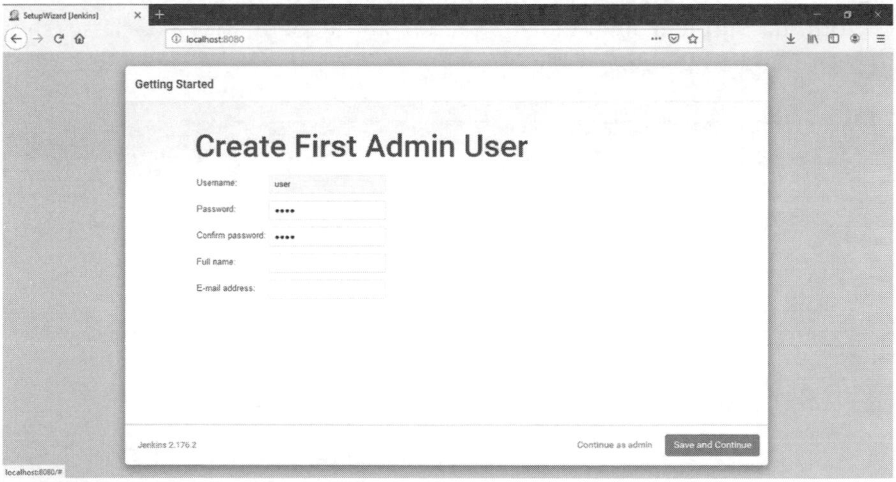

Figure 13.6 Creating the first admin user by providing new credentials

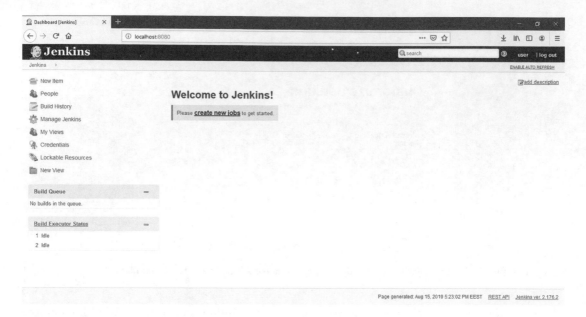

Figure 13.7   The Welcome to Jenkins page

13.3   *Practicing CI on a team*

The engineers at Tested Data Systems have decided to investigate using Jenkins for some of the projects developed inside the company. One of the projects under development is a flight-management application. John and Beth are developers working on this project, but have different tasks: John is responsible for developing the part concerning passengers, while Beth is responsible for developing the part concerning flights. They work independently and write their own code and tests.

John has implemented the Passenger and PassengerTest classes shown in listings 13.1 and 13.2, respectively.

Listing 13.1   Passenger class

```
[...]
public class Passenger {

    private String identifier;
    private String name;
    private String countryCode;
    [...]


    public Passenger(String identifier, String name,
                                    String countryCode) {
        if(!Arrays.asList(Locale.getISOCountries())
                            .contains(countryCode)) {
            throw new RuntimeException("Invalid country code");
```

```
        }
        this.identifier = identifier;
        this.name = name;                            ❷
        this.countryCode = countryCode;
    }

    public String getIdentifier() {
        return identifier;
    }

    public String getName() {
        return name;                       ❸
    }

    public String getCountryCode() {
        return countryCode;
    }

    @Override
    public String toString() {
        return "Passenger " + getName() + " with identifier: " +      ❹
               getIdentifier() + " from " + getCountryCode();
    }
}
```

In this listing:

- A passenger is described through an identifier, a name, and a country code ❶.
- The Passenger constructor checks the validity of the country code and, if this verification passes, sets the previously defined fields: identifier, name, and countryCode ❷.
- The class defines getters for the three previously defined fields: identifier, name, and countryCode ❸.
- The toString method is overridden to allow the information from a passenger to be displayed ❹.

Listing 13.2 PassengerTest class

```
[...]
public class PassengerTest {

    @Test
    public void testPassengerCreation() {
        Passenger passenger = new Passenger("123-45-6789",
                                            "John Smith", "US");      ❶
        assertNotNull(passenger);
    }

    @Test
    public void testInvalidCountryCode() {            ❷
        assertThrows(RuntimeException.class,
                ()->{
```

```
                        Passenger passenger = new Passenger("900-45-6789",
                                                "John Smith", "GJ");
                });
        }

        @Test
        public void testPassengerToString() {
            Passenger passenger = new Passenger("123-45-6789",
                                            "John Smith", "US");
            assertEquals("Passenger John Smith with identifier:
                        123-45-6789 from US",  passenger.toString());
        }
}
```

In this listing:

- A test checks the creation of a passenger with the correct parameters ❶.
- A test checks that the `Passenger` constructor throws an exception when the `countryCode` parameter is invalid ❷.
- A test checks the correct behavior of the `toString` method ❸.

Beth has implemented the `Flight` and `FlightTest` classes, shown in listings 13.3 and 13.4.

Listing 13.3 `Flight` class

```
[...]
public class Flight {

    private String flightNumber;
    private int seats;
    private Set<Passenger> passengers = new HashSet<>();

    private static String flightNumberRegex = "^[A-Z]{2}\\d{3,4}$";
    private static Pattern pattern =
                        Pattern.compile(flightNumberRegex);

    public Flight(String flightNumber, int seats) {
        Matcher matcher = pattern.matcher(flightNumber);
        if(!matcher.matches()) {
            throw new RuntimeException("Invalid flight number");
        }
        this.flightNumber = flightNumber;
        this.seats = seats;
    }

    public String getFlightNumber() {
        return flightNumber;
    }

    public int getNumberOfPassengers () {
        return passengers.size();
    }
```

```
    public boolean addPassenger(Passenger passenger) {
        if(getNumberOfPassengers() >= seats) {
            throw new RuntimeException("Not enough seats for flight "
                                       + getFlightNumber());
        }
        return passengers.add(passenger);
    }

    public boolean removePassenger(Passenger passenger) {
        return  passengers.remove(passenger);
    }
}
```
8
9

In this listing:

- A flight is described using the flight number, the number of seats, and the set of passengers **1**.
- `flightNumberRegex` provides the regular expression that describes a correctly formed flight number **2**. A *regular expression* is a sequence of characters that defines a search pattern. In this case, the regular expression requires that a flight number start with two capital letters followed by three or four digits. This regular expression is the same for all flights, so the field is static.
- A `Pattern` instance is created from the string regular expression **3**. The `Pattern` class belongs to the `java.util.regex` package and is the main access point of the Java regular expression API. Whenever you need to work with regular expressions in Java, you start by creating such an object. This field is also the same for all flights, so it is static.
- In the constructor of the `Flight` class, we create a `Matcher` object **4**. A `Matcher` is used to search through text for occurrences of a regular expression defined through a `Pattern`.
- If `flightNumber` does not match the required regular expression, an exception is thrown **5**. Otherwise, the instance fields are set with the values of the parameters **6**.
- The class defines getters for the flight number and the passenger number **7**.
- The `addPassenger` method tries to add a passenger to the current flight. If the number of passengers exceeds the number of seats, an exception is thrown. If the passenger is successfully added, it returns `true`. If the passenger already exists, it returns `false` **8**.
- The `removePassenger` method removes a passenger from the current flight. If the passenger is successfully removed, it returns `true`. If the passenger does not exist, it returns `false` **9**.

Listing 13.4 `FlightTest` class

```
[...]
public class FlightTest {
```

```
    @Test
    public void testFlightCreation() {
        Flight flight = new Flight("AA123", 100);          ❶
        assertNotNull(flight);
    }

    @Test
    public void testInvalidFlightNumber() {
        assertThrows(RuntimeException.class,
                ()->{                                       ❷
                    Flight flight = new Flight("AA12", 100);
                });
    }
}
```

In this listing:

- A test checks the creation of a flight with the correct parameters ❶.
- A test checks that the Flight constructor throws an exception when the flightNumber parameter is invalid ❷.

Additionally, Beth has written an integration test between the Passenger and Flight classes, because she is handling the Flight class (which also works with Passenger objects).

Listing 13.5   FlightWithPassengersTest class

```
[...]
public class FlightWithPassengersTest {
                                                            ❶
    private Flight flight = new Flight("AA123", 1);     ⟵

    @Test
    public void testAddRemovePassengers() throws IOException {   ❷
        Passenger passenger = new Passenger("124-56-7890",
                                    "Michael Johnson", "US");
        assertTrue(flight.addPassenger(passenger));         ❸
        assertEquals(1, flight.getNumberOfPassengers ());

        assertTrue(flight.removePassenger(passenger));      ❹
        assertEquals(0, flight.getNumberOfPassengers ());
    }

    @Test
    public void testNumberOfSeats() {
        Passenger passenger1 = new Passenger("124-56-7890",
                                    "Michael Johnson", "US");   ❺
        flight.addPassenger(passenger1);
        assertEquals(1, flight.getNumberOfPassengers ());
❻
        Passenger passenger2 = new Passenger("127-23-7991",
                                    "John Smith", "GB");        ❼
        assertThrows(RuntimeException.class,
                    () -> flight.addPassenger(passenger2));      ❽

    }
}
```

In this listing:

- We create a flight with a correct flight number and one seat—this is for convenient testing purposes ❶.
- A test creates a passenger ❷ to be added to ❸ and removed from ❹ the flight. At each step, we check that the operation is successful and the correct number of passengers are on the flight.
- A test creates a passenger to be added to a flight ❺, followed by another passenger that will exceed the number of seats on the flight ❼. We first check the correct number of passengers ❻ and then the fact that an exception is thrown when the number of passengers exceeds the number of seats ❽.

The code developed for this project is managed by Git on a CI machine. Git is a distributed version control system that tracks changes in source code. It can be downloaded from https://git-scm.com/downloads; the folder Git/cmd containing the `git` executable is on the path of the OS installed on the CI machine. For our examples, we'll use some basic Git commands and explain what they do and why. For more comprehensive details about Git, check the documentation.

The folder where the project sources reside is a Git repository. To make the folder a Git repository, the machine administrator ran the following command in the folder:

```
git init
```

This command creates a new Git repository. The folder is shown in figure 13.8: it contains the pom.xml Maven file, the src folder containing the Java sources, and the .git folder with meta-information for the Git distributed version control system.

Name	Date modified	Type	Size
.git	8/26/2019 6:04 PM	File folder	
src	8/26/2019 3:18 PM	File folder	
pom.xml	8/26/2019 4:16 PM	XML Document	2 KB

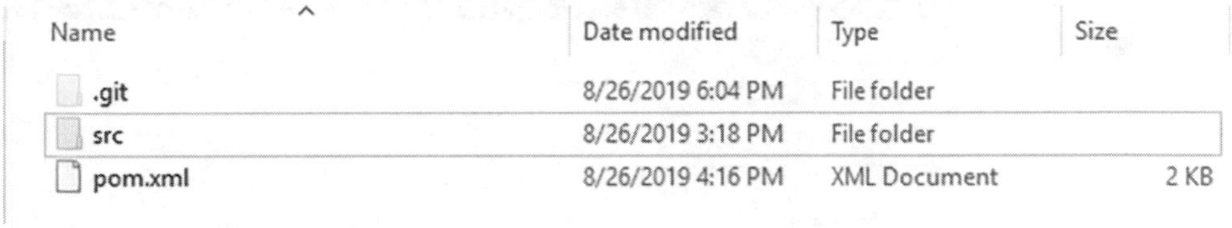

Figure 13.8 The src folder on the CI machine managed by Git

13.4 *Configuring Jenkins*

Configuring Jenkins is all done through the web interface. We would like to set up a project under its management. As Jenkins is running on the CI machine, we go back to its web interface, accessible at http://localhost:8080/ (figure 13.9). No item is defined so far, so we'll click the New Item option on the left side to create a new CI job.

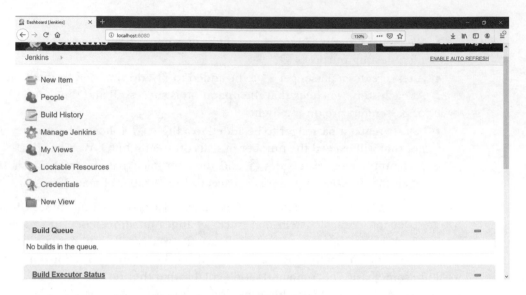

Figure 13.9   The Jenkins main page with no jobs created so far

We choose the Freestyle Project option, insert the item name ch13-continuous (figure 13.10), and then click the OK button. On the newly displayed page, we choose Git as the Source Code Management option; fill in the Repository URL (figure 13.11); go to the bottom of the page and choose Build > Add Build Step > Invoke Top Level Maven Targets; enter `clean install` (figure 13.12); and click the Save button.

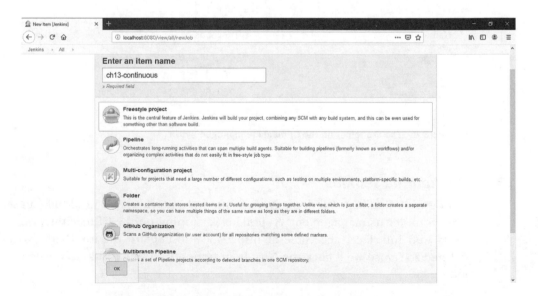

Figure 13.10   Creating a new CI job in Jenkins

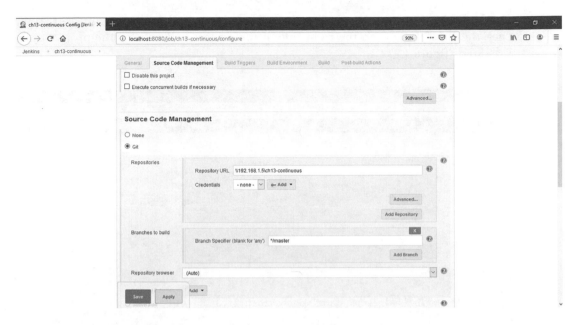

Figure 13.11   Defining the repository URL containing the source code

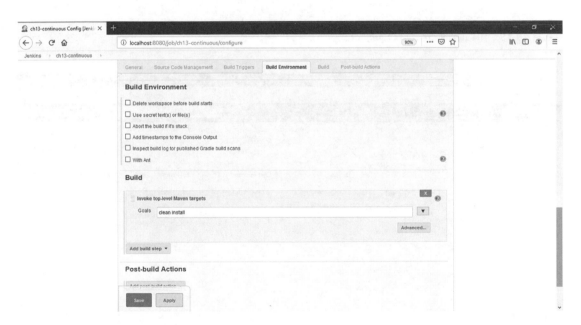

Figure 13.12   The build configuration for the newly created CI project

On the Jenkins main page, we now see the newly created CI project (figure 13.13). We click the Build button on the right side of the project and wait for the project to be executed (figure 13.14).

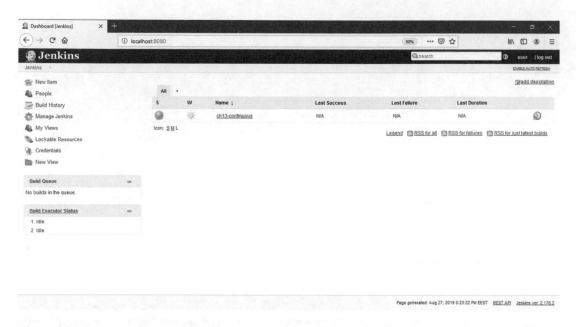

Figure 13.13   The newly created CI project

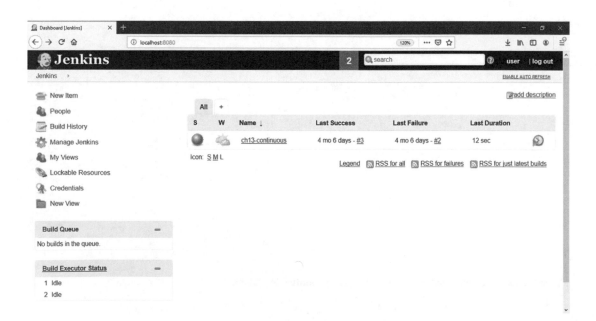

Figure 13.14   The result of the first execution of a build on the CI machine using Jenkins

Now we are sure that everything is fine from the CI point of view. The work created by John and Beth runs fine and also integrates well.

At the beginning of this chapter, we said that at development time, a programmer is usually focused on their module and wants to know that it is working as a single unit. At development time, the programmer only executes unit tests. Integration tests are executed independently from the development process—and now we have a fully configured Jenkins project to take care of this. We'll demonstrate how CI will help John and Beth quickly try their work head to head and easily fix any integration problems.

13.5 Working on tasks in a CI environment

John has a new task for the flight-management project: passengers must be able to join a flight themselves, not just be added to the flight. This is necessary because the new interactive system will allow passengers to choose their flights. Currently, we can add passengers to flights, but if we look at a Passenger object, we have no way to know which flight they are on.

To address this task, John considers introducing Flight as an instance variable of the Passenger class. This way, a passenger will be able to individually choose and join a flight, as the new interactive system requires. Note that there is a bidirectional reference between the Flight and Passenger classes. The Flight class already contains the set of Passengers:

```
private Set<Passenger> passengers = new HashSet<>();
```

John adds a test in the FlightWithPassengersTest class and modifies the existing testAddRemovePassengers.

> **Listing 13.6** `testPassengerJoinsFlight` **from** `FlightWithPassengersTest`

```
@Test
public void testPassengerJoinsFlight() {
    Passenger passenger = new Passenger("123-45-6789",
                                        "John Smith", "US");      ❶  ❷
    Flight flight = new Flight("AA123", 100);
    passenger.joinFlight(flight);
❸  assertEquals(flight, passenger.getFlight());
    assertEquals(1, flight.getNumberOfPassengers());             ❹
}                                                                ❺

@Test
public void testAddRemovePassengers() throws IOException {
    Passenger passenger = new Passenger("124-56-7890",
                            "Michael Johnson", "US");
    flight.addPassenger(passenger);
    assertEquals(1, flight.getNumberOfPassengers());             ❻
    assertEquals(flight, passenger.getFlight());

    flight.removePassenger(passenger);                           ❼
    assertEquals(0, flight.getNumberOfPassengers());
    assertEquals(null, passenger.getFlight());
}
```

In this listing:

- Johns creates a passenger ❶ and a flight ❷.
- He makes the passenger join the flight ❸.
- He checks that the passenger has the previously defined flight assigned ❹ and that the number of passengers from the flight is now one ❺.
- In the existing `testAddRemovePassengers`, after the flight has added a passenger, he checks whether the flight has been set on the passenger's side ❻. After the flight has removed a passenger, no flight is set on the passenger's side ❼.

John also adds the following code to the `Passenger` class.

Listing 13.7   Changes to the `Passenger` class

```
[...]
private Flight flight;                     <──┐
[...]                                         ❶

public Flight getFlight() {      ┐
    return flight;               ❷
}

public void setFlight(Flight flight) {            ┐
    this.flight = flight;                         ❸
}

public void joinFlight(Flight flight) {
    Flight previousFlight = this.flight;
    if (null != previousFlight) {
        if(!previousFlight.removePassenger(this)) {      ❹
            throw new RuntimeException("Cannot remove passenger");
        }
    }
 ┌─▷ setFlight(flight);
 ❺  if(null != flight) {
        if(!flight.addPassenger(this)) {                 ❻
            throw new RuntimeException("Cannot add passenger");
        }
    }
}
```

In this listing:

- John adds a `Flight` field to the `Passenger` class ❶.
- He creates a getter ❷ and a setter ❸ for the newly added field.
- In the `joinFlight` method, he checks whether a previous flight exists for the passenger and, if so, removes the passenger from it. If the removal is not successful, the method throws an exception ❹. Then it sets the flight for the passenger ❺. If the new flight is not null, the method adds the passenger to it. If the passenger cannot be added, the method throws an exception ❻.

John needs to push his code to the CI server located at 192.168.1.5. The local project is also under the management of a Git server; it is a clone of the code on the CI server. This clone was originally created using this Git command:

```
git clone \\192.168.1.5\ch13-continuous
```

To push the code, John executes a few Git commands, starting with this one:

```
git add *.java
```

The `git add` command includes updates to a particular file in the next commit. Executing this command will include all .java files that have been changed for the next commit. Changes are not actually recorded until we run `git commit`.

So, John will record the changes into his local repository by running the following command:

```
git commit -m "Allow the passenger to make the individual choice of a flight"
```

The changes are committed to the local repository with an informative message explaining the task the changes belong to: "Allow the passenger to make the individual choice of a flight."

Now, John needs to do just one more thing in order for the code to arrive on the CI server. He executes this command:

```
git push
```

After the code is pushed to the CI server, a new build is launched on this machine, and it will fail (figure 13.15). By accessing the console of the project from Jenkins

Figure 13.15   The result of the build execution after pushing the changes to the tests

(click the ch13-continuous link, then the build number dropdown icon in the Build
History, and then Console Output), we can see that the modified test fails (figure
13.16).

Figure 13.16   The console of the Jenkins project showing the failure after running the build

The error message says the following:

```
[INFO] Running
     com.manning.junitbook.ch13.flightspassengers.FlightWithPassengersTest
[ERROR] Tests run: 3, Failures: 1, Errors: 0, Skipped: 0,
Time elapsed: 0 s <<< FAILURE! - in
     com.manning.junitbook.ch13.flightspassengers.FlightWithPassengersTest
[ERROR] testAddRemovePassengers  Time elapsed: 0 s  <<< FAILURE!
org.opentest4j.AssertionFailedError: expected:
     <com.manning.junitbook.ch13.flights.Flight@c46bcd4> but was:
<null> at
     com.manning.junitbook.ch13.flightspassengers.FlightWithPassengersTest.
testAddRemovePassengers(FlightWithPassengersTest.java:29)
```

After the build fails and the console output is investigated, the programmers realize
that it is a problem of integration between Flight and Passenger. They need to
make sure the relationship between Passenger and Flight is bidirectional: if the
Passenger has a reference to a Flight, the Flight also has a reference to the
Passenger, and vice versa.

Beth is the developer working on `Flight`, so she will take care of this issue. Beth's local project is also under the management of Git. It is a clone of the code on the CI server. This clone was originally created using this Git command:

```
git clone \\192.168.1.5\ch13-continuous
```

To get the updated code from John, Beth executes the following Git command:

```
git pull
```

This way, Beth has the latest updates on her machine. To fix the issue, Beth modifies the existing `Flight` class: to be precise, the `addPassenger` and `removePassenger` methods.

Listing 13.8 Modified `Flight` class

```java
public boolean addPassenger(Passenger passenger) {
    if(getNumberOfPassengers() >= seats) {
        throw new RuntimeException("Not enough seats for flight "
                                    + getFlightNumber());
    }
    passenger.setFlight(this);          ◄─┐
    return passengers.add(passenger);      ❶
}

public boolean removePassenger(Passenger passenger) {
    passenger.setFlight(null);          ◄─┐
    return  passengers.remove(passenger);  ❷
}
```

Beth has added two lines of code to do the following:

- When a passenger is added to a flight, the flight is also set on the passenger's side ❶.
- When a passenger is removed from a flight, the flight is also removed from the passenger's side ❷.

Beth sends her changes to the CI server by executing the following Git commands:

```
git add *.java
git commit -m "Adding integration code for a passenger join/unjoin"
git push
```

After the code is pushed to the CI server, a new build is launched on this machine, and it succeeds (figure 13.17).

We can see the benefits of CI: integration problems are quickly signaled, and the developers can fix the issues immediately. JUnit 5 and Jenkins cooperate very effectively!

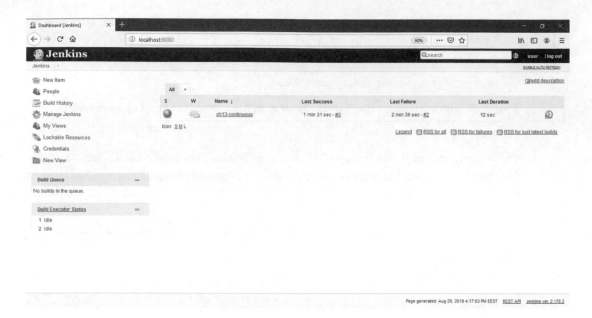

Figure 13.17   The Jenkins build after the necessary integration code is introduced in the `Flight` class

The next chapter will start part 4 of the book, which is dedicated to working with modern frameworks and JUnit 5. We'll begin by examining the JUnit 5 extension model.

Summary

This chapter has covered the following:

- Continuous integration, which is a software development practice that has members of a team integrate their work frequently.
- The benefits that CI provides for developing team Java applications: verifying each integration with an automated build that detects integration errors as quickly as possible, thus reducing integration problems and letting developers fix the issues immediately.
- Using Jenkins as a CI tool in collaborative projects. (Jenkins builds use JUnit 5 for execution).
- Demonstrating collaborative work on a team that practices CI: working on implementing tasks using Jenkins as a CI server and Git as a version control system.

Part 4

Working with modern frameworks and JUnit 5

This part of the book explores working with JUnit 5 and commonly used frameworks. Chapter 14 is dedicated to the implementation of JUnit 5 extensions as alternatives to JUnit 4 rules and runners. This is useful for working with custom test extensions as well as for easily working with modern frameworks that provide their own extensions for creating efficient JUnit 5 tests.

We continue by introducing HtmlUnit and Selenium in chapter 15. We will show you how to test the presentation layer with these tools. We go into detail about how to set up your projects and also some best practices for testing the presentation layer.

We dedicate chapters 16 and 17 to testing one of the most useful frameworks today: Spring. Spring is an open source application framework and inversion of control container for the Java platform. Spring is largely used today for creating Java SE and Java EE applications. It includes several separate frameworks, including the Spring Boot convention-over-configuration solution for creating applications that you can run directly.

Chapter 18 examines testing REST applications. Representational State Transfer represents an application program interface that uses HTTP requests to GET, PUT, PATCH, POST, and DELETE data. Chapter 19 discusses alternatives for testing database applications, including JDBC, Spring, and Hibernate.

JUnit 5 extension model

14

This chapter covers

- Creating JUnit 5 extensions
- Implementing JUnit 5 tests using available extension points
- Developing an application with tests extended by JUnit 5 extensions

The wheel is an extension of the foot, the book is an extension of the eye, clothing an extension of the skin, electric circuitry an extension of the central nervous system.

—Marshall McLuhan

In chapter 4, we demonstrated ways to extend the execution of tests. We examined JUnit 4 rules and JUnit 5 extensions face to face, and we analyzed how to migrate from the old JUnit 4 rules to the new extension model developed by JUnit 5. We also emphasized a fcw well-known extensions, such as `MockitoExtension` and `SpringExtension`. In chapter 8, we implemented tests using mock objects and `MockitoExtension`, and we'll implement more tests using `SpringExtension` in chapter 16. In this chapter, we demonstrate the systematic creation of custom extensions and their applicability to creating JUnit 5 tests.

14.1 *Introducing the JUnit 5 extension model*

Although JUnit 4 provides extension points through runners and rules (see chapter 3), the JUnit 5 extension model consists of a single concept: the `Extension` API. `Extension` itself is just a *marker interface* (or *tag* or *token interface*)—an interface with no fields or methods inside. It is used to mark the fact that the class implementing an interface of this category has some special behavior. Among the best-known Java marker interfaces are `Serializable` and `Cloneable`.

JUnit 5 can extend the behavior of tests' classes or methods, and these extensions can be reused by many tests. A JUnit 5 extension is connected to an occurrence of a particular event during the execution of a test. This kind of event is called an *extension point*. At the moment when such a point is reached in a test's life cycle, the JUnit engine automatically calls the registered extension.

The available extension points are as follows:

- *Conditional test execution*—Controls whether a test should be run
- *Life-cycle callback*—Reacts to events in the life cycle of a test
- *Parameter resolution*—At runtime, resolves the parameter received by a test
- *Exception handling*—Defines the behavior of a test when it encounters certain types of exceptions
- *Test instance postprocessing*—Executed after an instance of a test is created

Note that the extensions are largely used inside frameworks and build tools. They can also be used for application programming, but not to the same extent. The creation and usage of extensions follow common principles; this chapter will present examples appropriate for regular application development.

14.2 *Creating a JUnit 5 extension*

Tested Data Systems is developing a flight-management application. Harry is working on this project, developing and testing the part related to passengers. Currently, the `Passenger` and `PassengerTest` classes look like listings 14.1 and 14.2, respectively.

> #### Listing 14.1 Passenger class

```
public class Passenger {

    private String identifier;            ❶
    private String name;

    public Passenger(String identifier, String name) {
        this.identifier = identifier;      ❷
        this.name = name;
    }
```

```
    public String getIdentifier() {
        return identifier;
    }

    public String getName() {
        return name;
    }


    @Override
    public String toString() {
        return "Passenger " + getName() + " with identifier: " +
                getIdentifier();
    }
}
```

3 (marker beside getters)

4 (marker beside toString)

In this listing:

- A passenger is described through an identifier and a name **1**.
- The Passenger constructor sets the identifier and name fields **2**.
- The class defines getters for identifier and name **3**.
- The toString method is overridden to allow passenger information (the name and identifier) to be displayed **4**.

Listing 14.2 PassengerTest class

```
public class PassengerTest {

    @Test
    void testPassenger() throws IOException {
        Passenger passenger = new Passenger("123-456-789", "John Smith");
        assertEquals("Passenger John Smith with identifier: 123-456-789",
                    passenger.toString());
    }

}
```

This class has a single test that checks the behavior of the toString method.

Harry's next task involves the conditional execution of tests depending on the context. There are three types of contexts—regular, low, and peak—depending on the number of passengers during a certain period. The task requires the tests to be executed only in the regular and low contexts. The tests are not executed during peak periods, as an overloaded system would cause problems for the company.

To fulfill this task, Harry creates a JUnit extension that controls whether a test should be run. Then, he extends the tests with the help of this extension. Such an extension is defined by implementing the ExecutionCondition interface. Harry creates an ExecutionContextExtension class that implements the Execution-Condition interface and overrides the evaluateExecutionCondition() method.

The method verifies whether a property representing the current context name equals "regular" or "low" and, if not, disables the test.

Listing 14.3   ExecutionContextExtension class

```
public class ExecutionContextExtension implements ExecutionCondition {     ◁─┐
                                                                              ❶
    @Override
    public ConditionEvaluationResult                                         ❷
            evaluateExecutionCondition(ExtensionContext context) {
        Properties properties = new Properties();
        String executionContext = "";

        try {
            properties.load(ExecutionContextExtension.class
                                              .getClassLoader()             ❸
                    .getResourceAsStream("context.properties"));
            executionContext = properties.getProperty("context");
            if (!"regular".equalsIgnoreCase(executionContext) &&
                !"low".equalsIgnoreCase(executionContext)) {                ❹
                return ConditionEvaluationResult.disabled(
                    "Test disabled outside regular and low contexts");
            }
        } catch (IOException e) {
            throw new RuntimeException(e);
        }
        return ConditionEvaluationResult.enabled("Test enabled on the "+    ❺
                                  executionContext + " context");
    }
}
```

In this listing:

- Harry creates a conditional test execution extension by implementing the ExecutionCondition interface ❶.
- He overrides the evaluateExecutionCondition method, which returns a ConditionEvaluationResult to determine whether a test is enabled ❷.
- He creates a Properties object that loads the properties from the resource context.properties file. He keeps the value of the context property ❸.
- If the context property is something other than "regular" or "low", the returned ConditionEvaluationResult means the test is disabled ❹.
- Otherwise, the returned ConditionEvaluationResult means the test is enabled ❺.

The context is configured through the resources/context.properties configuration file:

```
context=regular
```

For the current business logic, the `"regular"` value means the tests will be executed in the current context.

The last thing to do is annotate the existing `PassengerTest` with the new extension:

```
@ExtendWith({ExecutionContextExtension.class})
public class PassengerTest {
[...]
```

Because the test executes in the current `"regular"` context configuration, the test will run just as it previously did. During peak periods, the context is set up differently (context=peak). If we try to execute the test during the peak period, we get the result shown in figure 14.1; the test is disabled, and it gives a reason.

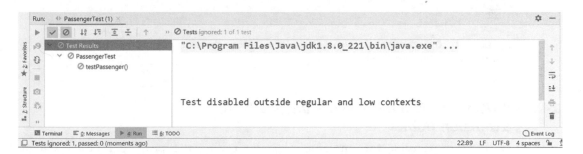

Figure 14.1 **The result of `PassengerTest` during the peak period, as extended with `ExecutionContext-Extension`**

We can instruct the Java Virtual Machine (JVM) to bypass the effects of conditional execution. To deactivate conditional execution, we set the `junit.jupiter.conditions.deactivate` configuration key to a pattern that matches the condition. From the Run > Edit Configurations menu, we can set `junit.jupiter.conditions.deactivate=*`, for example, and the result will be the deactivation of all conditions (figure 14.2). The result of the execution will not be influenced by any of the conditions, so all tests will run.

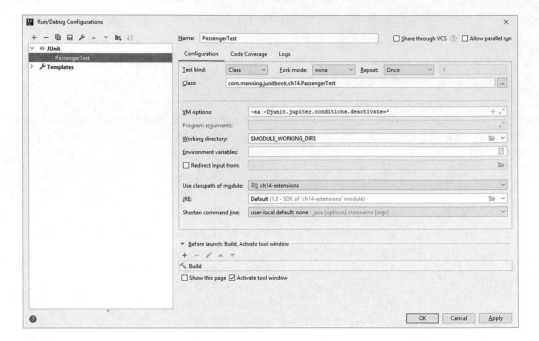

Figure 14.2   Deactivating conditional execution by setting the `junit.jupiter.conditions` `.deactivate` **configuration key**

14.3 Writing JUnit 5 tests using the available extension points

Harry is responsible for implementing and testing the passenger business logic, including persisting passengers to a database. This section follows his activity in implementing these tasks with the help of JUnit 5 extensions.

14.3.1 Persisting passengers to a database

Harry's next task is saving the passengers in a test database. Before the whole test suite is executed, the database must be reinitialized, and a connection to it must be open. At the end of the suite's execution, the connection to the database must be closed. Before executing a test, we have to set up the database in a known state so we can be sure that its content will be tested correctly. Harry decides to use the H2 database, JDBC, and JUnit 5 extensions.

H2 is a relational database management system developed in Java that permits the creation of an in-memory database. It can also be embedded in Java applications when required for testing purposes. JDBC is a Java API that defines how a client accesses a database; it's part of the Java Standard Edition platform.

To carry out this task, the first thing Harry needs to do is add the H2 dependency to the pom.xml file, as shown in the following listing.

Listing 14.4   H2 dependency added to the pom.xml file

```
<dependency>
  <groupId>com.h2database</groupId>
  <artifactId>h2</artifactId>
  <version>1.4.199</version>
</dependency>
```

To manage the connection to the database, Harry implements the `ConnectionManager` class.

Listing 14.5   ConnectionManager class

```
public class ConnectionManager {
    private static Connection connection;

    public static Connection getConnection() {          ❶
        return connection;
    }

    public static Connection openConnection() {
        try {                                           ❷
            Class.forName("org.h2.Driver"); // this is driver for H2   ⟵
            connection = DriverManager.
                getConnection("jdbc:h2:~/passenger",
                "sa", // login                          ❸
                "" // password
                );
            return connection;
        } catch(ClassNotFoundException | SQLException e) {
            throw new RuntimeException(e);
        }
    }

    public static void closeConnection() {
        if (null != connection) {
            try {                                       ❹
                connection.close();              ⟵
            } catch(SQLException e) {
                throw new RuntimeException(e);
            }
        }
    }
}
```

In this listing:

- Harry declares a `java.sql.Connection` field and a getter to return it ❶.
- The `openConnection` method loads the `org.h2.Driver` class, the driver for H2 ❷, and creates a connection to the database with the URL jdbc:h2:~/passenger and the default credentials `"sa"` and `" "` ❸. Normally, you do not want to store a user ID and password in plaintext in a configuration file, but it is OK

here because the database connection is only used for an in-memory database that is wiped after the tests are run.

■ The `closeConnection` method tries to close the previously opened connection ❹.

To manage the database tables, Harry implements the `TablesManager` class.

Listing 14.6   `TablesManager` class

```java
public class TablesManager {

    public static void createTable(Connection connection) {
        String sql =
            "CREATE TABLE IF NOT EXISTS PASSENGERS (ID VARCHAR(50), " +
            "NAME VARCHAR(50));";                                          ❶

        executeStatement(connection, sql);
    }

    public static void dropTable(Connection connection) {
        String sql = "DROP TABLE IF EXISTS PASSENGERS;";
                                                                          ❷
        executeStatement(connection, sql);
    }

    private static void executeStatement(Connection connection,
                                         String sql)
    {
        try(PreparedStatement statement =
            connection.prepareStatement(sql))
        {                                                                 ❸
            statement.executeUpdate();
        } catch (SQLException e) {
            throw new RuntimeException(e);
        }
    }

}
```

In this listing:

■ The `createTable` method creates the PASSENGERS table in the database. The table contains an ID and a NAME, both VARCHAR(50) ❶.

■ The `dropTable` method drops the PASSENGERS table from the database ❷.

■ The utility `executeStatement` method executes any SQL command against the database ❸.

To manage the execution of the queries against the database, Harry implements the `PassengerDao` interface (listing 14.7) and the `PassengerDaoImpl` class (listing 14.8). A data access object (DAO) provides an interface to a database and maps the application calls to specific database operations without exposing the details of the persistence layer.

Listing 14.7 `PassengerDao` **interface**

```java
public interface PassengerDao {
    public void insert(Passenger passenger);
    public void update(String id, String name);
    public void delete(Passenger passenger);
    public Passenger getById(String id);
}
```

In this listing, the insert ❶, update ❷, delete ❸, and getById ❹ methods declare the operations to be implemented against the database.

Listing 14.8 `PassengerDaoImpl` **class**

```java
public class PassengerDaoImpl implements PassengerDao {

    private Connection connection;

    public PassengerDaoImpl(Connection connection) {
        this.connection = connection;
    }

    @Override
    public void insert(Passenger passenger) {
        String sql = "INSERT INTO PASSENGERS (ID, NAME) VALUES (?, ?)";

        try (PreparedStatement statement = connection.prepareStatement(sql)){
            statement.setString(1, passenger.getIdentifier());
            statement.setString(2, passenger.getName());
            statement.executeUpdate();
        } catch (SQLException e) {
            throw new RuntimeException(e);
        }
    }

    @Override
    public void update(String id, String name) {
        String sql = "UPDATE PASSENGERS SET NAME = ? WHERE ID = ?";

        try (PreparedStatement statement = connection.prepareStatement(sql)){
            statement.setString(1, name);
            statement.setString(2, id);
            statement.executeUpdate();
        } catch (SQLException e) {
            throw new RuntimeException(e);
        }
    }

    @Override
    public void delete(Passenger passenger) {
        String sql = "DELETE FROM PASSENGERS WHERE ID = ?";

        try (PreparedStatement statement = connection.prepareStatement(sql)){
            statement.setString(1, passenger.getIdentifier());
```

```
                 statement.executeUpdate();
        } catch (SQLException e) {                          ⑩
            throw new RuntimeException(e);
        }
    }

    @Override                                               ⑪
    public Passenger getById(String id) {
        String sql = "SELECT * FROM PASSENGERS WHERE ID = ?";
        Passenger passenger = null;

        try (PreparedStatement statement = connection.prepareStatement(sql)){
            statement.setString(1, id);
            ResultSet resultSet = statement.executeQuery();  ⑫
                                                            ⑬
            if (resultSet.next()) {
                passenger = new Passenger(resultSet.getString(1),
                                          resultSet.getString(2));  ⑭
            }

        } catch (SQLException e) {
            throw new RuntimeException(e);
        }                           ⑮

        return passenger;
    }
}
```

In this listing:

- The Connection field is kept inside the class and provided as an argument of the constructor ❶.
- The insert method declares the SQL query to be executed ❷, sets the identifier and name of the passenger as parameters of the query ❸, and executes the query ❹.
- The update method declares the SQL query to be executed ❺, sets the identifier and name of the passenger as parameters of the query ❻, and executes the query ❼.
- The delete method declares the SQL query to be executed ❽, sets the identifier of the passenger as a parameter of the query ❾, and executes the query ❿.
- The getById method declares the SQL query to be executed ⑪, sets the identifier of the passenger as a parameter of the query ⑫, executes the query ⑬, and creates a new Passenger object with the parameters returned from the database ⑭. Then the new object is returned by the method ⑮.

Now Harry needs to implement the JUnit 5 extension to do the following:

1. Before the execution of the entire test suite, reinitialize the database and open a connection to it.
2. At the end of the execution of the suite, close the connection to the database.
3. Before executing a test, make sure the database is in a known state so the developer can be sure its content is tested correctly.

Looking at the requirements, which ask for actions based on the life cycle of the test suite, it is natural for Harry to choose to implement life-cycle callbacks. To implement the extensions concerning the test life cycle, Harry must add the following interfaces:

- `BeforeEachCallback` *and* `AfterEachCallback`—Executed before and after the execution of each of the test methods, respectively
- `BeforeAllCallback` *and* `AfterAllCallback`—Executed before and after the execution of all test methods, respectively

Harry implements the `DatabaseOperationsExtension` class shown in the next listing.

Listing 14.9 The `DatabaseOperationsExtension` class

```
public class DatabaseOperationsExtension implements
            BeforeAllCallback, AfterAllCallback, BeforeEachCallback,          ❶
            AfterEachCallback {

    private Connection connection;          ❷
    private Savepoint savepoint;

    @Override
    public void beforeAll(ExtensionContext context) {
        connection = ConnectionManager.openConnection();          ❸
        TablesManager.dropTable(connection);
        TablesManager.createTable(connection);
    }

    @Override
    public void afterAll(ExtensionContext context) {
        ConnectionManager.closeConnection();          ❹
    }

    @Override
    public void beforeEach(ExtensionContext context)
                          throws SQLException {          ❺
        connection.setAutoCommit(false);          
        savepoint = connection.setSavepoint("savepoint");          ❻
    }

    @Override
    public void afterEach(ExtensionContext context)          ❼
                          throws SQLException {
        connection.rollback(savepoint);          
    }

}
```

In this listing:

- The `DatabaseOperationsExtension` class implements four life-cycle interfaces: `BeforeAllCallback`, `AfterAllCallback`, `BeforeEachCallback`, and `AfterEachCallback` ❶.

- The class declares a `Connection` field to connect to the database and a `Save-point` field to track the state of the database before the execution of a test and to restore it after the test ❷.
- The `beforeAll` method, inherited from the `BeforeAllCallback` interface, is executed before the whole suite. It opens a connection to the database, drops the existing table, and re-creates it ❸.
- The `afterAll` method, inherited from the `AfterAllCallback` interface, is executed after the whole suite. It closes the connection to the database ❹.
- The `beforeEach` method, inherited from the `BeforeEachCallback` interface, is executed before each test. It disables autocommit mode, so the database changes resulting from the execution of the test should not be committed ❺. Then the method saves the state of the database before the execution of the test so that, after the test, the developer can roll back to it ❻.
- The `afterEach` method, inherited from the `AfterEachCallback` interface, is executed after each test. It rolls back to the state of the database that was saved before the execution of the test ❼.

Harry updates the `PassengerTest` class and introduces tests that verify the newly introduced database functionalities.

Listing 14.10   Updated `PassengerTest` class

```
@ExtendWith({ExecutionContextExtension.class,                    ❶
            DatabaseOperationsExtension.class })
public class PassengerTest {

    private PassengerDao passengerDao;

    public PassengerTest(PassengerDao passengerDao) {            ❷
        this.passengerDao = passengerDao;
    }

    @Test
    void testPassenger(){
        Passenger passenger = new Passenger("123-456-789", "John Smith");
        assertEquals("Passenger John Smith with identifier: 123-456-789",
                    passenger.toString());
    }

    @Test
    void testInsertPassenger() {
        Passenger passenger = new Passenger("123-456-789",       ❸
                                            "John Smith");
        passengerDao.insert(passenger);
        assertEquals("John Smith",                               ❺
            passengerDao.getById("123-456-789").getName());      ❹
    }

    @Test
    void testUpdatePassenger() {
```

```
        Passenger passenger = new Passenger("123-456-789",
                                        "John Smith");
        passengerDao.insert(passenger);
        passengerDao.update("123-456-789", "Michael Smith");
        assertEquals("Michael Smith",
                passengerDao.getById("123-456-789").getName());
    }

    @Test
    void testDeletePassenger() {
        Passenger passenger = new Passenger("123-456-789",
                                        "John Smith");
        passengerDao.insert(passenger);
        passengerDao.delete(passenger);
        assertNull(passengerDao.getById("123-456-789"));
    }

}
```

In this listing:

- The test is extended by DatabaseOperationsExtension ❶.
- The constructor of the PassengerTest class receives a PassengerDao as argument ❷. This PassengerDao will be needed to execute the tests against the database.
- The testInsertPassenger method creates a passenger ❸, inserts them in the database with passengerDao ❹, and checks whether they are found in the database ❺.
- The testUpdatePassenger method creates a passenger ❻, inserts them in the database with passengerDao ❼, updates the information about them ❽, and checks whether the update information is found in the database ❾.
- The testDeletePassenger method creates a passenger ❿, inserts them in the database with passengerDao ⓫, deletes them ⓬, and checks whether the passenger is found in the database ⓭.

If we run the tests at this time, we get the results shown in figure 14.3.

Figure 14.3 **The result of the updated PassengerTest after it is extended with DatabaseOperations-Extension**

The tests fail with this message:

```
org.junit.jupiter.api.extension.ParameterResolutionException:
No ParameterResolver registered for parameter
    [com.manning.junitbook.ch14.jdbc.PassengerDao arg0]
in constructor
```

This message appears because the constructor of the `PassengerTest` class is receiving a parameter of type `PassengerDao`, but this parameter is not provided by any `ParameterResolver`. To complete the task, Harry has to implement a `Parameter-Resolver` interface.

Listing 14.11 `DataAccessObjectParameterResolver` class

```
public class DataAccessObjectParameterResolver implements        ❶
        ParameterResolver{

    @Override
    public boolean supportsParameter(ParameterContext parameterContext,
                                ExtensionContext extensionContext)
        throws ParameterResolutionException {
      return parameterContext.getParameter()
        .getType()                                                 ❷
        .equals(PassengerDao.class);
    }

    @Override
    public Object resolveParameter(ParameterContext parameterContext,
                                ExtensionContext extensionContext)
        throws ParameterResolutionException {
      return new PassengerDaoImpl(ConnectionManager.getConnection());  ⟵
    }                                                                   ❸

}
```

In this listing:

- The class implements the `ParameterResolver` interface ❶.
- The `supportsParameter` method returns `true` if the parameter is of type `PassengerDao`. This is the missing parameter of the `PassengerTest` class constructor ❷, so the parameter resolver supports only a `PassengerDao` object.
- The `resolveParameter` method returns a newly initialized `PassengerDao-Impl` that receives as a constructor parameter the connection provided by the `ConnectionManager` ❸. This parameter will be injected into the test constructor at runtime.

Additionally, Harry extends the `PassengerTest` class with `DatabaseAccessObjectParameterResolver`. The first lines of the `PassengerTest` class are shown next.

Listing 14.12   Extending `PassengerTest`

```
@ExtendWith({ExecutionContextExtension.class,
             DatabaseOperationsExtension.class,
             DataAccessObjectParameterResolver.class})
public class PassengerTest {
[...]
```

The result of executing `PassengerTest` is shown in figure 14.4. All tests are green; the interaction with the database works properly. Harry has successfully implemented the additional behavior of the tests executed against a database with the help of the life-cycle callback and parameter-resolution extensions.

Figure 14.4   The result of the updated `PassengerTest` **after it is extended with** `DatabaseOperations-`
`Extension` **and** `DatabaseAccessObjectParameterResolver`

14.3.2 Checking the uniqueness of passengers

Next, Harry must prevent a passenger from being inserted into the database more than once. To implement this requirement, he decides to create his own custom exception, together with an exception-handling extension. He wants to introduce this custom exception because it is more expressive than the general `SQLException`. First, Harry creates the custom exception.

Listing 14.13   `PassengerExistsException` class

```
public class PassengerExistsException extends Exception {
    private Passenger passenger;                                    ❶

    public PassengerExistsException(Passenger passenger, String message) {
        super(message);                                            ❷
        this.passenger = passenger;                                ❸
    }
}
```

In this listing:

- Harry keeps the existing passenger as a field of the exception ❶.

- He invokes the constructor of the superclass, retaining the `message` parameter ❷, and then sets the passenger ❸.

Next, Harry changes the `PassengerDao` interface and the `PassengerDaoImpl` class so that the insert method throws `PassengerExistsException`.

Listing 14.14   Modified `insert` method from `PassengerDaoImpl`

```java
public void insert(Passenger passenger) throws PassengerExistsException {
    String sql = "INSERT INTO PASSENGERS (ID, NAME) VALUES (?, ?)";

    if (null != getById(passenger.getIdentifier()) ) {
      throw new PassengerExistsException                          ❶
              (passenger, passenger.toString());
    }

    try (PreparedStatement statement = connection.prepareStatement(sql)){
        statement.setString(1, passenger.getIdentifier());
        statement.setString(2, passenger.getName());
        statement.executeUpdate();
    } catch (SQLException e) {
        throw new RuntimeException(e);
    }
}
```

The `PassengerDaoImpl` insert method checks whether the passenger exists. If so, it throws `PassengerExistsException` ❶.

Harry wants to introduce a test that tries to insert the same passenger twice. Because he expects this test to throw an exception, he implements an exception-handling extension to log it.

Listing 14.15   `LogPassengerExistsExceptionExtension` class

```java
public class LogPassengerExistsExceptionExtension implements
            TestExecutionExceptionHandler {                          ❶
    private Logger logger = Logger.getLogger(this.getClass().getName());

    @Override
    public void handleTestExecutionException(ExtensionContext context,
                Throwable throwable) throws Throwable {              ❸
        if (throwable instanceof PassengerExistsException) {
            logger.severe("Passenger exists:" + throwable.getMessage());  ❹
            return;
        }
        throw throwable;                                            ❺
    }
}
```

❷

In this listing:

- The class implements the `TestExecutionExceptionHandler` interface ❶.

- Harry declares a logger of the class ❷ and overrides the `handleTest-ExecutionException` method inherited from the `TestExecution-ExceptionHandler` interface ❸.
- He checks whether the thrown exception is an instance of `Passenger-ExistsException`; if so, he simply logs it and returns from the method ❹. Otherwise, he rethrows the exception so it can be handled elsewhere ❺.

The updated `PassengerTest` class is shown in the following listing.

Listing 14.16 Updated `PassengerTest` class

```
@ExtendWith({ExecutionContextExtension.class,
             DatabaseOperationsExtension.class,
             DatabaseAccessObjectParameterResolver.class,
             LogPassengerExistsExceptionExtension.class})
public class PassengerTest {
[...]
```

The result of `PassengerTest` is shown in figure 14.5. All tests are green; the `PassengerExistsException` is caught and logged by the new extension. Table 14.1 summarizes the extension points and interfaces provided by JUnit 5.

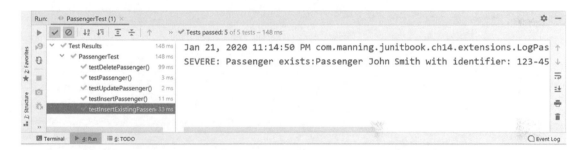

Figure 14.5   The result of the updated `PassengerTest` after it is extended with `LogPassengerExists-ExceptionExtension`

Table 14.1   Extension points and corresponding interfaces

Extension point	Interfaces to implement
Conditional test execution	`ExecutionCondition`
Life-cycle callbacks	`BeforeAllCallback`, `AfterAllCallback`, `BeforeEachCallback`, `AfterEachCallback`
Parameter resolution	`ParameterResolver`
Exception handling	`TestExecutionExceptionHandler`
Test instance postprocessing	`TestInstancePostProcessor`

Chapter 15 is dedicated to presentation-layer testing and finding bugs in an application's graphical user interface (GUI).

Summary

This chapter has covered the following:

- Introducing the JUnit 5 extension model and the available extension points: conditional test execution, life-cycle callbacks, parameter resolution, exception handling, and test instance postprocessing
- Demonstrating the development tasks that require the creation of JUnit 5 extensions: a context extension for conditional test execution; a passenger database setup extension for life-cycle callbacks; a parameter resolver for parameter resolution; and a logging exception extension for exception handling
- Using extensions to implement JUnit 5 tests required by the development scenario

Presentation-layer testing

This chapter covers

- Developing HtmlUnit tests
- Developing Selenium tests
- Comparing HtmlUnit and Selenium

If debugging is the process of removing software bugs, then programming must be the process of putting them in.

—Edsger Dijkstra

Simply stated, presentation-layer testing involves finding bugs in the graphical user interface (GUI) of an application. Finding errors here is as important as finding errors in other application tiers. A bad user experience can lose a customer or discourage a web surfer from visiting your site again. Furthermore, bugs in the user interface can cause other parts of the application to malfunction.

Due to its nature and user interaction, GUI testing presents unique challenges and requires its own set of tools and techniques. This chapter will cover the testing of web application user interfaces. We address what can be objectively—that is, programmatically—asserted about the GUI (by writing explicit Java code). Subjective elements like fonts, colors, and layout are outside the scope of this discussion.

Testing interaction with websites can be challenging from the point of view of stability. If the website content changes over time, or if you encounter problems with your internet connection, this kind of test may occasionally or permanently fail. The tests presented in this chapter have been designed to have high long-term stability by accessing known websites with less probability of changing in the near future.

We can test the following:

- The content of web pages to any level of detail (including spelling)
- The application structure or navigation (following links to their expected destination, for example)
- The ability to verify user stories with acceptance tests[1]

A *user story* is an informal, natural-language description of one or more features of a software system. An *acceptance test* is a test conducted to determine whether the requirements of a specification are met. We can also verify that the site works with the required browsers and operating systems.

15.1   Choosing a testing framework

We will look at two free, open source tools to implement the presentation-layer tests in JUnit 5: HtmlUnit and Selenium. HtmlUnit is a 100% Java headless browser framework that runs in the same virtual machine as our JUnit 5 tests. A *headless* browser is a browser without a GUI. We use HtmlUnit when our application is independent of OS features and browser-specific implementations of JavaScript, DOM, CSS, and so on.

Selenium drives various web browsers programmatically and checks the results from executing JUnit 5 tests. We use Selenium when we require validation of specific browsers and OSs, especially if the application takes advantage of or depends on a browser-specific implementation of JavaScript, DOM, CSS, and so on. Let's start with HtmlUnit.

15.2   Introducing HtmlUnit

HtmlUnit (http://htmlunit.sourceforge.net) is an open source Java headless browser framework. It allows tests to imitate the user of a browser-based web application programmatically. HtmlUnit JUnit 5 tests do not display a user interface. In the remainder of this section, when we talk about "testing with a web browser," it is with the understanding that we are really testing by emulating a specific web browser.

15.2.1   A live example

We'll first introduce the `ManagedWebClient` base class that we are going to use as the base class for HtmlUnit tests using JUnit 5 annotations.

---

[1] To learn about extreme programming acceptance tests, see www.extremeprogramming.org/rules/function-altests.html.

Listing 15.1 `ManagedWebClient` **base class**

```
[...]
import com.gargoylesoftware.htmlunit.WebClient;
[...]

public abstract class ManagedWebClient {              ❶
    protected WebClient webClient;                    ◁──┘

    @BeforeEach
    public void setUp() {
        webClient = new WebClient();                  ❷
    }

    @AfterEach
    public void tearDown() {
        webClient.close();                            ❸
    }
}
```

In this listing:

- We define a protected `WebClient` field to be inherited by the subclasses ❶. The `com.gargoylesoftware.htmlunit.WebClient` class is the main starting point of an HtmlUnit test.
- Before each test, we initialize a new `WebClient` object ❷. It simulates a web browser and will be used to execute all the tests.
- After each test, we make sure that the simulated browser is closed when the test is executed with a `WebClient` instance ❸.

Let's jump in with the example shown in listing 15.2. If you can connect to the internet, you can test. We will go to the HtmlUnit website and test the home page. We will also navigate to the Javadoc and make sure a class appears at the top of the list of documented classes.

Listing 15.2 Our first HtmlUnit example

```
[...]
public class HtmlUnitPageTest extends ManagedWebClient {

    @Test
    public void homePage() throws IOException {
        HtmlPage page = webClient.
                            getPage("http://htmlunit.sourceforge.net");   ❶
        assertEquals("HtmlUnit - Welcome to HtmlUnit",
                            page.getTitleText());

        String pageAsXml = page.asXml();
        assertTrue(pageAsXml.                                             ❷
                        contains("<div class=\"container-fluid\">"));
```

```
        String pageAsText = page.asText();
        assertTrue(pageAsText.contains(
            "Support for the HTTP and HTTPS protocols"));
    }

    @Test
    public void testClassNav() throws IOException {
        HtmlPage mainPage = webClient.getPage(
            "http://htmlunit.sourceforge.net/apidocs/index.html");
        HtmlPage packagePage = (HtmlPage)
            mainPage.getFrameByName("packageFrame").getEnclosedPage();
        HtmlListItem htmlListItem = (HtmlListItem)
            packagePage.getElementsByTagName("li").item(0);
        assertEquals("AboutURLConnection", htmlListItem.getTextContent());
    }
}
```

❸

❹

❺

❻

❼

In this listing:

- In the first test, we access the HtmlUnit website home page and check that the title of the page is as expected ❶.
- We get the home page of the HtmlUnit website as XML and check that it contains a particular tag ❷.
- We get the home page of the HtmlUnit website as text and check that it contains a particular string ❸.
- In the second test, we access a URL from the HtmlUnit website ❹.
- We get the page from inside the packageFrame ❺.
- Inside the page obtained at ❺, we look for the first element tagged as "li" ❻.
- We check that the text of the element obtained at ❻ is "AboutURL-Connection" ❼.

This example covers the basics: getting a web page, navigating the HTML object model, and asserting results. We'll look at more examples in the next section.

15.3 *Writing HtmlUnit tests*

When we write an HtmlUnit test, we write code that simulates the action of a user sitting in front of a web browser: we get a web page, enter data, read the text, and click buttons and links. Instead of manually manipulating the browser, we programmatically control an emulated browser. At each step, we can query the HTML object model and assert that values are what we expect. The framework will throw exceptions if it encounters a problem, which allows our test cases to avoid checking for these errors, thus reducing clutter.

15.3.1 *HTML assertions*

We know that JUnit 5 provides a class called Assertions to allow tests to fail when they detect an error condition. Assertions are the bread and butter of any unit test. HtmlUnit can work with JUnit 5, but it also provides a class in the same spirit called WebAssert, which contains standard assertions for HTML like assertTitle-Equals, assertTextPresent, and notNull.

15.3.2 *Testing for a specific web browser*

As of version 2.36, HtmlUnit supports the browsers listed in table 15.1.

Table 15.1 HtmlUnit-supported browsers

Web browser and version	HtmlUnit `BrowserVersion` constant
Internet Explorer 11	`BrowserVersion.INTERNET_EXPLORER`
Firefox 5.2 (deprecated)	`BrowserVersion.FIREFOX_52`
Firefox 6.0	`BrowserVersion.FIREFOX_60`
Latest Chrome	`BrowserVersion.CHROME`
The best-supported browser at the moment	`BrowserVersion.BEST_SUPPORTED`

By default, `WebClient` emulates `BrowserVersion.BEST_SUPPORTED`, which, at the time of writing this chapter, is Google Chrome (but this may change in the future, depending on the evolution of each browser). To specify which browser to emulate, we provide the `WebClient` constructor with a `BrowserVersion`. For example, for Firefox 6.0, we use

```
WebClient webClient = new WebClient(BrowserVersion.FIREFOX_60);
```

15.3.3 *Testing more than one web browser*

Our example company, Tested Data Systems, has many customers. Naturally, each customer uses its preferred browser to access the pages of applications developed for it. Consequently, the engineers at Tested Data Systems would like to test their applications with more than one browser version. John is in charge of writing tests for this purpose. He will define a test matrix to include all HtmlUnit-supported web browsers.

Listing 15.3 uses JUnit 5 parameterized tests to drive the same test with all browsers in the test matrix. The JUnit 5 parameterized tests will use Firefox 6.0, Internet Explorer 11, the latest Chrome (79 at the time of writing), and the best-supported browser (again, Chrome 79 at the time of writing, but this may change in the future).

Listing 15.3 Testing for all HtmlUnit-supported browsers

```
[...]
public class JavadocPageAllBrowserTest {

    private static Collection<BrowserVersion[]> getBrowserVersions() {
        return Arrays.asList(new BrowserVersion[][] {
                            { BrowserVersion.FIREFOX_60 },            ❶
                            { BrowserVersion.INTERNET_EXPLORER },
                            { BrowserVersion.CHROME },
                            { BrowserVersion.BEST_SUPPORTED } });
    }
                                    ❷
    @ParameterizedTest          ◄─┘
    @MethodSource("getBrowserVersions")    ◄─┐
                                             ❸
```

```
    public void testClassNav(BrowserVersion browserVersion)
                                     throws IOException          ❹
    {
        WebClient webClient = new WebClient(browserVersion);

        HtmlPage mainPage = (HtmlPage)webClient
                .getPage(                                          ❻
                "http://htmlunit.sourceforge.net/apidocs/index.html");
        WebAssert.notNull("Missing main page", mainPage);

        HtmlPage packagePage = (HtmlPage) mainPage              ❽
                .getFrameByName("packageFrame").getEnclosedPage();
        WebAssert.notNull("Missing package page", packagePage);

        HtmlListItem htmlListItem = (HtmlListItem) packagePage
                    .getElementsByTagName("li").item(0);          ❿
        assertEquals("AboutURLConnection",
                    htmlListItem.getTextContent());
    }
}
```

In this listing:

- John creates a `private static` method that will provide the collection of all web browsers supported by HtmlUnit ❶.
- He creates the `testClassNav` method that will receive as a parameter the `BrowserVersion` ❹. This is a parameterized test, as indicated by the `@ParameterizedTest` annotation ❷. The `BrowserVersion` parameters are injected by the `getBrowserVersion` method, as indicated by the `@Method-Source` annotation ❸.
- He creates a `WebClient` receiving as a constructor argument the injected `BrowserVersion` ❺, accesses a page on the internet ❻, and checks that the page exists ❼.
- Inside the page that John previously accessed, he looks for a frame with the name `packageFrame` ❽ and checks that it exists ❾.
- Inside the `packageFrame`, he looks for a list of all HtmlUnit classes and checks whether the first class on the list is named `AboutURLConnection` ❿.

15.3.4 *Creating standalone tests*

You may not always want to use the actual URLs of pages as input for tests because external pages may be subject to change without notice. A minor change in a website can make the tests break. In this section, we will show how to embed and run HTML in the unit test code itself.

The framework allows us to plug a mock (see chapter 8) HTTP connection into a web client. In listing 15.4, we create a JUnit 5 test that sets up a mock connection (an instance of the class `com.gargoylesoftware.htmlunit.MockWebConnection`) with a default HTML `String` response. The JUnit 5 test can then get this default page by using any URL value. We will test the title of the HTML response obtained by a web client with a mocked connection that avoids using an actual URL that may change without notice.

Listing 15.4   Configuring a standalone test

```
[...]
public class InLineHtmlFixtureTest extends ManagedWebClient {

    @Test
    public void testInLineHtmlFixture() throws IOException {          ❶
        final String expectedTitle = "Hello 1!";              ◄──
        String html = "<html><head><title>" +
                        expectedTitle +                   ❷
                        "</title></head></html>";                       ❸
        MockWebConnection connection = new MockWebConnection();  ◄──
        connection.setDefaultResponse(html);                         ❺
        webClient.setWebConnection(connection);                  ◄──
        HtmlPage page = webClient.getPage("http://page");     ◄──
        WebAssert.assertTitleEquals(page, expectedTitle);  ◄──
    }                                                        ❻
                                                         ❼
}
```
❹

In this listing:

- We create the expected HTML page title ❶ and the expected HTML response ❷.
- We create a `MockWebConnection` ❸ and set the HTML response as the default response for the mock connection ❹. We then set the web client connection to our mock connection ❺.
- We get the test page ❻. Any URL is fine here since we set up our HTML response as the default response.
- We check that the page title matches our HTML response ❼.

To configure a JUnit 5 test with multiple pages, we call one of the `MockWebConnection` `setResponse` methods for each page. The code in the next listing sets up three web pages in a mock connection. Again, we will test the titles of the HTML responses obtained by a web client with a mocked connection, thus avoiding using an actual URL that may change without notice.

Listing 15.5   Configuring a test with multiple page fixtures

```
@Test
public void testInLineHtmlFixtures() throws IOException {
    final URL page1Url = new URL("http://Page1/");
    final URL page2Url = new URL("http://Page2/");             ❶
    final URL page3Url = new URL("http://Page3/");
                                                         ❷
    MockWebConnection connection = new MockWebConnection();  ◄──
    connection.setResponse(page1Url,
```

```
            "<html><head><title>Hello 1!</title></head></html>");
    connection.setResponse(page2Url,
            "<html><head><title>Hello 2!</title></head></html>");
    connection.setResponse(page3Url,
        "<html><head><title>Hello 3!</title></head></html>");
    webClient.setWebConnection(connection);

    HtmlPage page1 = webClient.getPage(page1Url);
    WebAssert.assertTitleEquals(page1, "Hello 1!");

    HtmlPage page2 = webClient.getPage(page2Url);
    WebAssert.assertTitleEquals(page1, "Hello 2!");

    HtmlPage page3 = webClient.getPage(page3Url);
    WebAssert.assertTitleEquals(page1, "Hello 3!");
}
```

In this listing:

- We create three pages **1** and a mock connection **2** and set three responses for each of the URL pages **3**.
- We set the web client connection to our mock connection **4**.
- We test getting each page and verifying each page title **5**.

WARNING Do not forget the trailing / in the URL! http://Page1/ will work, but http://Page1 will not be found in the mock connection. The result will be an IllegalStateException with the message "No response specified that can handle URL."

15.3.5 *Testing forms*

HTML form support is built into the HtmlPage API, where form elements can be accessed with getForms (returns List<HtmlForm>) to get all form elements and getFormByName to get the first HtmlForm with a given name. We can call one of the HtmlForm getInput methods to get HTML input elements and then simulate user input with setValueAttribute.

The following example focuses on the HtmlUnit mechanics of driving a form. First, we create a simple page to display a form with an input field and a Submit button. We include form validation via JavaScript alerts.

Listing 15.6 Example form page

```html
<!doctype html>
<html lang="en">
<head>
<meta charset="utf-8">
<script>
function validate_form(form) {
    if (form.in_text.value=="") {
        alert("Please enter a value.");
        form.in_text.focus();
        return false;
    }
```

```
}
</script>
<title>Form</title></head>
<body>
<form name="validated_form" action="submit.html"
      onsubmit="return validate_form(this);" method="post">
  Value:
  <input type="text" name="in_text" id="in_text" size="30"/>
  <input type="submit" value="Submit" id="submit"/>
</form>
</body>
</html>
```

This form looks like figure 15.1 when we click the OK button without input.

Figure 15.1   Sample form with one input and one Submit button, and the alert triggered when we click the button without input

The next listing tests normal user interaction with the form.

Listing 15.7   Testing a form

```
[...]
public class FormTest extends ManagedWebClient {

@Test
public void testForm() throws IOException {
    HtmlPage page =
        webClient.getPage("file:src/main/webapp/formtest.html");      ❶
    HtmlForm form = page.getFormByName("validated_form");             ❷
    HtmlTextInput input = form.getInputByName("in_text");             ❸
    input.setValueAttribute("typing...");                            ❹
    HtmlSubmitInput submitButton = form.getInputByName("submit");
    HtmlPage resultPage = submitButton.click();                      ❺
    WebAssert.assertTitleEquals(resultPage, "Result");               ❻
}
}
```

In this listing:

- We use the web client inherited from the parent `ManagedWebClient` class to get the page containing the form ❶, and then we get the form ❷.
- We get the input text field from the form ❸, emulate the user typing in a value ❹, and then get and click the Submit button ❺.

- We get back a page from clicking the button, and we make sure it is the expected page ❻.

If at any step the framework does not find an object, the API throws an exception, and the test automatically fails. This allows us to focus on the test and let the framework handle failing the test if the page or form is not as expected.

15.3.6 *Testing JavaScript*

HtmlUnit processes JavaScript automatically. Even when, for example, HTML is generated with `Document.write()`, we follow the usual pattern: call `getPage`, find an element, click it, and check the result.

We can toggle JavaScript support on and off in a web client by calling

```
webClient.getOptions().setJavaScriptEnabled(true);
```

or

```
webClient.getOptions().setJavaScriptEnabled(false);
```

HtmlUnit enables JavaScript support by default. We can also set how long a script is allowed to run before being terminated, by calling

```
webClient.setJavaScriptTimeout(timeout);
```

To deal with JavaScript alert and confirm calls, we can provide the framework with callback routines. We will explore these next.

TESTING JAVASCRIPT ALERTS

Our tests can check which JavaScript alerts have taken place. We will reuse our example for testing forms from listing 15.7; it includes JavaScript validation code to alert the user about empty input values.

The test in listing 15.8 loads our form page and checks calling the alert when the form detects an error condition. Our test installs an alert handler that gathers all alerts and checks the result after the page has been loaded. The class `Collecting-AlertHandler` saves alert messages for later inspection.

Listing 15.8 Asserting expected alerts

```
[...]
public class FormTest extends ManagedWebClient {
[...]}

@Test
public void testFormAlert() throws IOException {
    CollectingAlertHandler alertHandler =
            new CollectingAlertHandler();            ❶      ❷
    webClient.setAlertHandler(alertHandler);
    HtmlPage page = webClient.getPage(                      ❸
            "file:src/main/webapp/formtest.html");
❹    HtmlForm form = page.getFormByName("validated_form");          ❺
    HtmlSubmitInput submitButton = form.getInputByName("submit");
```

```
       HtmlPage resultPage = submitButton.click();
       WebAssert.assertTitleEquals(resultPage, page.getTitleText());
  6    WebAssert.assertTextPresent(resultPage, page.asText());

       List<String> collectedAlerts =
                   alertHandler.getCollectedAlerts();
       List<String> expectedAlerts = Collections.singletonList(
                                 "Please enter a value.");
       assertEquals(expectedAlerts, collectedAlerts);
   }
}
```

6 ⟶ (from resultPage line)
7 ⟵ (from assertTitleEquals)
8 ⟵ (from assertTextPresent)
9 (from getCollectedAlerts)
10 (from singletonList)
11 (from assertEquals)

In this listing:

- We create the alert handler ❶, which we install in the web client inherited from the parent class ❷.
- We get the form page ❸, the form object ❹, and the Submit button ❺, and we click the button ❻. This invokes the JavaScript, which calls the alert.
- Clicking the button returns a page object, which we use to check that the page has not changed by comparing the current and previous page titles ❼. We also check that the page has not changed by comparing the current and previous page objects ❽.
- We get the list of alert messages that were raised ❾, create a list of expected alert messages ❿, and compare the expected and actual lists ⓫.

Next, we rewrite the original form test from listing 15.7 to make sure the form's normal operation doesn't raise alerts.

Listing 15.9 Asserting no alerts under normal operation

```
[...]
public class FormTest extends ManagedWebClient {
[...]

    @Test
    public void testFormNoAlert() throws IOException {
        CollectingAlertHandler alertHandler =
                                 new CollectingAlertHandler();          ❶
        webClient.setAlertHandler(alertHandler);
        HtmlPage page = webClient.getPage(
                "file:src/main/webapp/formtest.html");
        HtmlForm form = page.getFormByName("validated_form");           ❷
        HtmlTextInput input = form.getInputByName("in_text");
        input.setValueAttribute("typing...");
        HtmlSubmitInput submitButton = form.getInputByName("submit");
        HtmlPage resultPage = submitButton.click();
        WebAssert.assertTitleEquals(resultPage, "Result");
        assertTrue(alertHandler.getCollectedAlerts().isEmpty(),          ❸
                "No alerts expected");
    }

}
```

In this listing:

- We install a `CollectingAlertHandler` in the web client ❶.
- We simulate a user entering a value ❷ and, at the end of the test, check that the alert handler list of messages is empty ❸.

To customize the alert behavior, we need to implement our own `AlertHandler`. Setting `AlertHandler` as shown next will cause our test to fail when a script raises the first alert.

Listing 15.10   Custom alert handler

```
webClient.setAlertHandler((page, message) ->
                          fail("JavaScript alert: " + message));
```

Now we apply the same principles to test JavaScript confirm calls by installing a confirm handler in the web client with `setConfirmHandler`.

Listing 15.11   Asserting the expected confirmation messages

```
[...]
public class WindowConfirmTest extends ManagedWebClient {

    @Test
    public void testWindowConfirm() throws FailingHttpStatusCodeException,
                                           IOException {
        String html = "<html><head><title>Hello</title></head>           ❶
                       <body onload='confirm(\"Confirm Message\")'>
                       </body></html>";
        URL testUrl = new URL("http://Page1/");                          ❷
        MockWebConnection mockConnection = new MockWebConnection();      ❸
        final List<String> confirmMessages = new ArrayList<String>();    ❹

        webClient.setConfirmHandler((page, message) -> {
            confirmMessages.add(message);                                ❺
            return true;
        });
        mockConnection.setResponse(testUrl, html);                       ❻
        webClient.setWebConnection(mockConnection);                      ❼

        HtmlPage firstPage = webClient.getPage(testUrl);                 ❽
        WebAssert.assertTitleEquals(firstPage, "Hello");                 ❾
        assertArrayEquals(new String[] { "Confirm Message" },            ❿
                          confirmMessages.toArray());
    }
}
```

In this listing:

- We create the HTML page, including the confirm message ❶ and the test URL to be accessed ❷.
- We create a mock connection ❸ and initialize an empty confirm message list ❹.

- We set up the `webClient` inherited from the superclass with a confirm handler defined as a lambda expression that will simply add the message to the list ❺. We set the response of the connection when accessing the test URL ❻ and then set the web client connection to our mock connection ❼.
- We get the page ❽ and then check its title ❾ and the array of confirming messages ❿.

Next, we will modify the previous code to introduce a function in the JavaScript of the emulated website and a handler to collect alerts.

Listing 15.12 Asserting expected confirmation messages from a JavaScript function

```java
public class WindowConfirmTest extends ManagedWebClient {

  @Test
  public void testWindowConfirmAndAlert() throws
                FailingHttpStatusCodeException, IOException {
    String html = "<html><head><title>Hello</title>
                <script>function go(){
                    alert(confirm('Confirm Message'))
                }</script>\n" +
                "</head><body onload='go()'></body></html>";
    URL testUrl = new URL("http://Page1/");
    MockWebConnection mockConnection = new MockWebConnection();
    final List<String> confirmMessages = new ArrayList<String>();
    webClient.setAlertHandler(new CollectingAlertHandler());
    webClient.setConfirmHandler((page, message) -> {
        confirmMessages.add(message);
        return true;
    });
    mockConnection.setResponse(testUrl, html);
    webClient.setWebConnection(mockConnection);

    HtmlPage firstPage = webClient.getPage(testUrl);
    WebAssert.assertTitleEquals(firstPage, "Hello");
    assertArrayEquals(new String[] { "Confirm Message" },
                confirmMessages.toArray());
    assertArrayEquals(new String[] { "true" },
                ((CollectingAlertHandler)
                 webClient.getAlertHandler())
                .getCollectedAlerts().toArray());
  }
}
```

❶ ❷ ❸ ❹

In this listing:

- We create the HTML page, including a confirm message provided by a JavaScript function ❶.
- We set an alert handler for the `webClient` inherited from the superclass ❷. A `CollectingAlertHandler` is a simple alert handler that keeps track of alerts in a list.

- In addition to the list of confirmation messages ❸, we also check the collected alerts ❹.

> **TIP** Note that when you run some of the HtmlUnit tests in these sections, you may get a series of warnings. The problem is not in the test, but in the CSS of the web page that is accessed.

15.4 *Introducing Selenium*

Selenium (https://seleniumhq.org) is a free, open source tool suite used to test web applications. Selenium's strength lies in its ability to run tests against a real browser on a specific OS; this is unlike HtmlUnit, which emulates the browser in the same VM as your tests. Selenium lets you write tests in various programming languages, including Java with JUnit 5.

Selenium WebDriver is the name of the key interface against which tests should be written. Selenium WebDriver is a W3C Recommendation and is implemented by many current browsers, including Chrome, Firefox, and Internet Explorer. WebDriver makes direct calls to the browser, using each browser's native support for automation. How these direct calls are made, and the features they support, depends on the browser you are using. Every browser has different logic for performing actions on the browser. Figure 15.2 shows the various components of the Selenium WebDriver architecture.

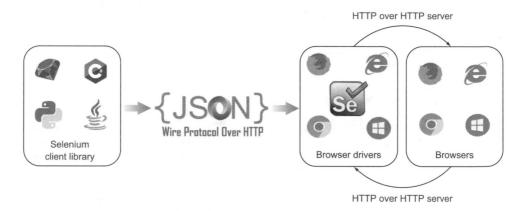

Figure 15.2   The Selenium WebDriver architecture, including the Selenium client library, the browser drivers, the browsers themselves, and HTTP communication

WebDriver includes the following four components:

- *Selenium client libraries*—Selenium supports multiple libraries for programming languages such as Java, C#, PHP, Python, Ruby, and so on.
- *JSON Wire Protocol over HTTP*—JavaScript Object Notation (JSON) is used to transfer data between servers and clients on the web. JSON Wire Protocol is a REST API that transfers the information to the HTTP server. Each WebDriver

(such as FirefoxDriver, ChromeDriver, InternetExplorerDriver, and so on) has its own HTTP server.

- *Browser drivers*—Each browser has a separate browser driver. Browser drivers communicate with the respective browser without revealing the internal logic of the browser functionality. When a browser driver receives a command, that command is executed on the browser, and the response goes back in the form of an HTTP response.
- *Browsers*—Selenium supports multiple browsers such as Firefox, Chrome, Internet Explorer, and Safari.

15.5 Writing Selenium tests

In this section, we will explore writing individual tests with Selenium. We will look at how to test for more than one browser and how to navigate the object model, and we will work through some example JUnit 5 tests. The first thing to do to set up a Selenium Java project is to include the Maven dependency into the project.

> **Listing 15.13 Selenium dependency in the pom.xml configuration**

```
<dependency>
    <groupId>org.seleniumhq.selenium</groupId>
    <artifactId>selenium-java</artifactId>
    <version>3.141.59</version>
</dependency>
```

As of version 3, Selenium supports the browsers listed in table 15.2.

Table 15.2 Browsers supported by Selenium

Web browser	Browser driver class
Google Chrome	ChromeDriver
Internet Explorer	InternetExplorerDriver
Safari	SafariDriver
Opera	OperaDriver
Firefox	FirefoxDriver
Edge	EdgeDriver

To be able to test for a specific browser, we will need to download the Selenium drivers for that specific browser and include the access path to it on the OS path. The links to download each driver can be found by visiting https://selenium.dev/downloads/, navigating to the Browsers section, and choosing the browser you are interested in.

For demonstration purposes, we are going to use three of the most popular browsers: Google Chrome, Internet Explorer, and Mozilla Firefox. So, we download the Selenium drivers for them and copy them into a dedicated folder, as shown in figure 15.3.

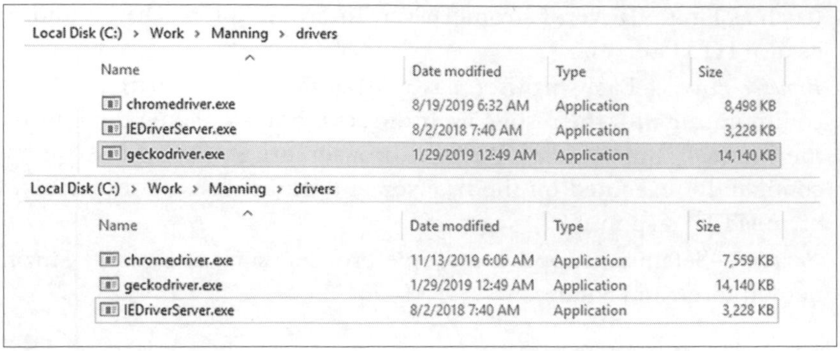

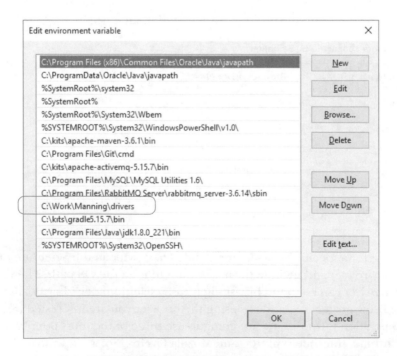

Figure 15.3   The folder containing the Selenium drivers

> **NOTE**   You must use the driver corresponding to the exact browser installed on your computer. For example, if your Google Chrome version is 79, you will only be able to use version 79 of the driver—versions such as 77, 78, and 80 will not work.

We need to include the folder with the Selenium drivers on the OS path. On Windows, we do this by choosing This PC > Properties > Advanced System Settings > Environment Variables > Path > Edit (figure 15.4). To do this on other OSs, consult the documentation.

Figure 15.4   The path to the Selenium drivers folder added on the OS path

We have now set up the environment and are ready to write Selenium tests.

15.5.1 *Testing for a specific web browser*

Our tests will use specific browsers at first. We'll try two tests that access the Manning home page and the Google home page and verify that their titles are as expected. Listings 15.14 and 15.15 use Chrome and Firefox in two separate test classes along with JUnit 5 annotated methods.

Listing 15.14 Accessing the Manning and Google home pages with Chrome

```
[...]
public class ChromeSeleniumTest {

    private WebDriver driver;                    ◁───┐
                                                     ❶
    @BeforeEach
    void setUp() {
        driver = new ChromeDriver();             ◁───┐
    }                                                ❷

    @Test
    void testChromeManning() {
        driver.get("https://www.manning.com/");
        assertThat(driver.getTitle(), is("Manning | Home"));   ❸
    }

    @Test
    void testChromeGoogle() {
        driver.get("https://www.google.com");
        assertThat(driver.getTitle(), is("Google"));    ❹
    }


    @AfterEach                      ❺
    void tearDown() {
        driver.quit();              ◁───┐
    }
}
```

Listing 15.15 Accessing the Manning and Google home pages with Firefox

```
[...]
public class FirefoxSeleniumTest {

    private WebDriver driver;                    ◁───┐
                                                     ❶'
    @BeforeEach
    void setUp() {
        driver = new FirefoxDriver();            ◁───┐
    }                                                ❷'
```

```
@Test
void testFirefoxManning() {
    driver.get("https://www.manning.com/");
    assertThat(driver.getTitle(), is("Manning | Home"));    ❸'
}

@Test
void testFirefoxGoogle() {
    driver.get("https://www.google.com");
    assertThat(driver.getTitle(), is("Google"));    ❹'
}

@AfterEach
void tearDown() {
    driver.quit();    ◁
}                                    ❺'
}
```

In these listings:

- We declare a web driver ❶ ❶', and we initialize it as ChromeDriver ❷ and as FirefoxDriver ❷', respectively.
- The first test accesses the Manning home page and checks that the title of the page is "Manning | Home" ❸ ❸'. We do this using Hamcrest matchers (see chapter 2).
- The second test accesses the Google home page and checks that the title of the page is "Google" ❹ ❹'. We also do this using Hamcrest matchers.
- After executing each JUnit 5 test, we make sure we call the quit method of the web driver, which closes all the open browser windows. The driver instance becomes garbage collectible, meaning it is available to be removed from memory ❺ ❺'.

If we run each of these tests, the execution opens Chrome and Firefox, respectively, accesses the Manning and Google websites, and validates their titles.

15.5.2 *Testing navigation using a web browser*

Our next test will access the Wikipedia website, find an element on the page, and click it. We'll use JUnit 5 annotations and Firefox to do this.

Listing 15.16   **Finding an element on a page with Firefox**

```
[...]
public class WikipediaAccessTest {

    private RemoteWebDriver driver;    ◁
                                          ❶
    @BeforeEach                              ❷
    void setUp() {
        driver = new FirefoxDriver();    ◁
    }
```

```
@Test
void testWikipediaAccess() {
    driver.get("https://en.wikipedia.org/");
    assertThat(driver.getTitle(),
               is("Wikipedia, the free encyclopedia"));

    WebElement contents = driver.findElementByLinkText("Contents");
    assertTrue(contents.isDisplayed());

    contents.click();
    assertThat(driver.getTitle(),
               is("Wikipedia:Contents - Wikipedia "));
}

@AfterEach
void tearDown() {
    driver.quit();
}
}
```

In this listing:

- We declare a web driver as `RemoteWebDriver` ❶. `RemoteWebDriver` is a class that implements the `WebDriver` interface and is extended by browser classes as `FirefoxDriver`, `ChromeDriver`, or `InternetExplorerDriver`. We declare the web driver as `RemoteWebDriver` in order to be able to call the method that finds elements on a web page and that is not declared by the `WebDriver` interface.
- We initialize the web driver as `FirefoxDriver` ❷.
- We access the Wikipedia home page and check that the title of the page is "Wikipedia, the free encyclopedia" ❸.
- We look for the Contents element and check that it is displayed ❹.
- We click the Contents element and check that the newly displayed page has the title "Wikipedia:Contents – Wikipedia" ❺.
- After executing the test, we make sure we call the `quit` method of the web driver, which closes all the open browser windows. The driver instance becomes garbage collectible, meaning it is available to be removed from memory ❻.

TIP You can easily change this program to use another web driver, such as `ChromeDriver` or `InternetExplorerDriver`. Try doing this as an exercise.

15.5.3 *Testing more than one web browser*

To emphasize the advantages of the new JUnit 5 features and put them in practice in our Selenium tests, we will run the same test class with more than one browser. The following listing reworks our example of accessing the Manning and Google home pages as JUnit 5 parameterized tests running with different browsers.

Listing 15.17   Accessing Manning and Google with different browsers

```java
public class MultiBrowserSeleniumTest {                              ❶

    private WebDriver driver;

    public static Collection<WebDriver> getBrowserVersions() {
        return Arrays.asList(new WebDriver[] {new FirefoxDriver(), new
                ChromeDriver(), new InternetExplorerDriver()});       ❷
    }

    @ParameterizedTest                                    ❸
    @MethodSource("getBrowserVersions")
    void testManningAccess(WebDriver driver) {
        this.driver = driver;
        driver.get("https://www.manning.com/");           ❹
        assertThat(driver.getTitle(), is("Manning | Home"));
    }

    @ParameterizedTest                                    ❸
    @MethodSource("getBrowserVersions")
    void testGoogleAccess(WebDriver driver) {
        this.driver = driver;
        driver.get("https://www.google.com");             ❺
        assertThat(driver.getTitle(), is("Google"));
    }

    @AfterEach
    void tearDown() {
        driver.quit();                   ◁
    }                                                    ❻

}
```

In this listing:

- We define a `WebDriver` field that will be initialized during test execution ❶.
- We create the `getBrowserVersions` method that will serve as a method source for injecting the argument of each parameterized test ❷. The method returns a collection of web drivers (`FirefoxDriver`, `ChromeDriver`, and `InternetExplorerDriver`) that are injected one by one into the parameterized tests.
- We define two parameterized tests, for which the `getBrowserVersions` method provides the test arguments ❸. This means each of the parameterized methods is executed a number of times equal to the size of the collection returned by `getBrowserVersions`—and it uses a different browser each time it runs.
- The first test saves a reference to the web driver in the field variable, accesses the Manning home page, and checks that the title of the page is "Manning | Home" ❹. We do this using Hamcrest matchers (see chapter 2). The JUnit 5

parameterized test is executed three times: once for each of the web drivers provided by the getBrowserVersions method. After executing each test, we make sure we call the quit method of the web driver, which closes all the open browser windows.

- The second test saves a reference to the web driver in the field variable, accesses the Google home page, and checks that the title of the page is "Google" **⑤**. The test is also executed three times, once for each of the web drivers provided by getBrowserVersions. We also do this using Hamcrest matchers.
- After executing each test, we call the quit method of the web driver **⑥**.

If we run this test class, the execution opens the Firefox, Chrome, and Internet Explorer browsers for each test, accesses the Manning and Google websites, and validates their titles. Two tests are executed through three browsers each—this is a total of six test executions.

15.5.4 Testing Google search and navigation using different web browsers

Next, we will see how to test a Google search by clicking one of the links we obtain from the search engine and navigating in the result. In the following listing, we search for "en.wikipedia.org" using Google, jump to the first result, and then navigate to an element inside it.

Listing 15.18   Testing Google search and navigating the Wikipedia website

```
public class GoogleSearchTest {                              ❶

    private RemoteWebDriver driver;          ◁─┘

    public static Collection<RemoteWebDriver> getBrowserVersions() {
        return Arrays.asList(new RemoteWebDriver[] {new FirefoxDriver(),    ❷
            new ChromeDriver(), new InternetExplorerDriver()});
    }

    @ParameterizedTest
    @MethodSource("getBrowserVersions")                      ❸
    void testGoogleSearch(RemoteWebDriver driver) {
        driver.get("http://www.google.com");
        WebElement element = driver.findElement(By.name("q"));          ❹
        element.sendKeys("en.wikipedia.org");
        driver.findElement(By.name("q")).sendKeys(Keys.ENTER);          ❺

        WebElement myDynamicElement = (new WebDriverWait(driver, 10))
                .until(ExpectedConditions                               ❻
                .presenceOfElementLocated(By.id("result-stats")));

        List<WebElement> findElements =
                driver.findElements(By.xpath("//*[@id='rso']//a/h3"));  ❼
```

```
        findElements.get(0).click();

        assertEquals("https://en.wikipedia.org/wiki/Main_Page",      ⑧
                            driver.getCurrentUrl());
        assertThat(driver.getTitle(),
                is("Wikipedia, the free encyclopedia"));

        WebElement contents = driver.findElementByLinkText("Contents");   ⑨
        assertTrue(contents.isDisplayed());

        contents.click();                                                ⑩
        assertThat(driver.getTitle(),
                        is("Wikipedia:Contents - Wikipedia"));
    }

@AfterEach
void tearDown() {
    driver.quit();                  �
}

}
```
                                            ⑪

In this listing:

- We declare a `RemoteWebDriver` field that will be initialized during test execution ❶.
- We create the `getBrowserVersions` method that serves as a method source for injecting the argument of each parameterized test ❷. The method returns a collection of `RemoteWebDrivers` (`FirefoxDriver`, `ChromeDriver`, and `InternetExplorerDriver`) that will be injected one by one into the parameterized tests. We need `RemoteWebDrivers` in order to call the method that finds elements on a web page and that is not declared by the `WebDriver` interface.
- We define one JUnit 5 parameterized test, for which `getBrowserVersions` provides the test argument ❸. This means the parameterized method will be executed a number of times equal to the size of the collection returned by `getBrowserVersions`.
- We access the http://www.google.com website and look for the element with the "q" name ❹. This is the name of the input edit box where we need to insert the text to search for; we can obtain it by right-clicking the element and choosing Inspect or Inspect Element (depending on the browser). We get the result shown in figure 15.5.
- We insert the text "en.wikipedia.org" to search for using Google, and we press Enter ❺.
- We wait until the Google page shows the result, but no longer than 10 seconds ❻.
- We use an XPath to get all the elements returned by the Google search ❼. XPath is a query language for finding elements in XML. Right now, all you

need to know is that the `//*[@id='rso']//a/h3` XPath provides the list of all elements returned by the Google search. For more about working with XPath in Selenium, see www.guru99.com/xpath-selenium.html.

- We click the first element on the list and check the URL and the title of the newly accessed page **8**.
- On this new page, we look for the element with the "Contents" text and check that it is displayed **9** Then, we click this element and check that the title of the newly accessed page is "Wikipedia:Contents—Wikipedia" **10**.
- After executing the test, we call the `quit` method of the web driver, which closes all the open browser windows. The driver instance becomes garbage collectible, meaning it is available to be removed from memory **11**.

Figure 15.5   Inspecting the name of the input edit box on the Google home page with the help of Firefox

If we run this test, the execution opens the Firefox, Chrome, and Internet Explorer browsers. We have one test executed through three browsers—a total of three test executions.

15.5.5 Testing website authentication

Many of Tested Data Systems' customers interact with their applications using websites where they need to authenticate. Authentication is critical for such applications because it verifies the identity of the user and allows access. Consequently, John needs to test authentication by writing tests to follow both successful and unsuccessful scenarios. John chooses Selenium, as he would also like to follow the interaction with the website visually.

John will use the website https://the-internet.herokuapp.com, which provides many functionalities that can be automatically tested, including form authentication. The class in the following listing represents the interaction with the https://the-internet .herokuapp.com home page (figure 15.6).

Figure 15.6   The https://the-internet.herokuapp.com home page

Listing 15.19   Class describing the home page of the tested website

```
[...]
public class Homepage {                                          ❶
    private WebDriver webDriver;

    public Homepage(WebDriver webDriver) {                       ❷
        this.webDriver = webDriver;
    }

    public LoginPage openFormAuthentication() {          ❸              ❹
        webDriver.get("https://the-internet.herokuapp.com/");
        webDriver.findElement(By.cssSelector("[href=\"/login\"]"))
                .click();
        return new LoginPage(webDriver);          ❺
    }
}
```

In this listing:

- The Homepage class contains a private WebDriver field that is used to interact with the website **①**. It is initialized by the constructor of the class **②**.
- In the openFormAuthentication class, John accesses https://the-internet .herokuapp.com/ **③**. He looks for the element having the login hyperlink (href) and clicks it **④**. He returns a new LoginPage **⑤** (described in the next listing) and receives the web driver as an argument of the constructor.

The class in the next listing represents the interaction with the https://the-internet .herokuapp.com/login login page (figure 15.7).

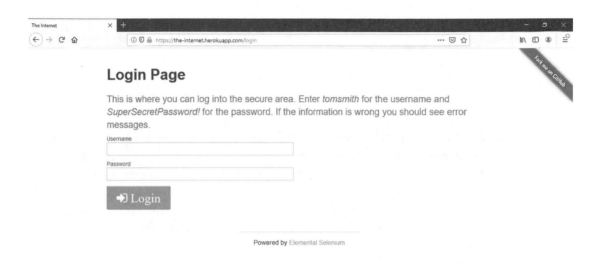

Figure 15.7   Login page at https://the-internet.herokuapp.com/login

Listing 15.20   Class describing the login page of the tested website

```
[...]
public class LoginPage {

    private WebDriver webDriver;                          ◁─┐ ❶

    public LoginPage(WebDriver webDriver) {               ❷
        this.webDriver = webDriver;                       ◁─┘
    }

    public LoginPage loginWith(String username, String password) {
        webDriver.findElement(By.id("username")).sendKeys(username);    ❸
        webDriver.findElement(By.id("password")).sendKeys(password);
```

```
        webDriver.findElement(By.cssSelector("#login button")).click();    ←┐
                                                                            ④
        return this;                      ←┐
    }                                      ⑤

    public void thenLoginSuccessful() {
        assertTrue(webDriver
                .findElement(By.cssSelector("#flash.success"))
                .isDisplayed());                                            ⑥
        assertTrue(webDriver
                .findElement(By.cssSelector("[href=\"/logout\"]"))
                .isDisplayed());
    }

    public void thenLoginUnsuccessful() {
     assertTrue(webDriver.findElement(By.id("username"))
                    .isDisplayed());                                        ⑦
     assertTrue(webDriver.findElement(By.id("password"))
                    .isDisplayed());
    }
}
```

In this listing:

- The `LoginPage` class contains a private `WebDriver` field that is used to interact with the website ❶. It is initialized by the constructor of the class ❷.
- The `loginWith` method finds the elements with the IDs `username` and `password` and writes in their content the string arguments `username` and `password` from the method ❸. Then, John finds the Login button using a CSS selector and clicks it ❹. The method returns the same object, as John intends to execute the `thenLoginSuccessful` and `thenLoginUnsuccessful` methods on it ❺.
- He checks for a successful login by verifying that the elements with the CSS selector `#flash.success` (the shaded bar in figure 15.8) and the hyperlink (`href`) `logout` (the Logout button in figure 15.8) are displayed on the page ❻. Remember that you can get the name of an element by right-clicking it and choosing Inspect or Inspect element (depending on the browser).
- He checks for an unsuccessful login by verifying that the elements with the IDs `username` and `password` are displayed on the page ❼. This is because after an unsuccessful login attempt, we remain on the same page (figure 15.9).

DEFINITION   *CSS selector*—The combination of an element selector and a selector value that identifies web elements within a web page. For now, you only need to know that the `#login button` CSS selector finds this element on the web page. For more about CSS selectors, see https://www.w3schools.com/css-ref/css_selectors.asp.

John uses the `Homepage` and `LoginPage` classes that he has created to run the successful and unsuccessful login testing scenarios, as shown in listing 15.21. Tom Smith

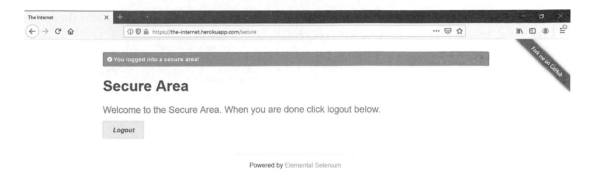

Figure 15.8   Successful login at https://the-internet.herokuapp.com/secure

Figure 15.9   Unsuccessful login at https://the-internet.herokuapp.com/secure

is a test user who accesses a web interface for the example flight-management application. The credentials that allow the login are username `tomsmith` and password `SuperSecretPassword!`. John will work with this test user (never use real credentials in a test—doing so is a breach of security): he will create a test with the test user's correct credentials (which should never be changed, as the test will fail otherwise) and another test with incorrect credentials.

Listing 15.21   Successful and unsuccessful login tests

```
[...]
public class LoginTest {

    private Homepage homepage;
    private WebDriver webDriver;                              ❶

    public static Collection<WebDriver> getBrowserVersions() {
        return Arrays.asList(new WebDriver[] {new FirefoxDriver(),   ❷
                new ChromeDriver(), new InternetExplorerDriver()});
    }

    @ParameterizedTest
    @MethodSource("getBrowserVersions")                      ❸
    public void loginWithValidCredentials(WebDriver webDriver) {
            this.webDriver = webDriver;                      ❹
        homepage = new Homepage(webDriver);
        homepage
                .openFormAuthentication()
                .loginWith("tomsmith", "SuperSecretPassword!")   ❺
                .thenLoginSuccessful();
    }

    @ParameterizedTest
    @MethodSource("getBrowserVersions")                      ❸
    public void loginWithInvalidCredentials(WebDriver webDriver) {
            this.webDriver = webDriver;                      ❹
        homepage = new Homepage(webDriver);
        homepage
                .openFormAuthentication()
                .loginWith("tomsmith", "SuperSecretPassword")    ❻
                .thenLoginUnsuccessful();
    }

    @AfterEach
    void tearDown() {                                        ❼
        webDriver.quit();
    }

}
```

In this listing:

- John declares a Homepage field and a WebDriver field that will be initialized during test execution ❶.
- He creates the getBrowserVersions method that will serve as a method source for injecting the argument of the parameterized tests ❷. The method returns a collection of WebDrivers (FirefoxDriver, ChromeDriver, and

> `InternetExplorerDriver`) that are injected one by one into the parameterized tests.

- He defines two JUnit 5 parameterized tests, for which `getBrowserVersions` provides the test arguments ❸. This means the parameterized method is executed a number of times equal to the size of the collection returned by the `getBrowserVersions` method.

- John starts each parameterized test by keeping a reference to the web driver inside the test and initializing a `Homepage` variable, passing its constructor the web driver as an argument ❹.

- The first test opens the form authentication, logs in with the valid username and password, and checks that the login is successful ❺.

- The second test opens the form authentication, logs in with an invalid username and password, and checks that the login is unsuccessful ❻.

- After executing each test, the `quit` method of the web driver is executed, which closes all the open browser windows. The driver instance becomes garbage collectible ❼.

John has now implemented two scenarios: successful and unsuccessful logins to the website. And he has done more than this: he has created, through the `Homepage` and `LoginPage` classes, the basics of a testing library that other developers who join the project will be able to use. In listing 15.21, the calls to the testing methods flow one after the other; the test scenario is easy for any newcomer to understand. This will really speed up the development of Selenium tests at Tested Data Systems!

15.6 *HtmlUnit vs. Selenium*

Let's recap the similarities and differences of HtmlUnit and Selenium. Both are free and open source, and both of their versions at the time of writing (HtmlUnit 2.36.0 and Selenium 3.141.59) require Java 8 as the minimum platform to run. The major difference between the two is that HtmlUnit emulates a specific web browser, whereas Selenium drives a real web browser process.

HtmlUnit's benefits are that, because it's a headless web browser, test execution is faster. It also provides its own domain-specific set of assertions.

Selenium's benefits are that the API is simpler and drives native browsers, which guarantees that the behavior of tests is as close as possible to interaction with real users. Selenium also supports multiple languages and provides a "visual effect" for executing larger scenarios by running the real browsers—a reason why it has been preferred for testing authentication functionality in the real world.

In general, use HtmlUnit when your application is independent of OS features and browser-specific implementations not accounted for by HtmlUnit. And use Selenium when you require validation of specific browsers and OSs, especially if the application takes advantage of or depends on a browser-specific implementation.

In the next chapter, we will start building and testing applications using one of the most popular Java frameworks today: Spring.

Summary

This chapter has covered the following:

- Examining presentation-layer testing
- Using HtmlUnit, an open source, headless browser tool
- Using Selenium, an open source tool that drives various browsers programmatically
- Testing HTML assertions (`assertTitleEquals`, `assertTextPresent`, `notNull`) and the functionality of different web browsers, and creating standalone tests using HtmlUnit
- Testing forms, web navigation and frames, and websites developed with JavaScript using HtmlUnit
- Testing the operation of searching on Google, selecting a link, and navigating on it using Selenium and different web browsers
- Creating and testing a website authentication scenario using Selenium

Testing Spring applications

16

This chapter covers

- Understanding dependency injection
- Building and testing a Spring application
- Using `SpringExtension` for JUnit Jupiter
- Testing Spring application features with JUnit 5

"Dependency Injection" is a 25-dollar term for a 5-cent concept.

—James Shore

Spring is a lightweight—but at the same time flexible and universal—open source set of frameworks for creating Java applications. It is not dedicated to any particular layer, which means it can be used at the level of any layer of a Java application. This chapter will focus on the basis of Spring: the dependency injection (or inversion of control) pattern; and how to test core Spring applications with the help of JUnit 5.

16.1 Introducing the Spring Framework

A *library* is a collection of classes or functions that enables code reuse: we can use code created by other developers. Usually, a library is dedicated to a domain-specific area. For example, there are libraries of computer graphics that let us quickly build three-dimensional scenes and display them on the computer screen.

On the other hand, a software *framework* is an abstraction in which software with generic functionality can be changed by code that the user writes. This enables the creation of specific software. A framework supports the development of software applications by providing a working paradigm. The key difference between a library and a framework is *inversion of control* (IoC). When you call a method from a library, you are in control. But with a framework, control is inverted: the framework calls *you* (see figure 16.1). You must follow the paradigm provided by the framework and fill out your own code. The framework defines a skeleton, and you insert the features to fill out that skeleton. Your code is under the control of the framework, and the framework calls it. This way, you can focus on implementing the business logic rather than on the design.

Rod Johnson created Spring in 2003, beginning with his book *Expert One-on-One J2EE Design and Development*. The basic idea behind Spring is to simplify the traditional approach to designing enterprise applications.

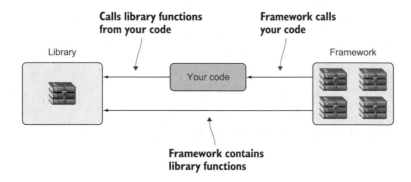

Figure 16.1   Your code calls a library. A framework calls your code.

The Spring Framework provides a comprehensive infrastructure for developing Java applications. It handles the infrastructure so that you can focus on your application and enables you to build applications from plain old Java objects (POJOs).

16.2 *Introducing dependency injection*

A Java application typically consists of objects that collaborate to form the application. The objects in an application have dependencies on each other. Java cannot organize the building blocks of an application and instead leaves that task to developers and architects. You can use design patterns (factory, builder, proxy, decorator, and so on) to compose classes and objects, but this burden is on the side of the developer.

Spring implements various design patterns. The Spring Framework dependency injection (also known as IoC) pattern provides a means of composing disparate components into a fully working application.

We'll start by demonstrating the traditional approach, where dependencies need to be managed by the developer at the level of the code. You will find the first examples in the ch16-traditional folder in the source code for this chapter. In our example flight-manage-ment application developed at Tested Data Sys-

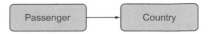

Figure 16.2 A passenger is from a country, and the `Passenger` **object is dependent on a** `Country` **object.**

tems, each passenger who is tracked comes from a country. In figure 16.2, a `Passenger` object is dependent on a `Country` object. We initialize this dependency directly in listings 16.1 and 16.2.

Listing 16.1 `Country` class

```
public class Country {                                    ❶
    private String name;                             ❷
    private String codeName;

    public Country(String name, String codeName) {
        this.name = name;                                    ❸
        this.codeName = codeName;
    }

    public String getName() {
        return name;                          ❶
    }

    public String getCodeName() {
        return codeName;              ❷
    }
}
```

In this listing:

- We create a `name` field together with a getter for it ❶ and a `codeName` field with a getter for it ❷.
- We create a constructor that initializes the `name` and `codeName` fields ❸.

Listing 16.2 `Passenger` class

```
public class Passenger {                                  ❶
    private String name;                     ❷
    private Country country;

    public Passenger(String name) {
        this.name = name;                                        ❸
        this.country = new Country("USA", "US");
    }

    public String getName() {
        return name;                          ❶
    }
```

```
public Country getCountry() {
    return country;
}

}
```
❷

In this listing:

- We create a name field together with a getter for it ❶ and a country field and with a getter for it ❷.
- We create a constructor that initializes the name and country fields ❸. The country is effectively initialized in the Passenger constructor, meaning there is a tight coupling between the country and the passenger.

With this approach, we are in the general situation shown in figure 16.3. This approach has several shortcomings:

- Class A directly depends on class B.
- It is impossible to test A separately from B.
- The lifetime of object B depends on A—it is impossible to use an object of type B in other places (although class B can be reused).
- It is not possible to replace B with another implementation.

A ⟶ B

Figure 16.3 The direct general dependency between objects A and B (Passenger and Country in the previous example)

These shortcomings favor a new approach: dependency injection.

With the dependency injection (DI) approach, objects are inserted into a container that injects the dependencies when it creates the object. This process is fundamentally the inverse of the traditional one: hence, the name *inversion of control*. Martin Fowler suggested the name *dependency injection* because it better reflects the essence of the pattern (https://www.martinfowler.com/articles/injection.html). The basic idea is to eliminate the dependency of application components on a certain implementation and to delegate to the container the rights to control class instantiation.

Moving to this new approach for the previous example, we will eliminate the direct dependency between the objects and rewrite the Passenger class. The next sources are found in the ch16-spring-junit4 folder from this chapter.

Listing 16.3 Passenger class, eliminating the tight coupling with Country

```
public class Passenger {
    private String name;
    private Country country;

    public Passenger(String name) {
        this.name = name;
    }
}
```
❶

```java
    public String getName() {
        return name;
    }

    public Country getCountry() {
        return country;
    }

    public void setCountry(Country country) {
        this.country = country;                    ❷
    }

}
```

The change in the code is at the level of its constructor: it no longer creates the dependent country itself ❶. The country can be set through the setCountry method ❷. As shown in figure 16.4, direct dependency has been removed.

Passenger   Country

Figure 16.4 The Passenger **and** Country **classes with no direct dependency**

XML is still the traditional way to configure Spring applications. It has the advantage of being nonintrusive—this means your code will be unaware of the fact that it is being used by a framework and is not mixed with external dependencies. In addition, when the configuration changes, the code does not need to be recompiled. This can be beneficial for testers who have less technical knowledge.

To be comprehensive, in this chapter we'll show alternatives for configuring Spring, and we'll start with XML—it is easier to understand and to follow, at least at the beginning. We'll delegate the management of dependencies to the container, which will be instructed how to do this through the configuration information in the application-context.xml file in listing 16.4. The Spring Framework will use this file to create and manage objects and their dependencies.

> **NOTE** Objects under the control of the Spring Framework container are generally called *beans*. According to the definition in the Spring Framework documentation, "a bean is an object from the backbone of the application, managed by a Spring IoC container."

Listing 16.4 application-context.xml configuration information

```xml
<bean id="passenger" class="com.manning.junitbook.spring.Passenger">    ⟵    ❶
    <constructor-arg name="name" value="John Smith"/>     ⟵
    <property name="country" ref="country"/>     ⟵                           ❷
</bean>                                                      ❸
                                                                ❹

<bean id="country" class="com.manning.junitbook.spring.Country">    ⟵
    <constructor-arg name="name" value="USA"/>               ❻         ❺
    <constructor-arg name="codeName" value="US"/>
</bean>                                                  ⟵
                                                            ❼
```

In this listing:

- We declare the `passenger` bean belonging to the class `com.manning.junit-book.spring.Passenger` ❶. We initialize it by passing to it `"John Smith"` as the argument of the constructor ❷, and we set the country by passing the reference to the `country` bean to the `setCountry` setter ❸. Then, we close the bean definition ❹.
- We declare the `country` bean belonging to the class `com.manning.junit-book.spring.Country` ❺. We initialize it by passing it `"USA"` and `"US"` as arguments of the constructor ❻. Then we close the bean definition ❼.

To access the beans created by the container, we do the following.

Listing 16.5   Accessing the beans defined in the application-context.xml file

```
ClassPathXmlApplicationContext context =
    new ClassPathXmlApplicationContext(                     ❶
            "classpath:application-context.xml");
Passenger passenger = (Passenger) context.getBean("passenger");   ❷   ❸
Country country = (Country) context.getBean("country");
```

In this listing:

- We create a `context` variable of type `ClassPathXmlApplicationContext` and initialize it to point to the application-context.xml file from the classpath ❶. The class `ClassPathXmlApplicationContext` belongs to the Spring Framework; a little later, we'll show how to introduce the dependency that it belongs to in the Maven pom.xml file.
- We request the `passenger` bean from the container ❷, and then we request the `country` bean ❸. From now on, we can use the `passenger` and `country` variables in our program.

The following are the advantages of this approach:

- When we request an object of any type, the container will return it.
- `Passenger` and `Country` are independent of each other and do not depend on any outer libraries—they are POJOs.
- The application-context.xml file documents the system and object dependencies.
- The container controls the lifetime of created objects.
- This approach facilitates the reuse of classes and components.
- The code is cleaner (classes do not initiate auxiliary objects).
- Unit testing is simplified; the classes are simpler and not cluttered with dependencies.
- It is very easy to make changes to object dependencies in the system. We simply need to change the application-context.xml file; we do not need to recompile the Java source files. It is recommended that you insert in the DI (IoC) container any objects for which the implementation may change.

Thus we have taken a step between the traditional approach, where the dependencies are in the code, to the DI (IoC) approach, where objects do not know anything about each other (figure 16.5).

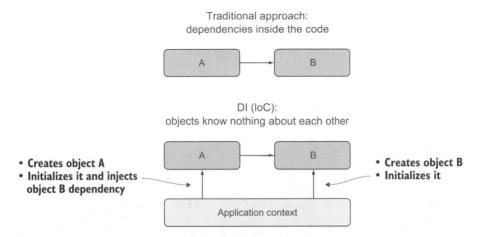

Figure 16.5   Moving from the traditional approach to DI (IoC)

In general, the work of a Spring container can be represented as shown in figure 16.6. When we instantiate and initiate the container, the application classes are combined with metadata (container configuration); as output, we get a fully configured, ready-to-work application.

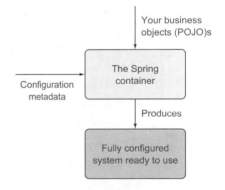

Figure 16.6   The functionality of the Spring container combines the POJOs and configuration metadata.

16.3   Using and testing a Spring application

As we mentioned earlier, due to the advantages of the Spring Framework, Tested Data Systems has introduced it into some of the company's projects, including the flight-management application. The introduction of Spring took place before the company began using JUnit 5, so we'll first look at how that took place.

16.3.1   Creating the Spring context programmatically

A few years ago, Ada was responsible for initially moving the flight-management application to Spring 4 and testing it using JUnit 4. It will be useful to see how Ada accomplished this task, because at some point you may need to work on an application using Spring 4 and/or JUnit 4 and continue its development or migrate it to Spring 5 and JUnit 5. Therefore, we closely examine what such an application looks like.

The first thing Ada had to do to work with Spring 4 and JUnit 4 was to introduce the needed dependencies in the Maven pom.xml file.

Listing 16.6   Spring 4 and JUnit 4 dependencies in pom.xml

```
<dependency>
    <groupId>org.springframework</groupId>
    <artifactId>spring-context</artifactId>          ❶
    <version>4.2.5.RELEASE</version>
</dependency>

<dependency>
    <groupId>org.springframework</groupId>
    <artifactId>spring-test</artifactId>             ❷
    <version>4.2.5.RELEASE</version>
</dependency>

<dependency>
    <groupId>junit</groupId>
    <artifactId>junit</artifactId>                   ❸
    <version>4.12</version>
</dependency>
```

In this listing:

- Ada adds the `spring-context` Maven dependency ❶. This is necessary in order to use classes such as `ClassPathXmlApplicationContext` that are needed to load the application context or the `@Autowired` annotation that we'll introduce later.
- She adds the `spring-test` Maven dependency ❷. This is needed in order to use the `SpringJUnit4ClassRunner` runner (we'll demonstrate its use).
- She also adds the JUnit 4.12 dependency ❸. Remember, Spring was added to the flight-management application a few years ago, before JUnit 5 existed.

The first test Ada wrote at that time loaded a passenger from the Spring container and verified its correctness.

Listing 16.7   First unit test for a Spring application

```
[...]                                  ❶
public class SimpleAppTest {

    private static final String APPLICATION_CONTEXT_XML_FILE_NAME =     ❷
            "classpath:application-context.xml";

    private ClassPathXmlApplicationContext context;      ❸

    private Passenger expectedPassenger;                 ❹

    @Before
    public void setUp() {
```

```
        context = new ClassPathXmlApplicationContext(          (5)       (6)
            APPLICATION_CONTEXT_XML_FILE_NAME);                          ◁
        expectedPassenger = getExpectedPassenger();
    }

    @Test                                                                     (7)
    public void testInitPassenger() {
        Passenger passenger = (Passenger) context.getBean("passenger");  ◁
        assertEquals(expectedPassenger, passenger);               ◁
    }
                                                                     (8)
}
```

In this listing:

- Ada creates a `SimpleAppTest` class ❶. It defines the string to access the application-context.xml file on the classpath ❷, the Spring context ❸, and the `expectedPassenger` ❹ to be constructed programmatically and compared with the one extracted from the Spring context.
- Before the execution of each test, she creates the context based on the string to access the application-context.xml file on the classpath ❺ and creates the `expectedPassenger` programmatically ❻.
- In the test, she gets the `passenger` bean from the context ❼ and compares it with the one constructed programmatically ❽. The configuration of the `passenger` bean from the Spring context is from listing 16.4.

To make an accurate comparison between the passenger extracted from the container and the one constructed programmatically, Ada overrides the `equals` and `hashCode` methods from the `Passenger` and `Country` classes (listings 16.8 and 16.9).

Listing 16.8 Overridden `equals` and `hashCode` methods from the `Passenger` class

```
public class Passenger {
    [...]
    @Override
    public boolean equals(Object o) {
        if (this == o) return true;
        if (o == null || getClass() != o.getClass()) return false;
        Passenger passenger = (Passenger) o;                              ❶
        return name.equals(passenger.name) &&
                Objects.equals(country, passenger.country);
    }

    @Override
    public int hashCode() {
        return Objects.hash(name, country);             ❷
    }
}
```

In this listing, Ada constructs the `Passenger` methods `equals` ❶ and `hashCode` ❷ based on the `name` and `country` fields.

Listing 16.9   Overridden `equals` and `hashCode` methods from the `Country` class

```java
public class Country {
    [...]
    @Override
    public boolean equals(Object o) {
        if (this == o) return true;
        if (o == null || getClass() != o.getClass()) return false;

        Country country = (Country) o;

        if (codeName != null ?
            !codeName.equals(country.codeName) :
            country.codeName != null) return false;
        if (name != null ?
            !name.equals(country.name) :
            country.name != null) return false;

        return true;
    }

    @Override
    public int hashCode() {
        int result = 0;
        result = 31 * result + (name != null ? name.hashCode() : 0);
        result = 31 * result + (codeName != null ?
                codeName.hashCode() : 0);
        return result;
    }
}
```

❶

❷

In this listing, Ada constructs the `Country` methods `equals` ❶ and `hashCode` ❷ based on the `name` and `codeName` fields.

The expected passenger is constructed programmatically through the get-ExpectedPassenger method from the `PassengerUtil` class.

Listing 16.10   `PassengerUtil` class

```java
public class PassengerUtil {

    public static Passenger getExpectedPassenger() {              ❶
        Passenger passenger = new Passenger("John Smith");    ←
                                                                  ❷
        Country country = new Country("USA", "US");           ←
        passenger.setCountry(country);                        ←
                                                                  ❸
        return passenger;                                     ←
    }                                                             ❹
}
```

In the `getExpectedPassenger` method, Ada first creates the passenger "John Smith" ❶ and the country "USA" ❷ and sets that as the country of the passenger ❸. She returns this passenger at the end of the method ❹.

Running the newly created `SimpleAppTest` is successful, as shown in figure 16.7. Ada has verified that the bean extracted from the Spring container is equal to the beans constructed programmatically.

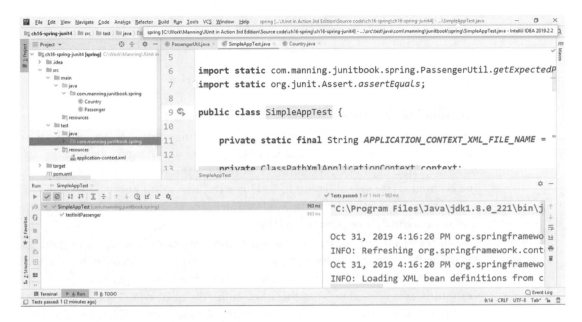

Figure 16.7 The result of running `SimpleAppTest`

16.3.2 *Using the Spring TestContext framework*

The Spring TestContext Framework offers unit and integration testing support independent of the testing framework in use: JUnit 3.x, JUnit 4.x, TestNG, and so on. The TestContext framework uses convention over configuration: it provides default behavior that can be overridden through configuration. For JUnit 4.5+, the TestContext framework also provides a custom runner.

Ada decided to refactor the initial test to use the capabilities of the TestContext framework.

Listing 16.11 `SpringAppTest` **class**

```
[...]
@RunWith(SpringJUnit4ClassRunner.class)
@ContextConfiguration("classpath:application-context.xml")
public class SpringAppTest {

    @Autowired
    private Passenger passenger;
    private Passenger expectedPassenger;
```
❶ ❷ ❸

```
@Before
public void setUp() {
   expectedPassenger = getExpectedPassenger();
}

@Test
public void testInitPassenger() {
   assertEquals(expectedPassenger, passenger);
}

}
```

In this listing:

- Ada runs the test with the help of `SpringJUnit4ClassRunner` ❶. She also annotates the test class to look for the context configuration in the application-context.xml file from the classpath ❷. These annotations belong to the `spring-test` dependency and serve to replace the programmatic creation of the context, as we saw in listing 16.7. Through these annotations, she takes care of creating the context from the application-context.xml file from the classpath and injects the defined beans into the test.
- She declares a field of type `Passenger` and annotates it as `@Autowired` ❸. Spring will automatically look in the container and try to autowire the declared `passenger` field to a unique injected bean of the same type, declared in the container. It is important that there is a single bean of type `Passenger` in the container; otherwise, there will be ambiguity, and the test will fail and throw an `UnsatisfiedDependencyException`.

`SpringAppTest` is shorter than `SimpleAppTest` because Ada has pushed even more control onto the Spring Framework by using the `@RunWith` and `@Context-Configuration` annotations that help to initialize the context automatically.

The result of running the newly created `SimpleAppTest` and `SpringAppTest` is successful, as shown in figure 16.8. Ada has verified in two ways that the bean extracted from the Spring container is equal to a bean constructed programmatically.

16.4 *Using SpringExtension for JUnit Jupiter*

`SpringExtension`, introduced in Spring 5, is used to integrate Spring TestContext with a JUnit 5 Jupiter test. `SpringExtension` is used with the JUnit 5 Jupiter `@ExtendWith` annotation.

Continuing her work on developing and testing the Spring-based flight-management application, Ada will first migrate to JUnit 5, following the steps we presented in chapter 4. Then, she will continue to add new features to the application that will now be tested with JUnit 5. You will find these examples in this chapter's ch16-spring-junit5 folder.

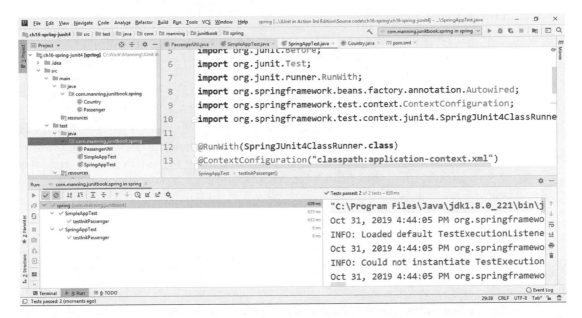

Figure 16.8 `SimpleAppTest` and `SpringAppTest` are successfully executed as Spring JUnit 4 tests.

The first thing Ada must do is replace the Spring 4 and JUnit 4 dependencies from the pom.xml file with the Spring 5 and JUnit 5 dependencies.

Listing 16.12 pom.xml file with Spring 5 and JUnit 5 dependencies

```
<dependency>
    <groupId>org.springframework</groupId>
    <artifactId>spring-context</artifactId>          ❶
    <version>5.2.0.RELEASE</version>
</dependency>
<dependency>
    <groupId>org.springframework</groupId>
    <artifactId>spring-test</artifactId>             ❷
    <version>5.2.0.RELEASE</version>
</dependency>
<dependency>
    <groupId>org.junit.jupiter</groupId>
    <artifactId>junit-jupiter-api</artifactId>       ❸
    <version>5.6.0</version>
    <scope>test</scope>
</dependency>
<dependency>
    <groupId>org.junit.jupiter</groupId>
    <artifactId>junit-jupiter-engine</artifactId>    ❹
    <version>5.6.0</version>
    <scope>test</scope>
</dependency>
```

In this listing:

- Ada introduces the `spring-context` ❶ and `spring-test` ❷ dependencies, version 5.2.0.RELEASE in both cases. `spring-context` is necessary to use the `@Autowired` annotation, while `spring-test` is necessary to use the `Spring-Extension` class and the `@ContextConfiguration` annotation. Ada has replaced the same dependencies from version 4.2.5.RELEASE.

- She introduces the `junit-jupiter-api` ❸ and `junit-jupiter-engine` ❹ dependencies that are needed to test the application with JUnit 5. She replaces the previously used JUnit 4.12 dependency, as we did for migration processes between JUnit 4 and JUnit 5 (see chapter 4).

Ada then migrates the code from using Spring 4 and JUnit 4 to using Spring 5 and JUnit 5.

Listing 16.13   SpringAppTest class

```
[...]
@ExtendWith(SpringExtension.class)                                    ◁
@ContextConfiguration("classpath:application-context.xml")    ◁        ❶
public class SpringAppTest {                                           ❷

    @Autowired
    private Passenger passenger;                        ❸
    private Passenger expectedPassenger;

    @BeforeEach
    public void setUp() {                               ◁
        expectedPassenger = getExpectedPassenger();     ❹
    }

    @Test
    public void testInitPassenger() {
        assertEquals(expectedPassenger, passenger);
        System.out.println(passenger);
    }
}
```

In this listing:

- Ada extends the test with the help of `SpringExtension` ❶. She also annotates the test class to look for the context configuration in the application-context.xml file from the classpath ❷. These annotations belong to the `spring-test` dependency (version 5.2.0.RELEASE this time) and serve to replace the work that has been done by JUnit 4 runners. Through these annotations, Ada takes care of creating the context from the application-context.xml file from the classpath and injects the defined beans into the test. For more details about JUnit 5 extensions, see chapter 14.

- She keeps the field of type `Passenger` and annotates it with `@Autowired` ❸. Spring will automatically look in the container and try to autowire the declared passenger field to a unique injected bean of the same type, declared in the container. It is important that there is a single bean of type `Passenger` in the container; otherwise, there will be ambiguity, and the test will fail and throw an `UnsatisfiedDependencyException`.

- She replaces the JUnit 4 `@Before` annotation with the JUnit 5 `@BeforeEach` annotation ❹. This is not specific to Spring applications, but it relates to the usual migration from JUnit 4 to JUnit 5 (see chapter 4).

The result of running the JUnit 5 `SpringAppTest` is successful, as shown in figure 16.9. Ada has verified the correct migration from working with Spring 4 and JUnit 4 to Spring 5 and JUnit 5. Now she is ready to continue her work and add new features to the Spring flight-management application.

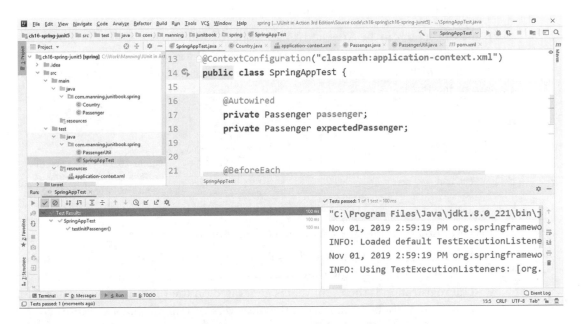

Figure 16.9 `SpringAppTest` **successfully executed as a Spring JUnit 5 test**

16.5 Adding a new feature and testing it with JUnit 5

Next, we will follow Ada as she adds a new feature to the current Spring 5 flight-management application and tests it with JUnit 5. In addition to what we have already presented, we will demonstrate some essential capabilities of the Spring Framework: creating beans through annotations, classes implementing essential interfaces, and implementing the observer pattern with the help of Spring 5–defined events and listeners.

> **NOTE** We started with an XML-based configuration as a gentle introduction. But the Spring Framework is a broad topic, and we are mostly discussing

things related to testing these applications with JUnit 5. For a comprehensive look at this subject, which also shows the configuration possibilities in detail, we recommend *Spring in Action* by Craig Walls (Manning, www.manning.com/books/spring-in-action-sixth-edition).

The feature that Ada has been assigned to implement requires tracking the registration of passengers through the registration manager of the flight-management system. The customer requires that whenever a new passenger is registered, the registration manager must answer with a confirmation. This functionality follows the idea of the observer pattern (figure 16.10), which we are going to examine and implement. You will find these examples in the chapter's ch16-spring-junit5-new-feature folder.

> **DEFINITION**   *Observer pattern*—A design pattern in which a subject maintains a list of dependents (observers or listeners). The subject will notify the observers about events on its side in which the observers are interested.

Such an observer can be attached to the side of the subject. Once attached, the observer will receive notifications about the events that are of interest to it. The events are announced by the subject, and, as a consequence, the observer will execute an update of its state.

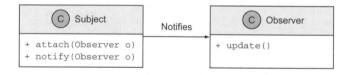

Figure 16.10   The subject notifies the observer about events of interest to it.

In this case, Ada identifies the following components of the system:

- The registration manager is the subject. It is where the event takes place and what needs to inform the observers.
- The registration is the event that is generated on the registration-manager side. This event must be broadcast to the observers (listeners) that are interested.
- The registration listener is the observer that will receive the registration event and confirm the registration by setting the passenger as registered in the system and by printing a message.

The functionality of this concrete registration system is shown in figure 16.11. Ada starts working on it by changing the `Passenger` class to be aware of the registration status.

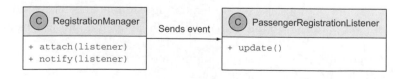

Figure 16.11 The registration manager informs the listener about registration events.

Listing 16.14 Modified `Passenger` class

```java
public class Passenger {
    [...]
    private boolean isRegistered;

    [...]
    public boolean isRegistered() {
        return isRegistered;
    }

    public void setIsRegistered(boolean isRegistered) {
        this.isRegistered = isRegistered;
    }

    @Override
    public String toString() {
        return "Passenger{" +
                "name='" + name + '\'' +
                ", country=" + country +
                ", registered=" + isRegistered +
                '}';
    }

    @Override
    public boolean equals(Object o) {
        if (this == o) return true;
        if (o == null || getClass() != o.getClass()) return false;
        Passenger passenger = (Passenger) o;
        return isRegistered == passenger.isRegistered &&
                Objects.equals(name, passenger.name) &&
                Objects.equals(country, passenger.country);
    }

    @Override
    public int hashCode() {
        return Objects.hash(name, country, isRegistered);
    }

}
```

❶ ❷ ❸ ❹

In this listing:

- Ada adds the `isRegistered` field to the `Passenger` class together with the getter and setter for it ❶.
- She modifies the `toString` ❷, `equals` ❸, and `hashCode` ❹ methods to also take into consideration the newly introduced `isRegistered` field.

Ada also modifies the application-context.xml file (listing 16.15). Declaring data beans in the XML configuration file is suitable for testing purposes, as in this case. The XML is easy to change, the code does not need to be recompiled, and we can have different configurations in different environments without touching the code.

Listing 16.15   Modified application-context.xml

```
<bean id="passenger" class="com.manning.junitbook.spring.Passenger">
    <constructor-arg name="name" value="John Smith"/>
    <property name="country" ref="country"/>                    ❶
    <property name="isRegistered" value="false"/>        ←┐
</bean>                                                        ❷
<context:component-scan base-package="com.manning.junitbook.spring" />    ←┘
```

In this listing:

- Ada adds the `isRegistered` field to the initialization of the `passenger` bean ❶.
- She inserts the directive to require Spring to also scan the package `com.manning.junitbook.spring` to find components ❷. As a result, in addition to the beans defined in the XML, other beans will be defined in the code from the indicated base package, using annotations.

Ada creates the `PassengerRegistrationEvent` class to define the custom event that is happening in the registration system.

Listing 16.16   `PassengerRegistrationEvent` class

```
public class PassengerRegistrationEvent extends ApplicationEvent {    ←┐
                                                                        ❶
    private Passenger passenger;                               ←┐
                                                                ❷
    public PassengerRegistrationEvent(Passenger passenger) {
        super(passenger);                           ❸
        this.passenger = passenger;
    }

    public Passenger getPassenger() {
        return passenger;
    }
                                                        ❷
    public void setPassenger(Passenger passenger) {
        this.passenger = passenger;
    }
}
```

In this listing:

- Ada defines the `PassengerRegistrationEvent` class that extends `ApplicationEvent` ❶. `ApplicationEvent` is the Spring abstract class to be extended by all application events.
- She keeps a reference to the `Passenger` object whose registration generated the event, together with a getter and a setter on it ❷.
- In the `PassengerRegistrationEvent`, she calls the constructor of the super-class `ApplicationEvent` that receives as an argument the source of the event: the passenger ❸.

We have mentioned that there are alternative ways to create Spring beans. The XML approach is suitable for data beans that may change for different executions and for different environments. We'll now show how to create beans using annotations, which is more appropriate for functional beans that generally do not change.

Ada creates the `RegistrationManager` class to serve as an event generator.

Listing 16.17   `RegistrationManager` **class**

```
[...]
@Service                                                          ❶
public class RegistrationManager implements ApplicationContextAware {     ❷
    private ApplicationContext applicationContext;

    public ApplicationContext getApplicationContext() {          ❸
        return applicationContext;
    }

    @Override
    public void setApplicationContext(ApplicationContext applicationContext)
                                    throws BeansException {       ❹
        this.applicationContext = applicationContext;
    }

}
```

In this listing:

- Ada annotates the class with the `@Service` annotation ❶. This means Spring will automatically create a bean of the type of this class. Remember that in the application-context.xml file, Ada inserted the `component-scan` directive with `base-package="com.manning.junitbook.spring"`, so Spring will look for annotation-defined beans in that package.
- The `RegistrationManager` class implements the `ApplicationContext-Aware` interface ❷. As a result, `RegistrationManager` will have a reference to the application context that it will use to publish events.
- In the class, Ada keeps a reference to the application context and a getter for it ❸.
- The `setApplicationContext` method inherited from `Application-ContextAware` initializes the field `applicationContext` as a reference to the `applicationContext` injected by Spring as an argument of this method ❹.

Ada creates the `PassengerRegistrationListener` class to serve as an observer of passenger registration events.

Listing 16.18   `PassengerRegistrationListener` **class**

```
[...]
@Service                                                          ❶
public class PassengerRegistrationListener {
```

```
@EventListener
public void confirmRegistration(PassengerRegistrationEvent          2
                                passengerRegistrationEvent) {
    passengerRegistrationEvent.getPassenger().setIsRegistered(true);
    System.out.println("Confirming the registration
                        for the passenger: "                        3
            + passengerRegistrationEvent.getPassenger());
    }
}
```

In this listing:

- Ada annotates the class with @Service ❶. As a result, Spring will automatically create a bean of the type of this class. Remember that, in the application-context.xml file, she inserted the component-scan directive with base-package="com.manning.junitbook.spring", so Spring will look for annotation-defined beans in that package.
- The confirmRegistration method receives as an argument a Passenger-RegistrationEvent and is annotated with @EventListener ❷. Thus Spring will automatically register this method as a listener (observer) for PassengerRegistrationEvent type events. Whenever such an event occurs, this method will be executed.
- In the method, once the passenger registration event is received, Ada confirms the registration by setting the passenger as registered in the system and printing a message ❸.

Ada finally creates the RegistrationTest class to verify the behavior of the code she has implemented.

Listing 16.19 RegistrationTest class

```
[...]
@ExtendWith(SpringExtension.class)
@ContextConfiguration("classpath:application-context.xml")           1
public class RegistrationTest {                                      2

    @Autowired
    private Passenger passenger;
                                                                     3
    @Autowired
    private RegistrationManager registrationManager;

    @Test
    public void testPersonRegistration() {
        registrationManager.getApplicationContext()
          .publishEvent(new PassengerRegistrationEvent(passenger));  4
        assertTrue(passenger.isRegistered());                        5
    }

}
```

In this listing:

- Ada extends the test with the help of SpringExtension ❶. She also annotates the test class to look for the context configuration in the application-context.xml file from the classpath ❷. Through these annotations, she takes care of creating the context from the application-context.xml file from the classpath and injecting the defined beans into the test.
- She declares a field of type Passenger and a field of type Registration-Manager and annotates them as @Autowired ❸. Spring will automatically look in the container and try to autowire the declared Passenger and Registration-Manager fields to unique injected beans of the same type, declared in the container. It is important that there is a single bean of each of these types in the container; otherwise, there will be ambiguity, and the test will fail and throw an UnsatisfiedDependencyException. Ada declares a Passenger bean in the application-context.xml file. And she annotates RegistrationManager with @Service, so Spring will automatically create a bean of the type of this class.
- In the test method, Ada uses the RegistrationManager field to publish an event of type PassengerRegistrationEvent with the help of the reference to the application context it is holding ❹. Then she checks that the registration status of the passenger has really changed ❺.

The result of running the newly created RegistrationTest is successful, as shown in figure 16.12. Ada has implemented and tested the passengers' registration feature using the capabilities of JUnit 5 and Spring 5.

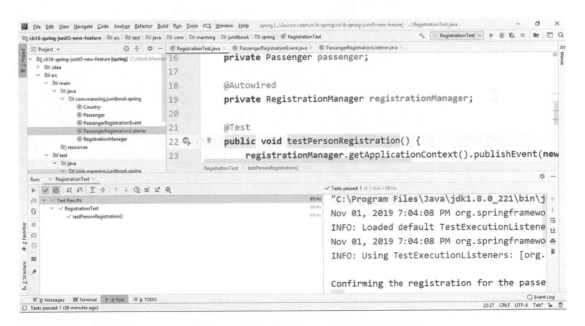

Figure 16.12 RegistrationTest **successfully executes as a Spring JUnit 5 test.**

In the next chapter, we will start building and testing software using Spring Boot, one of the extensions of the Spring Framework. Spring Boot eliminates the boilerplate configurations required for setting up a Spring application.

Summary

This chapter has covered the following:

- Introducing the Spring Framework, a widely used, lightweight, flexible, universal framework for creating Java applications.
- Demonstrating the dependency injection (inversion of control) pattern that is the basis of Spring. Objects are inserted into a container that injects dependencies when it creates the object.
- Introducing beans, the objects that form the backbone of a Spring application and that are instantiated, assembled, and managed by the Spring DI (IoC) container.
- Using and testing a Spring application both by creating the Spring context programmatically and by using the Spring TestContext framework.
- Using `SpringExtension` for JUnit Jupiter to create JUnit 5 tests for a Spring application.
- Developing a new feature for a Spring application using beans created through annotations, implementing the observer pattern with the help of Spring 5–defined events and listeners, and testing the application with JUnit 5.

17

Testing Spring Boot applications

This chapter covers

- Creating a project with Spring Initializr
- Moving a Spring application tested with JUnit 5 to Spring Boot
- Implementing a test-specific Spring Boot configuration
- Testing a Spring Boot application feature with JUnit 5

Working with Spring Boot is like pair-programming with the Spring developers.

—Anonymous

Spring Boot is a Spring convention-over-configuration solution. It enables the creation of Spring applications that are ready to run immediately. Spring Boot is an extension of the Spring Framework that strongly reduces the initial Spring application's configuration: a Spring Boot application is preconfigured and given dependencies to outside libraries so that we can start using it. Most Spring Boot applications need very little (or no) Spring configuration.

> **DEFINITION** *Convention over configuration*—A software design principle adopted by various frameworks to reduce the number of configuration actions a programmer using that framework needs to perform. The programmer only needs to specify the nonstandard configuration of the application.

17.1 Introducing Spring Boot

A shortcoming of the Spring Framework is that it takes some time to make an application ready for production. The configuration is time consuming and can be a little overwhelming for new developers.

Spring Boot is built on top of the Spring Framework as an extension of it. It strongly supports developers through a convention-over-configuration approach that can help with the rapid creation of an application. As most Spring Boot applications need little Spring configuration, you can focus on the business logic instead of infrastructure and configuration. The business logic is the part of the program focusing on the business rules that determine the way the application works.

In this chapter, we will examine the following Spring Boot features:

- Creating standalone Spring applications
- Automatically configuring Spring when possible
- Embedding web servers like Tomcat and Jetty directly (no need to deploy war files)
- Providing preconfigured Maven project object models (POMs)

17.2 Creating a project with Spring Initializr

In the Spring Boot spirit of supporting developers through the convention-over-configuration approach and supporting the rapid creation of applications, we will use Spring Initializr to generate a project with only what we need to start quickly. To do this, we go to https://start.spring.io/ and insert the configuration data of our new project on the web page. Spring Boot generates a skeleton for the application, and we transfer into it the business logic for tracking passenger registration through the registration manager of the example flight-management system we implemented in chapter 16.

As shown in figure 17.1, we choose to create a new Java project managed by Maven as a build tool. The group name is `com.manning.junitbook`, and the artifact ID is `spring-boot`. The Spring Boot version at the time of writing this chapter was 2.2.2; your version while studying this chapter may be higher. The application to be generated is found in the ch17-spring-boot-initializr folder of the source code for this chapter.

In figure 17.2, we provide more configuration for the newly created project. We leave the description as "Demo project for Spring Boot" and the packaging as .jar. We are given the chance to add new dependencies (Web, Security, JPA, Actuator, Devtools). We are not adding anything for the moment, as our first goal is to move the Spring application from chapter 16 to Spring Boot, but you should be aware of this possibility: with a few clicks, you can obtain the needed dependencies directly in the Maven pom.xml file.

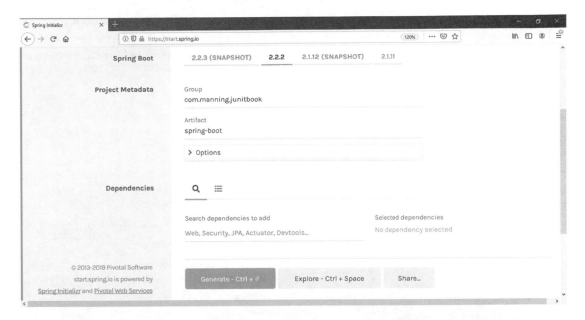

Figure 17.1 Creating a new Spring Boot project with the help of Spring Initializr. The project is managed by Maven as the build tool, the group name is com.manning.junitbook, and the artifact ID is spring-boot.

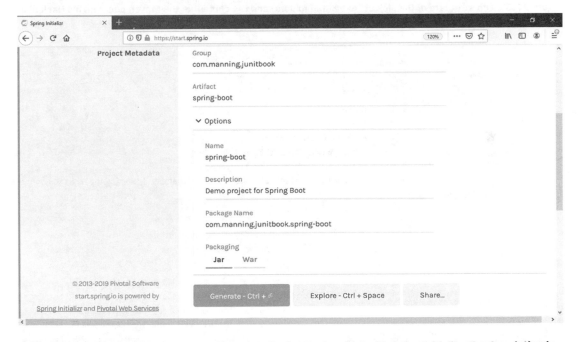

Figure 17.2 Available options when creating a new Spring Boot project with Spring Initializr: the description is "Demo project for Spring Boot," and the packaging is .jar. We can also add new dependencies (Web, Security, JPA, Actuator, Devtools).

When we click the Explore – Ctrl + Space button, we see a few details about what will be generated: the structure of the project and the content of the Maven pom.xml file (figure 17.3). We can click Download the ZIP or, on the previous screen, Generate - Ctrl +, and we'll get the archive containing the project.

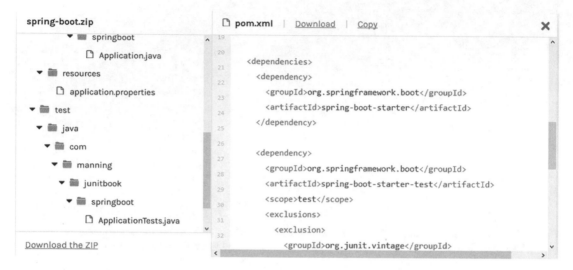

Figure 17.3   The structure of the project (expanded folders) and the content of the Maven pom.xml file (including the `spring-boot-starter` dependency)

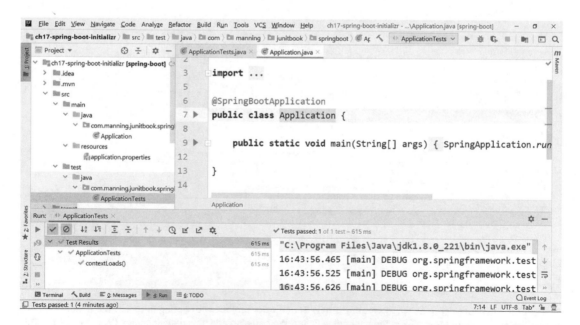

Figure 17.4   Loading the generated Spring Boot application into IntelliJ IDEA, and successfully running the test that is automatically provided

Opening the generated project, we see its structure containing the Maven pom.xml file, a `main` method in the `Application` class, a test in the `ApplicationTests` class, and an application.properties resource file (empty for now, but we'll use it later). So, with a few clicks and choices, in seconds we have a new Spring application. We can simply run the tests (figure 17.4), and then we'll focus on moving our previously created Spring application from chapter 16 to this new Spring Boot structure.

In this example, we use different ways to configure the Spring container. As we mentioned in chapter 16, XML is still the traditional approach for configurations, but recently there is a tendency for developers to work more with annotations. For our testing purposes, we'll use XML: it provides the advantage of being less intrusive. The classes do not need additional dependencies, and the configuration can be quickly changed for data beans meant for testing, without recompiling the code.

17.3 Moving the Spring application to Spring Boot

Now we'll begin moving our previously developed Spring application to the skeleton provided by Spring Boot. You will find this application in the chapter's ch17-spring-boot-initializr-old-feature folder. For a successfully systematic and organized migration, we'll do the following:

1 Introduce two new packages in the application generated by Spring Initializr: `com.manning.junitbook.springboot.model`, where we'll keep the domain classes `Passenger` and `Country`; and `com.manning.junitbook.spring-boot.registration`, where we'll keep the classes related to the registration events, `PassengerRegistrationEvent`, `PassengerRegistrationListener`, and `RegistrationManager`. The new structure is displayed in figure 17.5.

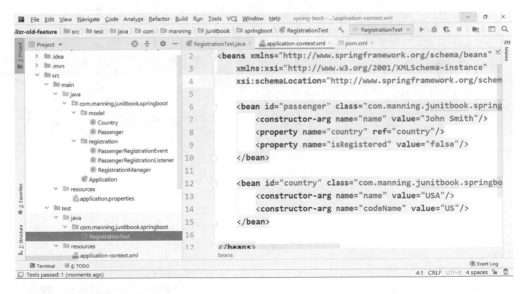

Figure 17.5 The new structure of the Spring Boot registration application. The classes have been distributed to two different packages.

2 The application-context.xml file will no longer contain the directive `<context :component-scan base-package="..." />`. We'll provide an equivalent using Spring annotations at the level of the test. The updated application-context.xml file will look as shown in listing 17.1.

3 Introduce new annotations in the `RegistrationTest` file to replace the directive that we eliminated from the application-context.xml file (listing 17.2).

4 Keep only the `RegistrationTest` class for testing our application, as the `SpringAppTest` class was just testing the behavior of a single passenger. We'll also adapt `RegistrationTest` to match the structure of the `Application-Tests` class initially provided by Spring Boot.

Listing 17.1   application-context.xml configuration file

```
<bean id="passenger"
        class="com.manning.junitbook.springboot.model.Passenger">
    <constructor-arg name="name" value="John Smith"/>
    <property name="country" ref="country"/>
    <property name="isRegistered" value="false"/>
</bean>

<bean id="country"
        class="com.manning.junitbook.springboot.model.Country">
    <constructor-arg name="name" value="USA"/>
    <constructor-arg name="codeName" value="US"/>
</bean>
```

The updated application-context.xml file keeps the definition of the `passenger` and `country` beans, but we remove the original directive `<context:component-scan base-package="..." />`. We'll provide an equivalent using Spring annotations at the level of the test.

Listing 17.2   Rewritten Spring Boot `RegistrationTest`

```
@SpringBootTest
@EnableAutoConfiguration
@ImportResource("classpath:application-context.xml")    ①②③
class RegistrationTest {

    [...]

    @Autowired
    private RegistrationManager registrationManager;     ④

    [...]
}
```

In this listing:

- We annotate our class with the `@SpringBootTest` annotation ① initially provided by the test generated by Spring Boot. This annotation provides a few features; we are using one that, together with `@EnableAutoConfiguration` ❷, searches in the current test class package and its subpackages for bean definitions. This way, it can discover and autowire the `RegistrationManager` bean ❹.

- There are still beans defined at the level of the XML configuration, which we import with the help of the `@ImportResource` annotation ❸.
- The rest of the original `RegistrationTest` class remains the same as the Spring Core application built in chapter 16.

Running the current test is successful, as shown in figure 17.6.

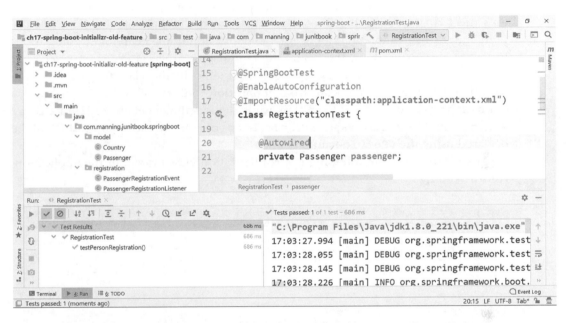

Figure 17.6 Successfully running `RegistrationTest`. **The registration functionality works fine after we move the application to Spring Boot.**

17.4 Implementing a test-specific configuration for Spring Boot

So far, we are using a Spring Boot application with the business logic of the original Spring Core application. The bean configuration is still at the level of the XML file. As we have mentioned, XML is the traditional approach for Spring configuration, as it is nonintrusive (the classes do not need external dependencies) and can be easily changed (the source files do not need to be recompiled). The `country` and `passenger` data beans are for testing purposes, so keeping them in an XML file will enable different testers with less programming skill to quickly create their own configurations. These examples are in the chapter's ch17-spring-boot-beans folder.

NOTE   We are focusing on the different configuration alternatives for testing Spring applications. For more comprehensive discussions of the topic, we recommend these two books by Craig Walls: *Spring in Action* (Manning, www.manning.com/books/spring-in-action-sixth-edition) and *Spring Boot in Action* (Manning, www.manning.com/books/spring-boot-in-action).

Now that the developers at Tested Data Systems have moved to Spring Boot, they would like to try a different configuration approach that is closer to the Spring Boot spirit. They also want to add more business logic. Mike is in charge of these tasks, and the first thing he decides to do is to introduce the test-specific configuration capabilities of Spring Boot.

Mike will replace the initial bean definitions from the application-context.xml file with the help of the Spring Boot `@TestConfiguration` annotation. The `@TestConfiguration` annotation can be used to define additional beans or customizations for a test. In Spring Boot, the beans configured in a top-level class annotated with `@TestConfiguration` must be explicitly registered in the class that contains the tests. The existing test data beans from application-context.xml will be moved to this `@TestConfiguration`-annotated class, while the functional beans (`Registration-Manager` and `PassengerRegistrationListener` from the code base) will be declared using the `@Service` annotation.

Mike introduces the following test configuration class instead of the application-context.xml file.

Listing 17.3   `TestBeans` class

```
[...]
@TestConfiguration
public class TestBeans {                      ❶

    @Bean                                     ❷
    Passenger createPassenger() {
        Passenger passenger = new Passenger("John Smith");
        passenger.setCountry(createCountry());               ❸
        passenger.setIsRegistered(false);
        return passenger;
    }
                                              ❹
    @Bean
    Country createCountry() {
        Country country = new Country("USA", "US");          ❺
        return country;
    }
}
```

In this listing:

- Mike introduces the new class `TestBeans` that replaces the existing application-context.xml file and annotates it with `@TestConfiguration` ❶. Its purpose is to provide the beans while executing the tests.

- He writes the `createPassenger` method ❸ and annotates it with `@Bean` ❷. Its purpose is to create and configure a `Passenger` bean that will be injected into the tests.
- He writes the `createCountry` method ❺ and annotates it with `@Bean` ❹. Its purpose is to create and configure a `Country` bean that will be injected into the tests.

Mike modifies the existing test to use the `@TestConfiguration`-annotated class instead of the application-context.xml file for the creation and configuration of the bean.

Listing 17.4 Modified `RegistrationTest` class

```
@SpringBootTest
@Import(TestBeans.class)                    ◄───┐
class RegistrationTest {                         ❶

    @Autowired
    private Passenger passenger;

    @Autowired
    private RegistrationManager registrationManager;

    @Test
    void testPersonRegistration() {
        registrationManager.getApplicationContext()
            .publishEvent(new PassengerRegistrationEvent(passenger));
        System.out.println("After registering:");
        System.out.println(passenger);
        assertTrue(passenger.isRegistered());
    }

}
```

In this listing, the change that is propagated in the test class is the replacement of the existing `@EnableAutoConfiguration` and `@ImportResource` annotations with `@Import(TestBeans.class)` ❶. This way, Mike explicitly registers the beans defined in `TestBeans` in the class that contains the tests.

The advantage of making the move to using the `@TestConfiguration` annotation is not only that this approach is more specific to Spring Boot or that we are replacing two annotations with one. Working with Java-based defined beans is *type-safe*: Java prevents errors, and the compiler will report issues if we configure incorrectly. Search and navigation are much simpler, because we take advantage of the IDE. Working with full Java code, you will also get a helping hand for refactoring, code completion, and finding references in the code.

Running the test in its new format is successful, as shown in figure 17.7. Notice that the application-context.xml configuration file has been removed.

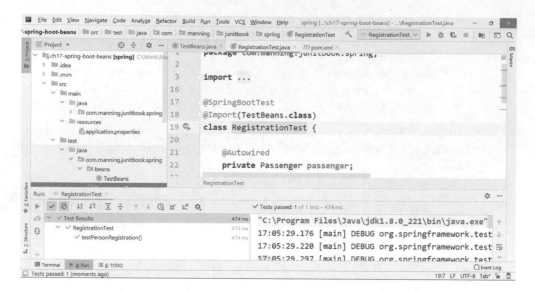

Figure 17.7 Successfully running `RegistrationTest`**. The registration functionality works fine after we implement a test-specific configuration for Spring Boot.**

17.5 *Adding and testing a new feature in the Spring Boot application*

Mike receives a requirement to introduce a new feature: the application must be able to create and set up flights, as well as add passengers to and remove them from flights. He will introduce a new class to model this case: `Flight`. He must check that a list of passengers can be correctly registered on a flight and that all the people on the list receive a registration confirmation. First, he has to introduce the `Flight` class. These examples are in the chapter's ch17-spring-boot-new-feature folder.

Listing 17.5 `Flight` class

```
public class Flight {

    private String flightNumber;                              ❶
    private int seats;
    private Set<Passenger> passengers = new HashSet< >();

    public Flight(String flightNumber, int seats) {           ❷
        this.flightNumber = flightNumber;
        this.seats = seats;
    }

    public String getFlightNumber() {
        return flightNumber;                                  ❸
    }

    public int getSeats() {
        return seats;
    }
```

```
public Set<Passenger> getPassengers() {
    return Collections.unmodifiableSet(passengers);    ◄── ❸
}                                                                      ❹
                                                                     ◄──
public boolean addPassenger(Passenger passenger) {
    if(passengers.size() >= seats) {
        throw new RuntimeException("Cannot add more
            passengers than the capacity of the flight!");
    }
    return passengers.add(passenger);
}                                                              ❺
                                                            ◄──
public boolean removePassenger(Passenger passenger) {
    return passengers.remove(passenger);
}
                                ❻
@Override                     ◄──
public String toString() {
    return "Flight " + getFlightNumber();
}

}
```

In this listing:

- Mike provides three fields—flightNumber, seats, and passengers—to describe a Flight ❶.
- He provides a constructor that has the first two parameters ❷.
- He also provides three getters ❸ that address the fields he defined. The getter of the passengers field will return an unmodifiable list of passengers so that the list cannot be changed from outside after being returned by the getter.
- The addPassenger method adds a passenger to the flight. It also compares the number of passengers with the number of seats so the flight will not be overbooked ❹.
- Mike provides the possibility to remove a passenger from a flight ❺.
- Finally, he overrides the toString method ❻.

Mike describes the list of passengers on the flight using the CSV file in the following listing. A passenger is described with a name and a country code. There are 20 passengers total.

Listing 17.6   flights_information.csv file

```
John Smith; UK
Jane Underwood; AU
James Perkins; US
Mary Calderon; US
Noah Graves; UK
Jake Chavez; AU
Oliver Aguilar; US
Emma McCann; AU
Margaret Knight; US
Amelia Curry; UK
Jack Vaughn; US
Liam Lewis; AU
```

```
Olivia Reyes; US
Samantha Poole; AU
Patricia Jordan; UK
Robert Sherman; US
Mason Burton; AU
Harry Christensen; UK
Jennifer Mills; US
Sophia Graham; UK
```

Mike will implement the `FlightUtilBuilder` class, which parses the CSV file and populates the flight with the corresponding passengers. The information is brought in from an external file to the application memory.

Listing 17.7   `FlightUtilBuilder` class

```
[...]
@TestConfiguration
public class FlightBuilder {                              ❶

    private static Map<String, Country> countriesMap =    ❷
            new HashMap<>();

    static {
        countriesMap.put("AU", new Country("Australia", "AU"));
        countriesMap.put("US", new Country("USA", "US"));    ❸
        countriesMap.put("UK", new Country("United Kingdom",
                                            "UK"));
    }

    @Bean
    Flight buildFlightFromCsv() throws IOException {       ❹                ❺
        Flight flight = new Flight("AA1234", 20);
        try(BufferedReader reader = new BufferedReader(
         new FileReader(                                         ❻
           "src/test/resources/flights_information.csv"))) {
             String line = null;
             do {                                            ❼
                 line = reader.readLine();
                 if (line != null) {
                     String[] passengerString =              ❾
                             line.toString().split(";");
                     Passenger passenger = new               ❿
                             Passenger(passengerString[0].trim());
❽                    passenger.setCountry(                   ⓫
                             countriesMap.get(
                                 passengerString[1].trim())));
                     passenger.setIsRegistered(false);
                     flight.addPassenger(passenger);     ⓭    ⓬
                 }
             } while (line != null);
        }
                                    ⓮
        return flight;
    }
}
```

In this listing:

- Mike creates the `FlightBuilder` class that will parse the CSV file and construct the list of flights. The class is annotated with the previously introduced annotation `@TestConfiguration` ❶. Thus, it signals that it defines the beans needed for a test.
- He defines the countries map ❷ and populates it with three countries ❸. The key of the map is the country code, and the value is its name.
- He creates the `buildFlightFromCsv` method and annotates it with `@Bean` ❹. Its purpose is to create and configure a `Flight` bean that will be injected into the tests.
- He creates a flight with the help of the constructor ❺ and then constructs it by parsing the CSV file ❻.
- He initializes the line variable with `null` ❼ and then parses the CSV file and reads it line by line ❽.
- The line is split by the `;` separator ❾. Mike creates a passenger with the help of the constructor, which has as an argument the part of the line before the separator ❿. He sets the passenger's country by taking from the countries map the value corresponding to the country code included in the part of the line after the separator ⓫.
- He sets the passenger as not registered ⓬, adds them to the flight ⓭, and, after he finishes parsing all the lines from the CSV file, returns the fully configured flight ⓮.

Mike will finally implement the `FlightTest` class, which registers all the passengers from a flight and checks that all of them are confirmed.

Listing 17.8 `FlightTest` class

```
[...]
@SpringBootTest
@Import(FlightBuilder.class)                          ❶
public class FlightTest {

    @Autowired
    private Flight flight;                             ❷

    @Autowired
    private RegistrationManager registrationManager;  ❸

    @Test
    void testFlightPassengersRegistration() {          ❹                    ❺
        for (Passenger passenger : flight.getPassengers()) {
            assertFalse(passenger.isRegistered());
            registrationManager.getApplicationContext().
                publishEvent(                                               ❼
                    new PassengerRegistrationEvent(passenger));
    }
```
❻

```
        for (Passenger passenger : flight.getPassengers()) {
            assertTrue(passenger.isRegistered());
        }
    }
}
```
8

In this listing:

- Mike creates the `FlightTest` class, annotates it with `@SpringBootTest`, and imports the beans from the `FlightBuilder` class ❶. Remember that `@SpringBootTest` searches in the current package of the test class and in its subpackages for bean definitions. This way, it will be able to discover and auto-wire the `RegistrationManager` bean ❸.
- He autowires the `Flight` bean injected by the `FlightBuilder` class ❷.
- He creates the `testFlightPassengersRegistration` method and annotates it with `@Test` ❹. In it, he browses all passengers from the injected `Flight` bean ❺ and first checks that they are not registered ❻. Then he uses the `RegistrationManager` field to publish an event of type `Passenger-RegistrationEvent` with the help of the reference to the application context that it is holding ❼.
- Finally, he browses all passengers from the injected `Flight` bean and checks that they are now registered ❽.

Running `FlightTest` is successful, as shown in figure 17.8.

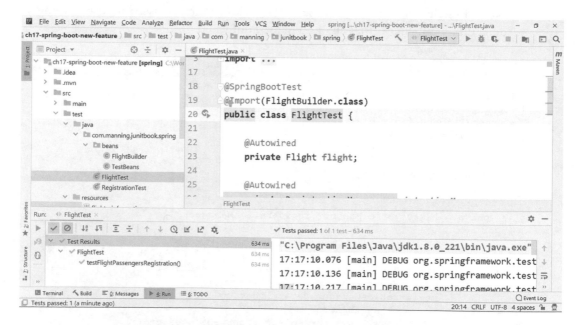

Figure 17.8   Successfully running `FlightTest`, which checks the registration of all passengers on a flight

In the next chapter, we will start building and testing a representational state transfer (REST) application with the help of Spring Boot.

Summary

This chapter has covered the following:

- Introducing Spring Boot as the Spring convention-over-configuration solution for creating Spring-based applications that you can simply run.
- Creating a ready-to-run Spring Boot project with Spring Initializr, a web application that helps to generate a Spring Boot project's structure.
- Moving our previously developed Spring application, which we tested with JUnit 5, to the skeleton provided by Spring Boot.
- Implementing a test-specific configuration for Spring Boot with the help of the @TestConfiguration annotation and Java-based beans, and taking advantage of the Spring Boot convention-over-configuration approach.
- Developing a new feature to create and set up flights and add and remove passengers, integrating it into a Spring Boot application, and testing it with JUnit 5.

Testing a REST API

This chapter covers

- Creating a RESTful API to manage one or more entities
- Testing a RESTful API

> *For now, let's just say that if your API is re-defining the HTTP verbs or if it is assigning new meanings to HTTP status codes or making up its own status codes, it is not RESTful.*
>
> —George Reese, *The REST API Design Handbook*

Representational state transfer (REST) is a software architectural style for creating web services; it also provides a set of constraints. The American computer scientist Roy Fielding first defined REST, presenting the REST principles in his PhD dissertation in 2000. (Fielding is also one of the authors of the HTTP specification.) Web services following this REST architectural style are called *RESTful web services*. RESTful web services allow interoperability between the internet and computer systems. Requesting systems can access and manipulate web resources represented as text using a well-known set of stateless operations. We'll study them in more detail in this chapter.

18.1 Introducing REST applications

We will first define the terms *client* and *resource* in order to shape what makes an API RESTful. A *client* may be a person or software using the RESTful API. For example, a programmer using a RESTful API to execute actions against the LinkedIn website is such a client. The client can also be a web browser. When you go to the LinkedIn website, your browser is the client that calls the website API and displays the obtained information on the screen.

A *resource* can be any object about which the API can obtain information. In the LinkedIn API, a resource can be a message, a photo, or a user. Each resource has a unique identifier.

The REST architecture style defines six constraints:

- *Client-server*—Clients are separated from servers, and each has its own concern. Most frequently, a client is concerned with the representation of the user, and a server is concerned with data storage and domain model logic—the conceptual model of a domain including data and behavior.
- *Stateless*—The server does not keep any information about the client between requests. Each request from a client contains all of the information necessary to respond to that request. The client keeps the state on its side.
- *Uniform interface*—The client and the server may evolve independently of each other. The uniform interface between them makes them loosely coupled.
- *Layered systems*—The client does not have any way to determine if it is interacting directly with the server or with an intermediary. Layers can be dynamically added and removed. They can provide security, load balancing, and shared caching.
- *Cacheable*—Clients can cache responses. Responses define themselves as cacheable or not.
- *Code on demand (optional)*—Servers can temporarily customize or extend the functionality of a client. The server can transfer to the client some logic that the client can execute: JavaScript client-side scripts and Java applets.

A RESTful web application provides information about its resources. Resources are identified with the help of URLs. The client can execute actions against such a resource: create, read, update, or delete the resource.

The REST architectural style is not protocol specific, but the most widely used is REST over HTTP. HTTP is a synchronous application network protocol based on requests and responses.

To make an API RESTful, you have to follow a set of rules while developing it. A RESTful API will transfer information to the client, which uses it as a representation of the state of the accessed resource. For example, when you call the LinkedIn API to access a specific user, the API will return the state of that user (name, biography, professional experience, posts). The REST rules make the API easier to understand and simpler for new programmers to use when they join a team.

The representation of the state can be in JSON, XML, or HTML format. The client uses the API to send the following to the server:

- The identifier (URL) of the resource you want to access.
- The operation you want the server to perform on that resource. This is an HTTP method. The common HTTP methods are GET, POST, PUT, PATCH, and DELETE.

For example, using the LinkedIn RESTful API to fetch a specific LinkedIn user requires that you have a URL that identifies the user and that you use the HTTP method GET.

18.2 *Creating a RESTful API to manage one entity*

The flight-management application developed at Tested Data Systems, as we left it at the end of chapter 17, allows us to register a list of passengers for a flight and test the confirmation of this registration. Mike, the programmer involved in developing the application, receives a new feature to implement: he has to create a REST API to manage a flight's passengers.

The first thing Mike will do is to create the REST API that will deal with countries. For that purpose, Mike will add new dependencies to the Maven pom.xml configuration file.

Listing 18.1   Newly added dependencies in the pom.xml configuration file

```
<dependency>
    <groupId>org.springframework.boot</groupId>
    <artifactId>spring-boot-starter-web</artifactId>          ❶
</dependency>
<dependency>
    <groupId>org.springframework.boot</groupId>
    <artifactId>spring-boot-starter-data-jpa</artifactId>     ❷
</dependency>
<dependency>
    <groupId>com.h2database</groupId>
    <artifactId>h2</artifactId>                               ❸
</dependency>
```

In this listing:

- Mike adds the spring-boot-starter-web dependency for building web (including RESTful) applications using Spring Boot ❶.
- Because he needs to use Spring and the Java Persistence API (JPA) for persisting information, he includes the spring-boot-starter-data-jpa dependency ❷.
- H2 is an open source, lightweight Java database that Mike will embed in the Java application and persist information to it. Consequently, he adds the h2 dependency ❸.

As the application will be a functional RESTful one that can be used to access, create, modify, and delete information about the list of passengers, Mike moves the Flight-Builder class from the test folder into the main folder. He also extends its functionality to provide access to managing countries.

Listing 18.2 `FlightBuilder` class

```
[...]
public class FlightBuilder {                                              ❶

    private Map<String, Country> countriesMap = new HashMap<>();    ◀─── ❷

    public FlightBuilder() throws IOException {                       ◀─
        try(BufferedReader reader = new BufferedReader(new                ❸
            FileReader("src/main/resources/countries_information.csv"))) {
      ▷  String line = null;
         do {                                                             ❻
❹            line = reader.readLine();
             if (line != null) {
❺                String[] countriesString = line.toString().split(";");  ◀─
                 Country country = new Country(countriesString[0].trim(), ❼
                                       countriesString[1].trim());
                 countriesMap.put(countriesString[1].trim(), country); ◀─
             }                                                            ❽
        } while (line != null);
        }
    }
    @Bean
    Map<String, Country> getCountriesMap() {
        return Collections.unmodifiableMap(countriesMap);                 ❾
    }

    @Bean                                                                 ❿
    public Flight buildFlightFromCsv() throws IOException {
      ▷  Flight flight = new Flight("AA1234", 20);
         try(BufferedReader reader = new BufferedReader(new               ⓬
           FileReader("src/main/resources/flights_information.csv"))) {
⓫        ▷  String line = null;
            do {                                                          ⓭
                line = reader.readLine();
                if (line != null) {
                    String[] passengerString = line.toString()           ⓯
                                                 .split(";");
                    Passenger passenger = new                            ⓰
                            Passenger(passengerString[0].trim());

⓮           ⓲   passenger.setCountry(
                        countriesMap.get(passengerString[1].trim()));    ⓱
             ▷  passenger.setIsRegistered(false);
                flight.addPassenger(passenger);                      ◀─
            }                                                            ⓳
        } while (line != null);
        }

    }
```

```
        return flight;        ⟵──┐
    }                             20
}
```

In this listing:

- Mike defines the countries map **1**.
- He populates the countries map in the constructor with three countries **2** by parsing the CSV file **3**.
- He initializes the `line` variable with `null` **4**, parses the CSV file, and reads it line by line **5**.
- The line is split with the `;` separator **6**. Mike creates a country with the help of the constructor, which has as an argument the part of the line before the separator **7**.
- He adds the parsed information to `countriesMap` **8**.
- He creates the `getCountriesMap` method and annotates it with `@Bean` **9**. Its purpose is to create and configure a `Map` bean that will be injected into the application.
- He creates the `buildFlightFromCsv` method and annotates it with `@Bean` **10**. Its purpose is to create and configure a `Flight` bean that will be injected into the application.
- He creates a flight with the help of the constructor **11** by parsing the CSV file **12**.
- He initializes the `line` variable with `null` **13**, parses the CSV file, and reads it line by line **14**.
- The line is split with the `;` separator **15**. Mike creates a passenger with the help of the constructor, which has as an argument the part of the line before the separator **16**. He sets the passenger's country by taking from the countries map the value corresponding to the country code included in the part of the line after the separator **17**.
- He sets the passenger as not registered **18** and adds them to the flight **19**. After all the lines from the CSV file are parsed, the fully configured flight is returned **20**.

The content of the countries_information.csv file used for building the countries map is shown next.

Listing 18.3 countries_information.csv file

```
Australia; AU
USA; US
United Kingdom; UK
```

Mike would like to start the RESTful application on the custom 8081 port to avoid possible port conflicts. Spring Boot allows the externalization of the configuration so that different people can work with the same application code in different environments. Various properties can be specified in the application.properties file; in this case, Mike only needs to set `server.port` as `8081`.

Listing 18.4   application.properties file

```
server.port=8081
```

Mike modifies the `Country` class to make it a model component of the RESTful application (see listing 18.5). The model is one of the components of the model-view-controller (MVC) pattern: it is the application's dynamic data structure, independent of the user interface. It directly manages the application's data.

> **DEFINITION**   *Model-view-controller (MVC)*—A software design pattern used for creating programs that access data through user interfaces. The program is split into three related parts: *model*, *view*, and *controller*. Thus the inner representation of information is separated from its presentation on the user side, and the system's parts are loosely coupled.

Listing 18.5   Modified `Country` class

```
[...]
@Entity
public class Country {          ◄──┐  ❶

    @Id
    private String codeName;         ❷
    private String name;


    // avoid "No default constructor for entity"
    public Country() {                       ❸
    }
    [...]
}
```

In this listing:

- Mike annotates the `Country` class with `@Entity` so it can represent objects that can be persisted ❶.
- He annotates the `codeName` field with `@Id` ❷. This means the `codeName` field is a primary key: it uniquely identifies an entity that is persisted.
- He adds a default constructor to the `Country` class ❸. Every class annotated with `@Entity` needs a default constructor, as the persistence layer will use it to create a new instance of this class through reflection. The compiler no longer provides the default constructor because Mike created one.

Next, Mike creates the `CountryRepository` interface, which extends `JpaRepository`.

Listing 18.6 `CountryRepository` interface

```
public interface CountryRepository extends JpaRepository<Country, Long> {
}
```

Defining this interface serves two purposes. First, by extending `JpaRepository`, Mike gets a bunch of generic CRUD (create, read, update, and delete) methods in the `CountryRepository` type that make it possible to work with `Country` objects. Second, this allows Spring to scan the classpath for this interface and create a Spring bean for it.

> **DEFINITION** *CRUD (create, read, update, delete)*—The four basic functions of persistence. In addition to REST, they are often used in database applications and user interfaces.

Mike now writes a controller for `CountryRepository`. A controller is responsible for controlling the application logic and acts as the coordinator between the view (the way data is displayed to the user) and the model (the data).

Listing 18.7 `CountryController` class

```
@RestController                                    ❶
public class CountryController {

    @Autowired                                     ❷
    private CountryRepository repository;

    @GetMapping("/countries")      ❸                ❹
    List<Country> findAll() {
        return repository.findAll();         ⟵
    }

}
```

In this listing:

- Mike creates the `CountryController` class and annotates it with `@Rest-Controller` ❶. The `@RestController` annotation was introduced in Spring 4.0 to simplify creating RESTful web services. It marks the class as a controller and also eliminates the need to annotate every one of its request-handling methods with the `@ResponseBody` annotation (as required before Spring 4.0).
- He declares a `CountryRepository` field and autowires it ❷. As `Country-Repository` extends `JpaRepository`, Spring will scan the classpath for this interface, create a Spring bean for it, and autowire it here.
- He creates the `findAll` method and annotates it with `@GetMapping("/coun-tries")` ❸. The `@GetMapping` annotation maps HTTP `GET` requests to the /countries URL onto the specific handler method. Because Mike uses the `@RestController` annotation on the class itself, he does not need to annotate

the response object of the method with @ResponseBody. As mentioned earlier, that was necessary before Spring 4.0, when we also had to use @Controller instead of @RestController on the class.

- The findAll method returns the result of executing repository .findAll() ❹. repository.findAll() is a CRUD method that is automatically generated because CountryRepository extends JpaRepository. As its name says, it will return all objects from the repository.

Mike now revises the Application class, previously created by Spring Boot (see chapter 17).

Listing 18.8 Modified `Application` class

```
[...]
@SpringBootApplication                              ❶
@Import(FlightBuilder.class)              ←─
public class Application {

    @Autowired
    private Map<String, Country> countriesMap;        ❷

    public static void main(String[] args) {
        SpringApplication.run(Application.class, args);
    }

    @Bean
    CommandLineRunner configureRepository                 ❸
                   (CountryRepository countryRepository) {
        return args -> {
            for (Country country: countriesMap.values()) {
                countryRepository.save(country);          ❹
            }
        };
    }

}
```

In this listing:

- Mike imports FlightBuilder, which created the countriesMap bean ❶, and autowires it ❷.
- He creates a bean of type CommandLineRunner ❸. CommandLineRunner is a Spring Boot functional interface (an interface with a single method) that gives access to application arguments as a string array. The created bean browses all the countries in countriesMap and saves them into countryRepository ❹. This CommandLineRunner interface is created, and its single method is executed, just before the run() method from SpringApplication completes.

Mike now executes Application. So far, the RESTful application only provides access to the /countries endpoint through the GET method. (An *endpoint* is a resource that can be referenced and to which client messages can be addressed.) We can test this REST API endpoint using the `curl` program. `curl` (which stands for *client URL*) is a command-line tool that transfers data using various protocols, including HTTP. We simply execute the following command

```
curl -v localhost:8081/countries
```

because the application is running on port 8081 and /countries is the only available endpoint. The result is shown in figure 18.1—the command lists the countries in JSON format.

```
C:\WINDOWS\system32\cmd.exe                                           —  □  ×
C:\Work>curl -v localhost:8081/countries
*   Trying ::1...
* TCP_NODELAY set
* Connected to localhost (::1) port 8081 (#0)
> GET /countries HTTP/1.1
> Host: localhost:8081
> User-Agent: curl/7.55.1
> Accept: */*
>
< HTTP/1.1 200
< Content-Type: application/json
< Transfer-Encoding: chunked
< Date: Sun, 15 Dec 2019 12:24:22 GMT
<
[{"codeName":"AU","name":"Australia"},{"codeName":"UK","name":"United Kingdom"},{"codeName":"US","name"
:"USA"}]* Connection #0 to host localhost left intact

C:\Work>
```

Figure 18.1   The result of running the `curl -v localhost:8081/countries` command is the list of created countries.

We can also test accessing this endpoint through the browser by going to local-host:8081/countries. Again, the result is provided in JSON format, as shown in figure 18.2.

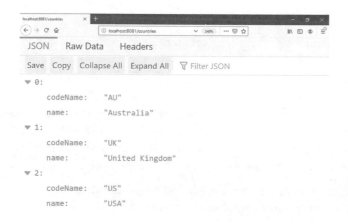

Figure 18.2   Accessing the localhost:8081/countries URL from the browser displays the list of created countries.

18.3   Creating a RESTful API to manage two related entities

Mike continues the implementation by modifying the `Passenger` class to make it a model component of the RESTful application.

Listing 18.9   Modified `Passenger` class

```
@Entity                                              <-- ❶
public class Passenger {

    @Id
    @GeneratedValue                                      ❷
    private Long id;
    private String name;
    @ManyToOne                                       <--
    private Country country;
    private boolean isRegistered;                        ❸

    // avoid "No default constructor for entity"
    public Passenger() {                                 ❹
    }
    [...]
}
```

In this listing:

- Mike annotates the `Passenger` class with `@Entity` so it has the ability to represent objects that can be persisted ❶.
- He introduces a new `Long` field, `id`, and annotates it with `@Id` and `@GeneratedValue` ❷. This means the `id` field is a primary key, and its value will be automatically generated for that field by the persistence layer.
- He annotates the `country` field with `@ManyToOne` ❸. This means many passengers can be mapped to a single country.
- He adds a default constructor to the `Passenger` class ❹. Every class annotated with `@Entity` needs a default constructor, as the persistence layer will use it to create a new instance of this class through reflection.

Mike next creates the `PassengerRepository` interface, which extends `Jpa-Repository`.

Listing 18.10   `PassengerRepository` interface

```
public interface PassengerRepository extends JpaRepository<Country, Long> {
}
```

Defining this interface serves two purposes. First, extending `JpaRepository` gives the `PassengerRepository` generic CRUD methods that let Mike work with `Passenger` objects. Second, this allows Spring to scan the classpath for this interface and create a Spring bean for it.

Mike now writes a custom exception to be thrown when a passenger is not found.

Listing 18.11 `PassengerNotFoundException` class

```
public class PassengerNotFoundException extends RuntimeException {              ◁──┐
                                                                                   ❶
    public PassengerNotFoundException(Long id) {
        super("Passenger id not found : " + id);          ❷
    }

}
```

In this listing, Mike declares `PassengerNotFoundException` by extending `Runtime-Exception` ❶ and creates a constructor that receives an `id` as a parameter ❷.

Next, Mike writes a controller for `PassengerRepository`.

Listing 18.12 `PassengerController` class

```
[...]
@RestController
public class PassengerController {           ❶

    @Autowired
    private PassengerRepository repository;           ❷

    @Autowired
    private Map<String, Country> countriesMap;           ❸

    @GetMapping("/passengers")
    List<Passenger> findAll() {
        return repository.findAll();           ❹
    }

    @PostMapping("/passengers")
    @ResponseStatus(HttpStatus.CREATED)           ◁── ❻          ❼
    Passenger createPassenger(@RequestBody Passenger passenger) {   ◁──
❺       return repository.save(passenger);
    }

    @GetMapping("/passengers/{id}")
──▷ Passenger findPassenger(@PathVariable Long id) {                           ❽
❾       return repository.findById(id)
                .orElseThrow(() -> new PassengerNotFoundException(id));
    }

    @PatchMapping("/passengers/{id}")
──▷ Passenger patchPassenger(@RequestBody Map<String, String> updates,        ❶❶
❿                @PathVariable Long id) {

        return repository.findById(id)
            .map(passenger -> {           ❶❷
```

```
                String name = updates.get("name");
                if (null!= name) {                          ⑬
                    passenger.setName(name);
                }

                Country country =
                    countriesMap.get(updates.get("country"));
                if (null != country) {                       ⑭
                    passenger.setCountry(country);
                }

                String isRegistered = updates.get("isRegistered");
                if(null != isRegistered) {                   ⑮
                  passenger.setIsRegistered(
                      isRegistered.equalsIgnoreCase("true")? true: false);
⑯                }
    └─ ▷     return repository.save(passenger);
        })
          .orElseGet(() -> {
              throw new PassengerNotFoundException(id);    ⑰
          });

    }

⑲
    @DeleteMapping("/passengers/{id}")
    void deletePassenger(@PathVariable Long id) {          ⑱
        repository.deleteById(id);
    }
}
```

In this listing:

- Mike creates the `PassengerController` class and annotates it with `@Rest-Controller` ❶.
- He declares a `PassengerRepository` field and autowires it ❷. Because `PassengerRepository` extends `JpaRepository`, Spring will scan the classpath for this interface, create a Spring bean for it, and autowire it here. Mike also declares a `countriesMap` field and autowires it ❸.
- He creates the `findAll` method and annotates it with `@GetMapping("/passengers")` ❹. This `@GetMapping` annotation maps HTTP `GET` requests to the /passengers URL onto the specific handler method.
- He declares the `createPassenger` method and annotates it with `@PostMapping("/passengers")` ❺. `@PostMapping`-annotated methods handle the HTTP `POST` requests matched with given URL expressions. Mike marks that method with `@ResponseStatus`, specifying the response status as `HttpStatus.CREATED` ❻. The `@RequestBody` annotation maps the `HttpRequest` body to the annotated domain object. The `HttpRequest` body is deserialized to a Java object ❼.
- Mike declares the `findPassenger` method that will look for the passenger by ID and annotates it with `@GetMapping("/passengers/{id}")` ❽. The

@GetMapping annotation maps HTTP GET requests to the /passengers/{id} URL onto the specific handler method. It searches for the passenger in the repository and returns them; or, if the passenger does not exist, it throws the custom declared PassengerNotFoundException. The id argument of the method is annotated with @PathVariable, meaning it will be extracted from the URL's {id} value ❾.

- Mike declares the patchPassenger method and annotates it with @Patch-Mapping("/passengers/{id}") ❿. The @PatchMapping annotation maps HTTP PATCH requests to the /passengers/{id} URL onto the specific handler method. He annotates the updates parameter with @RequestBody and the id parameter with @PathVariable ⓫. The @RequestBody annotation maps the HttpRequest body to the annotated domain object. The HttpRequest body is deserialized to a Java object. The id argument of the method, annotated with @PathVariable, will be extracted from the URL's {id} value.

- Mike searches the repository by the input id ⓬. He changes the name of an existing passenger ⓭, the country ⓮, and the registration status ⓯. The modified passenger is saved in the repository ⓰.

- If the passenger does not exist, the custom declared PassengerNotFound-Exception is thrown ⓱.

- Mike declares the delete method and annotates it with @DeleteMapping ("/passengers/{id}") ⓲. The @DeleteMapping annotation maps HTTP DELETE requests to the /passengers/{id} URL onto the specific handler method. It deletes the passenger from the repository. The id argument of the method is annotated with @PathVariable, meaning it will be extracted from the URL's {id} value ⓳.

Mike now modifies the Application class.

Listing 18.13 Modified Application class

```
@SpringBootApplication
@Import(FlightBuilder.class)
public class Application {

    @Autowired
    private Flight flight;                                          ❶

    @Autowired
    private Map<String, Country> countriesMap;

    public static void main(String[] args) {
        SpringApplication.run(Application.class, args);
    }

    @Bean
    CommandLineRunner configureRepository
                    (CountryRepository countryRepository,          ❷
                     PassengerRepository passengerRepository) {
        return args -> {
```

```
      for (Country country: countriesMap.values()) {
         countryRepository.save(country);
      }

      for (Passenger passenger : flight.getPassengers()) {        ❸
         passengerRepository.save(passenger);
      }
   };
}
```

}

In this listing:

- Mike autowires the `flight` bean ❶ imported from the `FlightBuilder`.
- He modifies the bean of type `CommandLineRunner` by adding a new parameter of type `PassengerRepository` to the `configureRepository` method that creates it ❷. `CommandLineRunner` is a Spring Boot interface that provides access to application arguments as a string array. The created bean will additionally browse all passengers in the `flight` and save them in `passenger-Repository` ❸. This `CommandLineRunner` interface is created, and its method is executed, just before the `run()` method from `SpringApplication` completes.

The list of passengers of the flight is shown in the following CSV file. A passenger is described using a name and a country code; there are 20 passengers total.

Listing 18.14　flights_information.csv file

```
John Smith; UK
Jane Underwood; AU
James Perkins; US
Mary Calderon; US
Noah Graves; UK
Jake Chavez; AU
Oliver Aguilar; US
Emma McCann; AU
Margaret Knight; US
Amelia Curry; UK
Jack Vaughn; US
Liam Lewis; AU
Olivia Reyes; US
Samantha Poole; AU
Patricia Jordan; UK
Robert Sherman; US
Mason Burton; AU
Harry Christensen; UK
Jennifer Mills; US
Sophia Graham; UK
```

When the application starts, the `FlightBuilder` class parses the file, creates the flight with the list of passengers, and injects the flight into the application. The application browses the list and saves each passenger in the repository.

Mike launches `Application` into execution. The RESTful application now also provides access to the /passengers endpoint. We can test the new functionalities of the REST API endpoint using the `curl` program:

```
curl -v localhost:8081/passengers
```

The application is running on port 8081, and /passengers is available as an endpoint. The result is shown in figure 18.3: a list of passengers in JSON format.

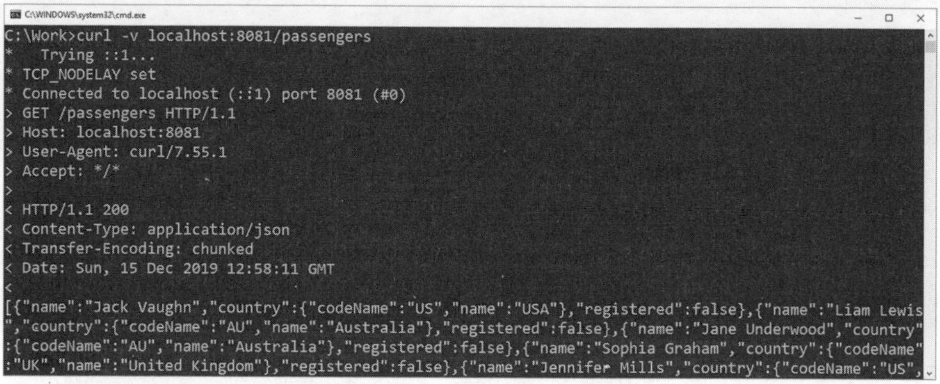

Figure 18.3   The result of running the `curl -v localhost:8081/passengers` command is the list of passengers.

We can also test the other functionalities implemented for the /passengers endpoint. For example, to get the passenger having ID 4, we execute this command:

```
curl -v localhost:8081/passengers/4
```

The result is shown in figure 18.4: the passenger information is provided in JSON format.

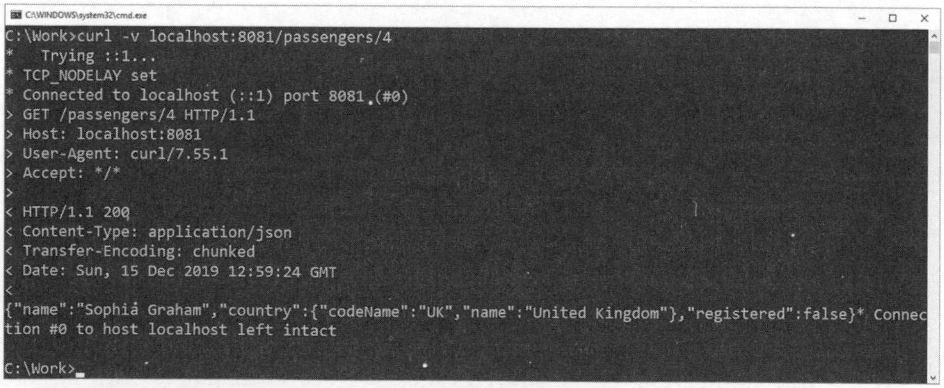

Figure 18.4   Running the `curl -v localhost:8081/passengers/4` command shows the passenger with ID 4.

We can update the name, country, and registered status of the passenger with ID 4 by executing this command:

```
curl -v -X PATCH localhost:8081/passengers/4
-H "Content-type:application/json"
-d "{\"name\":\"Sophia Jones\", \"country\":\"AU\",
    \"isRegistered\":\"true\"}"
```

The result is shown in figure 18.5.

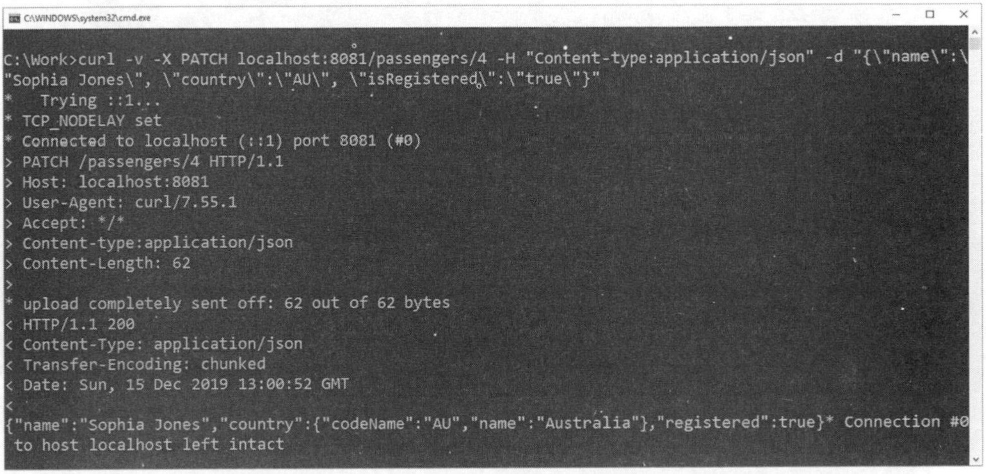

Figure 18.5   The result of successfully updating the information for the passenger with ID 4

To delete this passenger, we use this command:

```
curl -v -X DELETE localhost:8081/passengers/4
```

The result is shown in figure 18.6.

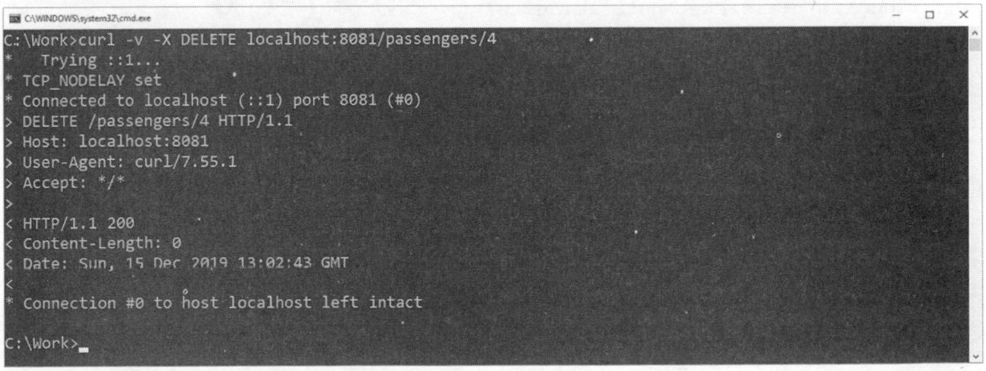

Figure 18.6   The passenger with ID 4 has been deleted.

Finally, we can post a new passenger:

```
curl -v -X POST localhost:8081/passengers
-H "Content-type:application/json"
-d "{\"name\":\"John Smith\"}"
```

The result is shown in figure 18.7.

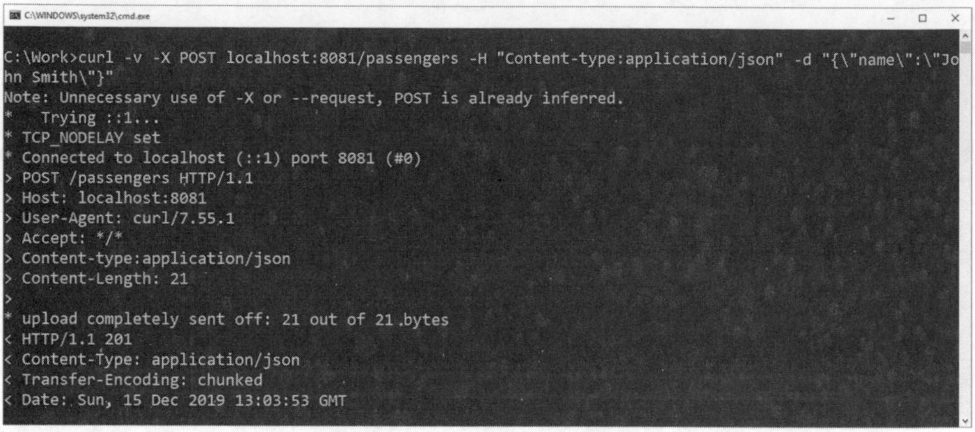

```
C:\Work>curl -v -X POST localhost:8081/passengers -H "Content-type:application/json" -d "{\"name\":\"Jo
hn Smith\"}"
Note: Unnecessary use of -X or --request, POST is already inferred.
*   Trying ::1...
* TCP_NODELAY set
* Connected to localhost (::1) port 8081 (#0)
> POST /passengers HTTP/1.1
> Host: localhost:8081
> User-Agent: curl/7.55.1
> Accept: */*
> Content-type:application/json
> Content-Length: 21
>
* upload completely sent off: 21 out of 21 bytes
< HTTP/1.1 201
< Content-Type: application/json
< Transfer-Encoding: chunked
< Date: Sun, 15 Dec 2019 13:03:53 GMT
```

Figure 18.7   We successfully posted a new passenger, John Smith.

18.4   *Testing the RESTful API*

Next, Mike writes the tests to automatically verify the behavior of the RESTful API.

Listing 18.15   `RestApplicationTest` class

```
[...]
@SpringBootTest
@AutoConfigureMockMvc
@Import(FlightBuilder.class)
public class RestApplicationTest {

    @Autowired
    private MockMvc mvc;

    @Autowired
    private Flight flight;

    @Autowired
    private Map<String, Country> countriesMap;

    @MockBean
    private PassengerRepository passengerRepository;

    @MockBean
    private CountryRepository countryRepository;
```

① ② ③ ④ ⑤ ⑥

```java
@Test
void testGetAllCountries() throws Exception {
    when(countryRepository.findAll()).thenReturn(new
            ArrayList<>(countriesMap.values()));
    mvc.perform(get("/countries"))
        .andExpect(status().isOk())
        .andExpect(content().contentType(MediaType.APPLICATION_JSON))
        .andExpect(jsonPath("$", hasSize(3)));

    verify(countryRepository, times(1)).findAll();
}

@Test
void testGetAllPassengers() throws Exception {
    when(passengerRepository.findAll()).thenReturn(new
            ArrayList<>(flight.getPassengers()));

    mvc.perform(get("/passengers"))
        .andExpect(status().isOk())
        .andExpect(content().contentType(MediaType.APPLICATION_JSON))
        .andExpect(jsonPath("$", hasSize(20)));

    verify(passengerRepository, times(1)).findAll();
}

@Test
void testPassengerNotFound() {
    Throwable throwable = assertThrows(NestedServletException.class,
            () -> mvc.perform(get("/passengers/30"))
                        .andExpect(status().isNotFound()));
    assertEquals(PassengerNotFoundException.class,
                throwable.getCause().getClass());
}

@Test
void testPostPassenger() throws Exception {

    Passenger passenger = new Passenger("Peter Michelsen");
    passenger.setCountry(countriesMap.get("US"));
    passenger.setIsRegistered(false);
    when(passengerRepository.save(passenger))
        .thenReturn(passenger);

    mvc.perform(post("/passengers")
        .content(new ObjectMapper().writeValueAsString(passenger))
        .header(HttpHeaders.CONTENT_TYPE, MediaType.APPLICATION_JSON))
        .andExpect(status().isCreated())
        .andExpect(jsonPath("$.name", is("Peter Michelsen")))
        .andExpect(jsonPath("$.country.codeName", is("US")))
        .andExpect(jsonPath("$.country.name", is("USA")))
        .andExpect(jsonPath("$.registered", is(Boolean.FALSE)));

verify(passengerRepository, times(1)).save(passenger);
}
```

7 **8** **9** **10** **11** **12** **13** **14** **15** **16** **17** **18**

```
@Test
void testPatchPassenger() throws Exception {
    Passenger passenger = new Passenger("Sophia Graham");
    passenger.setCountry(countriesMap.get("UK"));
    passenger.setIsRegistered(false);                        ⑲
    when(passengerRepository.findById(1L))
        .thenReturn(Optional.of(passenger));
    when(passengerRepository.save(passenger))               ⑳
        .thenReturn(passenger);
    String updates =
      "{\"name\":\"Sophia Jones\", \"country\":\"AU\",
      \"isRegistered\":\"true\"}";

    mvc.perform(patch("/passengers/1")                       ㉑
        .content(updates)
        .header(HttpHeaders.CONTENT_TYPE,
                         MediaType.APPLICATION_JSON))
        .andExpect(content().contentType(MediaType.APPLICATION_JSON))
        .andExpect(status().isOk());

    verify(passengerRepository, times(1)).findById(1L);      ㉒
    verify(passengerRepository, times(1)).save(passenger);
}


@Test
public void testDeletePassenger() throws Exception {

    mvc.perform(delete("/passengers/4"))                     ㉓
            .andExpect(status().isOk());

    verify(passengerRepository, times(1)).deleteById(4L);   ←
}                                                            ㉔

}
```

In this listing:

- Mike creates the RestApplicationTest class and annotates it with @Spring-
  BootTest ❶. @SpringBootTest searches the current package of the test class
  and its subpackages for bean definitions.

- He also annotates the class with @AutoConfigureMockMvc in order to enable
  all autoconfiguration related to the MockMvc objects used in the test ❷.

- He imports FlightBuilder, which creates a flight bean and a countries map
  bean ❸.

- He autowires a MockMvc object ❹. MockMvc is the main entry point for server-
  side Spring REST application testing: Mike will perform a series of REST operations against this MockMvc object during the tests.

- He declares a flight and a countriesMap field and autowires them ❺. These
  fields are injected from the FlightBuilder class.

- He declares countryRepository and passengerRepository fields and
  annotates them with @MockBean ❻. @MockBean is used to add mock objects to

the Spring application context; the mock will replace any existing bean of the same type in the application context. Mike will provide instructions for the behavior of the mock objects during the tests.

- In the `testGetAllCountries` test, he instructs the mock `country-Repository` bean to return the array of values from `countriesMap` when the `findAll` method is executed on it **❼**.
- Mike simulates the execution of the `GET` method on the `/countries` URL **❽** and verifies the returned status, expected content type, and returned JSON size **❾**. He also verifies that the method `findAll` has been executed exactly once on the `countryRepository` bean **❿**.
- In the `testGetAllPassengers` test, he instructs the mock `passenger-Repository` bean to return the passengers from the `flight` bean when the `findAll` method is executed on it **⓫**.
- He simulates the execution of the `GET` method on the `/passengers` URL and verifies the returned status, expected content type, and returned JSON size **⓬**. He also verifies that the method `findAll` has been executed exactly once on the `passengerRepository` bean **⓭**.
- In `testPassengerNotFound`, Mike tries to get the passenger having ID 30 and checks that a `NestedServletException` is thrown and that the returned status is "Not Found" **⓮**. He also checks that the cause of the `NestedServlet-Exception` is `PassengerNotFoundException` **⓯**.
- In `testPostPassenger`, Mike creates a `passenger` object, configures it, and instructs `passengerRepository` to return that object when a `save` is executed on that passenger **⓰**.
- He simulates the execution of the `POST` method on the `/passengers` URL and verifies that the content consists of the JSON string value of the `passenger` object, the header type, the returned status, and the content of the JSON **⓱**. He uses an object of type `com.fasterxml.jackson.databind.Object-Mapper`, which is the main class of the Jackson library (the standard JSON library for Java). `ObjectMapper` offers functionality for reading and writing JSON to and from basic POJOs.
- Mike also verifies that the `save` method has been executed exactly once on the previously defined passenger **⓲**.
- In `testPatchPassenger`, he creates a `passenger` object, configures it, and instructs `passengerRepository` to return that object when a passenger `findById` is executed with the argument 1 **⓳**. When the `save` method is executed on `passengerRepository`, that `passenger` is returned as well **⓴**.
- Mike sets a JSON object named `updates`, performs a `PATCH` on the `/passengers/1` URL using that update, and checks the content and the returned status **㉑**.
- He verifies that the `findById` and `save` methods have been executed exactly once on `passengerRepository` **㉒**.

- He performs a DELETE operation on the /passengers/4 URL, verifies that the returned status is OK ㉓, and verifies that the deleteById method has been executed exactly once ㉔.

Running RestApplicationTest is successful, as shown in figure 18.8.

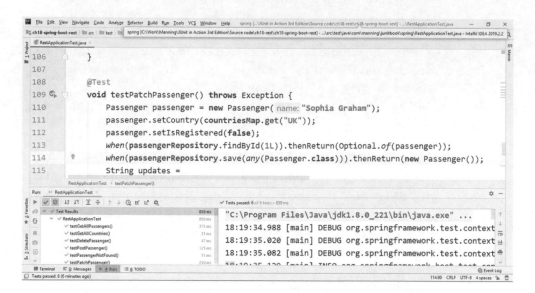

Figure 18.8   Successfully running RestApplicationTest, **which checks the RESTful application's functionality**

The next chapter will be dedicated to testing database applications and the various alternatives for doing so.

Summary

This chapter has covered the following:

- Introducing the REST architectural style and the concept of REST applications
- Demonstrating what makes an API RESTful, and the REST architecture constraints: client-server, stateless, uniform interface, layered system, cacheable, and code on demand
- Creating a RESTful API to manage a single entity—the country from the flight-management application—and executing GET operations against it to obtain the list of countries
- Creating a RESTful API to manage two related entities—the country and the passenger—and executing GET, PATCH, DELETE, and POST operations against it to get the list of passengers; to get a particular passenger by ID; and to create, update, or delete a passenger
- Testing the RESTful API that manages two related entities by creating and executing tests against a Spring REST MockMvc object to test the previously mentioned GET, PATCH, DELETE, and POST operations

Testing database applications

Dependency is the key problem in software development at all scales. . . . Eliminating duplication in programs eliminates dependency.

—Kent Beck, *Test-Driven Development: By Example*

The persistence layer (or, roughly speaking, database access code) is undoubtedly one of the most important parts of any enterprise project. Despite its importance, the persistence layer is hard to unit test, mainly due to the following three issues:

- Unit tests must exercise code in isolation; the persistence layer requires interaction with an external entity, the database.
- Unit tests must be easy to write and run; code that accesses the database can be cumbersome.

■ Unit tests must be fast to run; database access is relatively slow.

We call these issues the *database unit testing impedance mismatch*, in reference to the object-relational impedance mismatch (which describes the difficulties of using a relational database to persist data when an application is written using an object-oriented language). We'll discuss the issues in more detail in this chapter and show possible implementation and testing alternatives for Java database applications.

19.1 The database unit testing impedance mismatch

Let's take a deeper look at the three issues that make up the database unit testing impedance mismatch.

19.1.1 Unit tests must exercise code in isolation

From a purist's point of view, tests that exercise database access code cannot be considered unit tests because they depend on an external entity: the almighty database. What should they be called, then? Integration tests? Functional tests? Non-unit unit tests?

Well, the answer is that there is no secret ingredient! In other words, database tests can fit in many categories, depending on the context. Pragmatically speaking, though, database access code can be exercised by both unit and integration tests:

■ Unit tests are used to test classes that interact directly with the database (like DAOs). A data access object (DAO) is an object that provides an interface to a database and maps application calls to the specific database operations without exposing details of the persistence layer. Such tests guarantee that these classes execute the proper operation against the database. Although these tests depend on external entities (like the database and/or persistence frameworks), they exercise classes that are building blocks in a bigger application (and hence are units).

■ Similarly, unit tests can be written to test the upper layers (like facades) without the need to access the database. In these tests, the persistence layer can be emulated by mocks or stubs. Like a facade in architecture, the facade design pattern provides an object that serves as a front-facing interface masking a more complex underlying code.

There is still a practical question: can't the data in the database get in the way of the tests? Yes, it is possible, so before we run the tests, we must ensure that the database is in a known state—and we'll show how to do this in this chapter.

19.1.2 Unit tests must be easy to write and run

It does not matter how much a company, project manager, or technical leader praises unit tests—if they are not easy to write and run, developers will resist writing them. Moreover, writing code that accesses the database is not a straightforward task—we have to write SQL statements, mix many levels of `try/catch/finally` code, convert SQL types to and from Java, and so on.

Therefore, in order for database unit tests to thrive, it is necessary to alleviate the "database burden" on developers. We'll start our work using pure JDBC. Then, we'll introduce Spring as the framework used for our application. Finally, we'll move to ORM and Hibernate.

> **DEFINITIONS** *Java Database Connectivity (JDBC)*—A Java API that defines how a client can access a database. JDBC provides methods to query and update data in a relational database.
>
> *Object-relational mapping (ORM)*—A programming technique for converting data between relational databases and object-oriented programming languages and vice versa.
>
> *Hibernate*—An ORM framework for Java. It provides the facilities for mapping an object-oriented domain model to relational database tables. Hibernate manages the incompatibilities between the object-oriented model and the relational database model by replacing the direct database access with object manipulation.

19.1.3 *Unit tests must be fast to run*

Let's say you overcame the first two issues and have a nice environment with hundreds of unit tests exercising the objects that access the database, and where a developer can easily add new tests. Everything seems fine, but when a developer runs the build (and they should do that many times a day, at least after updating their workspace and before submitting changes to the source control system), it takes 10 minutes for the build to complete, 9 of them spent in the database tests. What should you do then?

This is the hardest issue because it cannot always be solved. Typically, the delay is caused by the database access per se, as the database is probably a remote server accessed by dozens of users. A possible solution is to move the database closer to the developer, by either using an embedded database (if the application uses standard SQL that enables a database switch or uses an ORM framework) or locally installing lighter versions of the database.

> **DEFINITION** *Embedded database*—A database that is bundled within an application instead of being managed by external servers (which is the typical scenario). A broad range of embedded databases are available for Java applications, most of them based on open source projects like H2 (https://h2database.com), HSQLDB (http://hsqldb.org), and Apache Derby (https://db.apache.org/derby). The fundamental characteristic of an embedded database is that it is managed by the application, not the language it is written in. For instance, both HSQLDB and Derby support client/server mode (in addition to the embedded option), while SQLite (which is a C-based product) could also be embedded in a Java application.

In the following sections, we will see how to start with a pure JDBC application and an embedded database. Then we will introduce Spring and Hibernate as ORM frameworks and also take steps to solve the database unit testing impedance mismatch.

19.2 *Testing a JDBC application*

JDBC is a Java API that defines how a client can access a database: it provides methods to query and update data in a relational database. It was first released as part of the Java Development Kit (JDK) 1.1 in 1997. Since then, it has been part of the Java Platform, Standard Edition (Java SE). Because it was one of the early APIs used in Java and was designed to be regularly used in database applications, it may still be encountered in projects and may not even be combined with any other technology.

In our example, we'll start from a pure JDBC application, then introduce Spring and Hibernate, and finally test all of these applications. This process will demonstrate how such database applications can be tested and also show how to reduce the database unit testing impedance mismatch.

At Tested Data Systems, the flight-management application we have seen in previous chapters persists information into a database. It is George's job to analyze the application and move it to present-day technologies. The JDBC application that George receives contains a Country class describing passengers' countries.

Listing 19.1 Country class

```java
public class Country {
    private String name;                              ❶
    private String codeName;

    public Country(String name, String codeName) {
        this.name = name;                             ❷
        this.codeName = codeName;
    }

    public String getName() {
        return name;
    }

    public void setName(String name) {
        this.name = name;                             ❶
    }

    public String getCodeName() {
        return codeName;
    }

    public void setCodeName(String codeName) {
        this.codeName = codeName;                     ❶
    }

    @Override
    public String toString() {
        return "Country{" +
                "name='" + name + '\'' +
                ", codeName='" + codeName + '\'' +    ❸
                '}';
    }
}
```

```
    @Override
    public boolean equals(Object o) {
        if (this == o) return true;
        if (o == null || getClass() != o.getClass()) return false;
        Country country = (Country) o;
        return Objects.equals(name, country.name) &&
                Objects.equals(codeName, country.codeName);
    }

    @Override
    public int hashCode() {
        return Objects.hash(name, codeName);
    }
}
```

❹

In this listing:

- George declares the name and codeName fields of the Country class, together with the corresponding getters and setters ❶.
- He creates a constructor of the Country class to initialize the name and code-Name fields ❷.
- He overrides the toString method to display a country ❸.
- He overrides the equals and hashCode methods to take into account the name and codeName fields ❹.

The application currently uses the embedded H2 database for testing purposes. The Maven pom.xml file includes the JUnit 5 dependencies and H2 dependencies.

Listing 19.2 Maven pom.xml dependencies

```xml
<dependencies>
    <dependency>
        <groupId>org.junit.jupiter</groupId>
        <artifactId>junit-jupiter-api</artifactId>
        <version>5.6.0</version>
        <scope>test</scope>
    </dependency>
    <dependency>
        <groupId>org.junit.jupiter</groupId>
        <artifactId>junit-jupiter-engine</artifactId>
        <version>5.6.0</version>
        <scope>test</scope>
    </dependency>
    <dependency>
        <groupId>com.h2database</groupId>
        <artifactId>h2</artifactId>
        <version>1.4.199</version>
    </dependency>
</dependencies>
```

The application manages connections to the database and operations against the database tables through the ConnectionManager and TablesManager classes (listings 19.3 and 19.4).

Listing 19.3   ConnectionManager class

```
[...]
public class ConnectionManager {                           ❶

    private static Connection connection;              ⟵

    public static Connection openConnection() {

        try {                                              ❷
            Class.forName("org.h2.Driver");        ⟵
            connection = DriverManager.getConnection(
                "jdbc:h2:~/country", "sa",                  ❸
                ""
                );
            return connection;
        } catch(ClassNotFoundException | SQLException e) {
❹           throw new RuntimeException(e);                  ❺
        }
    }

    public static void closeConnection() {     ❻
        if (null != connection) {                  ⟵       ❼
            try {
                connection.close();                    ⟵
            } catch(SQLException e) {
                throw new RuntimeException(e);   ❽
            }
        }
    }
}
```

In this listing:

- George declares a Connection type connection field ❶.
- In the openConnection method, he loads the H2 driver ❷ and initializes the previously declared connection field to access the H2 country database using JDBC, with sa as a user and no password ❸. If everything goes fine, he returns the initialized connection ❹.
- If the H2 driver class hasn't been found or the code encounters an SQL-Exception, George catches it and rethrows a RuntimeException ❺.
- In the closeConnection method, he first checks to be sure the connection is not null ❻ and then tries to close it ❼. If an SQLException occurs, he catches it and rethrows a RuntimeException ❽.

Listing 19.4   TablesManager class

```
[...]
public class TablesManager {

    public static void createTable() {
```

```
        String sql = "CREATE TABLE COUNTRY( ID IDENTITY,          ①
                        NAME VARCHAR(255), CODE_NAME VARCHAR(255) );";
        executeStatement(sql);                              ←────  ②
    }

    public static void dropTable() {
        String sql = "DROP TABLE IF EXISTS COUNTRY;";       ←────
        executeStatement(sql);                              ←────  ③
    }                                                         ④

    private static void executeStatement(String sql) {
      PreparedStatement statement;                          ←────
                                                              ⑤
      try {
          Connection connection = openConnection();         ←────     ←────
          statement = connection.prepareStatement(sql);     ←────          ⑥
          statement.exccuteUpdate();                        ←────    ⑦
          statement.close();                                  ⑧
      } catch (SQLException e) {
          throw new RuntimeException(e);                    ←────
      } finally {                                            ⑩
          closeConnection();                         ←────
      }                                               ⑪
    }
}

}
```

In this listing:

- In the `createTable` method, George declares an SQL `CREATE  TABLE` statement that creates the `COUNTRY` table with an `ID` identity field and the `NAME` and `CODE_NAME` fields of type `VARCHAR` ①. Then he executes this statement ②.
- In the `dropTable` method, he declares an SQL `DROP  TABLE` statement that drops the `COUNTRY` table if it exists ③. Then he executes this statement ④.
- The `executeStatement` method declares a `PreparedStatement` variable ⑤. Then it opens a connection ⑥, prepares the statement ⑦, executes it ⑧, and closes it ⑨. If an `SQLException` is caught, George rethrows a `RuntimeException` ⑩. Regardless of whether the statement is successfully executed, he closes the connection ⑪.

The application declares a `CountryDao` class, an implementation of the DAO pattern, which provides an abstract interface to the database and executes queries against it.

Listing 19.5 `CountryDao` class

```
[...]
public class CountryDao {
    private static final String GET_ALL_COUNTRIES_SQL =          ①
            "select * from country";
    private static final String GET_COUNTRIES_BY_NAME_SQL =      ②
            "select * from country where name like ?";
```

```
public List<Country> getCountryList() {
    List<Country> countryList = new ArrayList<>();                        ←  ③

    try {                                                            ④
        Connection connection = openConnection();        ←
        PreparedStatement statement =
                connection.prepareStatement(GET_ALL_COUNTRIES_SQL);      ⑤
        ResultSet resultSet = statement.executeQuery();

        while (resultSet.next()) {                                        ⑥
            countryList.add(new Country(resultSet.getString(2),
                            resultSet.getString(3)));
        }
        statement.close();                               ←
    } catch (SQLException e) {                       ⑧        ⑦
        throw new RuntimeException(e);
    } finally {
        closeConnection();                   ←
    }                                         ⑨
    return countryList;               ←
}                                      ⑩

public List<Country> getCountryListStartWith(String name) {   ⑪
    List<Country> countryList = new ArrayList<>();               ←

    try {                                          ⑫
        Connection connection = openConnection();        ←
        PreparedStatement statement =
                connection.prepareStatement(GET_COUNTRIES_BY_NAME_SQL);  ⑬
        statement.setString(1, name + "%");
        ResultSet resultSet = statement.executeQuery();

        while (resultSet.next()) {                                       ⑭
            countryList.add(new Country(resultSet.getString(2),
                            resultSet.getString(3)));
    ⑮    }
   →     statement.close();
    } catch (SQLException e) {                   ⑯
        throw new RuntimeException(e);
    } finally {
        closeConnection();                   ←
    }                                         ⑰
    return countryList;               ←
}                                      ⑱
}
```

In this listing:

- George declares two SQL SELECT statements to get all the countries from the COUNTRY table ❶ and to get the countries whose names match a pattern ❷.
- In the getCountryList method, he initializes an empty country list ❸, opens a connection ❹, prepares the statement, and executes it ❺.
- He passes through all the results returned from the database and adds them to the list of countries ❻. Then he closes the statement ❼. If an SQLException is

caught, he rethrows a `RuntimeException` **❽**. Regardless of whether the statement is successfully executed, he closes the connection **❾**. He returns the list of countries at the end of the method **❿**.

- In the `getCountryListStartWith` method, George initializes an empty country list **⓫**, opens a connection **⓬**, prepares the statement, and executes it **⓭**.

- He passes through all the results returned from the database and adds them to the list of countries **⓮**. Then he closes the statement **⓯**. If an `SQLException` is caught, he rethrows a `RuntimeException` **⓰**. Regardless of whether the statement is successfully executed, he closes the connection **⓱**. He returns the list of countries at the end of the method **⓲**.

Moving to the testing side, George has two classes: `CountriesLoader` (listing 19.6), which populates the database and makes sure it is in a known state; and `Countries-DatabaseTest` (listing 19.7), which effectively tests the interaction of the application with the database.

Listing 19.6 `CountriesLoader` **class**

```
[...]
public class CountriesLoader {                                       ❶

    private static final String LOAD_COUNTRIES_SQL =          <──┘
            "insert into country (name, code_name) values ";

    public static final String[][] COUNTRY_INIT_DATA = {
            { "Australia", "AU"}, { "Canada", "CA" }, { "France", "FR" },
            { "Germany", "DE" }, { "Italy", "IT" }, { "Japan", "JP" },
            { "Romania", "RO" },{ "Russian Federation", "RU" },       ❷
            { "Spain", "ES" }, { "Switzerland", "CH" },
            { "United Kingdom", "UK" }, { "United States", "US" } };

    public void loadCountries() {
        for (String[] countryData : COUNTRY_INIT_DATA) {
            String sql = LOAD_COUNTRIES_SQL + "('" + countryData[0] +      ❹
                    "', '" + countryData[1] + "');";

            try {
                Connection connection = openConnection();         <──┐
                PreparedStatement statement =
                    connection.prepareStatement(sql);             ❻    ❺
                statement.executeUpdate();
                statement.close();
            } catch (SQLException e) {                            ❼
                throw new RuntimeException(e);
            } finally {
                closeConnection();              <──┐
            }                                        ❽
        }
    }
}
```

In this listing:

- George declares one SQL INSERT statement to insert a country into the COUN-TRY table **1**. He then declares the initialization data for the countries to be inserted **2**.
- In the loadCountries method, he browses the initialization data for the coun-tries **3** and builds the SQL query that inserts each country **4**.
- He opens a connection **5**, prepares the statement, executes it, and closes it **6**. If an SQLException is caught, he rethrows a RuntimeException **7**. Regardless of whether the statement is successfully executed, he closes the connection **8**.

Listing 19.7   CountriesDatabaseTest class

```
import static
    com.manning.junitbook.databases.CountriesLoader.COUNTRY_INIT_DATA;
[...]


public class CountriesDatabaseTest {                                        1
    private CountryDao countryDao = new CountryDao();
    private CountriesLoader countriesLoader = new CountriesLoader();

    private List<Country> expectedCountryList = new ArrayList<>();
    private List<Country> expectedCountryListStartsWithA =          3        2
                        new ArrayList<>();

    @BeforeEach
    public void setUp() {                                    5
        TablesManager.createTable();
        initExpectedCountryLists();                                   6
        countriesLoader.loadCountries();
    }                                                       7


    @Test
    public void testCountryList() {                                  8
        List<Country> countryList = countryDao.getCountryList();          9
        assertNotNull(countryList);
        assertEquals(expectedCountryList.size(), countryList.size());
        for (int i = 0; i < expectedCountryList.size(); i++) {           11
10          assertEquals(expectedCountryList.get(i), countryList.get(i));
        }
    }


    @Test
    public void testCountryListStartsWithA() {
        List<Country> countryList =
                        countryDao.getCountryListStartWith("A");     12
        assertNotNull(countryList);
13      assertEquals(expectedCountryListStartsWithA.size(),          14
                        countryList.size());
```

```
        for (int i = 0; i < expectedCountryListStartsWithA.size();
                        i++) {
            assertEquals(expectedCountryListStartsWithA.get(i),
                         countryList.get(i));                          ⓯
        }
    }

    @AfterEach                                                         ⓰
    public void dropDown() {
        TablesManager.dropTable();                                     ⓱
    }

    private void initExpectedCountryLists() {
         for (int i = 0; i < COUNTRY_INIT_DATA.length; i++) {          ⓲
             String[] countryInitData = COUNTRY_INIT_DATA[i];
             Country country = new Country(countryInitData[0],
                                           countryInitData[1]);        ⓳
⓴            expectedCountryList.add(country);
             if (country.getName().startsWith("A")) {
                 expectedCountryListStartsWithA.add(country);          ㉑
             }
         }
    }
}
```

In this listing:

- George statically imports the countries data from `CountriesLoader` and initializes `CountryDao` and `CountriesLoader` ❶. He initializes an empty list of expected countries ❷ and an empty list of expected countries that start with *A* ❸. (He could do this for any letter, but the test is currently looking for the countries with names starting with *A*.)
- He marks the `setUp` method with the `@BeforeEach` annotation so it is executed before each test ❹. In it, he creates the empty `COUNTRY` table in the database ❺, initializes the expected list of countries ❻, and loads the countries in the database ❼.
- In the `testCountryList` method, he initializes the list of countries from the database by using `getCountryList` from the `CountryDao` class ❽. Then he checks that the list he has obtained is not null ❾, that it is the expected size ❿, and that its content is as expected ⓫.
- In the `testCountryListStartsWithA` method, George initializes the list of countries starting with *A* from the database by using `getCountryListStartWith` from the `CountryDao` class ⓬. Then he checks that the list he has obtained is not null ⓭, that it is the expected size ⓮, and that its content is as expected ⓯.
- He marks the `dropDown` method with the `@AfterEach` annotation so it is executed after each test ⓰. In it, he drops the `COUNTRY` table from the database ⓱.

- In the `initExpectedCountryLists` method, he browses the country initialization data ⑱, creates a `Country` object at each step ⑲, and adds it to the list of expected countries ⑳. If the name of the country starts with *A*, he also adds it to the list of expected countries whose names start with *A* ㉑.

The tests run successfully, as shown in figure 19.1.

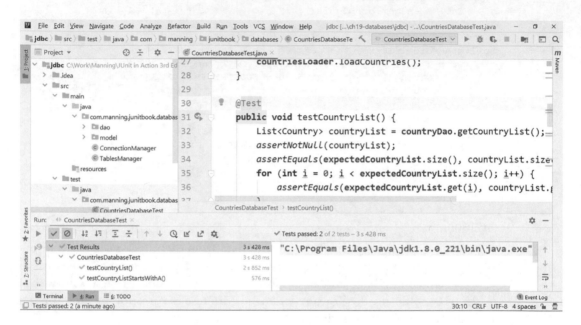

Figure 19.1   Successfully running the tests from the JDBC application to check the interaction with the COUNTRY **table**

This is the state of the application when it is assigned to George, and now he needs to improve the way it is tested. The application currently accesses and tests the database through JDBC, which requires a lot of tedious code to do the following:

- Create and open the connection
- Specify, prepare, and execute statements
- Iterate through the results
- Do the work for each iteration
- Process exceptions
- Close the connection

George will look for means to reduce the "database burden" so the developers can improve the way tests are written and reduce the database unit testing impedance mismatch.

19.3 *Testing a Spring JDBC application*

We introduced the Spring Framework and testing Spring applications in previous chapters. George has decided to introduce Spring into the flight-management database application, to reduce the database burden and to handle some of the tasks of interacting with the database via Spring inversion of control (IoC).

The application's `Country` class will remain untouched. George will make some other changes for the migration to Spring: first, he introduces the new dependencies in the Maven pom.xml file.

Listing 19.8   New dependencies introduced in the Maven pom.xml file

```
<dependency>
    <groupId>org.springframework</groupId>
    <artifactId>spring-context</artifactId>          ❶
    <version>5.2.1.RELEASE</version>
</dependency>
<dependency>
    <groupId>org.springframework</groupId>
    <artifactId>spring-jdbc</artifactId>             ❷
    <version>5.2.1.RELEASE</version>
</dependency>
<dependency>
    <groupId>org.springframework</groupId>           ❸
    <artifactId>spring-test</artifactId>
    <version>5.2.1.RELEASE</version>
</dependency>
```

In this listing, George adds the following dependencies:

- `spring-context`, the dependency for the Spring IoC container ❶.
- `spring-jdbc`, because the application is still using JDBC to access the database. Spring controls working with connections, preparing and executing statements, and processing exceptions ❷.
- `spring-test`, which provides support for writing tests with the help of Spring and which is necessary to use `SpringExtension` and the `@Context-Configuration` annotation ❸.

In the test/resources project folder, George inserts two files: one to create the database schema and one to configure the Spring context of the application (listings 19.9 and 19.10).

Listing 19.9   db-schema.sql file

```
create table country( id identity , name varchar (255) , code_name varchar
    (255) );
```

In this listing, George creates the COUNTRY table with three fields: ID (identity field), NAME, and CODE_NAME (VARCHAR type).

Listing 19.10   application-context.xml file

```xml
<jdbc:embedded-database id="dataSource" type="H2">
   <jdbc:script location="classpath:db-schema.sql"/>        ❶
</jdbc:embedded-database>

<bean id="countryDao"
      class="com.manning.junitbook.databases.dao.CountryDao">
        <property name="dataSource" ref="dataSource"/>       ❷
</bean>

<bean id="countriesLoader"
      class="com.manning.junitbook.databases.CountriesLoader">
   <property name="dataSource" ref="dataSource"/>            ❸
</bean>
```

In this listing, George instructs the Spring container to create three beans:

- dataSource, which points to a JDBC embedded database of type H2. He initializes the database with the help of the db-schema.sql file from listing 19.9, which is on the classpath ❶.
- countryDao, the DAO bean for executing SELECT queries to the database ❷. It has a dataSource property pointing to the previously declared dataSource bean.
- countriesLoader, which initializes the content of the database and brings it to a known state ❸. It also has a dataSource property pointing to the previously declared dataSource bean.

George changes the CountriesLoader class that loads the countries from the database and sets it in a known state.

Listing 19.11   CountriesLoader class

```java
public class CountriesLoader extends JdbcDaoSupport       ←┐
{                                                          ❶
    private static final String LOAD_COUNTRIES_SQL =      ←┐
            "insert into country (name, code_name) values ";  ❷

    public static final String[][] COUNTRY_INIT_DATA = {
            { "Australia", "AU"}, { "Canada", "CA" }, { "France", "FR" },
            { "Germany", "DE" }, { "Italy", "IT" }, { "Japan", "JP" },
            { "Romania", "RO" },{ "Russian Federation", "RU" },      ❸
            { "Spain", "ES" }, { "Switzerland", "CH" },
    { "United Kingdom", "UK" }, { "United States", "US" } };

                                                              ❹
    public void loadCountries() {
    for (String[] countryData : COUNTRY_INIT_DATA) {      ←┘
      String sql = LOAD_COUNTRIES_SQL + "('" + countryData[0] +
                    "','" + countryData[1] + "');";        ❺
        getJdbcTemplate().execute(sql);
      }
  }
}
```

In this listing:

- George declares the `CountriesLoader` class as extending `JdbcDaoSupport` **❶**.
- George declares one SQL `INSERT` statement, to insert a country in the COUN-TRY table **❷**. He then declares the initialization data for the countries to be inserted **❸**.
- In the `loadCountries` method, he browses the initialization data for the countries **❹**, builds the SQL query that inserts each particular country, and executes it against the database **❺**. With the Spring IoC approach, there is no need to perform the earlier tedious tasks: opening the connection, preparing the statement, executing and closing it, treating exceptions, and closing the connection.

Spring JDBC classes

`JdbcDaoSupport` is a Spring JDBC class that facilitates configuring and transferring database parameters. If a class extends `JdbcDaoSupport`, `JdbcDaoSupport` hides how a `JdbcTemplate` is created.

`JdbcTemplate` is the central class in the package `org.springframework.jdbc.core`. `getJdbcTemplate` is a `final` method from the `JdbcDaoSupport` class that provides access to an already initialized `JdbcTemplate` object that executes SQL queries, iterates over results, and catches JDBC exceptions.

George also changes the tested code to use Spring and reduce the database burden for the developers. He first implements the `CountryRowMapper` class that takes care of the mapping rules between the columns from the COUNTRY database table and the fields of the application `Country` class.

Listing 19.12 `CountryRowMapper` **class**

```
[...]
public class CountryRowMapper implements RowMapper<Country> {          ⟵─┐
    public static final String NAME = "name";                         ❷ │ ❶
    public static final String CODE_NAME = "code_name";

    @Override
    public Country mapRow(ResultSet resultSet, int i)
                                throws SQLException {                      ❸
        Country country = new Country(resultSet.getString(NAME),
            resultSet.getString(CODE_NAME));
        return country;                    ⟵─┐
    }                                        ❹
}
```

In this listing:

- George declares the `CountryRowMapper` class as implementing `RowMapper` **❶**. `RowMapper` is a Spring JDBC interface that maps the `ResultSet` obtained by accessing a database to certain objects.

- He declares the string constants to be used in the class, representing the names of the table columns ❷. The class will define once how to map the columns to the object fields and can be reused. There is no more need to set the statement parameters each time, as was necessary in the JDBC version.
- He overrides the mapRow method inherited from the RowMapper interface. He gets the two string parameters from the ResultSet coming from the database and builds a Country object ❸ that is returned at the end of the method ❹.

George modifies the existing CountryDao class to use Spring to interact with the database.

Listing 19.13   CountryDao class

```
[...]
public class CountryDao extends JdbcDaoSupport                    ❶
{
    private static final String GET_ALL_COUNTRIES_SQL =
            "select * from country";
    private static final String GET_COUNTRIES_BY_NAME_SQL =       ❷
            "select * from country where name like :name";

    private static final CountryRowMapper COUNTRY_ROW_MAPPER =    ❸
            new CountryRowMapper();

    public List<Country> getCountryList() {
        List<Country> countryList =
         getJdbcTemplate().
                        query(GET_ALL_COUNTRIES_SQL, COUNTRY_ROW_MAPPER);   ❹
        return countryList;
    }

    public List<Country> getCountryListStartWith(String name) {
        NamedParameterJdbcTemplate namedParameterJdbcTemplate =   ❺
            new NamedParameterJdbcTemplate(getDataSource());
        SqlParameterSource sqlParameterSource =                   ❻
            new MapSqlParameterSource("name", name + "%");
        return namedParameterJdbcTemplate.
                            query(GET_COUNTRIES_BY_NAME_SQL,       ❼
            sqlParameterSource, COUNTRY_ROW_MAPPER);
    }

}
```

In this listing:

- George declares the CountryDao class as extending JdbcDaoSupport ❶.
- He declares two SQL SELECT statements to get all the countries from the COUNTRY table and to get the countries whose names match a pattern ❷. In the second statement, he replaces the parameter with a named parameter (:name); it will be used this way in the class.
- He initializes a CountryRowMapper instance: the class he previously created ❸.

- In the `getCountryList` method, George queries the `COUNTRY` table using the SQL that returns all the countries and the `CountryRowMapper` that matches the columns from the table to the fields from the `Country` object. He directly returns a list of `Country` objects ❹.

- In the `getCountryListStartWith` method, George initializes a `Named-ParameterJdbcTemplate` variable ❺. `NamedParameterJdbcTemplate` allows the use of named parameters instead of the previously used `?` placeholders. The `getDataSource` method, which is the argument of the `Named-ParameterJdbcTemplate` constructor, is a `final` method inherited from `JdbcDaoSupport`; it returns the JDBC `DataSource` used by a DAO.

- He initializes an `SqlParameterSource` variable ❻. `SqlParameterSource` defines the functionality of the objects that can offer parameter values for named SQL parameters and can serve as an argument for `NamedParameter-JdbcTemplate` operations.

- He queries the `COUNTRY` table using the SQL that returns all the countries having names starting with *A* and the `CountryRowMapper` that matches the columns from the table to the fields from the `Country` object ❼.

Finally, George changes the existing `CountriesDatabaseTest` to take advantage of the Spring JDBC approach.

Listing 19.14 `CountriesDatabaseTest` class

```
[...]
@ExtendWith(SpringExtension.class)
@ContextConfiguration("classpath:application-context.xml")       ❶
public class CountriesDatabaseTest {                              ❷

    @Autowired
    private CountryDao countryDao;                      ❸

    @Autowired
    private CountriesLoader countriesLoader;                ❹

    private List<Country> expectedCountryList =
                              new ArrayList<Country>();          ❺
    private List<Country> expectedCountryListStartsWithA =
        new ArrayList<Country>();                       ❻

    @BeforeEach
    public void setUp() {                                   ❽
        initExpectedCountryLists();
        countriesLoader.loadCountries();
❼                                                      ❾
    }

                          ❿
    @Test
    @DirtiesContext
    public void testCountryList() {                             ⓫
        List<Country> countryList = countryDao.getCountryList();
```

```
              assertNotNull(countryList);
              assertEquals(expectedCountryList.size(), countryList.size());
              for (int i = 0; i < expectedCountryList.size(); i++) {
                  assertEquals(expectedCountryList.get(i),
                                                countryList.get(i));
              }
          }

          @Test
          @DirtiesContext
          public void testCountryListStartsWithA() {
              List<Country> countryList =
                          countryDao.getCountryListStartWith("A");
              assertNotNull(countryList);
              assertEquals(expectedCountryListStartsWithA.size(),
                          countryList.size());
              for (int i = 0; i < expectedCountryListStartsWithA.size();
                                                              i++) {
                  assertEquals(expectedCountryListStartsWithA.get(i),
                              countryList.get(i));
              }
          }

          private void initExpectedCountryLists() {
            for (int i = 0; i < CountriesLoader.COUNTRY_INIT_DATA.length; i++) {
                String[] countryInitData =
                              CountriesLoader.COUNTRY_INIT_DATA[i];
                Country country = new Country(countryInitData[0],
                        countryInitData[1]);
                expectedCountryList.add(country);
                if (country.getName().startsWith("A")) {
                    expectedCountryListStartsWithA.add(country);
                }
            }
          }
        }
```

12 **13** **14** **10** **16** **15** **17** **18** **19** **20** **21** **22**

In this listing:

- George annotates the test class to be extended with SpringExtension ❶. SpringExtension is used to integrate the Spring TestContext with the JUnit 5 Jupiter test.

- He also annotates the test class to look for the context configuration in the application-context.xml file from the classpath ❷.

- He autowires a CountryDao bean ❸ and a CountriesLoader bean ❹, which are declared in the application-context.xml file.

- He initializes an empty list of expected countries ❺ and an empty list of expected countries that start with *A* ❻.

- He marks the setUp method with the @BeforeEach annotation so it is executed before each test ❼. In it, he initializes the expected list of countries ❽ and loads the countries in the database ❾. The database is initialized by Spring; George has eliminated its manual initialization.

- He annotates the test methods with the @DirtiesContext annotation ❿. This annotation is used when a test has modified the context (in this case, the state of the embedded database). This reduces the database burden; subsequent tests will be supplied with a new, unmodified context.

- In the testCountryList method, George initializes the list of countries from the database by using getCountryList from the CountryDao class ⓫. Then he checks that the list he has obtained is not null ⓬, that it is the expected size ⓭, and that its content is as expected ⓮.

- In the testCountryListStartsWithA method, he initializes the list of countries starting with *A* from the database by using getCountryListStartWith from the CountryDao class ⓯. Then he checks that the list he has obtained is not null ⓰, that it is the expected size ⓱, and that its content is as expected ⓲.

- In the initExpectedCountryLists method, he browses the country initialization data ⓳, creates a Country object at each step ⓴, and adds it to the expected list of countries ㉑. If the name of the country starts with *A*, he also adds it to the expected list of countries whose names start with *A* ㉒.

The tests run successfully, as shown in figure 19.2.

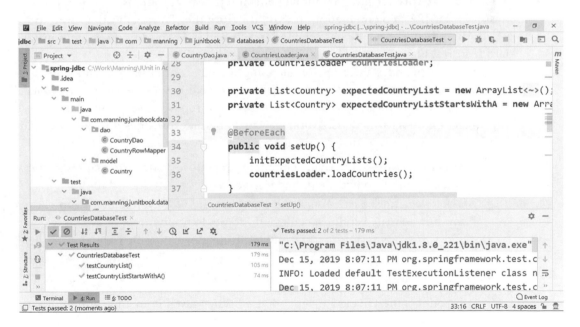

Figure 19.2   Successfully running the tests from the Spring JDBC application that check the interaction with the COUNTRY **table**

The application now accesses and tests the database through Spring JDBC. This approach has several advantages:

- It no longer requires the large amount of tedious code.

- We no longer create and open connections ourselves.
- We no longer prepare and execute statements, process exceptions, or close connections.
- Mainly, we must take care of the application context configuration to be handled by Spring, as well as the row mapper. Other than that, we only have to specify statements and iterate through the results.

Spring allows configuration alternatives, as we have demonstrated in earlier chapters. We use the XML-based configuration for tests here because it is easier to modify. As mentioned previously, for a comprehensive look at the Spring Framework and the configuration possibilities, we recommend *Spring in Action* by Craig Walls (Manning, www.manning.com/books/spring-in-action-sixth-edition).

Next, George will consider further alternatives to test the interaction with the database and to maintain the reduced database burden for the developers.

19.4 *Testing a Hibernate application*

The Java Persistence API (JPA) is a specification describing the management of relational data, the API the client will operate with, and metadata for ORM. Hibernate is an ORM framework for Java that implements the JPA specifications; it is currently the most popular JPA implementation. It existed before the JPA specifications were published; therefore, Hibernate has retained its old native API and offers some nonstandard features. For our example, we'll use the standard JPA.

Hibernate provides facilities for mapping an object-oriented domain model to relational database tables. It manages the incompatibilities between the object-oriented model and the relational database model by replacing direct database access with object-handling functions. Working with Hibernate provides a series of advantages for accessing and testing the database:

- *Faster development*—Hibernate eliminates repetitive code like mapping query result columns to object fields and vice versa.
- *Making data access more abstract and portable*—The ORM implementation classes know how to write vendor-specific SQL, so we do not have to.
- *Cache management*—Entities are cached in memory, thereby reducing the load on the database.
- *Generating boilerplate*—Hibernate generates code for basic CRUD operations.

George introduces the Hibernate dependency in the Maven pom.xml configuration.

> **Listing 19.15   Hibernate dependency introduced in the Maven pom.xml file**

```
<dependency>
    <groupId>org.hibernate</groupId>
    <artifactId>hibernate-core</artifactId>
    <version>5.4.9.Final</version>
</dependency>
```

Then, George changes the `Country` class by annotating it as an entity and annotating its fields as columns in a table.

Listing 19.16   Annotated `Country` class

```
@Entity                                              ◁─────        ❶
@Table(name = "COUNTRY")      ◁───
public class Country {                          ❷
     @Id
     @GeneratedValue(strategy = GenerationType.IDENTITY)        ◁──
❸    @Column(name = "ID")                         ◁──
     private int id;                                          ❹
                                                    ❺

     @Column(name = "NAME")      ◁──
     private String name;                      ❻

     @Column(name = "CODE_NAME")  ◁──
     private String codeName;

     [...]
}
```

In this listing:

- George annotates the `Country` class with `@Entity` so it can represent objects in a database ❶. The corresponding table in the database is provided by the `@Table` annotation and is named COUNTRY ❷.
- The `id` field is marked as the primary key ❸; its value is automatically generated using a database identity column ❹. The corresponding table column is ID ❺.
- He also marks the corresponding columns of the `name` and `codeName` fields in the class by annotating them with `@Column` ❻.

The persistence.xml file is the standard configuration for Hibernate. It is located in the test/resources/META-INF folder.

Listing 19.17   persistence.xml file

```
<persistence-unit name="manning.hibernate">                              ◁──
      <provider>org.hibernate.jpa.HibernatePersistenceProvider</provider>        ❶
      <class>com.manning.junitbook.databases.model.Country</class>    ◁──
❷     <properties>                                                          ❸
            <property name="javax.persistence.jdbc.driver"
                         value="org.h2.Driver"/>                   ❹
            <property name="javax.persistence.jdbc.url"
                         value="jdbc:h2:mem:test;DB_CLOSE_DELAY=-1"/>       ❺
          <property name="javax.persistence.jdbc.user" value="sa"/>
          <property name="javax.persistence.jdbc.password" value=""/>        ❻
          <property name="hibernate.dialect"
                         value="org.hibernate.dialect.H2Dialect"/>   ❼
❽         <property name="hibernate.show_sql" value="true"/>
```

```
                <property name="hibernate.hbm2ddl.auto" value="create"/>
        </properties>
</persistence-unit>
```

In this listing:

- George specifies the persistence unit as `manning.hibernate` ❶. The persistence.xml file must define a persistence unit with a unique name in the currently scoped class loader.

- He specifies the provider, meaning the underlying implementation of the JPA `EntityManager` ❷. An `EntityManager` manages a set of persistent objects and has an API to insert new objects and read/update/delete the existing ones. In this case, the `EntityManager` is Hibernate.

- He defines the entity class that is managed by Hibernate as the `Country` class from our application ❸.

- George specifies the JDBC driver as H2 because this is the database type in use ❹.

- He specifies the URL of the H2 database. In addition, `DB_CLOSE_DELAY=-1` keeps the database open and its content in-memory as long as the virtual machine is alive ❺.

- He specifies the credentials to access the database: a user and password ❻.

- He sets the SQL dialect for the generated query to `H2Dialect` ❼ and shows the generated SQL query on the console ❽.

- He creates the database schema from scratch every time he executes the tests ❾.

Finally, George rewrites the test that verifies the functionality of the database application, this time using Hibernate.

Listing 19.18   `CountriesHibernateTest` file

```
[...]
public class CountriesHibernateTest {

    private EntityManagerFactory emf;          ❶
                                               ❷
    private EntityManager em;

    private List<Country> expectedCountryList =
                        new ArrayList<>();
                                                        ❸
    private List<Country> expectedCountryListStartsWithA =
                        new ArrayList<>();

    public static final String[][] COUNTRY_INIT_DATA = {
        { "Australia", "AU" }, { "Canada", "CA" }, { "France", "FR" },
        { "Germany", "DE" }, { "Italy", "IT" }, { "Japan", "JP" },
        { "Romania", "RO" }, { "Russian Federation", "RU" },     ❹
        { "Spain", "ES" }, { "Switzerland", "CH" },
        { "United Kingdom", "UK" }, { "United States", "US" } };
```

```java
@BeforeEach
public void setUp() {
    initExpectedCountryLists();

    emf = Persistence.
                createEntityManagerFactory("manning.hibernate");
    em = emf.createEntityManager();

    em.getTransaction().begin();

    for (int i = 0; i < COUNTRY_INIT_DATA.length; i++) {
        String[] countryInitData = COUNTRY_INIT_DATA[i];
        Country country = new Country(countryInitData[0],
                            countryInitData[1]);
        em.persist(country);
    }

    em.getTransaction().commit();
}

@Test
public void testCountryList() {
    List<Country> countryList = em.createQuery(
            "select c from Country c").getResultList();
    assertNotNull(countryList);
    assertEquals(COUNTRY_INIT_DATA.length, countryList.size());
    for (int i = 0; i < expectedCountryList.size(); i++) {
        assertEquals(expectedCountryList.get(i), countryList.get(i));
    }

}

@Test
public void testCountryListStartsWithA() {
    List<Country> countryList = em.createQuery(
        "select c from Country c where c.name like 'A%'").
                                        getResultList();
    assertNotNull(countryList);
    assertEquals(expectedCountryListStartsWithA.size(),
                countryList.size());
    for (int i = 0; i < expectedCountryListStartsWithA.size();
                i++) {
        assertEquals(expectedCountryListStartsWithA.get(i),
                    countryList.get(i));
    }
}

@AfterEach
public void dropDown() {
    em.close();
    emf.close();
}

private void initExpectedCountryLists() {
    for (int i = 0; i < COUNTRY_INIT_DATA.length; i++) {
```

```
        String[] countryInitData = COUNTRY_INIT_DATA[i];
        Country country = new Country(countryInitData[0],
                                      countryInitData[1]);
        expectedCountryList.add(country);
        if (country.getName().startsWith("A")) {
            expectedCountryListStartsWithA.add(country);
        }
    }
  }
}
```

㉒

㉓

㉔

In this listing:

- George initializes `EntityManagerFactory` ❶ and `EntityManager` objects ❷. `EntityManagerFactory` provides instances of `EntityManager` for connecting to the same database, while `EntityManager` accesses a database in a particular application.

- He initializes an empty list of expected countries and an empty list of expected countries that start with *A* ❸. He then declares the initialization data for the countries to be inserted ❹.

- He marks the `setUp` method with the `@BeforeEach` annotation so it is executed before each test ❺. In it, he initializes the expected list of countries ❻, `EntityManagerFactory`, and `EntityManager` ❼.

- Within a transaction ❽, George initializes each country, one after the other ❾, and persists the newly created country to the database ❿.

- In the `testCountryList` method, he initializes the list of countries from the database by using the `EntityManager` and querying the `Country` entity using a JPQL `SELECT` ⓫. (Java Persistence Query Language [JPQL] is a platform-independent, object-oriented query language that is a part of the JPA specification.) Note that `Country` must be written exactly like the name of the class: an uppercase first letter followed by lowercase letters. Then George checks that the list he has obtained is not null ⓬, that it is the expected size ⓭, and that its content is as expected ⓮.

- In the `testCountryListStartsWithA` method, he initializes the list of countries starting with *A* from the database by using the `EntityManager` and querying the `Country` entity using a JPQL `SELECT` ⓯. Then he checks that the list he has obtained is not null ⓰, that it is the expected size ⓱, and that its content is as expected ⓲.

- George marks the `dropDown` method with the `@AfterEach` annotation so it is executed after each test ⓳. In it, he closes `EntityManagerFactory` and `EntityManager` ⓴.

- In the `initExpectedCountryLists` method, he browses the country initialization data ㉑, creates a `Country` object at each step ㉒, and adds it to the expected list of countries ㉓. If the name of the country starts with *A*, he also adds it to the expected list of countries whose names start with *A* ㉔.

The tests run successfully, as shown in figure 19.3.

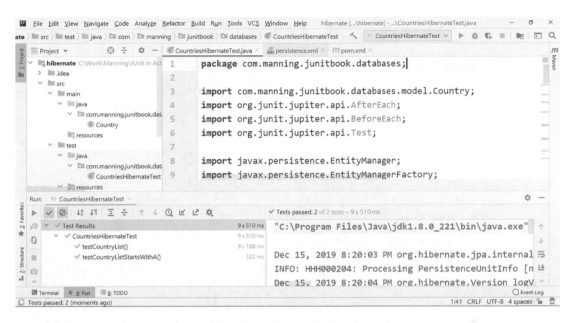

Figure 19.3 Successfully running the tests from the Hibernate application that check the interaction with the COUNTRY **table**

The application now accesses and tests the database through Hibernate. This approach comes with a few advantages:

- We no longer have to write SQL code in the application. We work only with Java code and JPQL, which are portable.
- We no longer need to map the query result columns to object fields and vice versa.
- Hibernate knows how to transform operations with implemented classes into vendor-specific SQL. So, if we change the underlying database, we will not have to touch the existing code; we'll only change the Hibernate configuration and the database dialect.

George will take one more step in considering alternatives to test interactions with the database: combining Spring and Hibernate. We'll see this approach in the next section.

19.5 *Testing a Spring Hibernate application*

Hibernate provides facilities for mapping an object-oriented domain model to relational database tables. Spring can take advantage of the IoC pattern to simplify database interaction tasks. To integrate Hibernate and Spring, George first adds the needed dependencies in the Maven pom.xml configuration file.

Listing 19.19   Spring and Hibernate dependencies in the Maven pom.xml file

```
<dependency>
    <groupId>org.springframework</groupId>
    <artifactId>spring-context</artifactId>
    <version>5.2.1.RELEASE</version>
</dependency>
<dependency>
    <groupId>org.springframework</groupId>
    <artifactId>spring-orm</artifactId>
    <version>5.2.1.RELEASE</version>
</dependency>
<dependency>
    <groupId>org.springframework</groupId>
    <artifactId>spring-test</artifactId>
    <version>5.2.1.RELEASE</version>
</dependency>
<dependency>
    <groupId>org.hibernate</groupId>
    <artifactId>hibernate-core</artifactId>
     <version>5.4.9.Final</version>
</dependency>
```
❶ ❷ ❸ ❹

In this listing, George adds the following dependencies:

- `spring-context`, the dependency for the Spring IoC container ❶.
- `spring-orm`, because the application is still using Hibernate as an ORM framework to access the database. Spring handles working with connections, preparing and executing statements, and processing exceptions ❷.
- `spring-test`, which provides support for writing tests with the help of Spring and which is necessary to use `SpringExtension` and the `@ContextConfiguration` annotation ❸.
- `hibernate-code`, for interacting with the database through Hibernate ❹.

George makes some changes to the persistence.xml file, the standard configuration for Hibernate. Only some minimal information will remain here, as database access control will be handled by Spring, and a good part of the information was moved to application-context.xml.

Listing 19.20   persistence.xml file

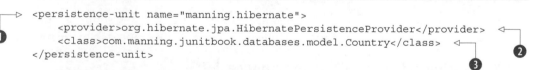

```
<persistence-unit name="manning.hibernate">
    <provider>org.hibernate.jpa.HibernatePersistenceProvider</provider>
    <class>com.manning.junitbook.databases.model.Country</class>
</persistence-unit>
```
❶ ❷ ❸

In this listing:

- George specifies the persistence unit as `manning.hibernate` ❶. The persistence.xml file must define a persistence unit with a unique name in the currently scoped class loader.

- He specifies the provider, meaning the underlying implementation of the JPA EntityManager ❷. In this case, the EntityManager is Hibernate.
- He defines the entity class that is managed by Hibernate as the Country class from the application ❸.

Next, George moves the database access configuration to the application-context.xml file that configures the Spring container.

Listing 19.21 application-context.xml file

```
                                                                        ❶
<tx:annotation-driven transaction-manager="txManager"/>    ⟵
<bean id="dataSource" class=                                            ❷
      "org.springframework.jdbc.datasource.DriverManagerDataSource">
❹     <property name="driverClassName" value="org.h2.Driver"/>    ⟵
  ⟶   <property name="url" value="jdbc:h2:mem:test;DB_CLOSE_DELAY=-1"/>   ❸
      <property name="username" value="sa"/>              ❺
      <property name="password" value=""/>
</bean>

<bean id="entityManagerFactory" class=                                 ❻
  "org.springframework.orm.jpa.LocalContainerEntityManagerFactoryBean">
      <property name="persistenceUnitName" value="manning.hibernate" />  ⟵
      <property name="dataSource" ref="dataSource"/>   ⟵              ❼
      <property name="jpaProperties">                   ❽
         <props>
           <prop key=                                                   ❾
           "hibernate.dialect">org.hibernate.dialect.H2Dialect</prop>
  ⟶        <prop key="hibernate.show_sql">true</prop>
❿          <prop key="hibernate.hbm2ddl.auto">create</prop>     ⟵
         </props>                                              ⓫
      </property>
</bean>

<bean id="txManager" class=                                 ⓬
      "org.springframework.orm.jpa.JpaTransactionManager">
      <property name="entityManagerFactory" ref="entityManagerFactory" />  ⟵
      <property name="dataSource" ref="dataSource" />    ⟵            ⓭
⓯                                                          ⓮
</bean>

<bean class="com.manning.junitbook.databases.CountryService"/>
```

In this listing:

- <tx:annotation-driven> tells the Spring context to use an annotation-based transaction management configuration ❶.
- George configures access to the data source ❷ by specifying the driver as H2, because this is the database type in use ❸. He specifies the URL of the H2 database. In addition, DB_CLOSE_DELAY=-1 keeps the database open and its content in memory as long as the virtual machine is alive ❹.

- He specifies the credentials to access the database: a user and password ❺.
- He creates an `EntityManagerFactory` bean ❻ and sets its properties: the persistence unit name (as defined in the persistence.xml file) ❼, the data source (defined previously) ❽, and the SQL dialect for the generated query (`H2Dialect`) ❾. He shows the generated SQL query on the console ❿ and creates the database schema from scratch every time he executes the tests ⓫.
- To process the annotation-based transaction configuration, a transaction manager bean needs to be created. George declares it ⓬ and sets its entity manager factory ⓭ and data source ⓮ properties.
- He declares a `CountryService` bean ⓯ because he'll create this class in the code and group the logic of the interaction with the database.

George next creates the `CountryService` class that contains the logic of the interaction with the database.

Listing 19.22   `CountryService` class

```
[...]
public class CountryService {

    @PersistenceContext
    private EntityManager em;                              ❶

    public static final String[][] COUNTRY_INIT_DATA =
        { { "Australia", "AU" }, { "Canada", "CA" }, { "France", "FR" },
          { "Germany", "DE" }, { "Italy", "IT" }, { "Japan", "JP" },
          { "Romania", "RO" }, { "Russian Federation", "RU" },        ❷
          { "Spain", "ES" }, { "Switzerland", "CH" },
          { "United Kingdom", "UK" }, { "United States", "US" } };

    @Transactional
    public void init() {
        for (int i = 0; i < COUNTRY_INIT_DATA.length; i++) {
            String[] countryInitData = COUNTRY_INIT_DATA[i];
            Country country = new Country(countryInitData[0],     ❹
                                          countryInitData[1]);
            em.persist(country);
        }                                                   ❸
    }

    @Transactional
    public void clear() {
        em.createQuery("delete from Country c").executeUpdate();   ←┐
    }                                                              ❺

    public List<Country> getAllCountries() {
        return em.createQuery("select c from Country c")      ❻
                 .getResultList();
    }
}
```

```
public List<Country> getCountriesStartingWithA() {
    return em.createQuery(
        "select c from Country c where c.name like 'A%'")
        .getResultList();
}
}
```
⑦

In this listing:

- George declares an `EntityManager` bean and annotates it with `@Persis-tenceContext` ❶. `EntityManager` is used to access a database and is created by the container using the information in the persistence.xml. To use it at runtime, George simply needs to request that it be injected into one of the components via `@PersistenceContext`.
- He declares the initialization data for the countries to be inserted ❷.
- He annotates the `init` and `clear` methods as `@Transactional` ❸. He does so because these methods modify the content of the database, and all such methods must be executed within a transaction.
- He browses the initialization data for the countries, creates each `Country` object, and persists it within the database ❹.
- The `clear` method deletes all countries from the `Country` entity using a JPQL `DELETE` ❺. As in listing 19.18, `Country` must be written exactly this way to match the class name.
- The `getAllCountries` method selects all the countries from the `Country` entity using a JPQL `SELECT` ❻.
- The `getCountriesStartingWithA` method selects all countries from the `Country` entity having names starting with *A* using a JPQL `SELECT` ❼.

Finally, George modifies the `CountriesHibernateTest` class that tests the logic of the interaction with the database.

Listing 19.23 `CountriesHibernateTest` class

```
[...]
@ExtendWith(SpringExtension.class)
@ContextConfiguration("classpath:application-context.xml")
public class CountriesHibernateTest {

    @Autowired
    private CountryService countryService;

    private List<Country> expectedCountryList = new ArrayList<>();
    private List<Country> expectedCountryListStartsWithA =
                            new ArrayList<>();

    @BeforeEach
    public void setUp() {
        countryService.init();
        initExpectedCountryLists();
    }
```
❶ ❷ ❸ ❹ ❺ ❻ ❼

```
    @Test
⑨  public void testCountryList() {                                              ⑧
        List<Country> countryList = countryService.getAllCountries();    ◄────┘
        assertNotNull(countryList);
   ▷  assertEquals(COUNTRY_INIT_DATA.length, countryList.size());
⑩      for (int i = 0; i < expectedCountryList.size(); i++) {              ⑪
            assertEquals(expectedCountryList.get(i), countryList.get(i));
        }
    }

    @Test
    public void testCountryListStartsWithA() {
        List<Country> countryList =                                      ⑫
                countryService.getCountriesStartingWithA();
   ▷  assertNotNull(countryList);
⑬      assertEquals(expectedCountryListStartsWithA.size(),              ⑭
                    countryList.size());
        for (int i = 0; i < expectedCountryListStartsWithA.size(); i++) { ⑮
            assertEquals(expectedCountryListStartsWithA.get(i),
                        countryList.get(i));
        }
    }
                              ⑯
    @AfterEach            ◄───┘
    public void dropDown() {                  ⑰
        countryService.clear();            ◄──┘
    }

    private void initExpectedCountryLists() {                            ⑱
        for (int i = 0; i < COUNTRY_INIT_DATA.length; i++) {         ◄──┘
            String[] countryInitData = COUNTRY_INIT_DATA[i];
            Country country = new Country(countryInitData[0],       ⑲
                                countryInitData[1]);
   ▷      expectedCountryList.add(country);
⑳          if (country.getName().startsWith("A")) {                 ㉑
                expectedCountryListStartsWithA.add(country);
            }
        }
    }
}
```

In this listing:

- George annotates the test class to be extended with SpringExtension ❶. SpringExtension is used to integrate the Spring TestContext with the JUnit 5 Jupiter test. This allows us to use other Spring annotations as well (such as @ContextConfiguration and @Transactional), but it also requires us to use JUnit 5 and its annotations.
- He annotates the test class to look for the context configuration in the application-context.xml file from the classpath ❷.
- He declares and autowires a CountryService bean. This bean is created and injected by the Spring container ❸.
- George initializes an empty list of expected countries and an empty list of expected countries that start with *A* ❹.

- He marks the `setUp` method with the `@BeforeEach` annotation so it is executed before each test ❺. In it, he initializes the database content through the `init` method from the `CountryService` class ❻ and initializes the expected list of countries ❼.

- In the `testCountryList` method, he initializes the list of countries from the database by using the `getAllCountries` method from the `CountryService` class ❽. Then he checks that the list he has obtained is not null ❾, that it is the expected size ❿, and that its content is as expected ⓫.

- In the `testCountryListStartsWithA` method, George initializes the list of countries starting with *A* from the database by using the `getCountriesStartingWithA` method from the `CountryService` class ⓬. Then he checks that the list he has obtained is not null ⓭, that it is the expected size ⓮, and that its content is as expected ⓯.

- He marks the `dropDown` method with the `@AfterEach` annotation so it is executed after each test ⓰. In it, he clears the `COUNTRY` table's contents using the `clear` method from the `CountryService` class ⓱.

- In the `initExpectedCountryLists` method, George browses the country initialization data ⓲, creates a `Country` object at each step ⓳, and adds it to the expected list of countries ⓴. If the name of the country starts with *A*, he also adds it to the expected list of countries whose names start with *A* ㉑.

The tests run successfully, as shown in figure 19.4.

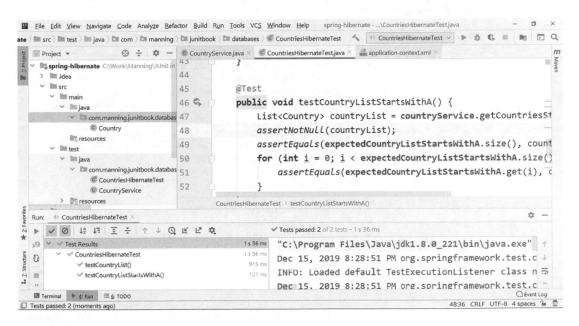

Figure 19.4 Successfully running the tests from the Spring Hibernate application that check the interaction with the `COUNTRY` table

The application now accesses and tests the database through Spring Hibernate. This approach offers several advantages:

- We no longer need to write SQL code in the application. We work only with Java code and JPQL, which are portable.
- We no longer have to create, open, or close connections ourselves.
- We do not have to process exceptions.
- We primarily take care of the application context to be handled by Spring, which includes the data source, transaction manager, and entity manager factory configuration.
- Hibernate knows how to transform operations with the implemented classes into vendor-specific SQL. So, if we change the underlying database, we will not have to touch the existing code; we'll only change the Hibernate configuration and the database dialect.

19.6   *Comparing the approaches for testing database applications*

We have followed George as he revised a simple JDBC application for use with Spring and Hibernate. We demonstrated how parts of the application were revised and how each approach simplified testing and interacting with the database. Our purpose was to analyze each approach and how the database burden can be reduced for developers. Table 19.1 summarizes the characteristics of these approaches.

Table 19.1   Comparison of working with a database application and testing it with JDBC, Spring JDBC, Hibernate, and Spring Hibernate

Application type	Characteristics

JDBC	<ul><li>SQL code needs to be written in the tests.</li><li>No portability between databases.</li><li>Full control over what the application is doing.</li><li>Manual work for the developer to interact with the database; for example:
	  – Creating and opening connections
	  – Specifying, preparing, and executing statements
	  – Iterating through the results
	  – Doing the work for each iteration
	  – Processing exceptions
	  – Closing the connection</li></ul>

Spring JDBC	<ul><li>SQL code needs to be written in the tests.</li><li>No portability between databases.</li><li>Need to take care of the row mapper and the application context configuration that is handled by Spring.</li><li>Control on the queries that the application is executing against the database.</li><li>Reduces the manual work to interact with the database:
	  – No creating/opening/closing connections ourselves
	  – No preparing and executing statements
	  – No processing exceptions</li></ul>

Table 19.1 Comparison of working with a database application and testing it with JDBC, Spring JDBC, Hibernate, and Spring Hibernate *(continued)*

Application type	Characteristics
Hibernate	■ No SQL code in the application; only JPQL, which is portable. ■ Developers work only with Java code. ■ No mapping query result columns to object fields and vice versa. ■ Portability between databases by changing the Hibernate configuration and the database dialect. ■ Database configuration is handled through Java code.
Spring Hibernate	■ No SQL code in the application; only JPQL, which is portable. ■ Developers work only with Java code. ■ No mapping query result columns to object fields and vice versa. ■ Portability between databases by changing the Hibernate configuration and the database dialect. ■ Database configuration is handled by Spring, based on information from the application context.

Notice that introducing at least one framework like Spring or Hibernate into the application greatly simplifies testing the database and developing the application itself. These are the most popular Java frameworks, and they provide many benefits (including testing interaction with a database, as we have demonstrated); we recommend that you consider adopting them into your project (if you haven't already).

This chapter has focused on alternatives for testing a database application with JUnit 5. The example tests covered only insertion and selection operations, but you can easily extend the tests offered here to include update and delete operations.

Chapter 20 will start the last part of the book, dedicated to the systematic development of applications with the help of JUnit 5. It will discuss one of the most widely used development techniques today: test-driven development (TDD).

Summary

This chapter has covered the following:

- Examining the database unit testing impedance mismatch, including these challenges: unit tests must exercise code in isolation; unit tests must be easy to write and run; and unit tests must be fast to run.
- Implementing tests for a JDBC application, which requires us to write SQL code in the tests and do a lot of tedious work: creating/opening/closing connections to the database; specifying, preparing, and executing statements; and handling exceptions.
- Implementing tests for a Spring JDBC application. This still requires us to write SQL code in the tests, but the Spring container handles creating/opening/closing connections; specifying, preparing, and executing statements; and handling exceptions.

- Implementing tests for a Hibernate application. No SQL code is required; we work only with Java code. The application is portable to another database with minimum configuration changes. The database configuration is handled through the Java code.

- Implementing tests for a Spring Hibernate application. No SQL code is required; we work only with Java code. The application is portable to another database with minimum configuration changes. Additionally, the database configuration is handled by Spring, based on information from the application context.

Part 5

Developing applications with JUnit 5

This part of the book examines working with JUnit 5 as part of the everyday activity of contemporary projects. Chapter 20 discusses project development using one of today's popular development techniques: test-driven development. We will demonstrate how to create safe applications whose functionality is driven by the tests.

Chapter 21 discusses developing projects using behavior-driven development. We will show how to create applications that address business needs: applications that not only do things right but also do the right thing.

In chapter 22, we build a test pyramid strategy with the help of JUnit 5. We will demonstrate testing from the ground level (unit testing) to the upper levels (integration testing, system testing, and acceptance testing).

20

Test-driven development with JUnit 5

This chapter covers

- Moving a non-TDD application to TDD
- Refactoring a TDD application
- Using TDD to implement new functionality

> *TDD helps you to pay attention to the right issues at the right time so you can make your designs cleaner, you can refine your designs as you learn. TDD enables you to gain confidence in the code over time.*
>
> —Kent Beck

In this chapter, we will show how to develop safe, flexible applications using test-driven development (TDD): a technique that can greatly increase development speed and eliminate much of the debugging nightmare—all with the help of JUnit 5 and its features. We will point out the main concepts involved in TDD and apply them in developing a Java application that Tested Data Systems (our example company) will use to implement the business logic for managing flights and passengers and following a set of policies. Our focus will be on clearly explaining TDD and proving its benefits by demonstrating how to put it in practice, step by step.

20.1 *TDD main concepts*

Test-driven development is a programming practice that uses a short, repeating development cycle in which requirements are converted into test cases, and then the program is modified to make the tests pass:

1 Write a failing test before writing new code.
2 Write the smallest piece of code that will make the new test pass.

The development of this technique is attributed to the American software engineer Kent Beck. TDD supports simple designs and inspires safety: it looks for "clean code that works."

This is different from traditional software development, where code may be added without having to verify that it meets requirements. In a classical approach, developing a program means we write code and then do some testing by observing its behavior. So, the conventional development cycle goes something like this:

```
[code, test, (repeat)]
```

TDD uses a surprising variation:

```
[test, code, (repeat)]
```

The test drives the design and becomes the first client of the method.

TDD's benefits include the following:

- We write code that is driven by clear goals, and we make sure we address exactly what our application needs to do.
- Introducing new functionality is much faster. On the one hand, tests drive us to implement code that does what it is supposed to do. On the other hand, tests will prevent us from introducing bugs into the existing working code.
- Tests act as documentation for the application. We can follow them and understand what problems our code is supposed to solve.

We said that TDD uses this development cycle:

```
[test, code, (repeat)]
```

In fact, it looks like this:

```
[test, code, refactor, (repeat)]
```

Refactoring is the process of modifying a software system in a way that does not impact its external behavior but does improve its internal structure. To make sure external behavior is not affected, we need to rely on the tests.

When we receive specifications to add new functionality to an application, we have to first understand them before we can add them to the code. What if we first implement a test that will show us *what* we have to do, and then think about *how* to do it? This is one of the fundamental principles of TDD.

When we begin working on an application, at the very least, we need to understand the fundamental idea of what the software is supposed to do. But if we want to check what classes or methods do, our choices are limited: read the documentation or look for sample code that invokes the functionality. Most programmers prefer to work with the code. And well-written unit tests do exactly this: they invoke our code and, consequently, provide a working specification for the code's functionality. As a result, TDD effectively helps to build a significant part of the application's technical documentation.

20.2 *The flight-management application*

As we have discussed throughout this book, Tested Data Systems (our example company) is developing a flight-management application for one of its customers. Currently, the application is able to create and set up flights, and add passengers to and remove them from flights.

In this chapter, we'll walk through scenarios that follow the developers' everyday work. We'll start with the non-TDD application, which is supposed to do several things such as follow company policies for regular and VIP passengers. We need to understand the application and make sure it is really implementing the expected operations. So, we have to cover the existing code with unit tests. Once we've done that, we'll address another challenge: adding new functionality by first understanding what needs to be done; next, writing tests that fail; and then, writing the code that fixes the tests. This work cycle is one of the foundations of TDD.

John is joining the development of the flight-management application, which is a Java application built with the help of Maven. The software must maintain a policy regarding adding passengers to and removing them from flights. Flights may be different types: currently, there are economy and business flights, but other types may be added later, depending on customer requirements. Both VIP passengers and regular customers may be added to economy flights, but only VIP passengers may be added to business flights (figure 20.1).

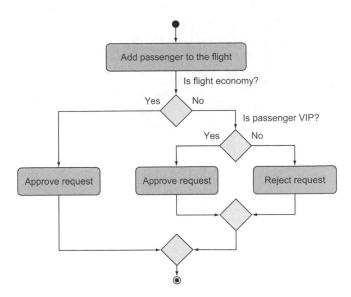

Figure 20.1 The business logic of adding passengers to a flight: if it is a business flight, only VIP passengers may be added to it. Any passenger can be added to an economy flight.

There is also a policy for removing passengers from flights: a regular passenger may be removed from a flight, but a VIP passenger cannot be removed (figure 20.2). As we can see from these two activity diagrams, the initial business logic focuses on decision making.

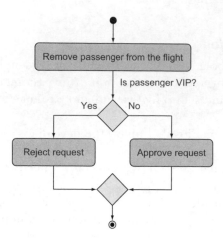

Figure 20.2   The business logic of removing passengers from a flight: only regular passengers may be removed.

Let's look at the initial design for this application (figure 20.3). It has a field called `flightType` in the `Flight` class. Its value determines the behavior of the `add-Passenger` and `removePassenger` methods. The developers need to focus on decision making at the level of the code for these two methods.

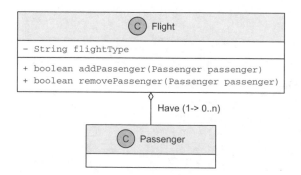

Figure 20.3   The class diagram for the flight-management application: the flight type is kept as a field in the `Flight` class.

The following listing shows the `Passenger` class.

Listing 20.1   `Passenger` class

```
public class Passenger {            ❶

    private String name;            ❷
    private boolean vip;
```

```java
    public Passenger(String name, boolean vip) {
        this.name = name;
        this.vip = vip;
    }

    public String getName() {
        return name;
    }

    public boolean isVip() {
        return vip;
    }

}
```

In this listing:

- The `Passenger` class contains a name field **1** together with a getter for it **4**.
- It also contains a `vip` field **2** together with a getter for it **5**.
- The constructor of the `Passenger` class initializes the `name` and `vip` fields **3**.

The next listing shows the `Flight` class.

Listing 20.2   `Flight` class

```java
public class Flight {                                        ❶
                                                             ❷
    private String id;              ←
    private List<Passenger> passengers = new ArrayList<Passenger>();   ←
    private String flightType;
❸
    public Flight(String id, String flightType) {
        this.id = id;                                        ❹
        this.flightType = flightType;
    }

    public String getId() {
        return id;                                           ❺
    }

    public List<Passenger> getPassengersList() {
        return Collections.unmodifiableList(passengers);     ❻
    }

    public String getFlightType() {
        return flightType;                                   ❼
    }


    public boolean addPassenger(Passenger passenger) {       ❽
        switch (flightType) {                       ←
            case "Economy":
                return passengers.add(passenger);            ❾
```

```
    case "Business":
       if (passenger.isVip()) {
          return passengers.add(passenger);                    ⑩
       }
       return false;
    default:
       throw new RuntimeException("Unknown type: " + flightType);   ⑪
    }

}

public boolean removePassenger(Passenger passenger) {            ⑫
   switch (flightType) {
      case "Economy":
         if (!passenger.isVip()) {
            return passengers.remove(passenger);               ⑬
         }
         return false;
      case "Business":
         return false;                  ⑭
      default:
         throw new RuntimeException("Unknown type: " + flightType);   ⑮
      }
   }

}
```

In this listing:

- The `Flight` class contains an identifier ❶ together with a getter for it ❺, a list of passengers initialized as an empty list ❷ together with a getter for it ❻, and a flight type ❸ together with a getter for it ❼.
- The constructor of the `Flight` class initializes the `id` and the `flightType` fields ❹.
- The `addPassenger` method checks the flight type ❽. If it is an economy flight, any passengers can be added ❾. If it is a business flight, only VIP passengers can be added ❿. Otherwise (if the flight is neither an economy nor a business flight), the method will throw an exception, as it cannot handle an unknown flight type ⑪.
- The `removePassenger` method checks the flight type ⑫. If it is an economy flight, only regular passengers can be removed ⑬. If it is a business flight, passengers cannot be removed ⑭. Otherwise (if the flight is neither an economy nor a business flight), the method will throw an exception, as it cannot handle an unknown flight type ⑮.

The application has no tests yet. Instead, the initial developers wrote some code in which they simply followed the execution and compared it with their expectations. For example, there is an `Airport` class, including a `main` method that acts as a client of the `Flight` and `Passenger` classes and works with the different types of flights and passengers.

Listing 20.3 `Airport` class, including the `main` method

```java
public class Airport {

    public static void main(String[] args) {
        Flight economyFlight = new Flight("1", "Economy");
        Flight businessFlight = new Flight("2", "Business");

        Passenger james = new Passenger("James", true);
        Passenger mike = new Passenger("Mike", false);

        businessFlight.addPassenger(james);
        businessFlight.removePassenger(james);
        businessFlight.addPassenger(mike);
        economyFlight.addPassenger(mike);

        System.out.println("Business flight passengers list:");
        for (Passenger passenger: businessFlight.getPassengersList()) {
            System.out.println(passenger.getName());
        }

        System.out.println("Economy flight passengers list:");
        for (Passenger passenger: economyFlight.getPassengersList()) {
            System.out.println(passenger.getName());
        }
    }
}
```

① ② ③ ④ ⑤ ⑥ ⑦

In this listing:

- We initialize an economy flight and a business flight ①. We also initialize James as a VIP passenger and Mike as a regular passenger ②.
- We try to add James to and remove him from the business flight ③, and then we try to add Mike to and remove him from the business flight ④ and the economy flight ⑤.
- We print the list of passengers on the business flight ⑥ and the economy flight ⑦.

The result of running this program is shown in figure 20.4. James, a VIP passenger, has been added to the business flight, and we could not remove him. Mike, a regular passenger, could not be added to the business flight, but we were able to add him to the economy flight.

```
Run:    Airport
    "C:\Program Files\Java\jdk1.8.0_221\bin\java.exe" ...
    Business flight passengers list:
    James
    Economy flight passengers list:
    Mike
```

Figure 20.4 The result of running the non-TDD flight-management application: the VIP passenger has been added to the business flight, and the regular passenger has been added to the economy flight.

So far, things are working as expected, following the policies that we previously defined. John is satisfied with the way the application works, but he needs to develop it further. To build a reliable application and to be able to easily and safely understand and implement the business logic, John considers moving the application to the TDD approach.

20.3   *Preparing the flight-management application for TDD*

To move the flight-management application to TDD, John first needs to cover the existing business logic with JUnit 5 tests. He adds the JUnit 5 dependencies we are already familiar with (junit-jupiter-api and junit-jupiter-engine) to the Maven pom.xml file.

Listing 20.4   JUnit 5 dependencies added to the pom.xml file

```
<dependencies>
   <dependency>
      <groupId>org.junit.jupiter</groupId>
      <artifactId>junit-jupiter-api</artifactId>
      <version>5.6.0</version>
      <scope>test</scope>
   </dependency>
   <dependency>
      <groupId>org.junit.jupiter</groupId>
      <artifactId>junit-jupiter-engine</artifactId>
      <version>5.6.0</version>
      <scope>test</scope>
   </dependency>
</dependencies>
```

Inspecting the business logic from figures 20.1 and 20.2, John understands that he has to check the add/remove passenger scenarios by providing tests for two flight types and two passenger types. So, multiplying two flight types by two passenger types, this means four tests in total. For each of the tests, he has to verify the possible add and remove operations.

John follows the business logic for an economy flight and uses the JUnit 5 nested test capability, as the tests share similarities between them and can be grouped: tests for economy flights and tests for business flights.

Listing 20.5   Testing the business logic for an economy flight

```
public class AirportTest {

    @DisplayName("Given there is an economy flight")      ❶
    @Nested
    class EconomyFlightTest {

        private Flight economyFlight;                      ❷

        @BeforeEach
```

```
void setUp() {
    economyFlight = new Flight("1", "Economy");       ②
}

@Test
public void testEconomyFlightRegularPassenger() {    ③
    Passenger mike = new Passenger("Mike", false);   ④

    assertEquals("1", economyFlight.getId());
    assertEquals(true, economyFlight.addPassenger(mike));
    assertEquals(1, economyFlight.getPassengersList().size());  ⑤
    assertEquals("Mike",
            economyFlight.getPassengersList().get(0).getName());

    assertEquals(true, economyFlight.removePassenger(mike));     ⑥
    assertEquals(0, economyFlight.getPassengersList().size());
}

@Test
public void testEconomyFlightVipPassenger() {         ⑦
    Passenger james = new Passenger("James", true);   ⑧

    assertEquals("1", economyFlight.getId());
    assertEquals(true, economyFlight.addPassenger(james));
    assertEquals(1, economyFlight.getPassengersList().size());   ⑨
    assertEquals("James",
            economyFlight.getPassengersList().get(0).getName());

    assertEquals(false, economyFlight.removePassenger(james));   ⑩
    assertEquals(1, economyFlight.getPassengersList().size());
}
    }
}
```

In this listing:

- John declares a nested test class EconomyFlightTest and labels it "Given there is an economy flight" with the help of the @DisplayName annotation ①.
- He declares an economy flight and initializes it before the execution of each test ②.
- When testing how the economy flight works with a regular passenger, he creates Mike as a regular passenger ③. Then, he checks the ID of the flight ④, whether he can add Mike on the economy flight and that he can find Mike there ⑤, and whether he can remove Mike from the economy flight and that Mike is no longer there ⑥.
- When testing how the economy flight works with a VIP passenger, he creates James as a VIP passenger ⑦. Then, he checks the ID of the flight ⑧, whether he can add James on the economy flight and that he can find James there ⑨, and whether he cannot remove James from the economy flight and that James is still there ⑩.

John follows the business logic for a business flight and translates it into the following tests.

Listing 20.6   Testing the business logic of the business flight

```java
public class AirportTest {
[...]

@DisplayName("Given there is a business flight")
@Nested                                                          ❶
class BusinessFlightTest {
    private Flight businessFlight;

    @BeforeEach
    void setUp() {                                               ❷
        businessFlight = new Flight("2", "Business");
    }

    @Test
    public void testBusinessFlightRegularPassenger() {          ❸
        Passenger mike = new Passenger("Mike", false);

        assertEquals(false, businessFlight.addPassenger(mike));      ❹
        assertEquals(0, businessFlight.getPassengersList().size());
        assertEquals(false, businessFlight.removePassenger(mike));   ❺
        assertEquals(0, businessFlight.getPassengersList().size());

    }

    @Test
    public void testBusinessFlightVipPassenger() {              ❻
        Passenger james = new Passenger("James", true);

        assertEquals(true, businessFlight.addPassenger(james));      ❼
        assertEquals(1, businessFlight.getPassengersList().size());
        assertEquals(false, businessFlight.removePassenger(james));  ❽
        assertEquals(1, businessFlight.getPassengersList().size());

    }
}
}
```

In this listing:

- John declares a nested test class BusinessFlightTest and labels it "Given there is a business flight" with the help of the @DisplayName annotation ❶.
- He declares a business flight and initializes it before the execution of each test ❷.
- When testing how the business flight works with a regular passenger, he creates Mike as a regular passenger ❸. Then, he checks that he cannot add Mike to the business flight ❹ and that trying to remove Mike from the business flight also has no effect ❺.

- When testing how the business flight works with a VIP passenger, he creates James as a VIP passenger ❻. Then, he checks that he can add James to the business flight and that he can find James there ❼ and that he cannot remove James from the business flight and that James is still there ❽.

If we run the tests with coverage from within IntelliJ IDEA, we get the results shown in figure 20.5. For more details about test coverage and how to run tests with coverage from IntelliJ IDEA, you can revisit chapter 6.

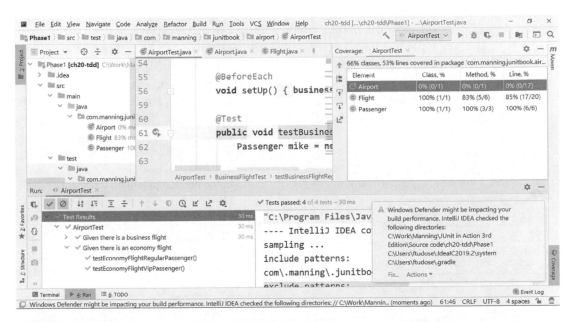

Figure 20.5 The result of running the economy and business flight tests with coverage using IntelliJ IDEA: the `Airport` class is uncovered (it contains the `main` method; we do not test it), and the `Flight` class has coverage of less than 100%.

John has successfully verified the functionality of the application by writing tests for all the scenarios that result from the business logic (figure 20.1 and 20.2). It is possible that in real life you may begin working with an application that has no tests and want to move to TDD. Before you do, you will have to test the application as it is.

John's work also provides additional conclusions. The `Airport` class is not tested—it served as a client for the `Passenger` and `Flight` classes. The tests are now serving as clients, so `Airport` can be removed. In addition, the code coverage is not 100%. The `getFlightType` method is not used, and the default case—when a flight is neither economy nor business type—is not covered. This suggests to John the need to refactor the application, to remove the elements that are not used. He is confident about doing this because the application is now covered with tests and, as we said earlier, TDD enables us to gain confidence in our code over time.

20.4   *Refactoring the flight-management application*

John has noticed that the lines of code that are not being executed are those related to using the `flightType` field. And the default case will never be executed, as the flight type is expected to be either economy or business; these default alternatives are needed because the code will not compile otherwise. Can John get rid of them by doing some refactoring and replacing the conditional statements with polymorphism?

The key to refactoring is to move the design to using polymorphism instead of procedural-style conditional code. With *polymorphism* (the ability of one object to pass more than one IS-A test), the method you are calling is determined not at compile time, but at runtime, depending on the effective object type (see chapter 6).

The principle in action here is called the *open/closed principle* (figure 20.6). Practically, it means the design shown on the left will require changes to the existing class each time we add a new flight type. These changes may reflect in each conditional decision made based on the flight type. In addition, we are forced to rely on the `flightType` field and introduce unexecuted default cases.

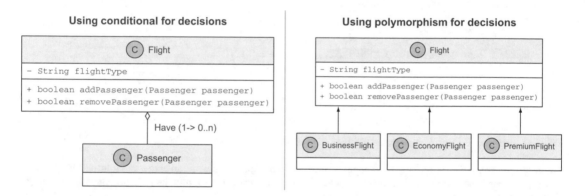

Figure 20.6   Refactoring the flight-management application by replacing the conditional with polymorphism: the `flightType` field is removed, and a hierarchy of classes is introduced.

With the design on the right—which is refactored by replacing conditional with polymorphism—we do not need a `flightType` evaluation or a default value in the `switch` instructions from listing 20.2. We can even add a new type—let's anticipate a little and call it `PremiumFlight`—by simply extending the base class and defining its behavior. According to the open/closed principle, the hierarchy will be open for extensions (we can easily add new classes) but closed for modifications (existing classes, starting with the `Flight` base class, will not be modified).

John will, of course, ask himself, "How can I be sure I am doing the right thing and not affecting already working functionality?" The answer is that passing the tests provides assurance that existing functionality is untouched. The benefits of the TDD approach really show themselves!

The refactoring will be achieved by keeping the base `Flight` class (listing 20.7) and, for each conditional type, adding a separate class to extend `Flight`. John will change `addPassenger` and `removePassenger` to abstract methods and delegate their implementation to subclasses. The `flightType` field is no longer significant and will be removed.

Listing 20.7 Abstract `Flight` class, the basis of the hierarchy

```
public abstract class Flight {                                    ◄──┐ ❶

    private String id;
    List<Passenger> passengers = new ArrayList<Passenger>();      ◄──┐ ❷

    public Flight(String id) {
        this.id = id;
    }

    public String getId() {
        return id;
    }

    public List<Passenger> getPassengersList() {
        return Collections.unmodifiableList(passengers);
    }

    public abstract boolean addPassenger(Passenger passenger);    ❸

    public abstract boolean removePassenger(Passenger passenger);

}
```

In this listing:

- John declares the class as abstract, making it the basis of the flight hierarchy ❶.
- He makes the `passengers` list package-private, allowing it to be directly inherited by the subclasses in the same package ❷.
- John declares `addPassenger` and `removePassenger` as abstract methods, delegating their implementation to the subclasses ❸.

John introduces an `EconomyFlight` class that extends `Flight` and implements the inherited `addPassenger` and `removePassenger` abstract methods.

Listing 20.8 `EconomyFlight` class, extending the abstract `Flight` class

```
public class EconomyFlight extends Flight {                       ◄──┐ ❶
    public EconomyFlight(String id) {
        super(id);                                                ❷
    }
```

```
    @Override
    public boolean addPassenger(Passenger passenger) {
        return passengers.add(passenger);                    ❸
    }

    @Override
    public boolean removePassenger(Passenger passenger) {
        if (!passenger.isVip()) {
            return passengers.remove(passenger);             ❹
        }
        return false;
    }

}
```

In this listing:

- John declares the EconomyFlight class extending the Flight abstract class ❶ and creates a constructor calling the constructor of the superclass ❷.
- He implements the addPassenger method according to the business logic: he simply adds a passenger to an economy flight with no restrictions ❸.
- He implements the removePassenger method according to the business logic: a passenger can be removed from a flight only if the passenger is not a VIP ❹.

John also introduces a BusinessFlight class that extends Flight and implements the inherited addPassenger and removePassenger abstract methods.

Listing 20.9   BusinessFlight class, extending the abstract Flight class

```
public class BusinessFlight extends Flight {              ❶

    public BusinessFlight(String id) {
        super(id);                                         ❷
    }

    @Override
    public boolean addPassenger(Passenger passenger) {
        if (passenger.isVip()) {
            return passengers.add(passenger);              ❸
        }
        return false;
    }

    @Override
    public boolean removePassenger(Passenger passenger) {
        return false;                                      ❹
    }

}
```

In this listing:

- John declares the BusinessFlight class extending the Flight abstract class **1** and creates a constructor calling the constructor of the superclass **2**.
- He implements the addPassenger method according to the business logic: only a VIP passenger can be added to a business flight **3**.
- He implements the removePassenger method according to the business logic: a passenger cannot be removed from a business flight **4**.

Refactoring by replacing the conditional with polymorphism, we immediately see that the methods now look much shorter and clearer, not cluttered with decision making. Also, we are not forced to treat the previous default case that was never expected and that threw an exception. Of course, the refactoring and the API changes propagate into the tests, as shown next.

Listing 20.10 Refactoring propagation into the AirportTest class

```java
public class AirportTest {

    @DisplayName("Given there is an economy flight")
    @Nested
    class EconomyFlightTest {
        private Flight economyFlight;

        @BeforeEach
        void setUp() {                                              1
            economyFlight = new EconomyFlight("1");   ←┘
        }
        [...]
    }

    @DisplayName("Given there is a business flight")
    @Nested
    class BusinessFlightTest {
        private Flight businessFlight;

        @BeforeEach
        void setUp() {                                              2
            businessFlight = new BusinessFlight("2");   ←┘
        }
        [...]
    }

}
```

In this listing, John replaces the previous Flight instantiations with instantiations of EconomyFlight **1** and BusinessFlight **2**. He also removes the Airport class that served as a client for the Passenger and Flight classes—it is no longer needed, now that John has introduced the tests. It previously served to declare the main method that created different types of flights and passengers and made them act together.

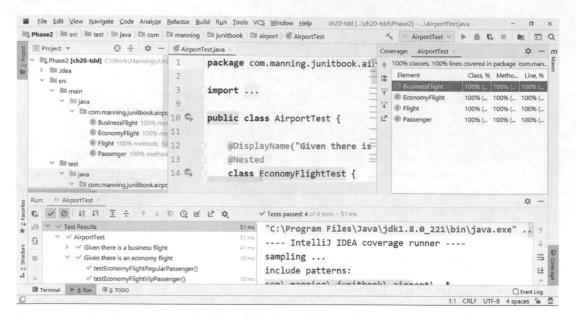

Figure 20.7   Running the economy and business flight tests after refactoring the flight-management application brings us to 100% code coverage.

If we run the tests now, we see that the code coverage is 100% (figure 20.7). So, refactoring the TDD application has helped both to improve the quality of the code and to increase the testing code coverage.

John has covered the flight-management application with tests and refactored it, resulting in better code quality and 100% code coverage. It is time for him to start introducing new features by working with TDD!

20.5   Introducing new features using TDD

After moving the software to TDD and refactoring it, John is responsible for the implementation of new features required by the customer that extend the application policies.

20.5.1   Adding a premium flight

The first new features that John will implement are a new flight type—premium—and policies concerning this flight type. There is a policy for adding a passenger: if the passenger is a VIP, the passenger should be added to the premium flight; otherwise, the request must be rejected (figure 20.8). There is also a policy for removing a passenger: if required, a passenger may be removed from a flight (figure 20.9). (The company is sorry; you may be an important person, but there are rules and restrictions, and the company may be forced to remove you from a flight.)

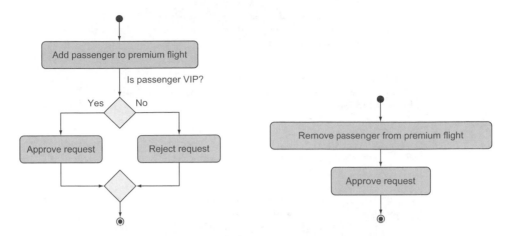

Figure 20.8   The extended business logic of adding a passenger to a premium flight: only VIP passengers are allowed to join.

Figure 20.9   The extended business logic of removing a passenger: any type of passenger may be removed from a premium flight.

John realizes that this new feature has similarities to the previous ones. He would like to take increased advantage of working TDD style and do more refactoring—this time, to the tests. This is in the spirit of the *Rule of Three*, as stated by Don Roberts (https://en.wikipedia.org/wiki/Rule_of_three_(computer_programming)):

> *The first time you do something, you just do it. The second time you do something similar, you wince at the duplication, but you do the duplicate thing anyway. The third time you do something similar, you refactor.*
>
> *So, three strikes and you refactor.*

John considers that, after receiving the requirement for the implementation of this third flight type, it is time to do some more grouping of the existing tests using the JUnit 5 @Nested annotation and then implement the premium flight requirement in a similar way. Following is the refactored AirportTest class before moving to the work for the premium flight.

Listing 20.11   Refactored `AirportTest` class

```java
public class AirportTest {

    @DisplayName("Given there is an economy flight")
    @Nested
    class EconomyFlightTest {

        private Flight economyFlight;
        private Passenger mike;
        private Passenger james;

        @BeforeEach
        void setUp() {
```
❶

```
            economyFlight = new EconomyFlight("1");
            mike  = new Passenger("Mike", false);        ❷
            james = new Passenger("James", true);
        }

        @Nested
        @DisplayName("When we have a regular passenger")
        class RegularPassenger {

            @Test
            @DisplayName(                                                    ❹
                "Then you can add and remove him from an economy flight")  ◁⎯
            public void testEconomyFlightRegularPassenger() {
                assertAll(
                            "Verify all conditions for a regular passenger
                            and an economy flight",
                        () -> assertEquals("1", economyFlight.getId()),
                        () -> assertEquals(true,
                            economyFlight.addPassenger(mike)),
                        () -> assertEquals(1,
                            economyFlight.getPassengersList().size()),      ❺
                        () -> assertEquals("Mike",
                            economyFlight.getPassengersList()
                                         .get(0).getName()),
                        () -> assertEquals(true,
                            economyFlight.removePassenger(mike)),
                        () -> assertEquals(0,
                            economyFlight.getPassengersList().size())
                );
            }
        }

        @Nested
        @DisplayName("When we have a VIP passenger")
        class VipPassenger {
            @Test
            @DisplayName("Then you can add him but
                          cannot remove him from an economy flight")        ❹
            public void testEconomyFlightVipPassenger() {
                assertAll("Verify all conditions for a VIP passenger
                            and an economy flight",
                        () -> assertEquals("1", economyFlight.getId()),
                        () -> assertEquals(true,
                economyFlight.addPassenger(james)),
                        () -> assertEquals(1,
                economyFlight.getPassengersList().size()),
                        () -> assertEquals("James",
                economyFlight.getPassengersList().get(0).getName()),
                        () -> assertEquals(false,
                economyFlight.removePassenger(james)),
                        () -> assertEquals(1,
                economyFlight.getPassengersList().size())
                );

            }
        }
    }
```

❸ (margin marker beside RegularPassenger block)

❺ (margin marker beside VipPassenger assertions)

```java
@DisplayName("Given there is a business flight")
@Nested
class BusinessFlightTest {
    private Flight businessFlight;
    private Passenger mike;                              ❶
    private Passenger james;

    @BeforeEach
    void setUp() {
        businessFlight = new BusinessFlight("2");
        mike = new Passenger("Mike", false);            ❷
        james = new Passenger("James", true);
    }

    @Nested
    @DisplayName("When we have a regular passenger")
    class RegularPassenger {

        @Test
        @DisplayName("Then you cannot add or remove him
                      from a business flight")            ❹
        public void testBusinessFlightRegularPassenger() {
            assertAll("Verify all conditions for a regular passenger
                       and a business flight",
                    () -> assertEquals(false,
                businessFlight.addPassenger(mike)),
                    () -> assertEquals(0,
                businessFlight.getPassengersList().size()),  ❺
                    () -> assertEquals(false,
                businessFlight.removePassenger(mike)),
                    () -> assertEquals(0,
                businessFlight.getPassengersList().size())
            );
        }
    }

    @Nested
    @DisplayName("When we have a VIP passenger")
    class VipPassenger {

        @Test
        @DisplayName("Then you can add him but cannot remove him
                      from a business flight")            ❹
        public void testBusinessFlightVipPassenger() {
            assertAll("Verify all conditions for a VIP passenger
                       and a business flight",
                    () -> assertEquals(true,
                        businessFlight.addPassenger(james)),
                    () -> assertEquals(1,
                        businessFlight.getPassengersList().size()),  ❺
                    () -> assertEquals(false,
                        businessFlight.removePassenger(james)),
                    () -> assertEquals(1,
                        businessFlight.getPassengersList().size())
            );
        }
    }
}
```

In this listing:

- In the existing nested classes `EconomyFlightTest` and `BusinessFlight-Test`, John groups the flight and passenger fields, as he would like to add one more testing level and reuse these fields for all tests concerning a particular flight type ❶. He initializes these fields before the execution of each test ❷.
- He introduces a new nesting level to test different passenger types. He uses the JUnit 5 `@DisplayName` annotation to label the classes in a way that is more expressive and easier to follow ❸. All of these labels start with the keyword `When`.
- He labels all existing tests with the help of the JUnit 5 `@DisplayName` annotation ❹. All of these labels start with the keyword `Then`.
- He refactors the checking of the conditions by using the `assertAll` JUnit 5 method and grouping all previously existing conditions, which can now be read fluently ❺.

This is how John has refactored the existing tests, to facilitate continuing to work in TDD style and to introduce the newly required premium flight business logic. If we run the tests now, we can easily follow the way they work and how they check the business logic (figure 20.10). Any new developer joining the project will find these tests extremely valuable as part of the documentation!

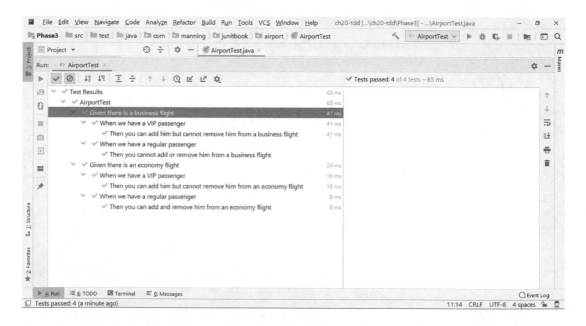

Figure 20.10   Running the refactored `AirportTest` for the economy flight and the business flight allows the developer to follow how the tests are working.

John moves now to the implementation of the `PremiumFlight` class and its logic. He will create `PremiumFlight` as a subclass of `Flight` and override the add-Passenger and `removePassenger` methods, but they act like stubs—they do not do anything and simply return `false`. Their behavior will be extended later. Working TDD style involves creating the tests first and then the business logic.

Listing 20.12 Initial design of the `PremiumFlight` class

```java
public class PremiumFlight extends Flight {                    ◄─┐  ❶

    public PremiumFlight(String id) {                        │ ❷
        super(id);
    }

    @Override
    public boolean addPassenger(Passenger passenger) {         │ ❸
        return false;
    }

    @Override
    public boolean removePassenger(Passenger passenger) {        │ ❹
        return false;
    }

}
```

In this listing:

- John declares the `PremiumFlight` class that extends `Flight` ❶, and he creates a constructor for it ❷.
- He creates the `addPassenger` ❸ and `removePassenger` ❹ methods as stubs, without any business logic. They simply return `false`.

John now implements the tests according to the premium flight business logic from figures 20.8 and 20.9.

Listing 20.13 Tests for the behavior of `PremiumFlight`

```java
public class AirportTest {
    [...]

    @DisplayName("Given there is a premium flight")
    @Nested                                                    │ ❶
    class PremiumFlightTest {
        private Flight premiumFlight;
        private Passenger mike;                              │ ❷
        private Passenger james;

        @BeforeEach
        void setUp() {
```

```
            premiumFlight = new PremiumFlight("3");
            mike = new Passenger("Mike", false);                    ❸
            james = new Passenger("James", true);
        }

        @Nested
        @DisplayName("When we have a regular passenger")            ❹
        class RegularPassenger {

            @Test
            @DisplayName("Then you cannot add or remove him          ❺
                         from a premium flight")
            public void testPremiumFlightRegularPassenger() {
                assertAll("Verify all conditions for a regular passenger    ❻
                          and a premium flight",
                        () -> assertEquals(false,
                            premiumFlight.addPassenger(mike)),      ❼
                        () -> assertEquals(0,
                            premiumFlight.getPassengersList().size()),
                        () -> assertEquals(false,
                            premiumFlight.removePassenger(mike)),   ❽
                        () -> assertEquals(0,
                            premiumFlight.getPassengersList().size())
                );
            }
        }

        @Nested
        @DisplayName("When we have a VIP passenger")                ❾
        class VipPassenger {
            @Test
            @DisplayName("Then you can add and remove him           ❿
                         from a premium flight")
            public void testPremiumFlightVipPassenger() {
                assertAll("Verify all conditions for a VIP passenger   ⓫
                          and a premium flight",
                        () -> assertEquals(true,
                            premiumFlight.addPassenger(james)),     ⓬
                        () -> assertEquals(1,
                            premiumFlight.getPassengersList().size()),
                        () -> assertEquals(true,
                            premiumFlight.removePassenger(james)),  ⓭
                        () -> assertEquals(0,
                            premiumFlight.getPassengersList().size())
                );
            }
        }
    }
}
```

In this listing:

- John declares the nested class `PremiumFlightTest` ❶ that contains the fields representing the flight and the passengers ❷ that are set up before each test ❸.

- He creates two classes nested at the second level in `PremiumFlightTest`: `RegularPassenger` ❹ and `VipPassenger` ❾. He uses the JUnit 5 `@Display-Name` annotation to label these classes starting with the keyword `When`.
- He inserts one test in each of the newly added `RegularPassenger` ❺ and `VipPassenger` ❿ classes. He labels these tests with the JUnit 5 `@DisplayName` annotation starting with the keyword `Then`.
- Testing a premium flight and a regular passenger, John uses the `assertAll` method to verify multiple conditions ❻. He checks that he cannot add a passenger to a premium flight and that trying to add a passenger does not change the size of the passenger list ❼. Then, he checks that he cannot remove a passenger from a premium flight and that trying to remove a passenger does not change the size of the passenger list ❽.
- Testing a premium flight and a VIP passenger, John again uses `assertAll` ⓫. He checks that he can add a passenger to a premium flight and that doing so increases the size of the passenger list ⓬. Then, he checks that he can remove a passenger from a premium flight and that doing so decreases the size of the passenger list ⓭.

After writing the tests, John runs them. Remember, he is working TDD style, so tests come first. The result is shown in figure 20.11.

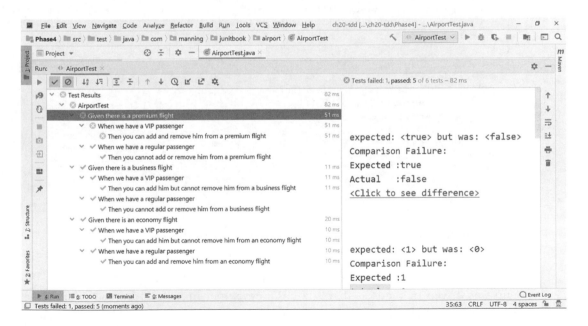

Figure 20.11 Running the newly added tests to check premium flights before the code implementation results in some test failures. We need to understand which behavior to introduce to fix the failing tests.

The fact that one of the tests is failing is not a problem. On the contrary: it is what John expected. Remember, working TDD style means being driven by tests, so we first create the test to fail and then write the piece of code that will make the test pass. But there is another remarkable thing here: the test for a premium flight and a regular passenger is already green. This means the existing business logic (the addPassenger and removePassenger methods returning false) is just enough for this case. John understands that he only has to focus on the VIP passenger. To quote Kent Beck again, "TDD helps you to pay attention to the right issues at the right time so you can make your designs cleaner, you can refine your designs as you learn. TDD enables you to gain confidence in the code over time."

So, John moves back to the PremiumFlight class and adds the business logic only for VIP passengers. Driven by tests, he gets straight to the point.

Listing 20.14   `PremiumFlight` class with the full business logic

```java
public class PremiumFlight extends Flight {

    public PremiumFlight(String id) {
        super(id);
    }

    @Override
    public boolean addPassenger(Passenger passenger) {
        if (passenger.isVip()) {
            return passengers.add(passenger);          ❶
        }
        return false;
    }

    @Override
    public boolean removePassenger(Passenger passenger) {
        if (passenger.isVip()) {
            return passengers.remove(passenger);        ❷
        }
        return false;
    }

}
```

In this listing:

- John adds a passenger only if the passenger is a VIP ❶.
- John removes a passenger only if the passenger is a VIP ❷.

The result of running the tests now is shown in figure 20.12. Everything went smoothly and was driven by the tests that guide the developer in writing the code that makes them pass. Additionally, the code coverage is 100%.

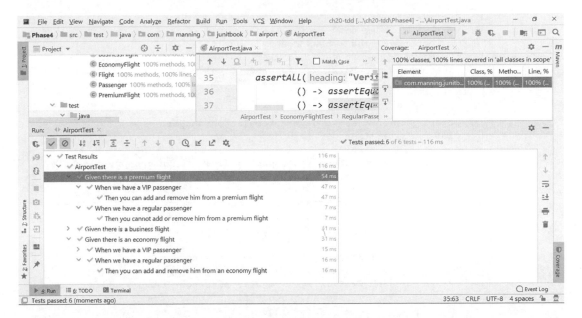

Figure 20.12   Running the full test suite (economy, business, and premium flights) after adding the business logic for `PremiumFlight`: code coverage is 100%.

20.5.2   Adding a passenger only once

Occasionally, on purpose or by mistake, the same passenger has been added to a flight more than once. This has caused problems with managing seats, and these situations must be avoided. John needs to make sure that whenever someone tries to add a passenger, if the passenger has been previously added to the flight, the request should be rejected. This is new business logic, and John will implement it TDD style.

John will begin the implementation of this new feature by adding the test to check it. He will try repeatedly to add the same passenger to a flight, as shown in the following listing. We'll detail only the case of a regular passenger repeatedly added to an economy flight, all other cases being similar.

> **Listing 20.15   Trying to add the same passenger repeatedly to the same flight**

```java
public class AirportTest {
    @DisplayName("Given there is an economy flight")
    @Nested
    class EconomyFlightTest {
        private Flight economyFlight;
        private Passenger mike;
        private Passenger james;
```

```
@BeforeEach
void setUp() {
    economyFlight = new EconomyFlight("1");
    mike  = new Passenger("Mike", false);
    james = new Passenger("James", true);
}


@Nested
@DisplayName("When we have a regular passenger")
class RegularPassenger {
    [...]
    @DisplayName("Then you cannot add him to an economy flight
                  more than once")                                    ❶
    @RepeatedTest(5)
    public void testEconomyFlightRegularPassengerAddedOnlyOnce
                    (RepetitionInfo repetitionInfo) {
        for (int i=0; i<repetitionInfo.getCurrentRepetition();
                                                      i++) {          ❸
            economyFlight.addPassenger(mike);
        }
        assertAll("Verify a regular passenger can be added
                   to an economy flight only once",                  ❹
                () -> assertEquals(1,
                    economyFlight.getPassengersList().size()),        ❺
                () -> assertTrue(
                 economyFlight.getPassengersList().
                               contains(mike)),                      ❻
                () -> assertTrue(
                    economyFlight.getPassengersList()                ❼
                    .get(0).getName().equals("Mike")));
    }
}
}
}
```

In this listing:

- John marks the test as @RepeatedTest five times ❶ and uses the RepetitionInfo parameter in it ❷.
- Each time a test is executed, he tries to add the passenger the number of times specified by the RepetitionInfo parameter ❸.
- He performs verifications using the assertAll method ❹: he checks that the list of passengers is size 1 ❺, that the list contains the added passenger ❻, and that the passenger is in the first position ❼.

If we run the tests, they fail. There is no business logic yet to prevent adding a passenger more than once (figure 20.13).

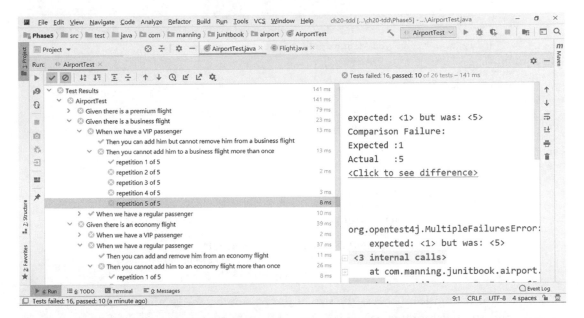

Figure 20.13 Running the tests that check whether a passenger can be added only once to a flight, before implementing the business logic, will result in failure.

To ensure the unicity of the passengers on a flight, John changes the passenger list structure to a set. So, he does some code refactoring that will also propagate across the tests. The `Flight` class changes as shown next.

> **Listing 20.16 `Flight` class after changing the list of passengers to a set**

```
public abstract class Flight {

    [...]
    Set<Passenger> passengers = new HashSet<>();      ①
    [...]

    public Set<Passenger> getPassengersSet() {        ②
        return Collections.unmodifiableSet(passengers);   ③
    }

    [...]
}
```

In this listing, John changes the type and the initialization of the `passengers` attribute to a sct ①, changes the name of the method ②, and returns an unmodifiable set ③.

John then creates a new test to check that a passenger can be added only once to a flight.

Listing 20.17   New test checking that a passenger can be added only once to a flight

```java
@DisplayName("Then you cannot add him to an economy flight
              more than once")
@RepeatedTest(5)
public void testEconomyFlightRegularPassengerAddedOnlyOnce
            (RepetitionInfo repetitionInfo) {
    for (int i=0; i<repetitionInfo.getCurrentRepetition(); i++){
        economyFlight.addPassenger(mike);
    }
    assertAll("Verify a regular passenger can be added
               to an economy flight only once",
        () -> assertEquals(1,
        economyFlight.getPassengersSet().size()),          ❶
        () -> assertTrue(
        economyFlight.getPassengersSet().contains(mike)),  ❷
        () -> assertTrue(
        new ArrayList<>(economyFlight.getPassengersSet())  ❸
          .get(0).getName().equals("Mike")));
}
```

In this listing, John checks the size of the passengers set ❶, the fact that this set contains the newly added passenger ❷, and that the passenger is in the first position ❸, after constructing a list from the existing set (he needs to do this because a set has no order for the elements).

Running the tests is now successful, with code coverage of 100% (figure 20.14). John has implemented this new feature in TDD style.

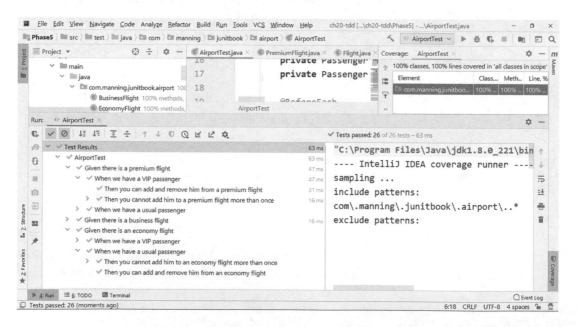

Figure 20.14   Successfully running the entire test suite after implementing the business logic to check that a passenger can be added only once to a flight

The next chapter is dedicated to another software development process that is frequently used today: behavior-driven development (BDD).

Summary

This chapter has covered the following:

- Examining the concept of TDD and demonstrating how it helps us develop safe applications because tests prevent the introduction of bugs into working code and act as part of the documentation
- Preparing a non-TDD application to be moved to TDD by adding hierarchical JUnit 5 tests that cover the existing business logic
- Refactoring and improving the code quality of this TDD application by replacing conditional with polymorphism while relying on the tests we developed
- Implementing new features in by working TDD style, starting by writing tests and then implementing the business logic

21

Behavior-driven development with JUnit 5

> *Some people refer to BDD as "TDD done right." You can also think of BDD as "how we build the right thing" and TDD as "how we build the thing right."*
>
> —Millard Ellingsworth

As we discussed in chapter 20, test-driven development (TDD) is an effective technique that uses unit tests to verify the code. Despite TDD's clear benefits, its usual loop

```
[test, code, refactor, (repeat)]
```

can cause developers to lose the overall picture of the application's business goals. The project may become larger and more complex, the number of unit tests will increase, and those tests will become harder to understand and maintain. The tests may also be strongly coupled with the implementation. They focus on the unit (the class or the method) that is tested, and the business goals may not be considered.

Starting from TDD, a new technique has been created: *behavior-driven development* (BDD). It focuses on the features themselves and makes sure they work as expected.

21.1 Introducing behavior-driven development

Dan North originated BDD in the mid-2000s. It is a software development technique that starts from the business requirements and goals and transforms them into working features. BDD encourages teams to interact, use concrete examples to communicate how the application must behave, and deliver software that matters, supporting cooperation between stakeholders. TDD helps us build software that works; BDD helps us build software that provides business value. Using BDD, we determine which features the organization really needs and focus on implementing them. We can also discover what users actually need, not just what they ask about.

> **NOTE** BDD is a large topic, and this chapter focuses on demonstrating how to use it in conjunction with JUnit 5 and how to effectively build features using this technique. For a comprehensive discussion of this subject, we recommend *BDD in Action* by John Ferguson Smart; the second edition of the book is in development at the time of writing this chapter (Manning, www.manning.com/books/bdd-in-action-second-edition).

Communication between people involved in the same project may lead to problems and misunderstandings. Usually, the flow works this way:

1. The customer communicates to the business analyst their understanding of the functionality of a feature.
2. The business analyst builds the requirements for the developer, describing the way the software must work.
3. The developer creates the code based on the requirements and writes unit tests to implement the new feature.
4. The tester creates the test cases based on the requirements and uses them to verify the way the new feature works.

But it is possible that the information may be misunderstood, modified, or ignored—and thus the new feature may not do exactly what was initially expected. We'll analyze how things evolve when a new feature is introduced.

21.1.1 Introducing a new feature

The business analyst talks with the customer to decide what software features will be able to address the business goals. These features are general requirements, like "Allow the traveler to choose the shortest way to the destination," and "Allow the traveler to choose the cheapest way to the destination."

These features need to be broken into *stories*. The stories might look like "Find the route between source and destination with the smallest number of flight changes," or "Find the quickest route between source and destination."

Stories are defined through concrete examples. These examples become the *acceptance criteria* for a story. Acceptance criteria are expressed BDD style through the keywords `Given`, `When`, and `Then`.

As an example, we may present the following acceptance criteria:

```
Given the flights operated by company X
When I want to find the quickest route from Bucharest to New York on
May 15 20...
Then I will be provided the route Bucharest—Frankfurt—New York,
    with a duration of...
```

21.1.2   *From requirements analysis to acceptance criteria*

For the company using the flight-management application, one business goal that we can formulate is "Increase sales by providing overall higher quality flight services." This is a very general goal, and it can be detailed through requirements:

- Provide an interactive application to choose flights.
- Provide an interactive application to change flights.
- Provide an interactive application to calculate the shortest route between source and destination.

To make the customer happy, the features generated by the requirements analysis need to achieve the customer business goals or deliver business value. The initial ideas need to be described in more detail. One way to describe the previous requirements would be

```
As a passenger
I want to know the flights for a given destination within a given period of
    time
So that I can choose the flight(s) that suit(s) my needs
```

or

```
As a passenger
I want to be able to change my initial flight(s) to a different one(s)
So that I can follow the changes in my schedule
```

A feature like "I can choose the flights that suit my needs" might be too large to be implemented at once—so, it must be divided. You may also want to get some feedback while passing through the milestones of the implementation of a feature.

The previous feature may be broken into smaller stories, such as the following:

```
Find the direct flights that suit my needs (if any).
Find the alternatives of flights with stopovers that suit my needs.
Find the one-way flights that suit my needs.
Find the there and back flights that suit my needs.
```

Generally, particular examples are used as acceptance criteria. Acceptance criteria express what will make the stakeholder agree that the application is working as expected.

In BDD, acceptance criteria are defined using the `Given/When/Then` keywords:

```
Given <a context>
When <an action occurs>
Then <expect a result>
```

Here's a concrete example:

```
Given the flights operated by the company
When I want to travel from Bucharest to London next Wednesday
Then I should be provided 2 possible flights: 10:35 and 16:20
```

21.1.3 *BDD benefits and challenges*

Here are some benefits of the BDD approach:

- *Addresses user needs*—Users care less about the implementation and are mainly interested in application functionality. Working BDD style, we get closer to addressing these needs.
- *Provides clarity*—Scenarios clarify what software should do. They are described in simple language that is easy for technical and nontechnical people to understand. Ambiguities can be clarified by analyzing the scenario or by adding another scenario.
- *Supports change*—Scenarios represent part of the software documentation: it's living documentation, as it evolves simultaneously with the application. It also helps locate incoming changes. Automated acceptance tests hinder the introduction of regressions when new changes are introduced.
- *Supports automation*—Scenarios can be transformed into automated tests, as the steps of the scenario are already defined.
- *Focuses on adding business value*—BDD prevents the introduction of features that are not useful to the project. We can also prioritize functionalities.
- *Reduces costs*—Prioritizing the importance of functionalities and avoiding unnecessary ones will prevent wasting resources and concentrate these resources on doing exactly what is needed.

The challenges of BDD are that it requires engagement, strong collaboration, interaction, direct communication, and constant feedback. This may be a challenge for some people and, in the context of present-day globalization and distributed teams, may require language skills and managing time zones.

21.2 *Working BDD style with Cucumber and JUnit 5*

In chapter 20, John, a programmer at Tested Data Systems, worked TDD style to develop the flight-management application to a stage where it can work with three types of flights: economy, business, and premium. In addition, he implemented the

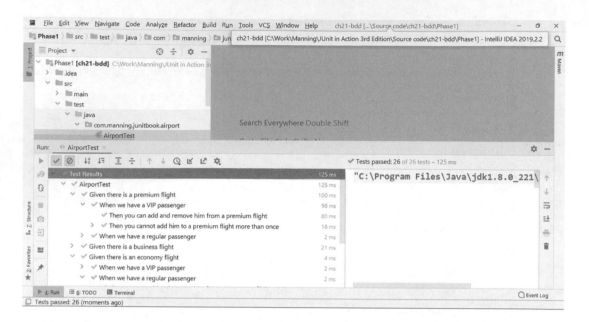

Figure 21.1   Successfully running the tests of the TDD flight-management application. Users can follow the execution of the annotated methods and read the scenarios.

requirement that a passenger can be added only once to a flight. The functionality of the application can be quickly reviewed by running the tests (figure 21.1).

John has already introduced, in a discrete way, a first taste of the BDD way of working. We can easily read how the application works by following the tests using the `Given`, `When`, and `Then` keywords. In this chapter, John will move the application to BDD with Cucumber and also introduce more new features.

21.2.1 *Introducing Cucumber*

Cucumber (https://cucumber.io/) is a BDD testing framework. It describes application scenarios in plain English using a language called Gherkin. Cucumber is easy for stakeholders to read and understand and allows automation.

The main capabilities of Cucumber are as follows:

- Scenarios or examples describe the requirements.
- A scenario is defined through a list of steps to be executed by Cucumber.
- Cucumber executes the code corresponding to the scenarios, checks that the software follows these requirements, and generates a report describing the success or failure of each scenario.

The main capabilities of Gherkin are as follows:

- Gherkin defines simple grammar rules that allow Cucumber to understand plain English text.

- Gherkin documents the behavior of the system. The requirements are always up to date, as they are provided through scenarios that represent living specifications.

Cucumber ensures that technical and nontechnical people can easily read, write, and understand the acceptance tests. The acceptance tests became an instrument of communication between the stakeholders of the project.

A Cucumber acceptance test looks like this:

```
Given there is an economy flight
When we have a regular passenger
Then you can add and remove him from an economy flight
```

Again, notice the `Given/When/Then` keywords for describing a scenario, which we introduced in our previous work with JUnit 5. We'll no longer use them just for labeling: Cucumber interprets sentences starting with these keywords and generates methods that it annotates using the annotations `@Given`, `@When`, and `@Then`.

The acceptance tests are written in Cucumber feature files. A *feature file* is an entry point to the Cucumber tests; in the file, we describe our tests in Gherkin. A feature file can contain one or many scenarios.

John makes plans for starting to work with Cucumber in the project. He will first introduce the Cucumber dependencies into the existing Maven configuration. He will create a Cucumber feature and generate the skeleton of the Cucumber tests. Then, he will move the existing JUnit 5 tests to fill in this Cucumber-generated test skeleton.

> **Listing 21.1   Cucumber dependencies added to the pom.xml file**

```
<dependency>
    <groupId>info.cukes</groupId>
    <artifactId>cucumber-java</artifactId>
    <version>1.2.5</version>
    <scope>test</scope>
</dependency>
<dependency>
    <groupId>info.cukes</groupId>
    <artifactId>cucumber-junit</artifactId>
    <version>1.2.5</version>
    <scope>test</scope>
</dependency>
```

In this listing, John introduces the two needed Maven dependencies: `cucumber-java` and `cucumber-junit`.

21.2.2 *Moving a TDD feature to Cucumber*

Now John will begin creating Cucumber features. He follows the Maven standard folder structure and introduces the features into the test/resources folder. He creates the test/resources/features folder and, in it, creates the passengers_policy.feature file (figure 21.2).

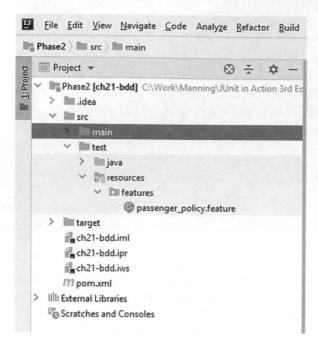

Figure 21.2   The new Cucumber passenger_policy.feature file is created in the test/resources/ features folder, following Maven rules.

John follows the Gherkin syntax and introduces a feature named `Passengers Policy`, together with a short description of what it should do. Then he follows the Gherkin syntax to write scenarios.

Listing 21.2   passenger_policy.feature file

```
Feature: Passengers Policy
  The company follows a policy of adding and removing passengers,
  depending on the passenger type and on the flight type

  Scenario: Economy flight, regular passenger
    Given there is an economy flight
    When we have a regular passenger
    Then you can add and remove him from an economy flight
    And you cannot add a regular passenger to an economy flight more than
      once

  Scenario: Economy flight, VIP passenger
    Given there is an economy flight
    When we have a VIP passenger
    Then you can add him but cannot remove him from an economy flight
    And you cannot add a VIP passenger to an economy flight more than once

  Scenario: Business flight, regular passenger
    Given there is a business flight
```

```
    When we have a regular passenger
    Then you cannot add or remove him from a business flight

  Scenario: Business flight, VIP passenger
    Given there is a business flight
    When we have a VIP passenger
    Then you can add him but cannot remove him from a business flight
    And you cannot add a VIP passenger to a business flight more than once

  Scenario: Premium flight, regular passenger
    Given there is a premium flight
    When we have a regular passenger
    Then you cannot add or remove him from a premium flight

  Scenario: Premium flight, VIP passenger
    Given there is a premium flight
    When we have a VIP passenger
    Then you can add and remove him from a premium flight
    And you cannot add a VIP passenger to a premium flight more than once
```

The keywords Feature, Scenario, Given, When, Then, and And are highlighted. Right-clicking this feature file shows the option to run it directly (figure 21.3).

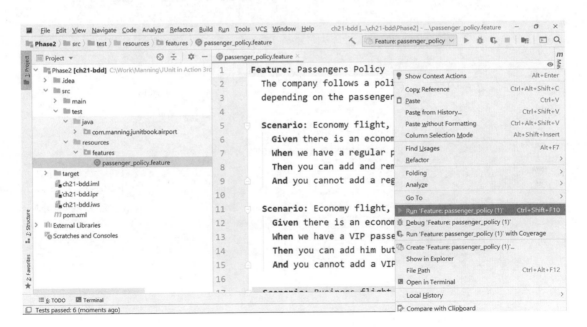

Figure 21.3 Directly running the passengers_policy.feature file by right-clicking the file

This is possible only if two requirements are fulfilled. First, the appropriate plugins must be activated. To do this in IntelliJ, go to File > Settings > Plugins and install the Cucumber for Java and Gherkin plugins (figures 21.4 and 21.5).

Figure 21.4   Installing the Cucumber for Java plugin from the File > Settings > Plugins menu

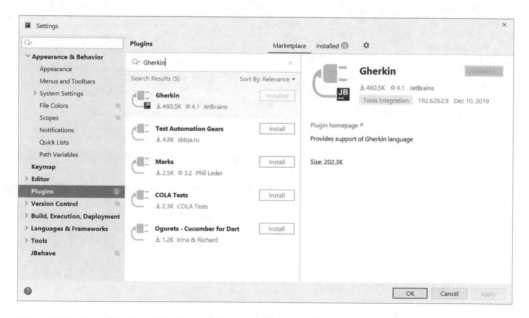

Figure 21.5   Installing the Gherkin plugin from the File > Settings > Plugins menu

Second, we must configure the way the feature is run. Go to Run > Edit Configurations, and set the following options (figure 21.6):

- Main Class: `cucumber.api.cli.Main`

- Glue (the package where step definitions are stored): `com.manning.junit-book.airport`
- Feature or Folder Path: the test/resources/features folder we have created
- Working Directory: the project folder

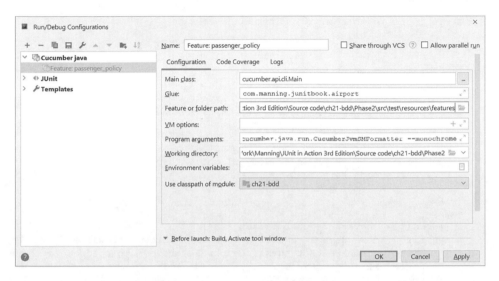

Figure 21.6 Setting the feature configuration by filling in the Main Class, Glue, Feature or Folder Path, and Working Directory fields

Running the feature directly generates the skeleton of the Java Cucumber tests (figure 21.7).

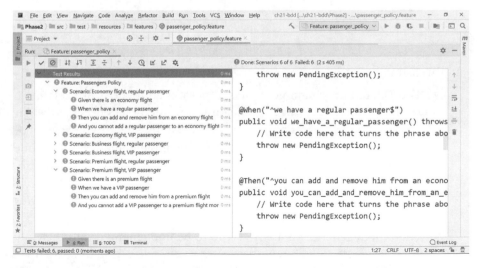

Figure 21.7 Getting the skeleton of the `Passengers Policy` feature by directly running the feature file. The annotated methods are executed to verify the scenarios.

John will now create a new Java class in the test/java folder, in the `com.manning` `.junitbook.airport` package. This class will be named `PassengersPolicy` and, at first, will contain the test skeleton (listing 21.3). The execution of such a test follows the scenarios described in the passengers_policy.feature file. For example, when executing the step

```
Given there is an economy flight
```

the program will execute the method annotated with

```
@Given("^there is an economy flight$")
```

Listing 21.3 Initial `PassengersPolicy` class

```
public class PassengerPolicy {                                       ❶
    @Given("^there is an economy flight$")              ◄─┐
    public void there_is_an_economy_flight() throws Throwable {
     // Write code here that turns the phrase above into concrete actions   ❷
     throw new PendingException();
    }
                                                         ❸
    @When("^we have a regular passenger$")              ◄─┐
    public void we_have_a_regular_passenger() throws Throwable {
    // Write code here that turns the phrase above into concrete actions    ❹
        throw new PendingException();
    }

    @Then("^you can add and remove him from an economy flight$")
    public void you_can_add_and_remove_him_from_an_economy_flight()
        throws Throwable {
    // Write code here that turns the phrase above into concrete actions    ❻
        throw new PendingException();
    }

    [...]

}
```

In this listing:

- The Cucumber plugin generates a method annotated with `@Given("^there is an economy flight$")`, meaning this method is executed when the step `Given there is an economy flight` from the scenario is executed ❶.
- The plugin generates a method stub to be implemented with the code addressing the step `Given there is an economy flight` from the scenario ❷.
- The plugin generates a method annotated with `@When("^we have a regular passenger$")`, meaning this method is executed when the step `When we have a regular passenger` from the scenario is executed ❸.
- The plugin generates a method stub to be implemented with the code addressing the step `When we have a regular passenger` from the scenario ❹.
- The plugin generates a method annotated with `@Then("^you can add and remove him from an economy flight$")`, meaning this method is executed

when the step Then you can add and remove him from an economy flight from the scenario is executed ❺.

- The plugin generates a method stub to be implemented with the code addressing the step Then you can add and remove him from an economy flight from the scenario ❻.
- The rest of the methods are implemented in a similar way; we have covered the Given, When, and Then steps of one scenario.

John follows the business logic of each step that has been defined and translates it into the tests from listing 21.4—the steps of the scenarios that need to be verified.

Listing 21.4 Implementing the business logic of the previously defined steps

```
public class PassengerPolicy {
    private Flight economyFlight;                    ❶
    private Passenger mike;
    [...]

    @Given("^there is an economy flight$")           ❷
    public void there_is_an_economy_flight() throws Throwable {
        economyFlight = new EconomyFlight("1");    ←┐
    }                                                ❸

    @When("^we have a regular passenger$")           ❹
    public void we_have_a_regular_passenger() throws Throwable {
        mike  = new Passenger("Mike", false);      ←┐
    }                                                ❺

    @Then("^you can add and remove him from an economy flight$")   ❻
    public void you_can_add_and_remove_him_from_an_economy_flight()
            throws Throwable {
        assertAll("Verify all conditions for a regular passenger
                and an economy flight",
            () -> assertEquals("1", economyFlight.getId()),
            () -> assertEquals(true, economyFlight.addPassenger(mike)),
            () -> assertEquals(1,
                    economyFlight.getPassengersSet().size()),        ❼
            () ->
            assertTrue(economyFlight.getPassengersSet().contains(mike)),
            () -> assertEquals(true, economyFlight.removePassenger(mike)),
            () -> assertEquals(0, economyFlight.getPassengersSet().size())
        );
    }
    [...]
}
```

In this listing:

- John declares the instance variables for the test, including economyFlight, and mike as a Passenger ❶.
- He writes the method corresponding to the Given there is an economy flight business logic step ❷ by initializing economyFlight ❸.

- He writes the method corresponding to the When we have a regular passenger business logic step ❹ by initializing the regular passenger mike ❺.
- He writes the method corresponding to the Then you can add and remove him from an economy flight business logic step ❻ by checking all the conditions using the assertAll JUnit 5 method, which can now be read fluently ❼.
- The rest of the methods are implemented in a similar way; we have covered the Given, When, and Then steps of one scenario.

To run the Cucumber tests, John will need a special class. The name of the class could be anything; he chooses CucumberTest.

Listing 21.5   CucumberTest class

```
[...]                                    ❶
@RunWith(Cucumber.class)
@CucumberOptions(                             ❸
    plugin = {"pretty"},
    features = "classpath:features")
public class CucumberTest {                ❷
                                              ❹
    /**
     * This class should be empty, step definitions should be in separate
     classes.
     */

}
```

In this listing:

- John annotates this class with @RunWith(Cucumber.class) ❶. Executing it like any JUnit test class runs all the features found on the classpath in the same package. As there is no Cucumber JUnit 5 extension at the moment of writing this chapter, we use the JUnit 4 runner.
- The @CucumberOptions annotation ❷ provides the plugin option ❸ that is used to specify different formatting options for the output reports. Using "pretty", the Gherkin source is printed with additional colors (figure 21.8). Other plugin options include "html" and "json", but "pretty" is appropriate for now. And the features option ❹ helps Cucumber locate the feature file in the project folder structure. It looks for the features folder on the classpath—and remember that the src/test/resources folder is maintained by Maven on the classpath!

By running the tests, we see that we have kept the test functionality that existed before moving to Cucumber.

There is another advantage of moving to BDD. Comparing the length of the pre-Cucumber AirportTest class, which has 207 lines, with the PassengersPolicy class, which has 157 lines, the testing code is only 75% of the pre-Cucumber size but has the same 100% coverage. Where does this gain come from? Remember that the

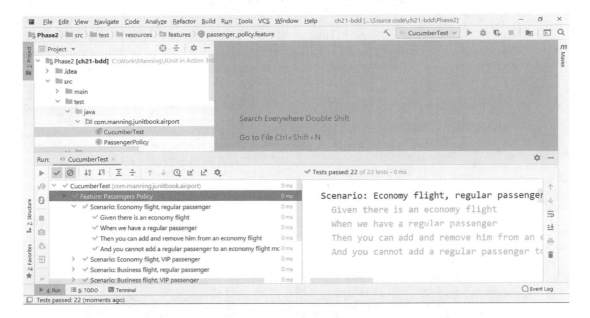

Figure 21.8 Running `CucumberTest`. The Gherkin source is pretty-printed, successful tests are displayed in green, and the code coverage is 100%.

`AirportTest` file contained seven classes on three levels: `AirportTest` at the top level; `EconomyFlightTest` and `BusinessFlightTest` at the second level; and, at the third level, two `RegularPassenger` and two `VipPassenger` classes. The code duplication is now really jumping to our attention, but that was the solution when we only had JUnit 5. With Cucumber, each step is implemented only once. If we have the same step in more than one scenario, we'll avoid the code duplication.

21.2.3 Adding a new feature with the help of Cucumber

John receives a new feature to implement concerning bonus points that are awarded to passengers. The specifications for calculating bonus points consider the mileage, meaning the distance traveled by each passenger. The bonus is calculated for all of the passenger's flights and depends on a factor: the mileage is divided by 10 for VIP passengers and by 20 for regular passengers (figure 21.9).

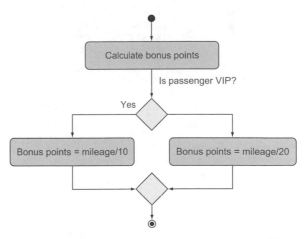

Figure 21.9 The business logic of awarding bonus points: the mileage is divided by 10 for VIP passengers and by 20 for regular passengers.

John moves to the BDD scenarios, tests, and implementation. He defines the scenarios for awarding bonus points (listing 21.6) and generates the Cucumber tests that describe the scenarios. They are expected to fail at first. Then he will add the code that implements the bonus award, run the tests, and expect them to be green.

Listing 21.6 The bonus_policy.feature file

```
Feature: Bonus Policy
  The company follows a bonus policy, depending on the passenger type and on
    the mileage

  Scenario Outline: Regular passenger bonus policy
    Given we have a regular passenger with a mileage
    When the regular passenger travels <mileage1> and <mileage2>
                                        and <mileage3>
    Then the bonus points of the regular passenger should be <points>

    Examples:
      | mileage1 | mileage2 | mileage3| points |
      |      349 |      319 |     623 |     64 |
      |      312 |      356 |     135 |     40 |
      |      223 |      786 |     503 |     75 |
      |      482 |       98 |     591 |     58 |
      |      128 |      176 |     304 |     30 |

  Scenario Outline: VIP passenger bonus policy
    Given we have a VIP passenger with a mileage
    When the VIP passenger travels <mileage1> and <mileage2>
                                    and <mileage3>
    Then the bonus points of the VIP passenger should be <points>

    Examples:
      | mileage1 | mileage2 | mileage3| points  |
      |      349 |      319 |     623 |     129 |
      |      312 |      356 |     135 |      80 |
      |      223 |      786 |     503 |     151 |
      |      482 |       98 |     591 |     117 |
      |      128 |      176 |     304 |      60 |
```

In this listing:

- We introduce a new capability of Cucumber: Scenario Outline ❶. With Scenario Outline, values do not need to be hardcoded in the step definitions.
- Values are replaced with parameters in the step definition itself—you can see <mileage1>, <mileage2>, <mileage3>, and <points> as parameters ❷.
- The effective values are defined in the Examples table at the end of the Scenario Outline ❸. The first row in the first table defines the values of three mileages (349, 319, 623). Adding them and dividing them by 20 (the regular passenger factor), we get the integer part 64 (the number of bonus points). This successfully replaces the JUnit 5 parameterized tests and has the advantages that the values are kept in the scenarios and can be easily understood by everyone.

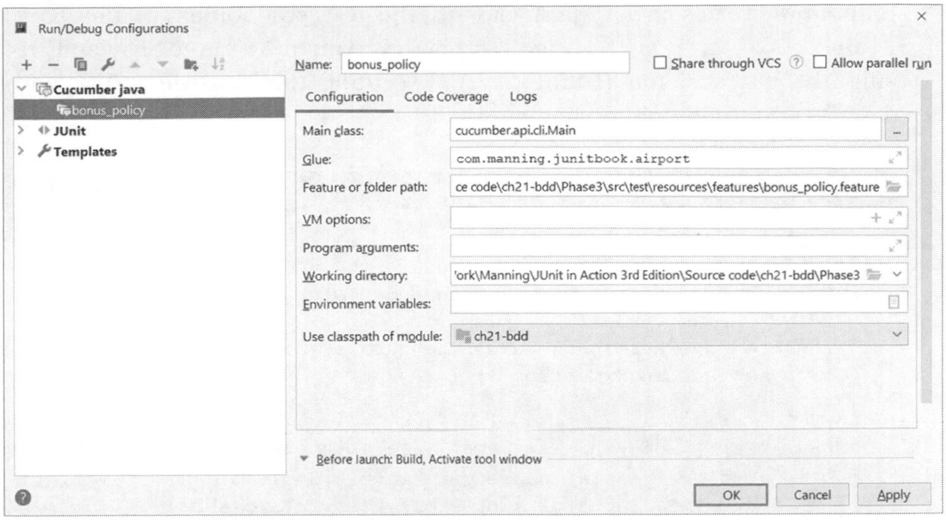

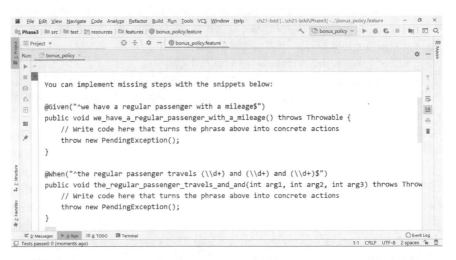

Figure 21.10 Setting the configuration for the new `Bonus_Policy` **feature by filling in the Main Class, Glue, Feature or Folder Path, and Working Directory fields**

To configure the way the feature is run, choose Run > Edit Configurations, and set the following options (figure 21.10):

- Main Class: `cucumber.api.cli.Main`
- Glue : `com.manning.junitbook.airport`
- Feature or Folder Path: test/resources/features/bonus_policy.feature
- Working Directory: the project folder

Running the feature directly generates the skeleton of the Java Cucumber tests (figure 21.11).

Figure 21.11 Getting the skeleton of the `Bonus Policy` **feature by directly running the feature file**

John now creates a new Java class in the test/java folder, in the `com.manning` `.junitbook.airport` package. This class is named `BonusPolicy` and, at first, contains the test skeleton (listing 21.7). Executing this test will follow the scenarios described in the bonus_policy.feature file.

Listing 21.7   Initial `BonusPolicy` class

```
public class BonusPolicy {
    @Given("^we have a regular passenger with a mileage$")
    public void we_have_a_regular_passenger_with_a_mileage()
            throws Throwable {
      // Write code here that turns the phrase above into concrete actions
      throw new PendingException();
    }

    @When("^the regular passenger travels (\\d+) and (\\d+) and (\\d+)$")
    public void the_regular_passenger_travels_and_and
            (int arg1, int arg2, int arg3) throws Throwable {
      // Write code here that turns the phrase above into concrete actions
      throw new PendingException();
    }

    @Then("^the bonus points of the regular passenger should be (\\d+)$")
    public void the_bonus_points_of_the_regular_passenger_should_be
                                                        (int arg1)
        throws Throwable {
      // Write code here that turns the phrase above into concrete actions
      throw new PendingException();
    }
    [...]

}
```

In this listing:

- The Cucumber plugin generates a method annotated with `@Given("^we have a regular passenger with a mileage$")`, meaning this method is executed when the step `Given we have a regular passenger with a mileage` from the scenario is executed ❶.
- The plugin generates a method to be implemented with the code addressing the step `Given we have a regular passenger with a mileage` from the scenario ❷.
- The plugin generates a method annotated with `@When("^the regular passenger travels (\\d+) and (\\d+) and (\\d+)$")`, meaning this method is executed when the step `When the regular passenger travels <mileage1> and <mileage2> and <mileage3>` from the scenario is executed ❸.
- The plugin generates a method to be implemented with the code addressing the step `When the regular passenger travels <mileage1> and <mileage2> and <mileage3>` from the scenario ❹. This method has three parameters corresponding to the three different mileages.

- The plugin generates a method annotated with @Then("^the bonus points of the regular passenger should be (\\d+)$"), meaning this method is executed when the step Then the bonus points of the regular passenger should be <points> from the scenario is executed **5**.
- The plugin generates a method to be implemented with the code addressing the step Then the bonus points of the regular passenger should be <points> from the scenario **6**. This method has one parameter corresponding to the points.
- The rest of the methods are implemented in a similar way; we have covered the Given, When, and Then steps of one scenario.

Next, John creates the Mileage class, declaring the fields and the methods but not implementing them yet. John needs to use the methods of this class for the tests, make these tests initially fail, and then implement the methods and make the tests pass.

Listing 21.8 Mileage class with no implementation of the methods

```java
public class Mileage {

    public static final int VIP_FACTOR = 10;          ❶
    public static final int REGULAR_FACTOR = 20;

    private Map<Passenger, Integer> passengersMileageMap =
                            new HashMap<>();            ❷
    private Map<Passenger, Integer> passengersPointsMap =
                            new HashMap<>();

    public void addMileage(Passenger passenger, int miles) {   ❸

    }

    public void calculateGivenPoints() {                ❹

    }

}
```

In this listing:

- John declares the VIP_FACTOR and REGULAR_FACTOR constants corresponding to the factor by which the mileage is divided for each type of passenger in order to get the bonus points ❶.
- He declares passengersMileageMap and passengersPointsMap, two maps having the passenger as a key and keeping as a value the mileage and points for that passenger, respectively ❷.
- He declares the addMileage method, which populates passengersMileage-Map with the mileage for each passenger ❸. The method does not do anything for now; it will be written later to fix the tests.

- He declares the `calculateGivenPoints` method, which populates the `passengersPointsMap` with the bonus points for each passenger ❹. Again, it will be written later to fix the tests.

John now turns his attention to writing the unimplemented tests from the `Bonus-Policy` class to follow the business logic of this feature.

Listing 21.9 Business logic of the steps from `BonusPolicy`

```
public class BonusPolicy {
    private Passenger mike;
    private Mileage mileage;                    ❶
    [...]

    @Given("^we have a regular passenger with a mileage$")    ❷
    public void we_have_a_regular_passenger_with_a_mileage()
                throws Throwable {
        mike    = new Passenger("Mike", false);       ❸
        mileage  = new Mileage();
    }

    @When("^the regular passenger travels (\\d+) and (\\d+) and (\\d+)$")   ❹
    public void the_regular_passenger_travels_and_and(int mileage1, int
                mileage2, int mileage3) throws Throwable {
        mileage.addMileage(mike, mileage1);
        mileage.addMileage(mike, mileage2);           ❺
        mileage.addMileage(mike, mileage3);
    }

    @Then("^the bonus points of the regular passenger should be (\\d+)$")   ❻
    public void the_bonus_points_of_the_regular_passenger_should_be
                (int points) throws Throwable {
        mileage.calculateGivenPoints();
        assertEquals(points,                          ❽
            mileage.getPassengersPointsMap().get(mike).intValue());
    }                                  ❼
    [...]
}
```

In this listing:

- John declares the instance variables for the test, including `mileage`, and `mike` as a `Passenger` ❶.
- He writes the method corresponding to the `Given we have a regular passenger with a mileage` business logic step ❷ by initializing the passenger and the mileage ❸.
- He writes the method corresponding to the `When the regular passenger travels <mileage1> and <mileage2> and <mileage3>` business logic step ❹ by adding mileages to the regular passenger `mike` ❺.
- He writes the method corresponding to the `Then the bonus points of the regular passenger should be <points>` business logic step ❻ by calculating the given points ❼ and checking that the calculated value is as expected ❽.

- The rest of the methods are implemented in a similar way; we have covered the `Given`, `When`, and `Then` steps of one scenario.

If we run the bonus point tests now, they fail (figure 21.12), as the business logic is not yet implemented (the `addMileage` and `calculateGivenPoints` methods are empty; the business logic is implemented after the tests). In fact, we get a `Null-PointerException` at ❽ in listing 21.9: the points map does not exist yet, and the `Mileage` class is not yet implemented. John moves on to the implementation of the two remaining business logic methods from the `Mileage` class (`addMileage` and `calculateGivenPoints`).

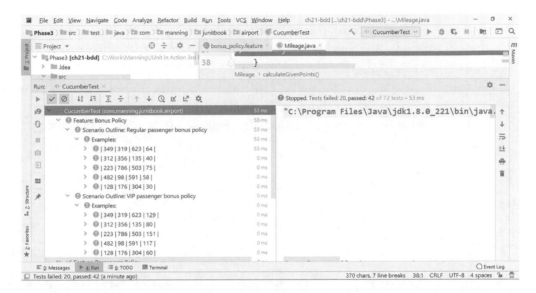

Figure 21.12 The bonus point tests fail when they are run before the business logic is implemented.

Listing 21.10 Implementing the business logic from the `Mileage` class

```
public void addMileage(Passenger passenger, int miles) {
    if (passengersMileageMap.containsKey(passenger)) {
        passengersMileageMap.put(passenger,
            passengersMileageMap.get(passenger) + miles);
    } else {
        passengersMileageMap.put(passenger, miles);
    }

}

public void calculateGivenPoints() {
    for (Passenger passenger : passengersMileageMap.keySet()) {
        if (passenger.isVip()) {
            passengersPointsMap.put(passenger,
                passengersMileageMap.get(passenger) / VIP_FACTOR);
```

❶ ❷ ❸ ❹ ❺

```
        } else {
            passengersPointsMap.put(passenger,
                passengersMileageMap.get(passenger) / REGULAR_FACTOR);
        }
    }
}
```
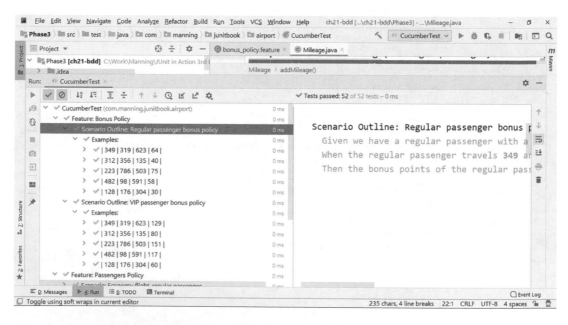

In this listing:

- In the `addMileage` method, John checks whether `passengersMileageMap` already contains a passenger ❶. If that passenger already exists, he adds the mileage to the passenger ❷; otherwise, he creates a new entry in the map having that passenger as a key and the miles as the initial value ❸.
- In the `calculateGivenPoints` method, he browses the passengers set ❹ and, for each passenger, if the passenger is a VIP, calculates the bonus points by dividing the mileage by the VIP factor ❺. Otherwise, he calculates the bonus points by dividing the mileage by the regular factor ❻.

Running the bonus point tests through `CucumberTest` is now successful. The results are nicely displayed, as shown in figure 21.13. John has successfully implemented the bonus policy feature while working BDD style with JUnit 5 and Cucumber.

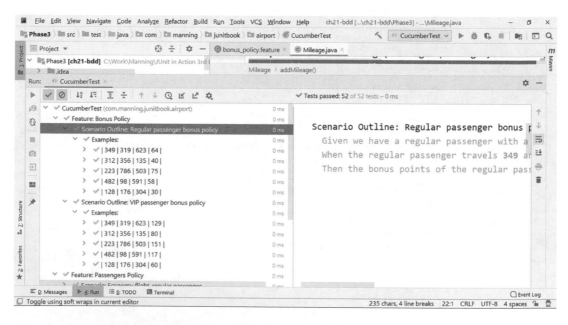

Figure 21.13   The bonus point tests succeed after the business logic is implemented.

21.3   *Working BDD style with JBehave and JUnit 5*

There are a few alternatives when choosing a BDD framework. In addition to Cucumber, we'll take a look at another very popular framework: JBehave.

21.3.1 Introducing JBehave

JBehave is a BDD testing framework that allows us to write stories in plain text that can be understood by everyone involved in the project. Through the stories, we can define scenarios that express the desired behavior.

Like other BDD frameworks, JBehave has its own terminology:

- *Story*—Covers one or more scenarios and represents an increment of business functionality that can be automatically executed
- *Scenario*—A real-life situation to interact with the application
- *Step*—Defined using the classic BDD keywords: `Given`, `When`, and `Then`

21.3.2 Moving a TDD feature to JBehave

With the help of JBehave, John would like to implement the same features and tests that he implemented with Cucumber. This will allow him to make some comparisons between the two BDD frameworks and decide which one to use.

John begins by introducing the JBehave dependency into the Maven configuration. He will first create a JBehave story, generate the test skeleton, and fill it in.

Listing 21.11   JBehave dependency added to the pom.xml file

```
<dependency>
    <groupId>org.jbehave</groupId>
    <artifactId>jbehave-core</artifactId>
    <version>4.1</version>
</dependency>
```

Next, John installs the plugins for IntelliJ. He goes to File > Settings > Plugins > Browse Repositories, types `JBehave`, and chooses JBehave Step Generator and JBehave Support (figure 21.14).

Figure 21.14   Installing the JBehave for Java plugins from the File > Settings > Plugins menu

John will now start creating the story. He follows the Maven standard folder structure and introduces the stories into the test/resources folder. He creates the folder com/manning/junitbook/airport and inserts the passengers_policy_story.story file. He also creates, in the test folder, the `com.manning.junitbook.airport` package containing the `PassengersPolicy` class (figure 21.15).

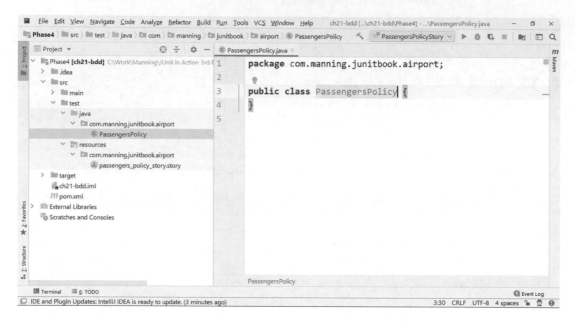

Figure 21.15   The newly added `PassengersPolicy` class corresponds to the story file found in the test/resources/com/manning/junitbook/airport folder.

The story contains meta-information about itself, the narrative (what it intends to do), and the scenarios.

Listing 21.12   passengers_policy_story.story file

```
Meta: Passengers Policy
      The company follows a policy of adding and removing passengers,
      depending on the passenger type and on the flight type

Narrative:
As a company
I want to be able to manage passengers and flights
So that the policies of the company are followed

Scenario: Economy flight, regular passenger
Given there is an economy flight
When we have a regular passenger
Then you can add and remove him from an economy flight
And you cannot add a regular passenger to an economy flight more than once
```

```
Scenario: Economy flight, VIP passenger
Given there is an economy flight
When we have a VIP passenger
Then you can add him but cannot remove him from an economy flight
And you cannot add a VIP passenger to an economy flight more than once

Scenario: Business flight, regular passenger
Given there is a business flight
When we have a regular passenger
Then you cannot add or remove him from a business flight

Scenario: Business flight, VIP passenger
Given there is a business flight
When we have a VIP passenger
Then you can add him but cannot remove him from a business flight
And you cannot add a VIP passenger to a business flight more than once

Scenario: Premium flight, regular passenger
Given there is a premium flight
When we have a regular passenger
Then you cannot add or remove him from a premium flight

Scenario: Premium flight, VIP passenger
Given there is a premium flight
When we have a VIP passenger
Then you can add and remove him from a premium flight
And you cannot add a VIP passenger to a premium flight more than once
```

To generate the steps into a Java file, John places the cursor on any not-yet-created test step (underlined in red) and presses Alt-Enter (figure 21.16).

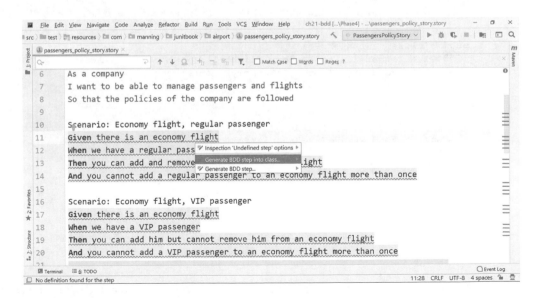

Figure 21.16   Pressing Alt-Enter and generating the BDD steps into a class

He generates all the steps in the newly created `PassengersPolicy` class (figure 21.17). The skeleton needs all the tests filled in.

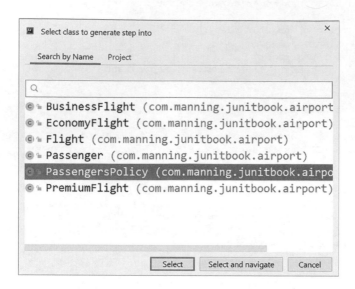

Figure 21.17   Choosing `PassengersPolicy` as the class in which to generate the steps of the story

The JBehave `PassengersPolicy` class is shown in the following listing with the tests skeleton filled in.

Listing 21.13   Skeleton of the JBehave `PassengersPolicy` test

```
[...]
public class PassengersPolicy {
    @Given("there is an economy flight")
    public void givenThereIsAnEconomyFlight() {

    }

    @When("we have a regular passenger")
    public void whenWeHaveARegularPassenger() {

    }

    @Then("you can add and remove him from an economy flight")
    public void thenYouCanAddAndRemoveHimFromAnEconomyFlight() {

    }
    [...]
}
```

John now implements the tests according to the business logic. He writes the code corresponding to each step defined through a method.

> **Listing 21.14** **Implemented tests from** `PassengersPolicy`

```
public class PassengersPolicy {
    private Flight economyFlight;          ❶
    private Passenger mike;
    [...]
                                           ❷
    @Given("there is an economy flight")        ❸
    public void givenThereIsAnEconomyFlight() {
        economyFlight = new EconomyFlight("1");
    }
                                           ❹
    @When("we have a regular passenger")        ❺
    public void whenWeHaveARegularPassenger() {
        mike  = new Passenger("Mike", false);
    }
                                                    ❻
    @Then("you can add and remove him from an economy flight")
    public void thenYouCanAddAndRemoveHimFromAnEconomyFlight() {
        assertAll("Verify all conditions for a regular passenger
                    and an economy flight",
            () -> assertEquals("1", economyFlight.getId()),
            () -> assertEquals(true,
                economyFlight.addPassenger(mike)),
            () -> assertEquals(1,
                economyFlight.getPassengersSet().size()),
            () -> assertEquals("Mike", new ArrayList<>(      ❼
              economyFlight.
                getPassengersSet()).get(0).getName()),
            () -> assertEquals(true,
                    economyFlight.removePassenger(mike)),
            () -> assertEquals(0,
                    economyFlight.getPassengersSet().size())
        );
    }
[...]

}
```

In this listing:

- John declares the instance variables for the test, including `economyFlight`, and `mike` as a `Passenger` ❶.
- He writes the method corresponding to the `Given there is an economy flight` business logic step ❷ by initializing `economyFlight` ❸.
- He writes the method corresponding to the `When we have a regular passenger` business logic step ❹ by initializing the regular passenger `mike` ❺.
- He writes the method corresponding to the `Then you can add and remove him from an economy flight` business logic step ❻ by checking all the conditions using the `assertAll` JUnit 5 method, which can now be read fluently ❼.
- The rest of the methods are implemented in a similar way; we have covered the `Given`, `When`, and `Then` steps of one scenario.

To be able to run these tests, John needs a special new class that represents the test configuration. He names this class `PassengersPolicyStory`.

Listing 21.15   `PassengersPolicyStory` class

```
[...]
public class PassengersPolicyStory extends JUnitStory {          ◁── ❶

    @Override
    public Configuration configuration() {         ❸
        return new MostUsefulConfiguration()       ◁──
                    .useStoryReporterBuilder(
                        new StoryReporterBuilder().
                            withDefaultFormats().              ❹
                        withFormats(Format.CONSOLE));
    }

    @Override                                                        ❺
    public InjectableStepsFactory stepsFactory() {     ◁──
        return new InstanceStepsFactory(configuration(),      ❻
                    new PassengersPolicy());
    }
}
```

❷ (pointing to the configuration method)

In this listing:

- John declares the `PassengersPolicyStory` class that extends `JUnitStory` ❶. A JBehave story class must extend `JUnitStory`.
- He overrides the `configuration` method ❷ and specifies that the configuration of the report is the one that works for the most situations that users are likely to encounter ❸ and that the report will be displayed on the console ❹.
- He overrides the `stepsFactory` method ❺ and specifies that the steps definition is to be found in the `PassengersPolicy` class ❻.

The result of running these tests is shown in figure 21.18. The tests are a success, and the code coverage is 100%. However, JBehave's reporting capabilities do not allow the same nice display as in the case of Cucumber.

We can compare the length of the pre-BDD `AirportTest` class, which has 207 lines, with the JBehave `PassengersPolicy` class, which has 157 lines (just like the Cucumber version). The testing code is now only 75% of the pre-BDD size, but it has the same 100% coverage. Where does this gain come from? Remember that the `AirportTest` file contained seven classes on three levels: `AirportTest` at the top level; one `EconomyFlightTest` and one `BusinessFlightTest` at the second level; and, at the third level, two `RegularPassenger` and two `VipPassenger` classes. The code duplication is now really jumping to our attention, but that was the solution that only had JUnit 5.

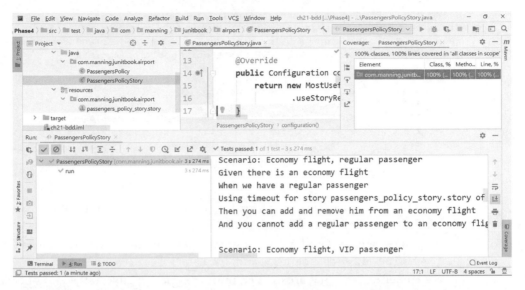

Figure 21.18 The JBehave passenger policy tests run successfully, and the code coverage is 100%.

21.3.3 Adding a new feature with the help of JBehave

John would like to implement, with the help of JBehave, the same new feature concerning the policy of bonus points awarded to passengers. John defines the scenarios for awarding bonus points in the bonus_policy_story.story file and generates JBehave tests that describe the scenarios. They are expected to fail at first.

Listing 21.16 bonus_policy_story.story file

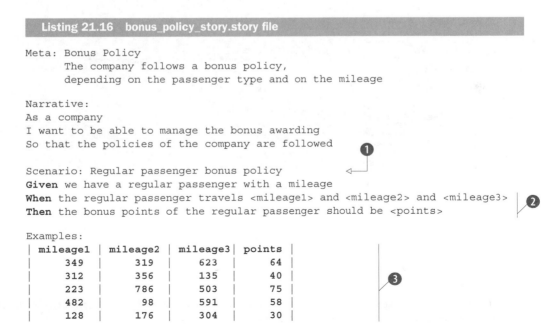

```
Meta: Bonus Policy
       The company follows a bonus policy,
       depending on the passenger type and on the mileage

Narrative:
As a company
I want to be able to manage the bonus awarding
So that the policies of the company are followed                ❶

Scenario: Regular passenger bonus policy                     ←
Given we have a regular passenger with a mileage
When the regular passenger travels <mileage1> and <mileage2> and <mileage3>   ❷
Then the bonus points of the regular passenger should be <points>

Examples:
| mileage1 | mileage2 | mileage3 | points |
|    349   |    319   |    623   |    64  |
|    312   |    356   |    135   |    40  |                    ❸
|    223   |    786   |    503   |    75  |
|    482   |     98   |    591   |    58  |
|    128   |    176   |    304   |    30  |
```

```
Scenario: VIP passenger bonus policy
Given we have a VIP passenger with a mileage
When the VIP passenger travels <mileage1> and <mileage2> and <mileage3>
Then the bonus points of the VIP passenger should be <points>

Examples:
| mileage1 | mileage2 | mileage3 | points |
|      349 |      319 |      623 |    129 |
|      312 |      356 |      135 |     80 |
|      223 |      786 |      503 |    151 |
|      482 |       98 |      591 |    117 |
|      128 |      176 |      304 |     60 |
```

In this listing:

- John introduces new scenarios for the bonus policy, using the Given, When, and Then keywords ❶.
- Values are replaced with parameters in the step definition: <mileage1>, <mileage2>, <mileage3>, and <points> ❷.
- The effective values are defined in the Examples table at the end of each Scenario ❸. The first row in the first table defines the values of three mileages (349, 319, 623). Adding them and dividing them by 20 (the regular passenger factor), we get the integer part 64 (the number of bonus points). This successfully replaces the JUnit 5 parameterized tests and has the advantage that the values are kept in the scenarios and are easy for everyone to understand.

In the test folder, John creates the BonusPolicy class in the com.manning.junitbook.airport package (figure 21.19).

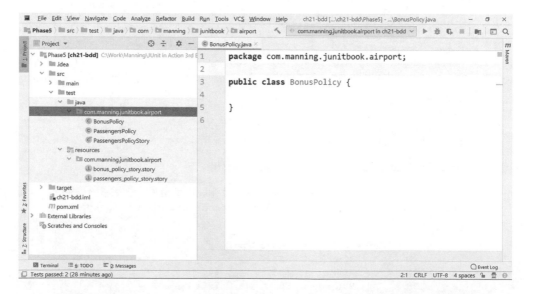

Figure 21.19   The newly introduced BonusPolicy class corresponds to the story file in the test/resources/com/manning/junitbook/airport folder.

To generate the steps in a Java file, John places the cursor on any not-yet-created step and presses Alt-Enter (figure 21.20). He generates all the steps in the newly created `BonusPolicy` class (figure 21.21). The `BonusPolicy` class is shown in listing 21.17 with the tests skeleton filled in.

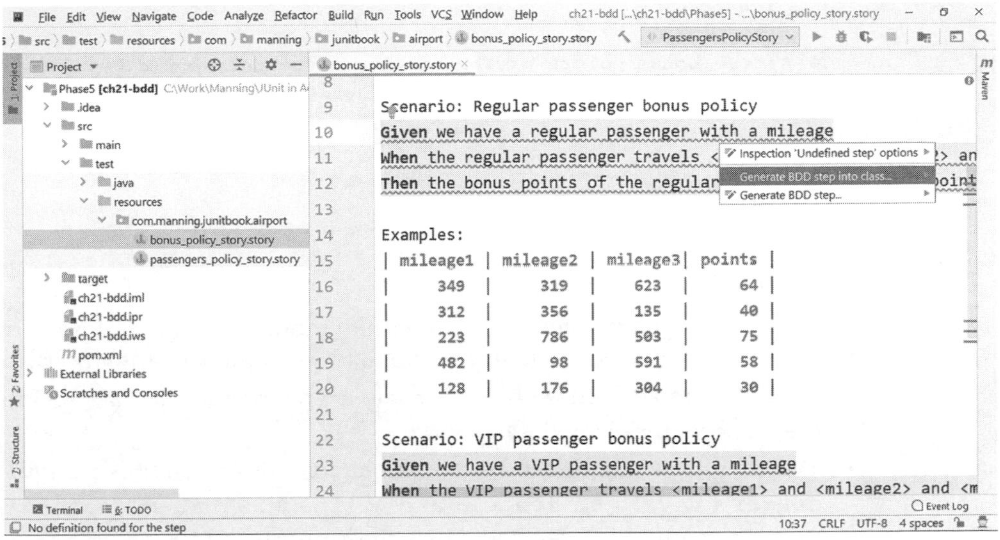

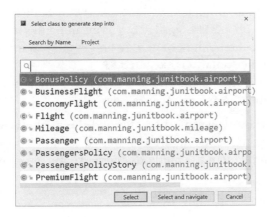

Figure 21.20 **Pressing Alt-Enter to generate the BDD steps in a class**

Figure 21.21 **Choosing** `BonusPolicy` **as the class in which to generate the steps of the story**

Listing 21.17 **Skeleton of the JBehave** `BonusPolicy` **test**

```
public class BonusPolicy {

    @Given("we have a regular passenger with a mileage")
    public void givenWeHaveARegularPassengerWithAMileage() {    ❶

    }
```

```
@When("the regular passenger travels <mileage1> and
        <mileage2> and <mileage3>")
public void whenTheRegularPassengerTravelsMileageAndMileageAndMileage(
        @Named("mileage1") int mileage1,
        @Named("mileage2") int mileage2,
        @Named("mileage3") int mileage3) {


}

@Then("the bonus points of the regular passenger should be <points>")
public void thenTheBonusPointsOfTheRegularPassengerShouldBePoints(
    @Named("points") int points) {


}
[...]
}
```

In this listing:

- The JBehave plugin generates a method annotated with `@Given("we have a regular passenger with a mileage")`, meaning this method is executed when the step `Given we have a regular passenger with a mileage` from the scenario is executed ❶.
- The plugin generates a method annotated with `@When("the regular passenger travels <mileage1> and <mileage2> and <mileage3>")`, meaning this method is executed when the step `When the regular passenger travels <mileage1> and <mileage2> and <mileage3>` from the scenario is executed ❷.
- The plugin generates a method annotated with `@Then("the bonus points of the regular passenger should be <points>")`, meaning this method is executed when the step `Then the bonus points of the regular passenger should be <points>` from the scenario is executed ❸.
- The rest of the methods generated by the JBehave plugin are similar; we have covered the `Given`, `When`, and `Then` steps of one scenario.

Next, John creates the `Mileage` class, declaring the fields and the methods but not implementing them yet. John needs to use the methods of this class for the tests, make these tests initially fail, and then implement the methods and make the tests pass.

Listing 21.18 `Mileage` class, with no implementation of the methods

```
public class Mileage {

    public static final int VIP_FACTOR = 10;
    public static final int REGULAR_FACTOR = 20;

    private Map<Passenger, Integer> passengersMileageMap =
                                new HashMap<>();
    private Map<Passenger, Integer> passengersPointsMap =
                                new HashMap<>();
```

```
    public void addMileage(Passenger passenger, int miles) {        ◄────┐
                                                                          ❸
    }

    public void calculateGivenPoints() {        ◄────┐
                                                      ❹
    }

}
```

In this listing:

- John declares the VIP_FACTOR and REGULAR_FACTOR constants corresponding to the factor by which the mileage is divided for each type of passenger in order to get the bonus points ❶.
- He declares passengersMileageMap and passengersPointsMap, two maps having the passenger as a key and keeping as a value the mileage and points for that passenger, respectively ❷.
- He declares the addMileage method, which populates passengersMileageMap with the mileage for each passenger ❸. The method does not do anything for now; it will be written later to fix the tests.
- He declares the calculateGivenPoints method, which populates passengersPointsMap with the bonus points for each passenger ❹. The method does not do anything for now; it will be written later to fix the tests.

John now turns his attention to writing the unimplemented tests from the BonusPolicy class to follow the feature's business logic.

Listing 21.19 Business logic of the steps from BonusPolicy

```
[...]
public class BonusPolicy {
    private Passenger mike;        ◄────┐
    private Mileage mileage;            ❶
    [...]
                                                                              ❷
    @Given("we have a regular passenger with a mileage")        ◄────┐
    public void givenWeHaveARegularPassengerWithAMileage() {
        mike    = new Passenger("Mike", false);                      ❸
        mileage  = new Mileage();
    }

    @When("the regular passenger travels <mileage1> and <mileage2> and              ❹
                                <mileage3>")
    public void the_regular_passenger_travels_and_and(@Named("mileage1")
                int mileage1, @Named("mileage2") int mileage2,
                @Named("mileage3") int mileage3) {
        mileage.addMileage(mike, mileage1);
        mileage.addMileage(mike, mileage2);        ❺
        mileage.addMileage(mike, mileage3);
    }
```

```
@Then("the bonus points of the regular passenger should be <points>")
public void the_bonus_points_of_the_regular_passenger_should_be
            (@Named("points") int points) {
    mileage.calculateGivenPoints();
    assertEquals(points,
        mileage.getPassengersPointsMap().get(mike).intValue());
}
[...]
}
```

In this listing:

- John declares the instance variables for the test, including `mileage`, and `mike` as a `Passenger` ❶.
- He writes the method corresponding to the `Given we have a regular passenger with a mileage` business logic step ❷ by initializing the passenger and the mileage ❸.
- He writes the method corresponding to the `When the regular passenger travels <mileage1> and <mileage2> and <mileage3>` business logic step ❹ by adding mileages to the regular passenger `mike` ❺.
- He writes the method corresponding to the `Then the bonus points of the regular passenger should be <points>` business logic step ❻ by calculating the points ❼ and checking that the calculated value is as expected ❽.
- The rest of the methods are implemented in a similar way; we have covered the `Given`, `When`, and `Then` steps of one scenario.

To run these tests, John needs a new special class that represents the test configuration. He names this class `BonusPolicyStory`.

Listing 21.20   BonusPolicyStory class

```
[...]
public class BonusPolicyStory extends JUnitStory {          ❶

    @Override
    public Configuration configuration() {
        return new MostUsefulConfiguration()                ❸
                .useStoryReporterBuilder(
                    new StoryReporterBuilder().
                        withDefaultFormats().                ❹
                        withFormats(Format.CONSOLE));
    }                                                        ❷

    @Override
    public InjectableStepsFactory stepsFactory() {           ❺
        return new InstanceStepsFactory(configuration(),
                new BonusPolicy());                          ❻
    }
}
```

In this listing:

- John declares the `BonusPolicyStory` class that extends `JUnitStory` ❶.
- He overrides the `configuration` method ❷ and specifies that the configuration of the report is the one that works for the most situations that users are likely to encounter ❸, and that the report will be displayed on the console ❹.
- He overrides the `stepsFactory` method ❺ and specifies that the step definition is found in the `BonusPolicy` class ❻.

If we run the bonus point tests now, they fail (figure 21.22), because the business logic is not yet implemented (the `addMileage` and `calculateGivenPoints` methods are empty).

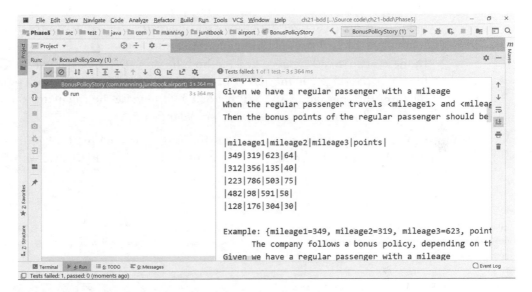

Figure 21.22   **The JBehave bonus point tests fail before the business logic is implemented.**

John goes back to the implementation of the two remaining business logic methods from the `Mileage` class (`addMileage` and `calculateGivenPoints`).

Listing 21.21   **Implementing business logic from the `Mileage` class**

```
public void addMileage(Passenger passenger, int miles) {
    if (passengersMileageMap.containsKey(passenger)) {
        passengersMileageMap.put(passenger,
            passengersMileageMap.get(passenger) + miles);          ❶
    } else {
        passengersMileageMap.put(passenger, miles);        ⟵
    }                                                              ❷
}
```

```
public void calculateGivenPoints() {
    for (Passenger passenger : passengersMileageMap.keySet()) {
        if (passenger.isVip()) {
            passengersPointsMap.put(passenger,
                passengersMileageMap.get(passenger)/ VIP_FACTOR);
        } else {
            passengersPointsMap.put(passenger,
                passengersMileageMap.get(passenger)/ REGULAR_FACTOR);
        }
    }
}
```

In this listing:

- In the `addMileage` method, John checks whether `passengersMileageMap` already contains a passenger ❶. If that passenger already exists, he adds the mileage to the passenger ❷; otherwise, he creates a new entry in the map with that passenger as a key and the miles as the initial value ❸.
- In the `calculateGivenPoints` method, he browses the passenger set ❸ and, for each passenger, if the passenger is a VIP, calculates the bonus points by dividing the mileage by the VIP factor ❹. Otherwise, he calculates the bonus points by dividing the mileage by the regular factor ❺.

Running the bonus point tests now is successful, as shown in figure 21.23. John has successfully implemented the bonus policy feature while working BDD style with JUnit 5 and JBehave.

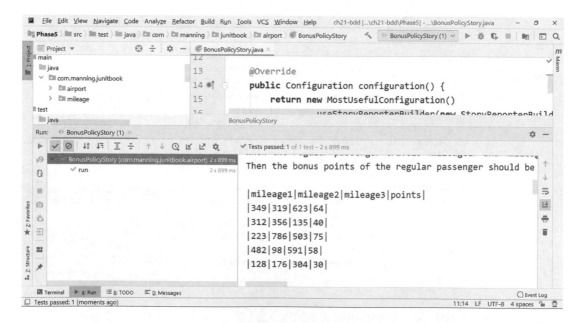

Figure 21.23   The JBehave bonus point tests succeed after the business logic has been implemented.

21.4 *Comparing Cucumber and JBehave*

Cucumber and JBehave have similar approaches and supporting BDD concepts. They are different frameworks but are built on the same well-defined BDD principles that we have emphasized.

They are based around features (Cucumber) or stories (JBehave). A feature is a collection of stories, expressed from the point of view of a specific project stakeholder. They use some of the same BDD keywords (`Given`, `When`, `Then`) but also have some variations in terms like `Scenario Outline` for Cucumber and `Scenario with Examples` for JBehave.

IntelliJ IDE support for both Cucumber and JBehave is provided through plugins that help from generating steps in Java code to checking code coverage. The Cucumber plugin produces nicer output, allowing us to follow the full testing hierarchy at a glance and displaying everything with significant colors. It also lets us run a test directly from the feature text file, which is easier to follow, especially for nontechnical people.

JBehave reached its maturity phase some time ago, while the Cucumber code base is still updated very frequently. For example, at the time of writing, the Cucumber GitHub displays tens of commits from the previous seven days, whereas the JBehave GitHub displays a single commit in the last seven days. Cucumber also has a more active community at the time of writing; articles on blogs and forums are more recent and frequent, which makes troubleshooting easier for developers. In addition, Cucumber is available for other programming languages. In terms of code size compared to the pre-BDD situation, both Cucumber and JBehave show similar performance, reducing the size of the initial code by the same proportion.

Choosing one of these frameworks is a matter of habit or preference (personal preference or project preference). We have shown them side by side in a very practical and comparable way so that you can eventually make your own choice.

The next chapter is dedicated to building a test pyramid strategy, from the low level to the high level, and applying it while working with JUnit 5.

Summary

This chapter has covered the following:

- Introducing BDD, a software development technique that encourages teams to deliver software that matters and supports cooperation between stakeholders
- Analyzing the benefits of BDD: addressing user needs, clarity, change support, automation support, focus on adding business value, and cost reduction
- Analyzing the challenges of BDD: it requires engagement and strong collaboration, interaction, direct communication, and constant feedback
- Moving a TDD application to BDD
- Developing business logic with the help of Cucumber by creating a separate feature, generating the skeleton of the testing code, writing the tests, and implementing the code

- Developing business logic with the help of JBehave by creating a separate story, generating the skeleton of the testing code, writing the tests, and implementing the code
- Comparing Cucumber and JBehave in terms of the BDD principles, ease of use, and code size needed to implement functionality

22

Implementing a test pyramid strategy with JUnit 5

This chapter covers

- Building unit tests for components in isolation
- Building integration tests for units as a group
- Building system tests for complete software
- Building acceptance tests and making sure software is compliant with business requirements

> *The test pyramid is a way of thinking about how different kinds of automated tests should be used to create a balanced portfolio. Its essential point is that you should have many more low-level UnitTests than high-level BroadStackTests running through a GUI.*
>
> —Martin Fowler

As we have discovered in the previous chapters, software testing has several purposes. Tests make us interact with the application and understand how it works. Testing helps us deliver software that meets expectations. It is a metric of the quality of the code and protects us against the possibility of introducing regressions. Consequently, effectively and systematically organizing the process of software testing is very important.

22.1   *Software testing levels*

The different levels of software tests can be regarded as a pyramid, as shown in figure 22.1. In this chapter, we'll discuss the following levels of software testing (from lowest to highest):

- *Unit testing*—Unit testing is at the foundation of the pyramid. It focuses on methods or classes (individual units) by testing each one in isolation to determine whether it works according to expectations.
- *Integration testing*—Individual, verified software components are combined in larger aggregates and tested together.
- *System testing*—Testing is performed on a complete system to evaluate its compliance with the specification. System testing requires no knowledge of the design or code but focuses on the functionality of the entire system.
- *Acceptance testing*—Acceptance testing uses scenarios and test cases to check whether the application satisfies the expectations of the end user.

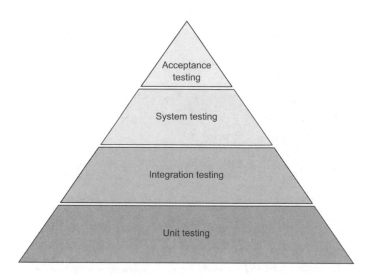

Figure 22.1   **The testing pyramid has many simple units at the bottom level, and fewer, more complicated units at the top.**

These levels represent a hierarchy built from simple to complex and also a view of the development process, from its beginning to the later phases. Low-level testing addresses individual components; it is concerned more with details and less with the broader view. High-level testing is more abstract; it verifies the overall goals and features of the system and is more focused on the user's interaction with the GUI and how the system works as a whole.

When it comes to what to test, we can identify the following:

- *Business logic*—How the program translates the business rules from the real world.
- *Bad input values*—For example, in our example flight-management application, we cannot assign a negative number of seats on a flight.

- *Boundary conditions*—Extremes of an input domain, such as the maximum or minimum. We might test flights having zero passengers or the maximum allowed number of passengers.
- *Unexpected conditions*—Conditions that are not part of the normal operation of a program. For instance, a flight cannot change its origin once it has taken off.
- *Invariants*—Expressions whose values do not change during program execution. For example, a person's identifier cannot change during the execution of the program.
- *Regressions*—Bugs introduced in an existing system after upgrades or patches.

We'll start now by analyzing the implementation of each testing level, starting from the bottom.

22.2 Unit testing: Basic components working in isolation

In this chapter, we'll demonstrate how Thomas, a developer with Tested Data Systems, builds a test pyramid strategy for the flight-management application. The application that Thomas is taking over is composed of two classes: `Passenger` (listing 22.1) and `Flight` (listing 22.2).

Listing 22.1 Passenger class

```java
public class Passenger {

    private String identifier;
    private String name;                                                    ❶
    private String countryCode;
    private String ssnRegex =
        "^(?!000|666)[0-8][0-9]{2}-(?!00)[0-9]{2}-(?!0000)[0-9]{4}$";        ❷
    private String nonUsIdentifierRegex =
        "^(?!000|666)[9][0-9]{2}-(?!00)[0-9]{2}-(?!0000)[0-9]{4}$";          ❸
    private Pattern pattern;                                                 ❹

    public Passenger(String identifier, String name, String countryCode){   ❺
        pattern = countryCode.equals("US")? Pattern.compile(ssnRegex):       ❻
                Pattern.compile(nonUsIdentifierRegex);
        Matcher matcher = pattern.matcher(identifier);
        if(!matcher.matches()) {                                             ❼
            throw new RuntimeException("Invalid identifier");
        }

        if(!Arrays.asList(Locale.getISOCountries()).contains(countryCode)){  ❽
            throw new RuntimeException("Invalid country code");
        }

        this.identifier = identifier;
        this.name = name;                                                    ❾
        this.countryCode = countryCode;
    }
}
```

```java
public String getIdentifier() {                              ⑩
    return identifier;
}

public void setIdentifier(String identifier) {
    Matcher matcher = pattern.matcher(identifier);
    if(!matcher.matches()) {
        throw new RuntimeException("Invalid identifier");    ⑪
    }

    this.identifier = identifier;
}

public String getName() {
    return name;
}

public void setName(String name) {                           ⑩
    this.name = name;
}

public String getCountryCode() {
    return countryCode;
}

public void setCountryCode(String countryCode) {
    if(!Arrays.asList(Locale.getISOCountries()).
                        contains(countryCode)){
        throw new RuntimeException("Invalid country code");  ⑫
    }

    this.countryCode = countryCode;
}

@Override
public String toString() {
    return "Passenger " + getName() + " with identifier: "   ⑬
            + getIdentifier() + " from " + getCountryCode();
}
}
```

In this listing:

- Thomas declares the `identifier`, `name`, and `countryCode` instance variables for `Passenger` ❶.
- If the passenger is a US citizen, the identifier is their Social Security number (SSN). `ssnRegex` describes the regular expression to be followed by the SSN. The SSN must conform to the following rules: the first three digits cannot be 000, 666, or between 900 and 999 ❷.
- If the passenger is not a US citizen, the identifier is generated by the company, following rules similar to those for an SSN. `nonUsIdentifierRegex` only allows identifiers with the first digits between 900 and 999 ❸. Thomas also declares a pattern that checks whether an `identifier` is following the rules ❹.

- In the constructor ❺, Thomas creates the pattern ❻, checks whether the identifier matches it ❼, checks whether the country code is valid ❽, and then constructs the passenger ❾.
- He provides getters and setters for the fields ❿, checking the validity of the input data for an identifier that has to match the pattern ⓫ and that the country code exists ⓬.
- He also overrides the toString method to include the name, identifier, and country code of the passenger ⓭.

Listing 22.2 Flight **class**

```
public class Flight {

    private String flightNumber;
    private int seats;
    private int passengers;
    private String origin;
    private String destination;
    private boolean flying;
    private boolean takenOff;
    private boolean landed;

    private String flightNumberRegex = "^[A-Z]{2}\\d{3,4}$";
    private Pattern pattern = Pattern.compile(flightNumberRegex);

    public Flight(String flightNumber, int seats) {
        Matcher matcher = pattern.matcher(flightNumber);
        if(!matcher.matches()) {
            throw new RuntimeException("Invalid flight number");
        }
        this.flightNumber = flightNumber;
        this.seats = seats;
        this.passengers = 0;
        this.flying = false;
        this.takenOff = false;
        this.landed = false;
    }

    public String getFlightNumber() {
        return flightNumber;
    }

    public int getSeats() {
        return seats;
    }

    public void setSeats(int seats) {
        if(passengers > seats) {
            throw new RuntimeException("Cannot reduce the number of
                    seats under the number of existing passengers!");
        }

        this.seats = seats;
    }
```

❶ ❷ ❸ ❹ ❺ ❻ ❼

```java
    public int getPassengers() {
        return passengers;
    }

    public String getOrigin() {
        return origin;
    }

    public void setOrigin(String origin) {
        if(takenOff){
            throw new RuntimeException("Flight cannot change its origin
                                        any longer!");
        }

        this.origin = origin;
    }

    public String getDestination() {
        return destination;
    }

    public void setDestination(String destination) {
        if(landed){
            throw new RuntimeException("Flight cannot change its
                                        destination any longer!");
        }

        this.destination = destination;
    }

    public boolean isFlying() {
        return flying;
    }

    public boolean isTakenOff() {
        return takenOff;
    }

    public boolean isLanded() {
        return landed;
    }

    @Override
    public String toString() {
        return "Flight " + getFlightNumber() + " from " + getOrigin()
                         + " to " + getDestination();
    }

    public void addPassenger() {
        if(passengers >= seats) {
            throw new RuntimeException("Not enough seats!");
        }
        passengers++;
    }
```

6

8

6

9

6

10

11

```
public void takeOff() {
    System.out.println(this + " is taking off");
    flying = true;
    takenOff = true;
}

public void land() {
    System.out.println(this + " is landing");
    flying = false;
    landed = true;
}

}
```

⑫

⑬

In this listing:

- Thomas declares the instance variables for a `Flight` ❶.
- The flight number needs to match a regular expression: a code for an airline service consists of a two-character airline designator and a three- or four-digit number ❷. Thomas also declares a `pattern` that checks whether a flight number is following the rules ❸.
- In the constructor, he checks whether the flight number matches the pattern ❹ and then constructs the flight ❺.
- He provides getters and setters for the fields ❻, checking that there are not more passengers than seats ❼, that the origin cannot change after the plane has taken off ❽, and that the destination cannot change after the plane has landed ❾.
- He overrides the `toString` method to display the flight number, origin, and destination ❿.
- When he adds a passenger to the plane, he checks that there are enough seats ⓫.
- When the plane takes off, he prints a message and changes the state of the plane ⑫. He also prints a message and changes the state of the plane when the plane lands ⑬.

The functionality of the `Passenger` class is verified in the `PassengerTest` class.

Listing 22.3   `PassengerTest` class

```
public class PassengerTest {

    @Test
    public void testPassengerCreation() {
        Passenger passenger = new Passenger("123-45-6789",
                                            "John Smith", "US");
        assertNotNull(passenger);
    }
```

❶

```java
@Test
public void testNonUsPassengerCreation() {
    Passenger passenger = new Passenger("900-45-6789",
                                "John Smith", "GB");
    assertNotNull(passenger);
}


@Test
public void testCreatePassengerWithInvalidSsn() {
    assertThrows(RuntimeException.class,
            ()->{
                Passenger passenger = new Passenger("123-456-789",
                                        "John Smith", "US");
            });
    assertThrows(RuntimeException.class,
            ()->{
                Passenger passenger = new Passenger("900-45-6789",
                                        "John Smith", "US");
            });
}


@Test
public void testCreatePassengerWithInvalidNonUsIdentifier() {
    assertThrows(RuntimeException.class,
            ()->{
                Passenger passenger = new Passenger("900-456-789",
                                        "John Smith", "GB");
            });
    assertThrows(RuntimeException.class,
            ()->{
                Passenger passenger = new Passenger("123-45-6789",
                                        "John Smith", "GB");
            });
}


@Test
public void testCreatePassengerWithInvalidCountryCode() {
    assertThrows(RuntimeException.class,
            ()->{
                Passenger passenger = new Passenger("900-45-6789",
                                        "John Smith", "GJ");
            });
}


@Test
public void testSetInvalidSsn() {
    assertThrows(RuntimeException.class,
            ()->{
                Passenger passenger = new Passenger("123-45-6789",
                                        "John Smith", "US");
                passenger.setIdentifier("123-456-789");
            });

}
```

```java
@Test
public void testSetValidSsn() {
        Passenger passenger = new Passenger("123-45-6789",
                                "John Smith", "US");
        passenger.setIdentifier("123-98-7654");
        assertEquals("123-98-7654", passenger.getIdentifier());
}
```
7

```java
@Test
public void testSetValidNonUsIdentifier() {
    Passenger passenger = new Passenger("900-45-6789",
                        "John Smith", "GB");
    passenger.setIdentifier("900-98-7654");
    assertEquals("900-98-7654", passenger.getIdentifier());
}
```
8

```java
@Test
public void testSetInvalidCountryCode() {
    assertThrows(RuntimeException.class,
            () ->{
                Passenger passenger = new Passenger("123-45-6789",
                                "John Smith", "US");
                passenger.setCountryCode("GJ");
            });

}
```
9

```java
@Test
public void testSetValidCountryCode() {
        Passenger passenger = new Passenger("123-45-6789",
                                "John Smith", "US");
        passenger.setCountryCode("GB");
        assertEquals("GB", passenger.getCountryCode());
}
```
10

```java
@Test
public void testPassengerToString() {
    Passenger passenger = new Passenger("123-45-6789",
                        "John Smith", "US");
    passenger.setName("John Brown");
    assertEquals("Passenger John Brown with identifier:
                123-45-6789 from US",  passenger.toString());
}

}
```
11

In this listing:

- Thomas checks the correct creation of a US passenger ❶ and a non-US passenger ❷, with correct identifiers.
- He checks that he cannot set an invalid identifier for a US citizen ❸ or a non-US citizen ❹.
- He checks that he cannot set an invalid country code ❺ or an invalid SSN ❻.

- He checks that he can set a valid SSN for a US citizen ❼ and a valid identifier for a non-US citizen ❽.
- He checks setting an invalid country code ❾ and a valid country code ❿.
- He checks the behavior of the `toString` method ⓫.

The functionality of the `Flight` class is verified in the `FlightTest` class.

Listing 22.4   `FlightTest` class

```java
public class FlightTest {

    @Test
    public void testFlightCreation() {
        Flight flight = new Flight("AA123", 100);           ❶
        assertNotNull(flight);
    }

    @Test
    public void testInvalidFlightNumber() {
        assertThrows(RuntimeException.class,
                ()->{
                    Flight flight = new Flight("AA12", 100);
                });                                          ❷
        assertThrows(RuntimeException.class,
                ()->{
                    Flight flight = new Flight("AA12345", 100);
                });
    }

    @Test
    public void testValidFlightNumber() {
        Flight flight = new Flight("AA345", 100);
        assertNotNull(flight);                              ❸
        flight = new Flight("AA3456", 100);
        assertNotNull(flight);
    }

    @Test
    public void testAddPassengers() {
        Flight flight = new Flight("AA1234", 50);
        flight.setOrigin("London");
        flight.setDestination("Bucharest");
        for(int i=0; i<flight.getSeats(); i++) {
            flight.addPassenger();
        }                                                   ❹
        assertEquals(50, flight.getPassengers());
        assertThrows(RuntimeException.class,
                ()->{
                    flight.addPassenger();
                });

    }
```

```
@Test
public void testSetInvalidSeats() {
    Flight flight = new Flight("AA1234", 50);
    flight.setOrigin("London");
    flight.setDestination("Bucharest");
    for(int i=0; i<flight.getSeats(); i++) {
        flight.addPassenger();
    }
    assertEquals(50, flight.getPassengers());
    assertThrows(RuntimeException.class,
            ()->{
                flight.setSeats(49);
            });
}
```

```
@Test
public void testSetValidSeats() {
    Flight flight = new Flight("AA1234", 50);
    flight.setOrigin("London");
    flight.setDestination("Bucharest");
    for(int i=0; i<flight.getSeats(); i++) {
        flight.addPassenger();
    }
        assertEquals(50, flight.getPassengers());
    flight.setSeats(52);
        assertEquals(52, flight.getSeats());
}
```

```
@Test
public void testChangeOrigin() {
    Flight flight = new Flight("AA1234", 50);
    flight.setOrigin("London");
    flight.setDestination("Bucharest");
    flight.takeOff();
    assertEquals(true, flight.isFlying());
    assertEquals(true, flight.isTakenOff());
    assertEquals(false, flight.isLanded());
    assertThrows(RuntimeException.class,
            ()->{
                flight.setOrigin("Manchester");
            });
}
```

```
@Test
public void testChangeDestination() {
 Flight flight = new Flight("AA1234", 50);
    flight.setOrigin("London");
    flight.setDestination("Bucharest");
    flight.takeOff();
    flight.land();
    assertThrows(RuntimeException.class,
            ()->{
                flight.setDestination("Sibiu");
            });
}
```

```
@Test
public void testLand() {
    Flight flight = new Flight("AA1234", 50);
    flight.setOrigin("London");
    flight.setDestination("Bucharest");
    flight.takeOff();
    assertEquals(true, flight.isTakenOff());
    assertEquals(false, flight.isLanded());
    flight.land();
    assertEquals(true, flight.isTakenOff());
    assertEquals(true, flight.isLanded());
    assertEquals(false, flight.isFlying());
}

}
```

In this listing:

- Thomas checks the creation of a flight ❶.
- He checks that he cannot set an invalid flight number ❷ but can set a valid one ❸.
- He checks that he can add passengers only within the seat limit ❹.
- He checks that he cannot set the number of seats less than the number of passengers ❺, but he can set it greater than the number of passengers ❻.
- He checks that he cannot change the origin after the plane has taken off ❼ or the destination after the plane has landed ❽.
- He checks that the plane has changed its state after taking off ❾ and again after landing ❿.

The result of running the unit tests for the `Passenger` and `Flight` classes is successful, and the code coverage is 100%, as shown in figure 22.2.

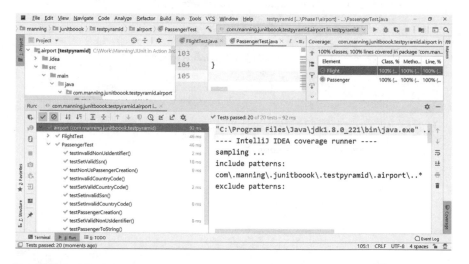

Figure 22.2   The unit tests for `Passenger` and `Flight` check the correct behavior of the individual classes and run successfully.

Thomas has successfully created the application consisting of the `Passenger` and `Flight` classes and has checked that each class works fine individually. Using JUnit 5 tests, he has checked the following:

- Passenger identifier and country code restrictions
- Flight number restrictions (verifying that they start with two letters, followed by three of four digits)
- Bad input values (such as a flight with a negative number of seats)
- Boundary conditions (he cannot add more passengers than there are available seats)

From here, Thomas will move on to integrate the functionality of the two classes.

22.3 *Integration testing: Units combined into a group*

Integration testing combines individual units to check their interactions. The fact that units work fine in isolation does not necessarily mean they work fine together.

Thomas will now investigate how the `Passenger` and `Flight` classes cooperate. They represent two different units; to cooperate, they need to expose appropriate interfaces (APIs). However, interfaces can have defects that prevent interactions, such as missing methods or methods that do not receive the appropriate types of arguments.

When Thomas analyzes the current interfaces, he finds that a passenger should be added to a flight and removed from a flight. Currently, he is only modifying the number of passengers: the current interface is missing an `addPassenger` method as well as a `removePassenger` method. The `Flight` class should be more integrated with `Passenger` and maintain the set of recorded passengers. The changes to the `Flight` class are shown in the following listing.

Listing 22.5 Modified `Flight` class

```java
public class Flight {                                    ❶

    Set<Passenger> passengers = new HashSet< >();    ←

    [...]
    public boolean addPassenger(Passenger passenger) {   ❷   ←
        if(passengers.size() >= seats) {
            throw new RuntimeException(                              ❸
         "Cannot add more passengers than the capacity of the flight!");
        }
        return passengers.add(passenger);           ←
    }                                            ❹

    public boolean removePassenger(Passenger passenger) {   ❺
        return passengers.remove(passenger);
    }

    public int getPassengersNumber() {
        return passengers.size();                    ❻
    }
    [...]
}
```

In this listing:

- Thomas adds a `passengers` field to hold the set of passengers ❶. This replaces the integer `passengers` field, and consequently the `this.passengers = 0` initialization is no longer needed.
- He adds an `addPassenger` method ❷ that checks whether there are enough seats ❸ and then adds a passenger to the set of passengers ❹.
- He adds a `removePassenger` method that removes a passenger from the set of passengers ❺ and the `getPassengersNumber` method that returns the size of the passengers set ❻.

To perform integration testing, Thomas decides to use Arquillian—a testing framework for Java that uses JUnit to execute test cases against a Java container. We introduced Arquillian in chapter 9, and we will revisit it now in the context of integration testing.

Arquillian does not have a JUnit 5 extension at this time, but it is very popular and has been frequently adopted in projects up to JUnit 4. It greatly simplifies the task of managing containers, deployments, and framework initializations.

Arquillian tests Java EE applications. Using it in our examples requires some basic knowledge of Contexts and Dependency Injection (CDI), a Java EE standard for the inversion of control design pattern. We'll explain the most important ideas as we go so that you can quickly adopt Arquillian within your projects.

ShrinkWrap is an external dependency used with Arquillian and a simple way to create archives in Java. Using the fluent ShrinkWrap API, developers at Tested Data Systems can assemble jar, war, and ear files to be deployed directly by Arquillian during testing. Such files are archives that can contain all classes needed to run an application. ShrinkWrap helps define the deployments and the descriptors to be loaded to the Java container being tested against.

Thomas will use a list of 50 passengers on the flight, to be described by identifier, name, and country. The list is stored in the following CSV file.

Listing 22.6   flights_information.csv file

```
123-45-6789; John Smith; US
900-45-6789; Jane Underwood; GB
123-45-6790; James Perkins; US
900-45-6790; Mary Calderon; GB
123-45-6791; Noah Graves; US
900-45-6791; Jake Chavez; GB
123-45-6792; Oliver Aguilar; US
900-45-6792; Emma Mccann; GB
123-45-6793; Margaret Knight; US
900-45-6793; Amelia Curry; GB
123-45-6794; Jack Vaughn; US
900-45-6794; Liam Lewis; GB
123-45-6795; Olivia Reyes; US
900-45-6795; Samantha Poole; GB
```

```
123-45-6796; Patricia Jordan; US
900-45-6796; Robert Sherman; GB
123-45-6797; Mason Burton; US
900-45-6797; Harry Christensen; GB
123-45-6798; Jennifer Mills; US
900-45-6798; Sophia Graham; GB
123-45-6799; Bethany King; US
900-45-6799; Isla Taylor; GB
123-45-6800; Jacob Tucker; US
900-45-6800; Michael Jenkins; GB
123-45-6801; Emily Johnson; US
900-45-6801; Elizabeth Berry; GB
123-45-6802; Isabella Carpenter; US
900-45-6802; William Fields; GB
123-45-6803; Charlie Lord; US
900-45-6803; Joanne Castaneda; GB
123-45-6804; Ava Daniel; US
900-45-6804; Linda Wise; GB
123-45-6805; Thomas French; US
900-45-6805; Joe Wyatt; GB
123-45-6806; David Byrne; US
900-45-6806; Megan Austin; GB
123-45-6807; Mia Ward; US
900-45-6807; Barbara Mac; GB
123-45-6808; George Burns; US
900-45-6808; Richard Moody; GB
123-45-6809; Victoria Montgomery; US
900-45-6809; Susan Todd; GB
123-45-6810; Joseph Parker; US
900-45-6810; Alexander Alexander; GB
123-45-6811; Jessica Pacheco; US
900-45-6811; William Schneider; GB
123-45-6812; Damian Reid; US
900-45-6812; Daniel Hart; GB
123-45-6813; Thomas Wright; US
900-45-6813; Charles Bradley; GB
```

Listing 22.7 implements the `FlightBuilderUtil` class, which parses the CSV file and populates the flight with the corresponding passengers. Thus, the code brings the information from an external file to the memory of the application.

Listing 22.7 `FlightBuilderUtil` class

```
public class FlightBuilderUtil {

    public static Flight buildFlightFromCsv() throws IOException {
        Flight flight = new Flight("AA1234", 50);
        flight.setOrigin("London");                          ❶
        flight.setDestination("Bucharest");

        try(BufferedReader reader =
            new BufferedReader(new FileReader(               ❷
                "src/test/resources/flights_information.csv")))
        {
```

```
        String line = null;
        do {                                            ❸
            line = reader.readLine();                  ◁─────┘
            if (line != null) {
              String[] passengerString = line.toString().split(";");
              Passenger passenger =
❹                     new Passenger(passengerString[0].trim(),
                                    passengerString[1].trim(),      ❺
                                    passengerString[1].trim());
              flight.addPassenger(passenger);           ◁─────
            }                                                       ❻
        } while (line != null);


    }

    return flight;          ◁─────┐
    }                           ❼
}
```

In this listing:

- Thomas creates a flight and sets its origin and destination ❶.
- He opens the CSV file to parse ❷.
- He reads the file line by line ❸, splits each line ❹, creates a passenger based on the information that has been read ❺, and adds the passenger to the flight ❻.
- He returns the fully populated flight from the method ❼.

So far, all the classes that have been implemented during development of the flight- and passenger-management tasks are pure Java classes; no particular framework or technology has been used. As we mentioned, the Arquillian testing framework executes test cases against a Java container, so using it requires some understanding of notions related to Java EE and CDI. Arquillian abstracts the container or application startup logic and deploys the application to the targeted runtime (an application server, embedded or managed) to execute test cases.

For this example, the following listing shows the dependencies that Thomas needs to add to the Maven pom.xml configuration file to work with Arquillian.

Listing 22.8   Required pom.xml dependencies

```xml
<dependencyManagement>
     <dependencies>
        <dependency>
            <groupId>org.jboss.arquillian</groupId>
            <artifactId>arquillian-bom</artifactId>        ❶
            <version>1.4.0.Final</version>
            <scope>import</scope>
            <type>pom</type>
        </dependency>
     </dependencies>
</dependencyManagement>
```

```
<dependencies>
     <dependency>
          <groupId>org.jboss.spec</groupId>
          <artifactId>jboss-javaee-7.0</artifactId>        ❷
          <version>1.0.3.Final</version>
          <type>pom</type>
          <scope>provided</scope>
     </dependency>
     <dependency>
          <groupId>org.junit.vintage</groupId>
          <artifactId>junit-vintage-engine</artifactId>    ❸
          <version>5.4.2</version>
          <scope>test</scope>
     </dependency>
     <dependency>
          <groupId>org.jboss.arquillian.junit</groupId>
          <artifactId>arquillian-junit-container</artifactId>  ❹
          <scope>test</scope>
     </dependency>
     <dependency>
          <groupId>org.jboss.arquillian.container</groupId>
          <artifactId>arquillian-weld-ee-embedded-1.1</artifactId>  ❺
          <version>1.0.0.CR9</version>
          <scope>test</scope>
     </dependency>
     <dependency>
          <groupId>org.jboss.weld</groupId>
          <artifactId>weld-core</artifactId>               ❻
          <version>2.3.5.Final</version>
          <scope>test</scope>
     </dependency>
</dependencies>
```

This listing adds the following:

- The Arquillian API dependency ❶.
- The Java EE 7 API dependency ❷.
- The JUnit Vintage Engine dependency ❸. As mentioned earlier, at least for the moment, Arquillian is not yet integrated with JUnit 5. Because Arquillian lacks a JUnit 5 extension, Thomas has to use JUnit 4 dependencies and annotations to run the tests.
- The Arquillian JUnit integration dependency ❹.
- The container adapter dependencies ❺ ❻. To execute tests against a container, Thomas must include the dependencies that correspond to that container. This requirement demonstrates one of the strengths of Arquillian: it abstracts the container from the unit tests and is not tightly coupled to specific tools that implement in-container unit testing.

An Arquillian test, as implemented next, looks just like a unit test, with some additions. The test is named `FlightWithPassengersTest` to show the goal of the integration testing between the two classes.

Listing 22.9   FlightWithPassengersTest class

```
[...]
@RunWith(Arquillian.class)                          ⬅──┐
public class FlightWithPassengersTest {                 ❶

    @Deployment
    public static JavaArchive createDeployment() {
        return ShrinkWrap.create(JavaArchive.class)                    ❷
                .addClasses(Passenger.class, Flight.class)
                .addAsManifestResource(EmptyAsset.INSTANCE, "beans.xml");
    }

    @Inject                    ❸
    Flight flight;

    @Test(expected = RuntimeException.class)
    public void testNumberOfSeatsCannotBeExceeded() throws IOException {    ❹
        assertEquals(50, flight.getPassengersNumber());
        flight.addPassenger(new Passenger("124-56-7890",
                                "Michael Johnson", "US"));
    }

    @Test
    public void testAddRemovePassengers() throws IOException {    ❺
        flight.setSeats(51);
        Passenger additionalPassenger =
            new Passenger("124-56-7890", "Michael Johnson", "US");
        flight.addPassenger(additionalPassenger);
        assertEquals(51, flight.getPassengersNumber());
        flight.removePassenger(additionalPassenger);
        assertEquals(50, flight.getPassengersNumber());
        assertEquals(51, flight.getSeats());
    }
}
```

As this listing shows, an Arquillian test case must have three things:

- A @RunWith(Arquillian.class) annotation on the class ❶. The @RunWith annotation tells JUnit to use Arquillian as the test controller.
- A public static method annotated with @Deployment that returns a Shrink-Wrap archive ❷. The purpose of the test archive is to isolate the classes and resources that the test needs. The archive is defined with ShrinkWrap. The microdeployment strategy lets us focus on precisely the classes we want to test. As a result, the test remains very lean and manageable. For the moment, Thomas includes only the Passenger and Flight classes. He tries to inject a Flight object as a class member using the CDI @Inject annotation ❸. The @Inject annotation allows us to define injection points in classes. In this case, @Inject instructs CDI to inject into the test a field of type reference to a Flight object.

- At least one method annotated with `@Test` ❹ ❺. Arquillian looks for a public static method annotated with the `@Deployment` annotation to retrieve the test archive. Then each `@Test`-annotated method is run in the container environment.

When the ShrinkWrap archive is deployed to the server, it becomes a real archive. The container has no knowledge that the archive was packaged by ShrinkWrap.

Now that the infrastructure is in place for using Arquillian in the project, we can run the integration tests with its help! If we run the tests now, we get an error (figure 22.3).

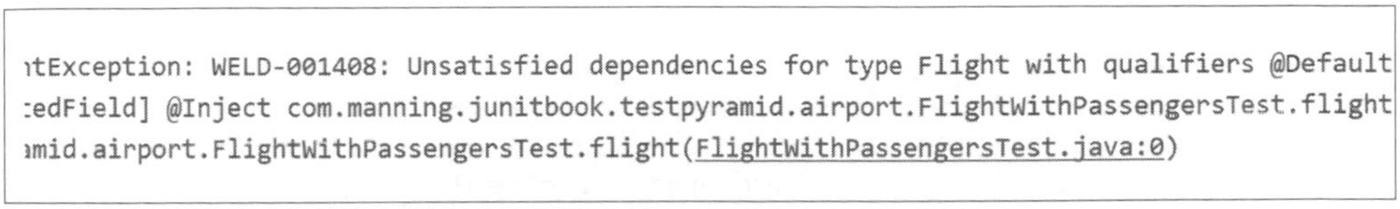

```
tException: WELD-001408: Unsatisfied dependencies for type Flight with qualifiers @Default
:edField] @Inject com.manning.junitbook.testpyramid.airport.FlightWithPassengersTest.flight
mid.airport.FlightWithPassengersTest.flight(FlightWithPassengersTest.java:0)
```

Figure 22.3 The result of running `FlightWithPassengersTest`. **There is no default dependency for type** `Flight`.

The error says `Unsatisfied dependencies for type Flight with qualifiers @Default`. It means the container is trying to inject the dependency, as it has been instructed to do through the CDI `@Inject` annotation, but it is unsatisfied. Why? What has Thomas missed? The `Flight` class provides only a constructor with arguments, and it has no default constructor to be used by the container for the creation of the object. The container does not know how to invoke the constructor with parameters and which parameters to pass to it to create the `Flight` object that must be injected.

What is the solution in this case? Java EE offers producer methods that are designed to inject objects that require custom initialization. The solution in the next listing fixes the issue and is easy to put into practice, even for a junior developer.

Listing 22.10 `FlightProducer` class

```
[...]
public class FlightProducer {

    @Produces
    public Flight createFlight() throws IOException {
        return FlightBuilderUtil.buildFlightFromCsv();
    }
}
```

In this listing, Thomas creates the `FlightProducer` class with the `createFlight` method, which invokes `FlightBuilderUtil.buildFlightFromCsv()`. He can use this method to inject objects that require custom initialization: in this case, he injects a flight that has been configured based on the CSV file. Thomas annotates the `createFlight` method with `@Produces`, which is also a Java EE annotation. The container automatically invokes this method to create the configured flight; then it injects the method into the `Flight` field, annotated with `@Inject` from the `Flight-WithPassengersTest` class.

Now Thomas adds the `FlightProducer` class to the ShrinkWrap archive.

Listing 22.11   Modified deployment method from `FlightWithPassengersTest`

```
@Deployment
public static JavaArchive createDeployment() {
    return ShrinkWrap.create(JavaArchive.class)
            .addClasses(Passenger.class, Flight.class,
                    FlightProducer.class)
            .addAsManifestResource(EmptyAsset.INSTANCE,
                    "beans.xml");
}
```

If we run the tests now, they are green, and the code coverage is 100%. The container injected the correctly configured flight (figure 22.4). Thomas has successfully created the integration layer of the test pyramid and is ready to move to the next level.

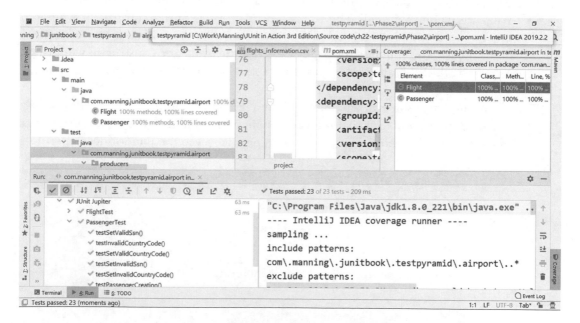

Figure 22.4   Successfully executing the integration tests from `FlightWithPassengersTest`. The code coverage is 100% after Arquillian is fully configured.

22.4   *System testing: Looking at the complete software*

System testing tests the entire system to evaluate its compliance with the specification and to detect inconsistencies between units that are integrated together. Mock objects (see chapter 8) can simulate the behavior of complex, real objects and are therefore useful when it is impractical to incorporate a real object (for example, some depended-on component) into a test, or impossible—at least for the moment—as the depended-on component is not yet available (figure 22.5). For example, our system may depend on a device providing measurements of out-side conditions (temperature, humidity). The results offered by this device influence our tests and are nondeterministic—we cannot simply decide the meteorological conditions that we need at a given time.

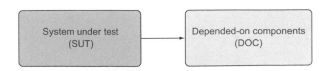

Figure 22.5   The system under test (SUT) needs a depended-on component (DOC) that is not available at the beginning of system development.

When developing a program, we may need to create mock objects that simulate the behavior of complex, real objects to achieve our testing goals. Common uses of mock objects include communicating with an external or internal service that is not yet available. These kinds of services may not be fully available, or they might be maintained by different teams, which makes accessing them slow or difficult. That's why a test double is handy: it saves our tests from having to wait for the availability of that service. We want to make these mock objects an accurate representation of the external service. It is important that the DOC keeps its contract—the expected behavior and an API that our system may use.

When the DOC is created in parallel by a different team, it is useful to use a consumer-driven contract approach. This means the provider must follow an API or a behavior expected by the consumer.

22.4.1 *Testing with a mock external dependency*

The flight-management application is currently at the level of integration testing. Thomas now needs to add a new feature that will award bonus points to passengers, depending on the distances they travel with the company. The bonus policy is simple: a passenger gets 1 bonus point for every 10 kilometers they travel.

The management of the bonus policy is externalized to another team that will provide the `DistancesManager` class. So far, Thomas knows that the interface forms the contract between the consumer and the provider. The application is following a consumer-driven contract.

He knows that the `DistancesManager` API provides the following methods:

- `getPassengersDistancesMap` provides a map that has the passenger as a key and the traveled distance as a value.
- `getPassengersPointsMap` provides a map that has the passenger as a key and the bonus points as a value.

- `addDistance` adds a traveled distance to the passenger.
- `calculateGivenPoints` calculates the bonus points for a passenger.

Thomas does not know the implementations yet, so he provides dummy implementations and mocks the behavior of the class.

Listing 22.12   Dummy implementation of the `DistancesManager` class

```
public class DistancesManager {

    public Map<Passenger, Integer> getPassengersDistancesMap() {
        return null;
    }

    public Map<Passenger, Integer> getPassengersPointsMap() {
        return null;
    }

    public void addDistance(Passenger passenger, int distance) {
    }

    public void calculateGivenPoints() {
    }

}
```

Thomas has one flight description in a CSV file, but this is not enough. To make sure the calculations are consistent, he needs passengers who have participated in more than one flight. So, he introduces two more CSV files describing two other flights that have passengers in common with the first flight (the following listing shows partial passenger lists).

Listing 22.13   flights_information2.csv and flights_information3.csv files

```
123-45-6789; John Smith; US
900-45-6789; Jane Underwood; GB
123-45-6790; James Perkins; US
[...]

123-45-6790; James Perkins; US
900-45-6790; Mary Calderon; GB
123-45-6792; Oliver Aguilar; US
[...]
```
The Flight class is modified to include a distance field together with a getter and a setter for it.

Listing 22.14   The modified `Flight` class

```
private int distance;

public int getDistance() {
    return distance;
}
```

```
public void setDistance(int distance) {
    this.distance = distance;
}
```

To determine that the same passenger is on different flights, Thomas has to override the equals and hashCode methods in the Passenger class. He'll know that two passengers are the same if they have the same identifier.

Listing 22.15 Overridden equals and hashCode methods in the Passenger class

```
public class Passenger {

    [...]
    @Override
    public boolean equals(Object o) {
        if (this == o) return true;
        if (o == null || getClass() != o.getClass()) return false;
        Passenger passenger = (Passenger) o;
        return Objects.equals(identifier, passenger.identifier);
    }

    @Override
    public int hashCode() {
        return Objects.hash(identifier);
    }

}
```

To distinguish between different flights, Thomas introduces the FlightNumber annotation, which receives the flight number as a parameter.

Listing 22.16 FlightNumber annotation

```
[...]
@Qualifier                          ❶   ❷
@Retention(RUNTIME)                       ❸
@Target({FIELD, METHOD})                      ❶
public @interface FlightNumber {
    String number();
}                                   ❹
```

In this listing:

- Thomas creates the FlightNumber annotation ❶. The information it provides about the annotated elements is kept during runtime ❷.
- This annotation can be applied to fields and methods ❸ and has a number parameter ❹.

In the FlightProducer class, Thomas annotates the createFlight method with the new FlightNumber annotation, using "AA1234" as an argument to give the flight an identity.

Listing 22.17   Modified `FlightProducer` class

```java
public class FlightProducer {

    @Produces
    @FlightNumber(number= "AA1234")
    public Flight createFlight() throws IOException {
        return FlightBuilderUtil.buildFlightFromCsv("AA1234",
                50,"src/test/resources/flights_information.csv");
    }
}
```

Thomas also changes the `FlightWithPassengersTest` class to annotate the injected flight and writes a test for the distance manager.

Listing 22.18   Modified `FlightWithPassengersTest` class

```java
@RunWith(Arquillian.class)
public class FlightWithPassengersTest {
    [...]

    @Inject
    @FlightNumber(number= "AA1234")                          ❶
    Flight flight;

    @Mock
    DistancesManager distancesManager;                       ❷

    @Rule
    public MockitoRule mockitoRule = MockitoJUnit.rule();    ❸

    private static Map<Passenger, Integer> passengersPointsMap =   ❹
        new HashMap<>();

    @BeforeClass
    public static void setUp() {
        passengersPointsMap.put(new Passenger("900-45-6809",
                                "Susan Todd", "GB"), 210);
        passengersPointsMap.put(new Passenger("900-45-6797",   ❺
                                "Harry Christensen", "GB"), 420);
        passengersPointsMap.put(new Passenger("123-45-6799",
                                "Bethany King", "US"), 630);
    }

    [...]

    @Test
    public void testFlightsDistances() {                      ❻
      when(distancesManager.getPassengersPointsMap()).        ❼
          thenReturn(passengersPointsMap);

      assertEquals(210, distancesManager.getPassengersPointsMap().
      get(new Passenger("900-45-6809", "Susan Todd", "GB")).longValue());   ❽
      assertEquals(420, distancesManager.getPassengersPointsMap().
```

```
        get(new Passenger("900-45-6797", "Harry Christensen", "GB"))
            .longValue());
    assertEquals(630, distancesManager.getPassengersPointsMap()
            .get(new Passenger("123-45-6799", "Bethany King", "US"))
            .longValue());
    }
}
```

In this listing:

- Thomas annotates the `flight` field with the `FlightNumber` annotation ❶ to give an identity to the injected flight.
- He provides a mock implementation of the `DistancesManager` object and annotates it with `@Mock` ❷.
- He declares a `MockitoRule` `@Rule` annotated object, which is needed to allow the initialization of mocks annotated with `@Mock` ❸. Remember that Thomas is using Arquillian, which is not compatible with JUnit 5, and he needs to use the rules from JUnit 4.
- He declares `passengersPointsMap` to keep the bonus points for the passengers ❹ and populates it with some expected values ❺.
- He creates `testFlightsDistances` ❻, where he instructs the mock object to return `passengersPointsMap` when he calls `distancesManager.get-PassengersPointsMap()` ❼. Then he checks that the bonus points are as expected ❽. For now, he only inserts some data into the map and checks that it is correctly retrieved. However, he defines a tests skeleton and expects new functionalities from the provider side.

22.4.2 *Testing with a partially implemented external dependency*

From the provider side, Thomas receives the partial implementation of the `DistancesManager` class.

Listing 22.19 Modified implementation of the `DistancesManager` class

```
public class DistancesManager {

    private static final int DISTANCE_FACTOR = 10;     ❶

    private Map<Passenger, Integer> passengersDistancesMap =
                            new HashMap<>();
    private Map<Passenger, Integer> passengersPointsMap = new HashMap<>();

    public Map<Passenger, Integer> getPassengersDistancesMap() {
        return Collections.unmodifiableMap(passengersDistancesMap);  ❷
    }

    public Map<Passenger, Integer> getPassengersPointsMap() {
        return Collections.unmodifiableMap(passengersPointsMap);
    }
```

```
    public void addDistance(Passenger passenger, int distance) {   ⟵
    }                                                                        ❸

    public void calculateGivenPoints() {
        for (Passenger passenger : getPassengersDistancesMap().keySet()) {   ❹
            passengersPointsMap.put(passenger,
                getPassengersDistancesMap().get(passenger)/ DISTANCE_FACTOR);
        }
    }

}
```

In this listing:

- Thomas defines the DISTANCE_FACTOR constant by which to divide the distances, in order to get the number of bonus points ❶.
- He keeps passengersDistancesMap and passengersPointsMap and provides getters for them ❷.
- The addDistance method is still not implemented ❸. The calculate-GivenPoints method has an implementation that browses passengers-DistancesMap and divides the distances by DISTANCE_FACTOR to populate passengersPointsMap ❹.

In real applications, you may receive some fully implemented packages or classes while another part is still under construction but follows the agreed-on contract. To simplify, we have reduced our example situation to a class with four methods, of which only one does not have an implementation. What is important is that the API contract is respected.

How will this change the tests on the consumer side? Thomas knows how to get the bonus based on the distance, so he doesn't keep passengersPointsMap, but rather passengersDistancesMap. The changes to FlightWithPassengersTest are shown in the following listing.

Listing 22.20   Modified FlightWithPassengersTest class

```
[...]
@RunWith(Arquillian.class)
public class FlightWithPassengersTest {
    [...]

    @Spy
    DistancesManager distancesManager;                              ❶

    private static Map<Passenger, Integer> passengersDistancesMap =   ❷
        new HashMap<>();
```

```
@BeforeClass
public static void setUp() {
    passengersDistancesMap.put(new Passenger("900-45-6809",
                                "Susan Todd", "GB"), 2100);
    passengersDistancesMap.put(new Passenger("900-45-6797",
                                "Harry Christensen", "GB"), 4200);
    passengersDistancesMap.put(new Passenger("123-45-6799",
                                "Bethany King", "US"), 6300);

}

[...]

@Test
public void testFlightsDistances() {
  when(distancesManager.getPassengersDistancesMap()).
      thenReturn(passengersDistancesMap);

  distancesManager.calculateGivenPoints();

  assertEquals(210, distancesManager.getPassengersPointsMap().
  get(new Passenger("900-45-6809", "Susan Todd", "GB")).longValue());
  assertEquals(420, distancesManager.getPassengersPointsMap().
      get(new Passenger("900-45-6797", "Harry Christensen", "GB"))
      .longValue());
    assertEquals(630, distancesManager.getPassengersPointsMap()
      .get(new Passenger("123-45-6799", "Bethany King", "US"))
      .longValue());
  }
}
```

In this listing:

- Thomas changes the annotation of the DistancesManager object to @Spy ❶. With the previous @Mock annotation, he was mocking the whole distances- Manager object. In order to indicate that he would like to mock only some methods and to keep the functionality of others, he replaces the @Mock annotation with @Spy.
- He initializes passengersDistancesMap ❷ and populates it before the execution of the tests ❸.
- In testFlightsDistances, he instructs the distancesManager object to return passengersDistancesMap when he calls distancesManager.get- PassengersDistancesMap() ❹. Then he calls the already implemented calculateGivenPoints ❺ and checks that the bonus points are as expected after this calculation ❻.

If we run the tests now, they are green. The code coverage is not 100%, as we are still waiting for the implementation of a method from DistancesManager to be able to test everything (figure 22.6).

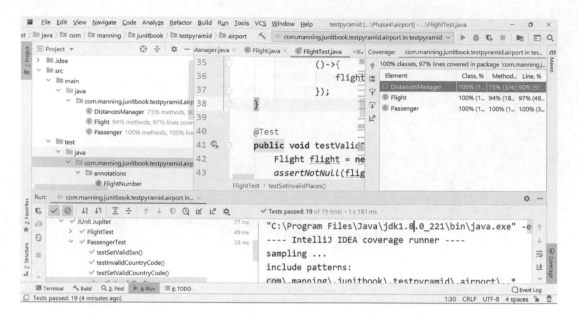

Figure 22.6 `PassengerTest`, `FlightTest`, **and** `FlightWithPassengersTest` **run successfully with a partial implementation of the** `DistancesManager` **class. The code coverage is not yet 100%, as some functionality is still missing.**

22.4.3 *Testing with the fully implemented external dependency*

On the consumer side, the real system is now fully available. Thomas needs to test the functionality against this real provider service. The full implementation of the `DistancesManager` class has introduced the `addDistance` method.

Listing 22.21   Modified implementation of the `DistancesManager` **class**

```java
public class DistancesManager {
  [...]

  public void addDistance(Passenger passenger, int distance) {       ❶
      if (passengersDistancesMap.containsKey(passenger)) {       ◁──
        passengersDistancesMap.put(passenger,
            passengersDistancesMap.get(passenger) + distance);       ❷
      } else {
        passengersDistancesMap.put(passenger, distance);       ◁──
      }
  }                                                              ❸

}
```

In this listing:

- In the `addDistance` method, Thomas checks whether `passengers-DistanceMap` already contains a passenger ❶.

- If that passenger already exists, he adds the distance to the passenger ❷; otherwise, he creates a new entry in the map with that passenger as a key and the distance as the initial value ❸.

Because Thomas will use the real passenger set for each flight and populate `passengersDistancesMap` based on the passengers' information, he introduces the `getPassengers` method into the `Flight` class.

Listing 22.22 Modified implementation of the `Flight` class

```java
public class Flight {

    [...]
    private Set<Passenger> passengers = new HashSet<Passenger>();    ⟵❶

    public Set<Passenger> getPassengers() {
        return Collections.unmodifiableSet(passengers);    ❷
    }
    [...]
}
```

In this listing, Thomas makes passengers private ❶ and exposes it through a getter ❷.

Thomas now goes back to the test that previously mocked a behavior and introduces real behavior. He removes the Mockito dependencies from the pom.xml file, as they are no longer needed. He also removes the initialization of `passengersDistancesMap` before executing the tests. The changes to `FlightWithPassengersTest` are shown in the following listing.

Listing 22.23 Modified `FlightWithPassengersTest` class

```java
@RunWith(Arquillian.class)
public class FlightWithPassengersTest {
    @Deployment
    public static JavaArchive createDeployment() {
        return ShrinkWrap.create(JavaArchive.class)
            .addClasses(Passenger.class, Flight.class,                    ❶
                        FlightProducer.class, DistancesManager.class)    ⟵
            .addAsManifestResource(EmptyAsset.INSTANCE, "beans.xml");
    }

    @Inject
    @FlightNumber(number= "AA1234")
    Flight flight;

    @Inject
    @FlightNumber(number= "AA1235")    ❷
    Flight flight2;

    @Inject
    @FlightNumber(number= "AA1236")
    Flight flight3;
```

```
@Inject
DistancesManager distancesManager;                          3

[...]
@Test
public void testFlightsDistances() {

    for (Passenger passenger : flight.getPassengers()) {
      distancesManager.addDistance(passenger, flight.getDistance());
    }

    for (Passenger passenger : flight2.getPassengers()) {
      distancesManager.addDistance(passenger, flight2.getDistance());    4
    }

    for (Passenger passenger : flight3.getPassengers()) {
      distancesManager.addDistance(passenger, flight3.getDistance());
    }
                                                            5
    distancesManager.calculateGivenPoints();          <—

    assertEquals(210, distancesManager.getPassengersPointsMap()
       .get(new Passenger("900-45-6809", "Susan Todd", "GB"))
       .longValue());
    assertEquals(420, distancesManager.getPassengersPointsMap()
       .get(new Passenger("900-45-6797", "Harry Christensen", "GB"))    6
       .longValue());
    assertEquals(630, distancesManager.getPassengersPointsMap()
       .get(new Passenger("123-45-6799", "Bethany King", "US"))
       .longValue());
    }
}
```

In this listing:

- Thomas adds `DistancesManager.class` to the ShrinkWrap archive **1** so that the `DistancesManager` class can be injected into the test.
- He injects three flights into the test and annotates and differentiates them with the `@FlightNumber` annotation. The annotations have different arguments for each flight **2**. He also injects a `DistancesManager` field **3**.
- He changes the `testFlightsDistance` test to browse all passengers from the three flights and adds the distances they have traveled to `distancesManager` **4**. Based on the traveled distances, he calculates the bonus points **5** and checks that the bonus points are as expected after this calculation **6**.

If we run the tests now, they are green, and the code coverage is 100% (figure 22.7).

Thomas has successfully tested the entire system using a consumer-driven contract and has moved from a mock implementation of the external functionality to using the real thing. He is ready to proceed to the last step in building the test pyramid strategy: acceptance testing.

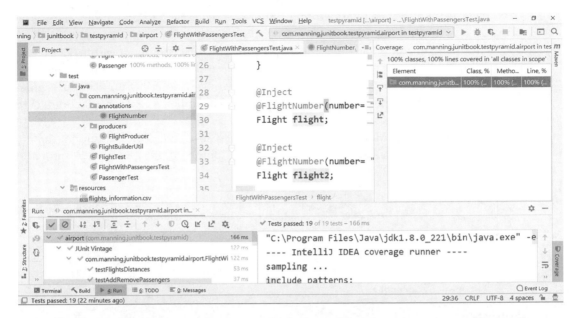

Figure 22.7 `PassengerTest`, `FlightTest`, and `FlightWithPassengersTest` run successfully with a full implementation of the `DistancesManager` class, and the code coverage is 100%.

22.5 Acceptance testing: Compliance with business requirements

Acceptance testing is the level of software testing where a system is tested for compliance with business requirements. Once the system testing has been fulfilled, acceptance testing is executed to confirm that the software is ready for delivery and will satisfy the needs of the end users.

In chapter 21, we discussed the working features that give business value to software, and the communication challenges that exist between customer, business analyst, developer, and tester. We have emphasized that acceptance criteria may be expressed as scenarios in a way that can be automated later. The keywords are `Given`, `When`, and `Then`:

```
Given <a context>
When <an action occurs>
Then <expect a result>
```

Thomas needs to implement a new feature in the application. This feature concerns the company policy regarding adding passengers to and removing them from flights. Because the number of seats and the type of passenger must be considered, the company defines the following policy: in case of constraints, regular passengers may be removed from a flight and added to another one, whereas VIP passengers cannot be removed from a flight.

This is the business logic that the application must be compliant with to satisfy the end user. To fulfill the acceptance testing, Thomas will use Cucumber, the acceptance testing framework that we used in chapter 21. Cucumber describes application scenarios in plain English, using the Gherkin language. Cucumber is easy for stakeholders to read and understand and allows automation.

To start working with Cucumber, Thomas first introduces the additional dependencies that are needed at the level of the Maven pom.xml file: `cucumber-java` and `cucumber-junit`.

Listing 22.24 Cucumber dependencies in the Maven pom.xml file

```
<dependency>
    <groupId>info.cukes</groupId>
    <artifactId>cucumber-java</artifactId>
    <version>1.2.5</version>
    <scope>test</scope>
</dependency>
<dependency
    <groupId>info.cukes</groupId>
    <artifactId>cucumber-junit</artifactId>
    <version>1.2.5</version>
    <scope>test</scope>
</dependency>
```

Thomas will introduce the new feature by working TDD/BDD style, as we demonstrated in chapters 20 and 21. This means he will first write the acceptance tests in Cucumber. Then he will write the tests in Java. Finally, he will write the code that fixes the tests and consequently provides the feature implementation.

Thomas introduces the two types of passengers: regular and VIP. This changes the `Passenger` class by adding a `boolean vip` field, together with a getter and a setter.

Listing 22.25 Modified `Passenger` class

```
public class Passenger {

    [...]
    private boolean vip;

    public boolean isVip() {
        return vip;
    }

    public void setVip(boolean vip) {
        this.vip = vip;
    }
[...]
}
```

Next, to build the scenarios that express the acceptance criteria, Thomas creates the passengers_policy.feature file in the new test/resources/features folder. He reuses the three CSV flight files that were used for the system integration testing. The scenarios that Thomas defines are presented in the following listing and can be read using natural language. To review the capabilities of Cucumber, see chapter 21.

Listing 22.26 passengers_policy.feature file

```
Feature: Passengers Policy
  The company follows a policy of adding and removing passengers, depending
    on the passenger type

  Scenario Outline: Flight with regular passengers
    Given there is a flight having number "<flightNumber>" and
          <seats> seats with passengers defined into "<file>"
    When we have regular passengers
    Then you can remove them from the flight
    And add them to another flight

    Examples:
      |flightNumber | seats | file                      |
      |   AA1234    | 50    | flights_information.csv   |
      |   AA1235    | 50    | flights_information2.csv  |
      |   AA1236    | 50    | flights_information3.csv  |

  Scenario Outline: Flight with VIP passengers
    Given there is a flight having number "<flightNumber>" and
          <seats> seats with passengers defined into "<file>"
    When we have VIP passengers
    Then you cannot remove them from the flight

    Examples:
      |flightNumber | seats | file                      |
      |   AA1234    | 50    | flights_information.csv   |
      |   AA1235    | 50    | flights_information2.csv  |
      |   AA1236    | 50    | flights_information3.csv  |
```

To generate the skeleton of the Java tests, Thomas makes sure the Cucumber and Gherkin plugins are installed by accessing the File > Settings > Plugins menu (figures 22.8 and 22.9).

Figure 22.8   Installing the Cucumber for Java plugin from the File > Settings > Plugins menu

Figure 22.9   Installing the Gherkin plugin from the File > Settings > Plugins menu

Now he must configure the way the feature is run by going to Run > Edit Configurations and choosing a few settings (figure 22.10):

- Main Class: `cucumber.api.cli.Main`
- Glue (the package where step definitions are stored): `com.manning.junit-book.testpyramid.airport`

- Feature or Folder Path: the newly created file test/resources/features/passengers_policy.feature
- Working Directory: the project folder

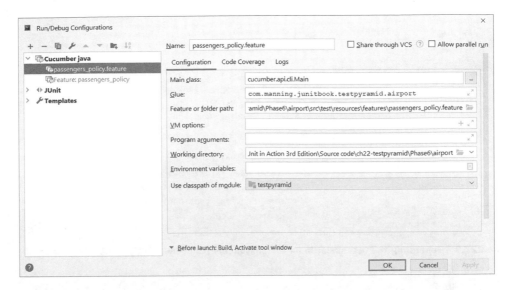

Figure 22.10 Setting the feature configuration by filling in the Main Class, Glue, Feature or Folder Path, and Working Directory fields

After setting this configuration, Thomas can run the feature file directly by right-clicking it (figure 22.11). He gets the skeleton of the Java tests (figure 22.12).

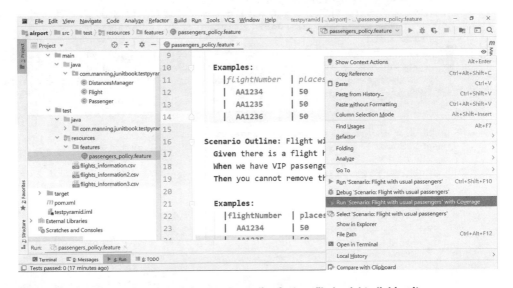

Figure 22.11 Directly running the passengers_policy.feature file by right-clicking it

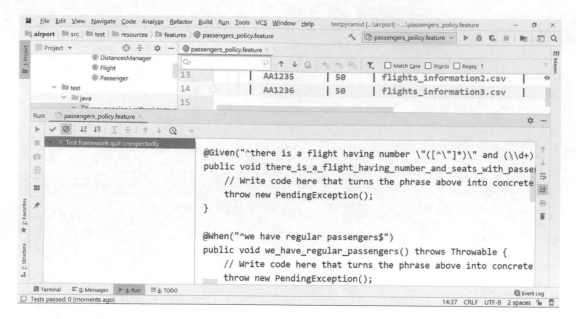

Figure 22.12   Generating the test skeleton for the passengers policy by directly running the feature file

Thomas now creates the `PassengersPolicy` file that contains the skeleton of the tests to be executed.

Listing 22.27   Skeleton of the `PassengersPolicy` test

```
[...]
public class PassengersPolicy {
    @Given("^there is a flight having number \"([^\"]*)\" and (\\d+) seats
            with passengers defined into \"([^\"]*)\"$")
    public void
      there_is_a_flight_having_number_and_seats_with_passengers_defined_into(
        String arg1, int arg2, String arg3) throws Throwable {
        // Write code here that turns the phrase above into concrete actions
        throw new PendingException();
    }

    @When("^we have regular passengers$")
    public void we_have_regular_passengers() throws Throwable {
        // Write code here that turns the phrase above into concrete actions
        throw new PendingException();
    }

    @Then("^you can remove them from the flight$")
    public void you_can_remove_them_from_the_flight() throws Throwable {
        // Write code here that turns the phrase above into concrete actions
        throw new PendingException();
    }
```

```
@Then("^add them to another flight$")
public void add_them_to_another_flight() throws Throwable {
    // Write code here that turns the phrase above into concrete actions
    throw new PendingException();
}

@When("^we have VIP passengers$")
public void we_have_VIP_passengers() throws Throwable {
    // Write code here that turns the phrase above into concrete actions
    throw new PendingException();
}

@Then("^you cannot remove them from the flight$")
public void you_cannot_remove_them_from_the_flight() throws Throwable {
    // Write code here that turns the phrase above into concrete actions
    throw new PendingException();
}
}
```

To run the Cucumber tests, Thomas needs a special class. The name of the class could be anything; he chooses CucumberTest.

Listing 22.28 CucumberTest class

```
[...]
@RunWith(Cucumber.class)          ①
@CucumberOptions(                 ②
    plugin = {"pretty"},
    features = "classpath:features")   ④
public class CucumberTest {       ③
    /**
     * This class should be empty, step definitions should be in separate
          classes.
     */

}
```

In this listing:

- Thomas annotates this class with @RunWith(Cucumber.class) ①. Executing it like any JUnit test class will run all features found on the classpath in the same package. As there is no Cucumber JUnit 5 extension at the time of writing, he uses the JUnit 4 runner.
- The @CucumberOptions ② annotation provides the plugin option ③ that is used to specify different formatting options for the output reports. Using "pretty" prints the Gherkin source with additional colors. The features option ④ helps Cucumber to locate the feature file in the project folder structure. It looks for the features folder on the classpath—and remember that the src/test/resources folder is maintained by Maven on the classpath!

Thomas next turns back to the `PassengersPolicy` class and writes the tests to check the functionality of the `PassengersPolicy` feature to be introduced.

Listing 22.29   `PassengersPolicy` test class

```java
public class PassengersPolicy {                          ❶
    private Flight flight;                               ⟵
    private List<Passenger> regularPassengers = new ArrayList<>();     ❷
    private List<Passenger> vipPassengers = new ArrayList<>();
    private Flight anotherFlight = new Flight("AA7890", 48);           ⟵
                                                                        ❸
    @Given("^there is a flight having number \"([^\"]*)\" and (\\d+)
            seats with passengers defined into \"([^\"]*)\"$")
    public void
    there_is_a_flight_having_number_and_seats_with_passengers_defined_into(
        String flightNumber, int seats, String fileName) throws Throwable {
        flight = FlightBuilderUtil.buildFlightFromCsv(flightNumber,    ❹
                seats,"src/test/resources/" + fileName);
    }

    @When("^we have regular passengers$")
    public void we_have_regular_passengers() {
        for (Passenger passenger: flight.getPassengers()) {
            if (!passenger.isVip()) {                                  ❺
                regularPassengers.add(passenger);
            }
        }
    }

    @Then("^you can remove them from the flight$")
    public void you_can_remove_them_from_the_flight() {
        for(Passenger passenger: regularPassengers) {
            assertTrue(flight.removePassenger(passenger));             ❻
        }
    }

    @Then("^add them to another flight$")
    public void add_them_to_another_flight() {
        for(Passenger passenger: regularPassengers) {
            assertTrue(anotherFlight.addPassenger(passenger));         ❼
        }
    }

    @When("^we have VIP passengers$")
    public void we_have_VIP_passengers() {
        for (Passenger passenger: flight.getPassengers()) {
            if (passenger.isVip()) {                                   ❽
                vipPassengers.add(passenger);
            }
        }
    }
```

```
@Then("^you cannot remove them from the flight$")
public void you_cannot_remove_them_from_the_flight(){
    for(Passenger passenger: vipPassengers) {
        assertFalse(flight.removePassenger(passenger));
    }
}
}
```

⑨

In this listing:

- Thomas defines as fields the flight from which passengers are moved ❶, the list of regular and VIP passengers ❷, and the second flight to which the passengers are moved ❸.
- The step labeled `Given there is a flight having number "<flight-Number>" and <seats> seats with passengers defined into "<file>"` initializes the flight from the CSV file ❹.
- Thomas browses the list of all passengers, adds the regular passengers to their list ❺, checks that he can remove them from a flight ❻, and adds them to another flight ❼.
- He browses the list of all passengers, adds the VIP passengers to their list ❽, and checks that he cannot remove them from a flight ❾.

Running the tests now by executing `CucumberTest`, Thomas obtains the result shown in figure 22.13.

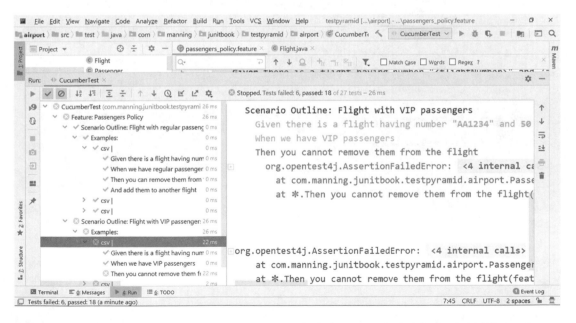

Figure 22.13 Running the newly introduced `PassengersPolicy` tests results in failure only for VIP passengers.

Only the tests concerning VIP passengers fail, so Thomas knows that he only needs to change the code regarding this type of passenger: he will modify the addPassenger method from the Flight class.

Listing 22.30   Modified Flight class

```java
public class Flight {

[...]
    public boolean removePassenger(Passenger passenger) {
        if(passenger.isVip()) {
            return false;                              ❶
        }
        return  passengers.remove(passenger);
    }
}
```

In this listing, Thomas introduces the condition that a VIP passenger cannot be removed from a flight ❶. Running the tests now by executing CucumberTest, Thomas obtains the result shown in figure 22.14—all tests execute successfully.

To check the code coverage, Thomas executes all of the tests that form the test pyramid. When he does, the code coverage is 100% (figure 22.15). He has successfully implemented a test pyramid for the flight-management application including unit tests, integration tests, system tests, and acceptance tests.

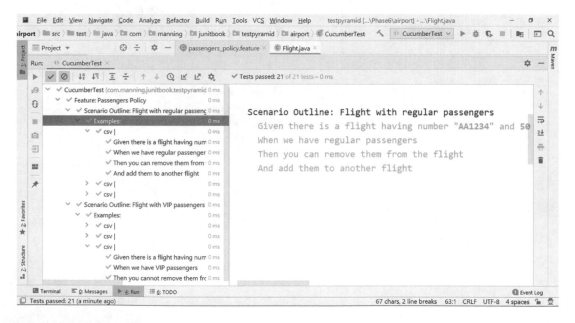

Figure 22.14   Successfully running the newly introduced PassengersPolicy test after writing the business logic

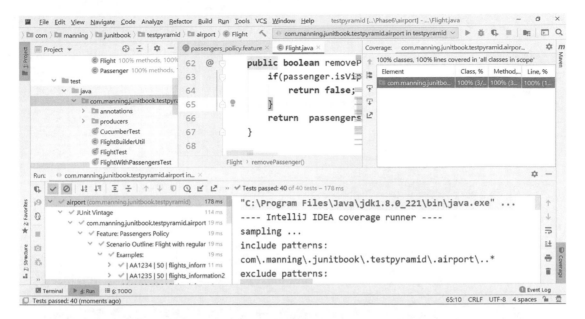

Figure 22.15 The code coverage is 100% after implementing the entire test pyramid.

Summary

This chapter has covered the following:

- Introducing the software testing levels (unit, integration, system, and acceptance) and the concept of a test pyramid (from simpler levels to more complex ones)
- Analyzing what software tests should verify: business logic, bad input values, boundary conditions, unexpected conditions, invariants, and regressions
- Developing unit tests, and testing values restrictions, bad input values, and boundary conditions
- Developing tests to verify the integration between two classes using the Arquillian framework, and testing how these classes interact
- Developing system tests using a consumer-driven contract and moving from a mock implementation of an external functionality to using the real thing
- Developing acceptance tests for a new feature to satisfy external policies with the help of JUnit 5 and Cucumber

appendix A
Maven

Maven (https://maven.apache.org) can be regarded a source-building *environment*. To better understand how Maven works, you need to understand the key points (principles) that stand behind Maven. From the very beginning of the Maven project, certain ground rules were created for software architecture. These rules aimed to simplify development with Maven and make it easier for developers to implement the build system. One of the fundamental ideas of Maven is that the build system should be as simple as possible: software engineers should not spend a lot of time implementing the build system. It should be easy to start a new project from scratch and then rapidly begin developing the software, rather than spending valuable time designing and implementing a build system. This appendix describes the core Maven principles in detail and explains what they mean from a developer's point of view.

A.1 Convention over configuration

Convention over configuration is a software design principle that aims to decrease the number of configurations a software engineer needs to make, instead of introducing conventional rules that we must follow strictly. This way, we can skip the tedious configuration that needs to be done for every single project and focus on the more important parts of our work.

Convention over configuration is one of the strongest principles of the Maven project. One example of its application is the folder structure of the build process. With Maven, all the directories we need are already defined for us. src/main/java/, for example, is the Maven convention for where Java code for the project resides, src/test/java is where the unit tests for the project reside, target is the build folder, and so on.

That sounds great, but aren't we losing the flexibility of the project? What if we want our source code to reside in another folder? Maven is easy to configure: it provides the convention, but at any point, we can override the convention and use the configuration of our choice.

A.2   *Strong dependency management*

Strong dependency management is the second key point that Maven introduced. When the Maven project began, the de facto build system for Java projects was another build tool, Ant. With Ant, we have to distribute the dependencies of our project, which means each project must take care of the dependencies it requires, and the dependencies of the same project may be distributed across different locations. Also, the same dependency may be used by different projects but located in a different place for each project, causing duplication of resources.

Maven introduced the notion of a *central repository*: a location on the internet where all kinds of artifacts (dependencies) are stored. The Maven build tool resolves these artifacts by reading a project's build descriptor, downloading the necessary versions of the artifacts, and including them in the classpath of the application. This way, we need to list our dependencies only once, in the dependencies section of our build descriptor. For example:

```
<dependencies>
    <dependency>
        <groupId>org.junit.jupiter</groupId>
        <artifactId>junit-jupiter-api</artifactId>
        <version>5.6.0</version>
        <scope>test</scope>
    </dependency>
    <dependency>
        <groupId>org.jmock</groupId>
        <artifactId>jmock-junit5</artifactId>
        <version>2.12.0</version>
    </dependency>
  </dependencies>
```

Thereafter, we are free to build the software on any other machine. We don't need to bundle the dependencies with our project.

Maven also introduced the concept of the local repository: a folder on a hard disk (~/.m2/repository/ in UNIX and C:\Documents and Settings\<UserName>\.m2\ repository\ in Windows) where Maven keeps the artifacts that it just downloaded from the central repository. After we build our project, our artifacts are installed in the local repository for later use by other projects, which is simple and neat.

A developer might join a project managed by Maven and need access only to the sources of the project. Maven downloads the needed dependencies from the central repository and brings them to the local repository, where they will be available for other projects that the same developer may work on.

A.3   *Maven build life cycles*

Another very strong principle in Maven is the *build life cycle*. The Maven project is built around the idea of defining the process of building, testing, and distributing a particular artifact. A Maven project can produce only one artifact. This way, we can use Maven to build the project artifact, clean the project's folder structure, or generate the project documentation. Following are the three built-in Maven life cycles:

- *Default*—For generating the project artifact
- *Clean*—For cleaning the project
- *Site*—For generating the project documentation

Each of these life cycles is composed of several phases. To navigate a certain life cycle, the build follows its phases (figure A.1).

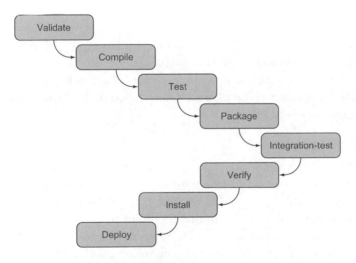

Figure A.1   The phases of Maven's default life cycle, from validate to deploy

Following are the phases of the default life cycle:

1. *Validate*—Validate that the project is correct and all necessary information is available.
2. *Compile*—Compile the source code of the project.
3. *Test*—Test the compiled source code using a suitable unit testing framework (perhaps JUnit 5, in this case). The test should not require the code to be packaged or deployed.
4. *Package*—Package the compiled code in its distributable format, such as a jar file.

5 *Integration-test*—Process and deploy the package (if necessary) into an environment where integration tests can be run.

6 *Verify*—Run any checks to verify that the package is valid and meets quality criteria.

7 *Install*—Install the package in the local repository for use as a dependency in other projects locally.

8 *Deploy*—In an integration or release environment, copy the final package to the remote repository for sharing with other developers and projects.

Here, again, is the convention-over-configuration principle promoted by Maven. These phases are already defined in the order in which they are listed here. Maven invokes these phases in a very strict order; the phases are executed sequentially in the order in which they are listed here, to complete the life cycle. If we invoke any of these phases—if we type

```
mvn compile
```

on the command line in our project home directory, for example—Maven first validates the project and then tries to compile the sources of the project.

One last thing: it is useful to think of all these phases as extension points. We can attach additional Maven plugins to the phases and orchestrate the order and the way in which these plugins are executed.

A.4   *Plugin-based architecture*

The last feature of Maven that we will mention here is its plugin-based architecture. We mentioned that Maven is a source-building environment. More specifically, Maven is a plugin-execution source-building environment. The core of the project is very small, but the architecture of the project allows multiple plugins to be attached to the core. This way, Maven builds an environment in which different plugins can be executed.

Each phase in a given life cycle has several plugins attached, and Maven invokes them when passing through the given phase in the order in which the plugins are declared. Here are some of the core Maven plugins:

- *Clean*—Cleans up after the build
- *Compiler*—Compiles Java sources
- *Deploy*—Deploys the built artifact to the remote repository
- *Install*—Installs the built artifact in the local repository
- *Resources*—Copies the resources to the output directory for inclusion in the jar file
- *Site*—Generates a site that includes information about the current project
- *Surefire*—Runs the JUnit tests in an isolated classloader
- *Verifier*—Verifies the existence of certain conditions (useful for integration tests)

In addition to these core Maven plugins, other Maven plugins are available for many situations, such as WAR (for packaging a web application) and Javadoc (for generating project documentation).

Plugins are declared in the `plugins` section of the build configuration file, as in this example:

```
<build>
    <plugins>
        <plugin>
            <artifactId>maven-surefire-plugin</artifactId>
            <version>2.22.2</version>
        </plugin>
    </plugins>
</build>
```

A plugin declaration can have a `groupId`, `artifactId`, and `version`. This way, the plugins look like dependencies. In fact, plugins are handled the same way as dependencies; they are downloaded to the local repository like dependencies. When we specify a plugin, the `groupId` and `version` parameters are optional; if we do not declare them, Maven looks for a plugin with the specified `artifactId` and one of the following `groupId`s: `org.apache.maven.plugins` or `org.codehaus.mojo`. As the version is optional, Maven tries to download the latest available plugin version. Specifying the plugin versions is highly recommended to prevent auto-updates and nonreproducible builds. We may have built our project with the most recently updated Maven plugin; but later, if another developer tries to make the same build with the same configuration, and if the Maven plugin has since been updated, using the newest update may result in a nonreproducible build.

A.5 The Maven project object model (POM)

Maven has a build descriptor called pom.xml (short for *project object model*) by default. We do not imperatively specify the things we want to do. We declaratively specify general information for the project itself, as in the following listing.

> **Listing A.1 Very simple pom.xml**

```
<project>
    <modelVersion>4.0.0</modelVersion>
    <groupId>com.manning.junitbook</groupId>
    <artifactId>example-pom</artifactId>
    <packaging>jar</packaging>
    <version>1.0-SNAPSHOT</version>
</project>
```

This code looks really simple, doesn't it? But one big question may arise: how is Maven capable of building source code with so little information?

The answer lies in the inheritance feature of the pom.xml files. Every simple pom.xml inherits most of its functionality from a Super POM. As in Java, in which every class inherits certain methods from the `java.lang.Object` class, the Super POM empowers each pom.xml with Maven features.

We can see the analogy between Java and Maven. To take this analogy even further, Maven pom.xmls can inherit from one another; just as in Java, some classes can act as parents for others. If we want to use the pom from listing A.1 for our parent, all we have to do is change its packaging value to pom. Parent and aggregation (multimodule) projects can have pom only as a packaging value. We also need to define in our parent which modules are the children.

Listing A.2 Parent pom.xml with a child module

```
<project>
   <modelVersion>4.0.0</modelVersion>
   <groupId>com.manning.junitbook</groupId>
   <artifactId>example-pom</artifactId>          ❶
   <packaging>pom</packaging>                      ←┘
   <version>1.0-SNAPSHOT</version>
   <modules>
         <module>example-module</module>          ←┐
   </modules>
</project>                                          ❷
```

Listing A.2 is an extension of listing A.1. We declare that this pom is an aggregation module by declaring the package to be of pom type ❶ and adding a modules section ❷. The modules section lists all the children modules that our module has by providing the relative path to the project folder (example-module, in this case). The following listing shows the child pom.xml.

Listing A.3 pom.xml that inherits the parent pom.xml

```
<project>
  <modelVersion>4.0.0</modelVersion>
  <parent>
    <groupId>com.manning.junitbook</groupId>
    <artifactId>example-pom</artifactId>
    <version>1.0-SNAPSHOT</version>
  </parent>
  <artifactId>example-child</artifactId>
</project>
```

Remember that this pom.xml resides in the folder that the parent XML has declared (example-module, in this case).

Two things are worth noticing here. First, because we inherit from some other pom, we don't need to specify groupId and version for the child pom; second, Maven expects the values to be the same as in the parent.

Going further with the analogy of Java, it seems reasonable to ask what kinds of objects poms can inherit from their parents. Here are all the elements that a pom can inherit from its parent:

- Dependencies
- Developers and contributors
- Plugins and their configurations
- Reports lists

Each of these elements specified in the parent pom is automatically specified in the child pom.

A.6 *Installing Maven*

Installing Maven is a three-step process:

1 Download the latest distribution from https://maven.apache.org, and unzip/untar it in the directory of your choice.

2 Define an M2_HOME environment variable pointing to where you have installed Maven.

3 Add M2_HOME\bin (M2_HOME/bin on UNIX) to your PATH environment variable so that you can type mvn from any directory.

appendix B
Gradle

B.1   Installing Gradle

Gradle runs on all major OSs and requires only an installed Java JDK or JRE version 8 or higher. You can download the Gradle distribution from https://gradle.org/releases. At the time of writing, the latest version was 6.0.1. For our purpose, downloading the binary distribution will be enough. You can choose to make operations with the help of the IDE and the Gradle plugin, but our demonstration will be made through the command line, better touching the functionalities.

As Windows is the most commonly used OS, our example configuration details are on Windows. Concepts such as the path, environment variables, and the command prompt also exist in other OSs. Please follow your documentation guidelines if you run the examples on an OS other than Windows.

Unzip the downloaded file into a folder of your choice; we'll call it GRADLE_HOME. Then add the GRADLE_HOME\bin folder to your path. To do this in Windows, go to This PC, right-click it, and choose Properties > Advanced System Settings. Click Environment Variables, and you will get the window shown in figure B.1.

From here, choose Path and click Edit. This will open the window in figure B.2. Click the New button on the right, and choose to add the GRADLE_HOME\bin folder to your path. On our machine, we unzipped Gradle in the C:\kits\gradle-6.0.1 folder, so this is our GRADLE_HOME. We have added C:\kits\gradle-6.0.1\bin to the path.

To check the results, open a command prompt and type `gradle -version`. On our machine, we got the result shown in figure B.3.

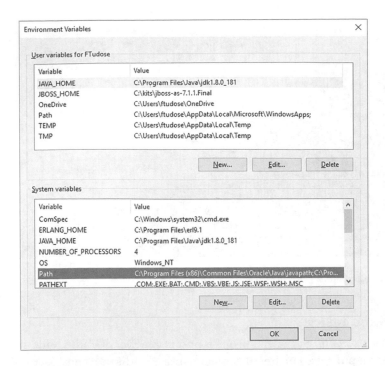

Figure B.1 Accessing the Environment Variables window

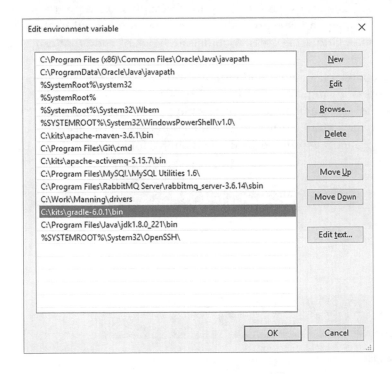

Figure B.2 Adding the GRADLE_HOME\bin folder to the path

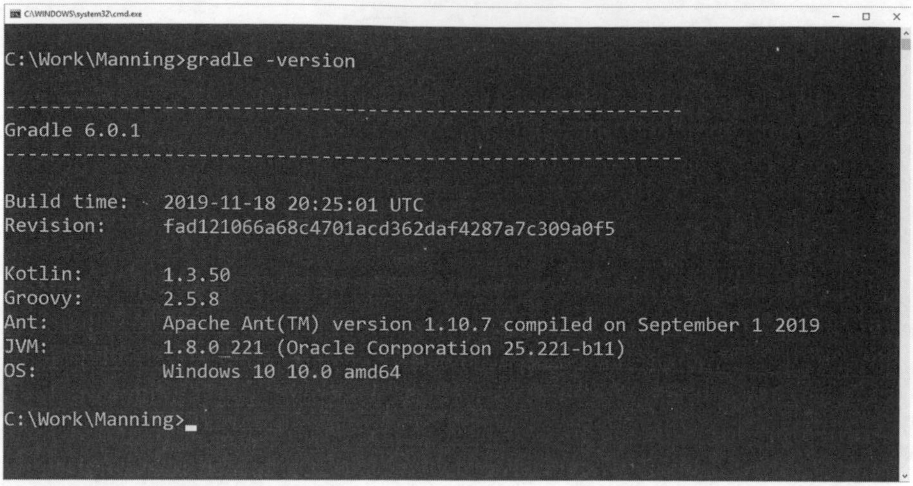

Figure B.3   Executing `gradle -version` at the command prompt

B.2   *Creating Gradle tasks*

Gradle manages a *build file* to handle projects and tasks. Every Gradle build file represents one or more projects. Further, a project consists of different tasks. A *task* represents a piece of work performed by running a build file. A task may compile some classes, create a JAR, generate a Javadoc, or publish archives to a repository. Tasks give us control over defining and executing the actions that are needed for building and testing the project. A Gradle *closure* is a standalone block of code that can take arguments or return values.

The Gradle build file is named build.gradle by default. To describe builds, Gradle uses a domain-specific language (DSL) based on Groovy. Listing B.1 shows a script defining a simple task named `junit` containing a closure that prints "JUnit in Action." If you create a build.gradle file with the content from this listing and execute the `gradle -q junit` command in the containing folder, you will get the result shown in figure B.4.

> **Listing B.1   build.gradle file containing one simple task**

```
task junit {
    println "JUnit in Action"
}
```

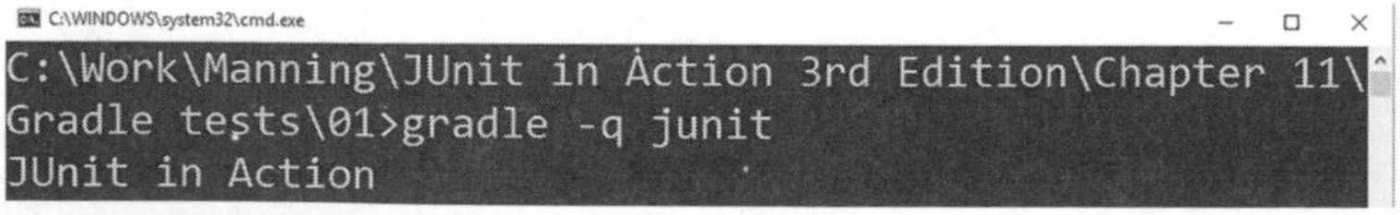

Figure B.4   Executing the command `gradle -q junit`

A task may be dependent on another task. This means a dependent task can start only when the task it depends on is finished. Each task is defined using a task name.

Listing B.2 defines two tasks called `junit` and `third`. The `third` task depends on the `junit` task. Each task contains one closure, each of which prints a message. So, if you save this content into a build.gradle file and execute `gradle -q third` in the containing folder, you will get the result shown in figure B.5.

Listing B.2 build.gradle file containing two dependent tasks

```
task junit {
    print "JUnit in Action"            ◄─┐
}                                         ❶

task third (dependsOn: 'junit'){                 ❷
    println ", third edition"          ◄─
}
```

```
C:\Work\Manning\JUnit in Action 3rd Edition\Chapter 11\
Gradle tests\02>gradle -q third
JUnit in Action, third edition
```

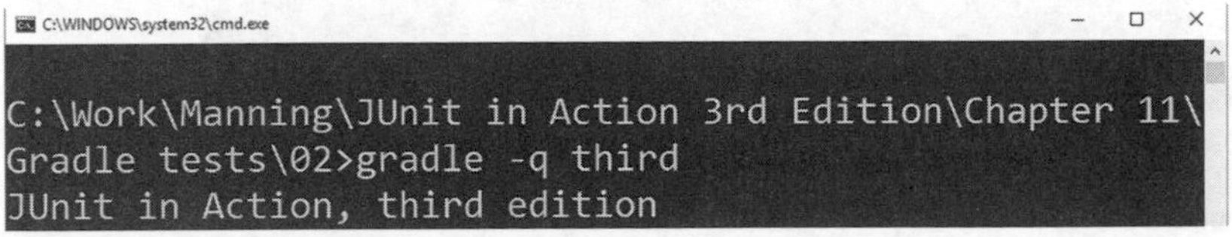

Figure B.5 Executing the command `gradle -q third`

In this listing:

- We try to execute the task `third`. It is dependent on the task `junit`. So, first, the closure ❶ from this task is executed.
- The closure ❷ of the task `third` is executed.

Working with tasks, Gradle defines different phases. First there is a configuration phase, where the code, which is specified directly in the task closure, is executed. The configuration block is executed for every available task, not only for those tasks that are executed later. After the configuration phase, the execution phase runs the code in the `doFirst` or `doLast` closure of those tasks, which are executed. If you save this content into a build.gradle file and execute the `gradle -q third` command in the containing folder, you will get the result shown in figure B.6.

Listing B.3 build.gradle file with two dependent tasks, each with multiple phases

```
task junit {
    print "JUnit "            ◄─┐
                                 ❶              ❷
    doFirst {
        print "Action"        ◄─
    }
```

```
        doLast {
            print ", "                ◀─┐
        }                              ❸
}

task third (dependsOn: 'junit') {      ❹
    print "in "                       ◀─┘

    doFirst {                          ❺
        print "third "                ◀─┘
    }

    doLast {                           ❻
        println "edition"             ◀─┘
    }
}
```

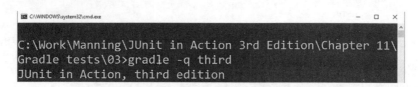

Figure B.6   Executing the command `gradle -q junit` **with tasks containing multiple phases**

In this listing:

- We try to execute the task `third`. It is dependent on the task `junit`. So, first, the configuration phase ❶ of this task is executed.
- The configuration phase ❹ of the task `third` is executed.
- The `doFirst` phase ❷ of the task `junit` is executed.
- The `doLast` phase ❸ of the task `junit` is executed.
- The `doFirst` phase ❺ of the task `third` is executed.
- The `doLast` phase ❻ of the task `third` is executed.

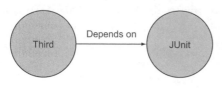

Figure B.7   The directed acyclic graph built by Gradle for listing B.3

Gradle determines the order in which tasks are run by using a directed acyclic graph. For the particular case of listing B.3, it is shown in figure B.7.

Gradle provides many possibilities to create and configure tasks. A detailed discussion of them would exceed the purpose of this appendix. For more information regarding Gradle tasks, we recommend *Gradle in Action* by Benjamin Muschko (Manning, https://www.manning.com/books/gradle-in-action). What we have discussed here is the "just-in-time" information you need to pursue the road to using the Gradle tasks for working with JUnit 5.

appendix C
IDEs

Theoretically, developing Java programs is possible with the help of a simple editor, while compiling and executing can be done at the command line. Practically, this process represents a significant burden and is extremely time consuming. You would have to struggle with the infrastructure and with tedious activities, instead of focusing on writing code.

There still may be some benefit to writing code without an IDE—for learning purposes. Writing very simple applications consisting of one or two short classes and compiling and executing them through the command line may be an excellent introduction for a new Java programmer. Otherwise, you should take advantage of all the benefits of comfortably working with your favorite IDE, which will greatly speed up your development process.

An IDE generally consists of at least a source code editor, build-automation tools, the compiler, and the debugger. A *debugger* is a computer program that is used to test and debug the program under development, usually through step-by-step execution.

Additionally, modern IDEs provide features like these:

- Syntax highlighting
- Code completion
- Navigating between classes
- Easy find and replace
- Automatic generation of pieces of code
- Information about potential problems within the code
- Integration with source control version tools
- Support for refactoring (changing the internal structure of the code while keeping its observable behavior)

IDEs are intended to maximize productivity: all development is done in the same place, including creating, modifying, compiling, deploying, and debugging software.

C.1   *Installing IntelliJ IDEA*

The official website of IntelliJ IDEA is www.jetbrains.com. You can download either of the two versions—Community (Apache licensed) or Ultimate (proprietary commercial)—from www.jetbrains.com/idea/download. The Community edition is enough for our examples because it includes full support for JUnit 5.

To install IntelliJ, you have to run the downloaded installation kit. IntelliJ IDEA has supported running JUnit 5 tests since version 2016.2. At the time of writing, the latest version is 2019.2, so that's what we will use. The installation will produce a Jet-Brains/IntelliJ IDEA Community Edition 2019.2 folder, and the executable that will launch the IDE is found in JetBrains/IntelliJ IDEA Community Edition 2019.2/bin. Depending on the OS, you can choose to launch either the `idea` executable (for 32-bits OSs) or `idea64` (for 64-bits OSs). Figure C.1 shows a piece of the installation on the Windows 10 OS.

Program Files › JetBrains › IntelliJ IDEA Community Edition 2019.2 › bin

Name	Date modified	Type	Size
append.bat	7/23/2019 9:15 AM	Windows Batch File	1 KB
appletviewer.policy	7/23/2019 9:15 AM	POLICY File	1 KB
breakgen.dll	7/23/2019 9:15 AM	Application extens...	82 KB
breakgen64.dll	7/23/2019 9:15 AM	Application extens...	93 KB
elevator.exe	7/23/2019 9:15 AM	Application	149 KB
format.bat	7/23/2019 9:15 AM	Windows Batch File	1 KB
fsnotifier.exe	7/23/2019 9:15 AM	Application	97 KB
fsnotifier64.exe	7/23/2019 9:15 AM	Application	111 KB
idea.bat	7/23/2019 9:15 AM	Windows Batch File	5 KB
idea.exe	7/23/2019 9:15 AM	Application	1,276 KB
idea.exe.vmoptions	7/23/2019 9:15 AM	VMOPTIONS File	1 KB
idea.ico	7/23/2019 9:15 AM	Icon	348 KB
idea.properties	7/23/2019 9:15 AM	PROPERTIES File	12 KB
idea.svg	7/23/2019 9:15 AM	SVG Document	3 KB
idea64.exe	7/23/2019 9:15 AM	Application	1,302 KB
idea64.exe.vmoptions	7/23/2019 9:15 AM	VMOPTIONS File	1 KB
IdeaWin32.dll	7/23/2019 9:15 AM	Application extens...	87 KB
IdeaWin64.dll	7/23/2019 9:15 AM	Application extens...	98 KB

Figure C.1   A piece of the IntelliJ IDEA Community Edition 2019.2 installation

C.2   *Installing Eclipse*

The official website of Eclipse is www.eclipse.org. You can download it from www.eclipse.org/downloads. To install Eclipse, run the downloaded installation kit. Both Eclipse IDE for Java Developers and Eclipse IDE for Enterprise Java Developers provide support for JUnit 5, starting from Eclipse Oxygen.1a (4.7.1a) release. At the time of writing, the latest version was 2019-06, so that's what we will use. The installation will produce an eclipse/jee-2019-06/eclipse folder, and the executable that will launch the IDE is in this folder. Figure C.2 shows a piece of the installation on the Windows 10 OS.

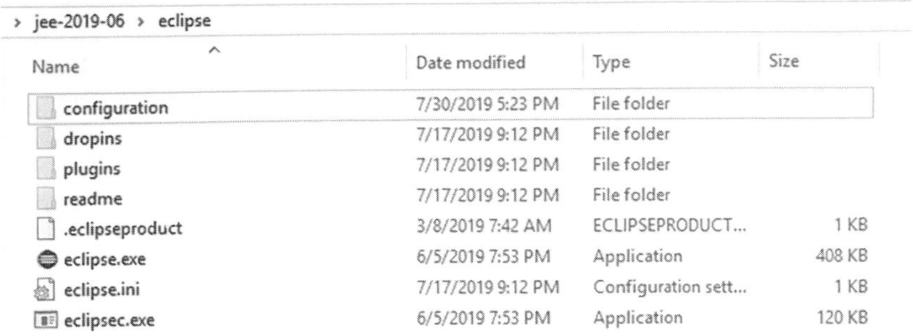

Figure C.2   A piece of the Eclipse 2019-06 installation

C.3   *Installing NetBeans*

The official website of NetBeans is https://netbeans.org/. You can download it from https://netbeans.apache.org/download/index.html. NetBeans can be downloaded as a zip archive and needs to be unpacked. It provides support for JUnit 5 starting from release 10.0. At the time of writing, the latest version was 11.1, so that's what we will use. Unpacking the archive will produce a netbeans folder, and the executable that will launch the IDE is in netbeans/bin. Figure C.3 shows a piece of the installation on the Windows 10 OS.

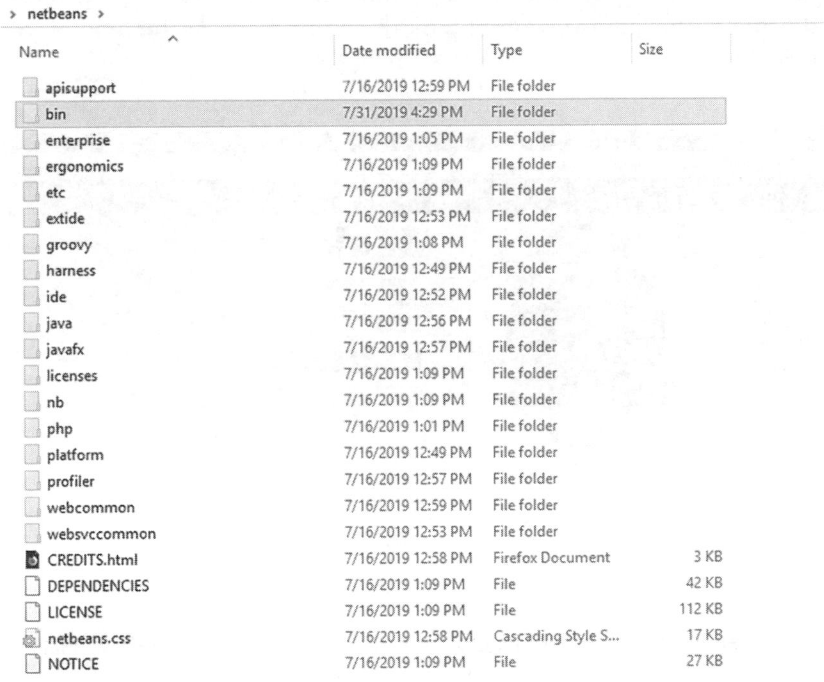

Figure C.3   A piece of the NetBeans 11.1 installation

appendix D
Jenkins

Jenkins (https://jenkins.io/) is an open source project for continuous builds. Like any other software for continuous builds, it relies on the idea of being able to continuously poll the source code from the source control system. If changes are detected, it fires up a build. It is very popular and is used in many projects.

Before installing Jenkins, make sure you have Java version 8 or 11 already installed. Older versions of Java are not supported, and versions 9, 10, and 12 are also not supported. The JAVA_HOME environment variable must point to the location where Java is installed.

The installation procedure itself is straightforward. Go to the project website, and download the latest version of Jenkins (figure D.1). At the time of writing, the latest version is 2.176.2.

Figure D.1 The Jenkins continuous integration tool can be downloaded from the official website.

Running on Windows, the Jenkins distribution comes as an installer file. Executing it will launch a wizard that will guide you through the setup (figure D.2). In our example, we are installing Jenkins into its default folder on Windows (figure D.3).

Figure D.2   Launching the Jenkins Setup Wizard

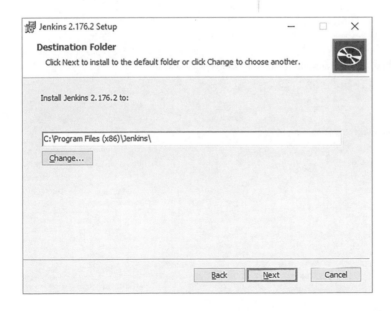

Figure D.3   Installing Jenkins in the Windows default folder

After the installation is completed, Windows creates a folder structure. The most important piece is the jenkins.war file (figure D.4).

Program Files (x86) > Jenkins >			
Name	Date modified	Type	Size
users	8/15/2019 5:22 PM	File folder	
war	8/15/2019 5:14 PM	File folder	
workflow-libs	8/15/2019 5:19 PM	File folder	
.lastStarted	8/15/2019 5:15 PM	LASTSTARTED File	0 KB
.owner	8/15/2019 9:26 PM	OWNER File	1 KB
config.xml	8/15/2019 5:23 PM	XML Document	2 KB
hudson.model.UpdateCenter.xml	8/15/2019 5:14 PM	XML Document	1 KB
hudson.plugins.git.GitTool.xml	8/15/2019 5:19 PM	XML Document	1 KB
identity.key.enc	8/15/2019 5:14 PM	Wireshark capture...	2 KB
jenkins.err.log	8/15/2019 8:49 PM	Text Document	157 KB
jenkins.exe	7/17/2019 6:08 AM	Application	363 KB
jenkins.exe.config	4/5/2015 10:05 AM	CONFIG File	1 KB
jenkins.install.InstallUtil.lastExecVersion	8/15/2019 5:23 PM	LASTEXECVERSIO...	1 KB
jenkins.install.UpgradeWizard.state	8/15/2019 5:23 PM	STATE File	1 KB
jenkins.model.JenkinsLocationConfigura...	8/15/2019 5:22 PM	XML Document	1 KB
jenkins.out.log	8/15/2019 5:14 PM	Text Document	1 KB
jenkins.pid	8/15/2019 5:13 PM	PID File	1 KB
jenkins.telemetry.Correlator.xml	8/15/2019 5:14 PM	XML Document	1 KB
jenkins.war	7/17/2019 6:08 AM	WAR File	75,566 KB
jenkins.wrapper.log	8/15/2019 9:57 PM	Text Document	3 KB
jenkins.xml	7/17/2019 6:08 AM	XML Document	3 KB
nodeMonitors.xml	8/15/2019 5:14 PM	XML Document	1 KB
secret.key	8/15/2019 5:14 PM	KEY File	1 KB
secret.key.not-so-secret	8/15/2019 5:14 PM	NOT-SO-SECRET ...	0 KB

Figure D.4   The Jenkins installation folder with the jenkins.war file

index